Praise for Joby W

RED LINE

"A detailed look at an excruciating moment for Syria, the United States, and the world—the time in 2013 when the United States concluded that Syria's government had used chemical weapons in its long-running civil war." —*Morning Edition*, NPR

"[An] engrossing account of chemical warfare in the Syrian civil war. . . . [A] gripping investigation of the challenges of Middle East politics." —*Library Journal* (starred review)

"*Red Line* can grip as tightly as any thriller." —*The Washington Post*

"*Red Line* is a forensic examination of the moral culpability of the Assad government and its Russian backers. . . . Warrick combines the novelist's gift for storytelling with the journalist's gift for hard research." —*The Tablet*

"[An] electric tale." —*Publishers Weekly*

"The virtue of Warrick's book is that it provides a panoramic reconstruction of the [2013] chemical attack and its aftermath. We see it from the eyes of survivors, doctors, activists, disarmament experts, diplomats, and policymakers. The book cuts from scenes on the ground in Eastern Ghouta, to the UN inspectors in Damascus, to National Security Council meetings in the White House, telling the story with urgency and clarity." —*Newlines*

"An unsettling look at the extraordinarily brutal civil war that has engulfed Syria since 2011. . . . Warrick delivers a vivid account."

—*Kirkus Reviews*

"A valuable addition to the growing literature on the war in Syria. . . . The book includes . . . compelling accounts with characters ranging from UN weapons inspectors and Syrian doctors to Islamic State operatives planning their own chemical attacks. In Warrick's hands, their experiences come alive." —*The National Interest*

"Lively and easily accessible. . . . [*Red Line*] contains powerful material that should serve as a warning to us all." —*The New Arab*

"A meticulously reported, gripping story." —Literary Hub

"[President Biden] may wish to read Joby Warrick's *Red Line*. . . . [It] has important implications for countering proliferation."

—*The Wall Street Journal*

"Riveting. . . . Warrick's vivid portraits of so many of the diverse individuals involved, from victims to American engineers and U.N. investigators, provide a devastating perspective on the civil war in Syria." —*The National Book Review*

"The power of Warrick's account derives from his exceptional ability to tell the Syrian disarmament story through the lives of individuals. . . . At the basic human level, Warrick lays bare two contrasting dimensions of the Syrian [chemical-weapons] story: resourcefulness and resilience—reflected in the brilliant solutions that the book's protagonists, at the Syrian local level as much as in the U.S. government, developed to meet the [challenge]—but also the sheer suffering of those exposed to chemical attacks."

—*The Nonproliferation Review*

"You come away from the pages both entertained and informed. . . . More so than with [a] novel, the hard facts are sought, observed and metabolized. More so than most nonfiction, there is a narration of the facts that makes it come alive." —*Corriere della Sera* (Italy)

JOBY WARRICK

RED LINE

Joby Warrick has been a reporter for *The Washington Post* since 1996. He is a two-time winner of the Pulitzer Prize, having been awarded the 1996 Pulitzer Prize for Public Service for a series of newspaper articles and the 2016 Pulitzer Prize for General Nonfiction for his book *Black Flags: The Rise of ISIS*. He is also the author of *The Triple Agent*.

Also by Joby Warrick

Black Flags

The Triple Agent

RED
LINE

RED LINE

THE UNRAVELING OF SYRIA AND AMERICA'S RACE TO DESTROY THE MOST DANGEROUS ARSENAL IN THE WORLD

JOBY WARRICK

ANCHOR BOOKS
A Division of Penguin Random House LLC
New York

FIRST ANCHOR BOOKS EDITION, FEBRUARY 2022

 Published in the United States by Anchor Books, a division of Penguin Random House LLC, New York, and distributed in Canada by Penguin Random House Canada Limited, Toronto. Originally published in hardcover in the United States by Doubleday, a division of Penguin Random House LLC, New York, in 2021.

The Library of Congress has cataloged the Doubleday edition as follows:
Names: Warrick, Joby, author.
Title: Red line : the unraveling of Syria and America's race to destroy the most dangerous arsenal in the world / Joby Warrick.
Description: First edition. | New York : Doubleday, 2021. | Includes bibliographical references (pages 311–331) and index.
Identifiers: LCCN 2020017981 (print) | LCCN 2020017982 (ebook)
Subjects: LCSH: IS (Organization). | Chemical weapons—Syria. | Chemical weapons disposal—Syria. | Terrorism—Prevention—Government policy—United States. | Syria—History—Civil War, 2011– | Syria—History—Civil War, 2011—Atrocities. | Syria—History—Civil War, 2011—Participation, Russian. | United States—Foreign relations—Syria. | Syria—Foreign relations—United States.
Classification: LCC DS98.6 .W38 2020 (print) | LCC DS98.6 (ebook) | DDC 956.9104/23—dc23
LC record available at https://lccn.loc.gov/2020017981
LC ebook record available at https://lccn.loc.gov/2020017982

Anchor Books Trade Paperback ISBN: 978-0-525-56481-2
eBook ISBN: 978-0-385-54447-4

www.anchorbooks.com

Printed in the United States of America
10 9 8 7 6 5 4 3 2 1

In memory of my parents,
Barbara and Eugene

The more decisive a weapon is, the more surely it will be used.

—Edward Teller, father of the hydrogen bomb

CONTENTS

List of Principal Characters *xiii*
Key Locations in *Red Line* *xvi*
Prologue: *The Chemist* 1

PART I

1. *"Like watching a freight train coming"* 11
2. *"Something fell from the sky"* 18
3. *The Machine* 43
4. *"Help, please—they're dying!"* 59
5. *"No one is coming out alive"* 72
6. *"We go in again"* 84
7. *"The eye of a hurricane"* 101
8. *The Deal* 116
9. *"No one is coming to help you"* 127

PART II

10. *"An elephant with a tick on its back"* 137
11. *"A technical delay"* 154
12. *Ghost Armies* 169

13. *"A perfect loophole"* 185
14. *Race to the Coast* 195
15. *"The number we will never know . . ."* 211

PART III

16. *A Day "perfect for a chemical attack"* 231
17. *A "catastrophic success"* 247
18. *An ISIS "wonder weapon"* 259
19. *"Like Judgment Day"* 272
20. *A Smoking Gun* 282
21. *The Unraveling* 298

Acknowledgments 307
Notes 311
Index 332

LIST OF PRINCIPAL CHARACTERS

UNITED NATIONS/ORGANIZATION FOR THE PROHIBITION OF CHEMICAL WEAPONS

Ban Ki-moon, UN secretary-general
Susana Malcorra, UN Secretariat chef de cabinet
Angela Kane, UN high representative for disarmament affairs
Ahmet Üzumcü, OPCW director-general
Åke Sellström, scientist, leader of August 2013 Syria investigation
Scott Cairns, Sellström mission and OPCW team leader
Diarmuid O'Donovan, security adviser to Sellström, Joint Mission teams
Sigrid Kaag, special coordinator, OPCW-UN Joint Mission to Syria
Julian Tangaere, Joint Mission deputy leader, OPCW operations chief
Abdullah Fadil, Joint Mission deputy leader, UN official
Jerry Smith, head of field operations, Joint Mission
Edmond Mulet, head of OPCW/UN Joint Investigative Mechanism

WHITE HOUSE

Barack Obama, president, 2009–2017
Donald J. Trump, president, 2017–2021
Susan Rice, national security adviser
Benjamin Rhodes, deputy national security adviser
Tony Blinken, deputy national security adviser

Denis McDonough, chief of staff
Laura Holgate, senior director on weapons of mass destruction (WMD) terrorism, NSC
John Bolton, national security adviser

DEFENSE DEPARTMENT

Chuck Hagel, Defense Secretary
Ash Carter, Deputy Defense Secretary
Major Gen. Jay Santee, deputy director, Defense Threat Reduction Agency
Col. John D. Cinnamon, chief of plans, DTRA
Andrew C. Weber, assistant secretary for nuclear, chemical, and biological defense programs
Rebecca Hersman, deputy assistant secretary for countering weapons of mass destruction
Gen. Sean MacFarland, commander of the coalition against ISIS in Syria and Iraq
Gen. Joe Votel, commander, U.S. Special Operations command
Gen. James Mattis, Defense Secretary

STATE DEPARTMENT

John F. Kerry, Secretary of State
Thomas Countryman, assistant secretary for international security and nonproliferation
Robert Ford, U.S. Ambassador to Syria
Samantha Power, UN ambassador
Wa'el Alzayat, senior policy adviser to UN ambassador
Brett McGurk, Special Presidential Envoy for the Global Coalition to Counter ISIS

EDGEWOOD CHEMICAL BIOLOGICAL CENTER AND *CAPE RAY* OFFICERS

Tim Blades, director of operations, Chemical Biological Application and Risk Reduction
Rick Jordan, master mariner and captain, MV *Cape Ray*

Navy Capt. Richard Dromerhauser, mission leader and commodore, MV *Cape Ray*

INTERNATIONAL

Vladimir Putin, president, Russian Federation
Qasem Soleimani, commander, Quds Force, Islamic Revolutionary Guard Corps of Iran
Ayatollah Ali Khamenei, Iranian supreme leader
Nouri al-Maliki, Iraqi prime minister
Torben Mikkelsen, Danish naval commodore in charge of maritime task force to Syria
Hamish de Bretton-Gordon, commander, WMD defense regiment, UK (ret.)
Vitaly Churkin, Russian UN ambassador
Azamat Kulmuhametov, Russian ambassador to Syria
Abu Bakr al-Baghdadi, caliph and commander, Islamic State
Suleiman al-Afari, Islamic State chemical weapons scientist
Basil Hassan, ISIS coordinator of Australian airliner plot
Khaled Khayat, leader of Australian airliner plot

SYRIA

Bashar al-Assad, president, Syrian Arab Republic
Walid al-Muallem, foreign minister
Hassan al-Sharif, Syrian brigadier general, liaison to OPCW-UN Joint Mission
Faisal Mekdad, deputy foreign minister
Bashar Jaafari, Syrian ambassador to the UN
Kassem Eid, Syrian activist and blogger
Houssam Alnahhas, Syrian physician, chemical weapons defense group coordinator
Mamoun Morad, physician, Khan Sheikhoun, Syria

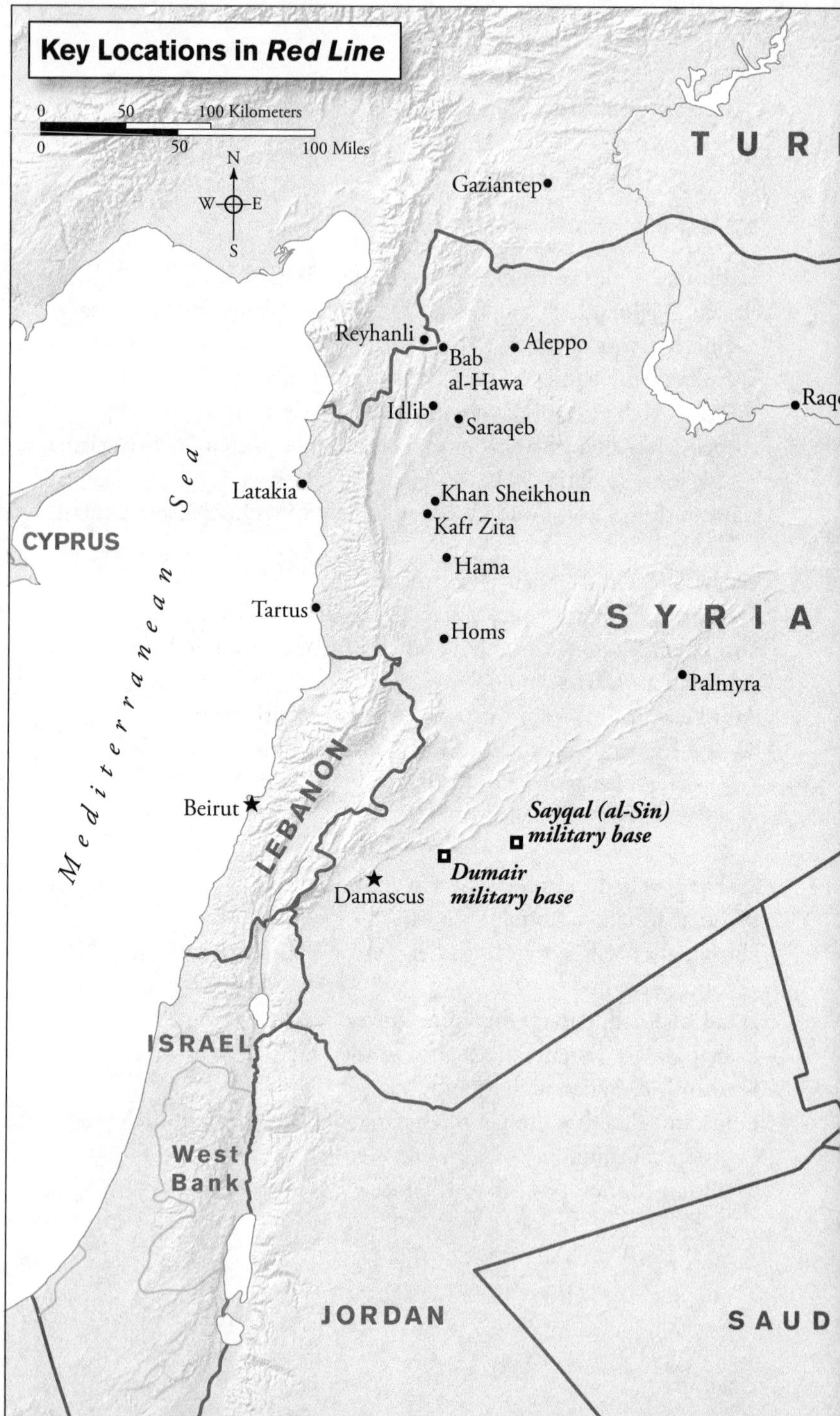

Key Locations in *Red Line*
0
50
100 Kilometers
0
50
100 Miles
N
W
E
S
TUR
Gaziantep
Reyhanli
Bab
al-Hawa
Aleppo
Idlib
Saraqeb
Raq
Latakia
Khan Sheikhoun
Kafr Zita
Hama
CYPRUS
Mediterranean Sea
Tartus
Homs
SYRIA
Palmyra
LEBANON
Beirut
Sayqal (al-Sin)
military base
Dumair
military base
Damascus
ISRAEL
West
Bank
JORDAN
SAUD

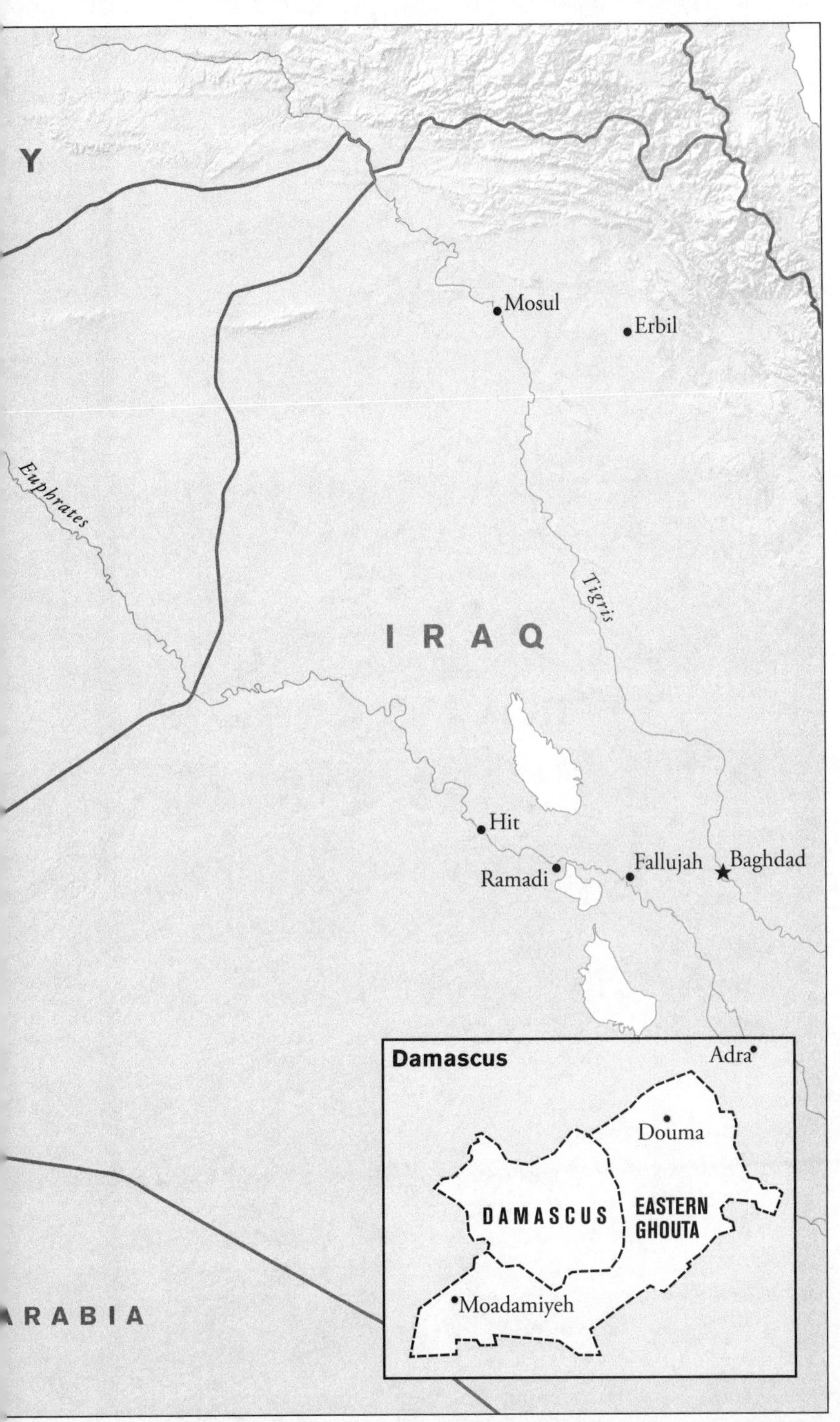
Y
Mosul
Erbil
Euphrates
Tigris
I R A Q
Hit
Ramadi
Fallujah
Baghdad
ARABIA
Damascus
Adra
Douma
DAMASCUS
EASTERN
GHOUTA
Moadamiyeh

RED LINE

PROLOGUE

The Chemist

DAMASCUS, SYRIA. 1986

He was known to the CIA's clandestine service as "the chemist," and few at headquarters would ever know his real name. A professor and a gifted scientist, he had been perfectly positioned for spy work, with a job that entitled him to privileges not accorded to ordinary Syrians, including a broad latitude to travel and to meet with foreigners in the crowded souks and smoke-filled cafés of the old city. He drew little attention to himself as he moved about, a small, clean-shaven man in his late thirties with owlish glasses and gray-flecked hair, in a modest suit that might have belonged to a salesman or bureaucrat. Only when he spoke English was there a hint of something exotic: a distinct American accent. It was the only detectable residue from a youth spent partly in the United States, where he attended school, ate cheeseburgers, played sports, and even joined the Boy Scouts, all before returning to his homeland to become an expert in making chemicals designed to kill human beings.

He was proud of his professional work—so proud, in fact, that analysts suspected at times that his spying was motivated less by patriotism or greed than by a compulsion to boast. His first attempt at establishing contact had occurred at a scientific conference in Europe, where he had asked a friend to pass along a note to an American at the U.S. embassy. Many months passed before the CIA followed through, yet he seemed unsurprised when a stranger approached him after one of his evening lectures at Damascus University.

I've been expecting you, he told the visitor, a twentysomething CIA case officer who would soon be entrusted with an extraordinary military secret. Call me Ayman.

The chemist seemed to take an instant liking to the American, and the two spent long hours in conversation as each quietly sized up the other. One day the scientist invited the young officer to his home in downtown Damascus, a small apartment he shared with two different women he had wed legally under Syria's permissive polygamy laws. He seemed compelled to justify his living arrangements, as another man might explain an extravagant impulse purchase: his first wife was an excellent cook, he said, but he had decided to marry a second, considerably younger woman—his secretary—out of a purely carnal attraction. Who could have foreseen such turmoil? The two women squabbled constantly, except for the times when they united to direct their scorn at him. He had wanted a spicier love life and ended up with a case of perpetual heartburn. I don't recommend it, the scientist counseled his guest.

The two wives politely served coffee as Ayman spoke of his high school and college years in the United States, and of the kindly American couple who took care of him when he arrived as a wide-eyed teenager with a suitcase and an academic scholarship. He showed off his stereo and musical collection, playing a few tracks of moody electronica from his favorite artist, French new-age composer Jean-Michel Jarre. And then, after the women left the room, the Syrian turned to the subject that he had waited anxiously to talk about. That evening, in the first of multiple meetings between the two men, he told his incredible story as the case officer sat transfixed, the sludgy coffee turning cold in his cup.

On a hill overlooking the capital stood a complex of laboratories where Syria's military carried out experiments on new weapons. Foreign intelligence services were well familiar with the Scientific Studies and Research Center—commonly known as CERS, its French initials—as the place that supplied the engineering muscle behind Syria's modest line of missiles designed to deliver conventional warheads to Tel Aviv or Jerusalem. But hidden within CERS was a secret unit called Institute 3000, and Ayman was one of its senior researchers. Its primary work was making a line of exceedingly lethal poisons to be placed inside those warheads. The scientists called their project al-Shakush, or, in English, "The Hammer."

In part because of his own contributions, Institute 3000 had made remarkable strides, the chemist said. Syria's chemical weapons program had started simply, with mustard gas, famously used in the trenches of Europe during the epic battles of World War I. But now it had moved to a far deadlier class of poisons called nerve agents, which Institute 3000 was beginning to produce in an underground factory just outside the capital. These were nightmare weapons, and the Syrians had created multiple variations so they could adjust to changing battlefield conditions. One of them, sarin, had been around for half a century and still was regarded as one of the deadliest substances ever made. Another one, called VX, was even deadlier than sarin, and longer lasting. It left behind an invisible oily coating that could kill for days, since the slightest brush against bare skin is nearly always fatal.

The case officer listened thoughtfully. The CIA had long known of Syria's interest in making chemical weapons, but the extent of Damascus's progress was unclear. Twice in public statements in the late 1980s, Syrian officials had hinted about a new "deterrent," a made-in-Syria answer to Israel's nuclear bombs. Was this what they meant?

If the chemist felt the slightest ambivalence about his work, he gave no sign of it. The United States and the Soviet Union had developed entire weapons systems based on such poisons in the 1950s and 1960s. Why shouldn't Syria have the same right to deter aggression by its nuclear-armed neighbor? Whenever Israel came up in conversation, it was clear that subject was intensely personal. Twice in the chemist's lifetime, Syria had endured the humiliation of having its southern border overrun by Israeli tanks: in 1967, when the Jewish state captured the Golan Heights; and again during the 1973 Yom Kippur War, when the Israeli army chased retreating Syrian battalions to within twenty-five miles of Damascus. From now on, things would be different, the scientist said. Future invaders would find themselves engulfed in a fog of suffocating gases that would leave their bodies strewn across the dusty valleys of Syria's southwestern frontier. Those who survived would be among the first to see the contrails of Syrian missiles heading south to deliver the same fate to distant Israeli cities.

The chemist eyed his guest with deadly earnestness.

"You should warn the Jews," he said.

The chemist became particularly animated whenever the conversation turned to sarin. Of all the weapons under development within Institute 3000, the chemist was clearly proudest of his sarin work. Sarin is a perfect killer, as the Nazis learned when they inadvertently discovered the compound while testing new kinds of pesticides in the 1930s. Military-grade sarin is twenty-six times deadlier than cyanide, and it works by attacking the nervous system, quickly paralyzing the muscles used in breathing, so that the victim dies an agonizing death of asphyxiation. Just a whiff of vapor and the poison would grasp a man with the deadly intensity of a python's embrace, squeezing him until he lacked even the breath with which to utter a final prayer.

But making pure sarin—the kind that the Soviets and Americans manufactured by the ton during the Cold War—is hard for a small country with a modest industrial base. And lesser grades of the poison tended to deteriorate with time. So the chemist devised a clever workaround. His laboratories would make a form of binary sarin: two stable liquids that could be stored separately and blended only at the last minute. One of the two liquids was ordinary isopropyl alcohol. The other, a toxic brew called DF, contained all the other ingredients, including an exclusive additive—which Ayman helped discover—that helped ensure that the sarin lost none of its potency during the short interval between the mixing and the arrival at the target. Over the decades, perhaps a dozen countries had manufactured sarin for use as a weapon. But no one had developed a formula exactly like this one.

After the meetings, the case officer relayed the gist of the conversations via secret cable to CIA headquarters, where analysts pondered the chemist's assertions with astonishment and concern. The information was extraordinarily detailed and credible—almost too good. The agency's new spy was now being paid for his information, in cash transfers to a foreign bank account, but he was asking the Americans to take him at his word. Where was the evidence?

The chemist appeared to anticipate the question. One late December day, he sent a cryptic signal to the case officer requesting a meeting. He had something to give the young American, but it had to be in private—not at his house, and not in a café or another public place where the exchange might be seen.

The arrangements were set. On the agreed evening, the spy and the case officer sat together in the front seat of a Peugeot parked on a quiet Damascus street a few blocks from the U.S. embassy. After a brief exchange of pleasantries, the scientist produced a small package.

"It's nearly Christmas. You're a Christian," the chemist said. "Here's a Christmas present." A few minutes later, the American was left alone to ponder what was inside the parcel's plain wrapping.

The younger man had an inkling, so the CIA arranged to send a pair of technical specialists to his Damascus apartment to help with the initial assessment. Donning protective suits, the specialists removed the outer packaging to reveal a small box.

Inside the box was a sealed plastic vial. And within it, visible through the plastic casing, was a clear liquid. The chemist had boasted of his prowess in making exceedingly effective nerve agents. Now he had given the Americans a sample.

Days passed before the liquid could be fully analyzed. The vial was first repackaged and placed in a shatterproof container, then flown out of the country. Once in the United States, it was rushed to a military laboratory, where scientists in hazmat suits gingerly opened the vial for a first look at what was inside.

The results of the tests caused a sensation at CIA outposts on both sides of the Atlantic. In a bare-bones lab, in a backward, autocratic state that had been shunned and blacklisted by the West, the Syrian chemist had produced a weapon of astonishing quality and elegant simplicity—a deadly chemical masterpiece.

Now the CIA faced a wrenching decision: whether to keep its spy operation under wraps or to share Ayman's secrets with the country most likely to become a target of Syria's chemical bombs. To reveal the existence of a high-level mole was extremely risky, but there were other costs to be weighed. Experts ran the numbers and concluded that a sarin attack on Tel Aviv could inflict fifteen thousand casualties. Finally the White House's National Security Council decided the matter. Israel would be told.

The first attempt to broach the subject with Israeli intelligence did not go well. An American delegation flew to Tel Aviv armed with reports and charts and was greeted with skeptical stares. Israel's Mossad spy agency certainly knew that Syria had tinkered with chemical weapons. But binary sarin? In tanker-sized quantities? It was impossible. Perhaps the CIA had fallen for a Syrian ruse.

Two weeks later, a second U.S. delegation brought photos and other hard evidence. Then, to dispel any doubts, the Americans delivered a vial containing a tiny sample of Ayman's sarin. See for yourselves, the Mossad was told.

The Israelis, one knowledgeable official later said, "went ballistic."

In an odd way, the revelation ended up helping preserve peace along the border. Syria now possessed a formidable deterrent, so all-out war was unthinkable. Yet the Americans knew that Israel's Mossad would not allow the program to go unchallenged. Military officers and scientists with ties to the labs died under mysterious circumstances. A Russian general who delivered equipment to the Syrians was found dead in his airplane seat after a flight from Damascus. The Americans worried frantically that Ayman might be next.

Then give us the name of your mole, the Mossad insisted. The CIA refused, but then the two agencies reached a compromise. A list of five names was transmitted to Tel Aviv. Four were Syrian officials picked almost at random. The fifth was the CIA's prized informant. If these five were protected, America's spy would be safe.

The Israelis gave their word. All five Syrians were spared. And Ayman never knew how close he came to being killed.

Years passed, and the hilltop laboratory complex steadily grew. By the early 2000s, the network of laboratories and production centers gradually blossomed into a mature manufacturing complex that encompassed some forty buildings and bunkers at two dozen secret locations scattered across the country. The lab's researchers still experimented with new products, but by the early 2000s the program had achieved a kind of equilibrium: a steady reserve of up to 1,500 tons of sarin, mustard gas, and VX. With Syria at peace, there was no need to make more.

The meetings in the alleys and cafés also went on, for fourteen years, though the faces on the American side changed as new handlers came and went. Over time new methods were devised for communicating, so that Ayman could transmit messages to the CIA simply by passing the U.S. embassy building. The cash transfers continued as well, and the spy became a wealthy man, with a bank account grown fat with American dollars as well as dinars he received as kickbacks from vendors. The sound system and Western music collection grew larger, and Ayman, approaching fifty now and gray-haired, moved his querulous wives into separate, lavishly appointed households. He was on top of the world professionally: respected by peers and admired by younger scientists. He commanded a large staff and a generous budget, and he led a highly successful military program that was prized by Syria's leaders, including the president himself.

But something, somewhere, went wrong. The chemist could see it in the faces of the security men who arrived at CERS unannounced one morning in late 2001, looking to speak to him. Could the scientist accompany them to their office for a private meeting?

Ayman froze. Did these men suspect something?

The interrogation began at the headquarters of Syria's Mukhabarat intelligence service, where a high-ranking officer—Assef Shawkat, the deputy director of military intelligence and the president's own brother-in-law—laid out his cards at once.

You have been betrayed, Ayman was told.

Shawkat proceeded to explain to the frightened scientist that the government knew all about his secret activities. It would be far better for you, Shawkat said, if you confessed and asked for leniency on account of your years of service to the Republic.

So Ayman confessed—to everything. He told his interrogators about his many years of contact with the CIA. He talked about the meetings with his handlers, the secrets he had passed, and the large sum of money he had amassed in an offshore bank. No one else had been aware of his spying, he said; not his coworkers, or his business associates, or even his wives. He had done it all by himself.

Shawkat and the other security men listened, confused at first, and then fascinated. The intelligence chief had decided to question the scientist after learning of a bribery scheme in which Ayman, in his greed, had demanded payoffs in return for contracts to sell supplies to his institute. That was the entire reason for his arrest.

Of the far more consequential betrayal—the selling of state secrets to the CIA—the intelligence service had known nothing at all.

—

At that moment, throughout the Middle East, a new era was dawning, and old battles were being refought with new ferocity. The United States had been attacked by al-Qaeda, and within eighteen months Washington would launch a military invasion of Iraq that would mire the country in an unpopular war and unleash cascading disasters on the region. In northern Iraq, an obscure Jordanian terrorist called Abu Musab al-Zarqawi opened a training camp in a mountain refuge and dreamed of a day when his tiny band—the forerunner of the Islamic State, or ISIS—could claim territory and battle a superpower. In Moscow, a newly elected president, Vladimir Putin, was restructuring the Kremlin in preparation for a new age of assertive engagement in the Middle East and around the world. And Syria's new president, Bashar al-Assad, had just ended his flirtation with free expression, a brief flowering of dissent that became known as the Damascus Spring. Eerily foreshadowing the events that would occur a decade later, Assad firmly cast his lot with the security forces who kept his father in power for nearly thirty years, giving his police free rein to arrest, torture, and murder until the last tendrils of the fledgling movement had been ripped from the earth.

From hard men such as these, there would be no leniency for an accomplished scientist and poison-maker who had betrayed his own country. Ayman was found guilty of treason, a verdict rendered in a closed proceeding that was kept out of the public eye but described in detail, as a warning to the other scientists at CERS. Prisoners convicted of capital offenses in Syria are usually executed by hanging, but Ayman, who had been a national hero as well as a traitor, was given special treatment. His two wives and their children were permitted to leave the country to start new lives abroad. Then, on the gray, blustery morning of April 7, he was awakened in his cell at the country's infamous Adra Prison and escorted into a courtyard where a firing squad stood waiting. He was blindfolded, tied to a post, and shot to death.

As he died, teams of workers in protective suits were mixing a new batch of the chemist's binary sarin in an underground factory in the Adra hills, less than five miles from the prison. In a locked chamber beyond the production hall, the finished product sat in gleaming two-thousand-liter tanks, arrayed in row after tidy row, waiting for the unthinkable day when they would be put to use.

PART I

1

"Like watching a freight train coming"

Long before Syria's civil war—before the uprising and the bloody street clashes, before the massacres, the gassings and the thousand brutal acts that followed—the government's Military Intelligence Directorate built a large torture palace for political prisoners on the southern outskirts of Damascus. The Branch 235 headquarters was a modern building that stood nine stories tall, not counting the three underground floors where inmates were locked away in coffin-like cells. Within the city's small dissident community, it was dubbed the "Sheraton," although many a guest who disappeared behind its imposing outer wall was never heard from again.

The start of the war brought Branch 235 a flood of new business, and in the spring of the war's second year, its grim practitioners were busier than ever. On the steamy morning of May 10, 2012, the line of commuters arriving to work the day shift stretched around the block, mingling with the modest sedans of teachers and families heading toward the elementary school on the same street. No one seemed to notice the young man who pulled up to the curb by the security gate at exactly 7:10 a.m., pausing for an instant before reaching for the detonator attached by wires to a large cache of explosives in the trunk.

The blast was so powerful that it flattened a section of the concrete wall and turned nearby cars into infernos. Dazed commuters abandoned their vehicles to stare at the ruined wall as police, soldiers, and rescue workers scrambled over the broken concrete to search for victims.

Then came a second explosion, vastly larger than the first. A separate car bomb, later calculated to contain at least a ton of explosives and shrapnel, cut through the crowd of bystanders and peeled off the Branch 235 building's entire nine-story facade. It gouged a bus-sized crater in the asphalt and shook homes and offices in downtown Damascus, more than two miles away. By the evening, rescue workers had treated nearly four hundred wounded and recovered fifty-six bodies, making the attack the deadliest of the war so far.

Blame quickly coalesced around a single suspect, and the following day, May 11, the shadowy group that called itself al-Nusra Front confirmed the suspicions by taking credit for the killings in a brief video message. The video was simply a white screen with an unseen narrator reading words that appeared in Arabic characters. In the background was a recording of a *nasheed,* a chanted prayer in an a cappella style popular among Islamist extremists.

"We kept our promise," the narrator said. "What is coming will be more calamitous, God willing."

Within minutes, the warning was being translated and parsed in dozens of capitals around the world. It commanded a prominent spot in President Barack Obama's daily intelligence briefing at the White House, and echoed through secure conference rooms at CIA headquarters in Langley, Virginia, where analysts had followed the emergence of the mysterious terrorist group with foreboding. At the Pentagon, U.S. secretary of defense Leon Panetta stopped to ponder the meaning of the twin explosions. Until now, there had been no instances in Syria of this kind of expertly timed, double suicide bombing on a crowded street at rush hour. None of Syria's secular rebel groups had ever killed in such an indiscriminate way. These were the unmistakable hallmarks of al-Qaeda in Iraq, the bloodthirsty jihadist group that had unleashed mayhem on U.S. troops and tens of thousands of ordinary Iraqi civilians for nearly a decade. Its leader, Abu Bakr al-Baghdadi, now called his band of murderers the Islamic State, and al-Nusra Front was the group's first official Syrian franchise.

"An al-Qaeda presence in Syria," Panetta mused. It was an ominous sign.

Only a handful of analysts knew Baghdadi's name, and no one in the West had fully grasped the terrorist leader's plans for Syria. But at that moment, in a cramped office a short walk from Panetta's suite, a small team of Pentagon analysts was beginning to grapple with a chilling possibility. The scenario had been discussed hypothetically for months. Now, in the opinion of the team's fifty-three-year-old leader, the threat had become alarmingly real.

Andrew C. Weber was, in the spring of 2012, the Pentagon's assistant secretary for nuclear, chemical, and biological defense programs. He was slim and wiry, with a receding hairline and intelligent blue eyes, and a quiet, understated demeanor that belied an adventurous past. In an earlier life, Weber had personally led operations to smuggle loose nuclear weapons components from former Soviet republics after the fall of the communist government in Moscow. What Weber was seeing now in Syria troubled him nearly as much as anything he had witnessed in his years overseas.

His office, at the end of a long corridor on the Pentagon's third floor, was adorned with oversized windows that looked out onto a courtyard. Weber kept the shades drawn at all times because of the highly sensitive intelligence stored inside. There were paper maps, delivered every morning with the day's classified briefing materials, and special computers from which the most restricted electronic files could be accessed. From his reading, Weber had come to appreciate the exquisite detail contained in page after page of secret memos from the CIA's files on Syria's chemical weapons program. Thanks to the dead spy, the agency knew all about Syria's 1,300-ton stockpile, including where it was made and how it was kept. Tens of thousands of gallons of binary sarin and VX lay scattered across nearly two dozen military bases and storage depots, nominally controlled by an embattled Syrian regime that, in the estimation of every leading intelligence agency in the world, was on the verge of collapse. If the consensus view was correct, Syria's dictator could topple within weeks, perhaps even days. What would happen to all those weapons then?

Weber had followed the events in Syria since the earliest days of the uprising, with a single-minded focus on the security of the regime's arsenal of poisons. What had begun as civil protests had become a true civil war, with government troops fighting pitched battles against an army of its own citizens. If President Bashar al-Assad's government truly began to falter, he reasoned, things could go bad very quickly. A desperate Assad might decide to use his weapons or give them to Iran or another ally. The government might lose control of a few liters of sarin, or the entire stockpile. For such deadly weapons to go missing in the Middle East would be a crisis of the first order. Of all the reasons to worry about Syria, Weber believed, none posed a more urgent threat to Americans than this.

There are multiple potential disasters, Weber thought. *And on top of all of it, now you have al-Nusra.*

With the bombings in Damascus, the thought of terrorists hauling tankers of liquid sarin through Turkey and into the heart of Europe did not seem far-fetched. In the weeks after the attack, Weber sat with his staff in a small conference room to study the maps and ponder the awful possibilities. If al-Nusra could penetrate the most secure corners of Syria's capital, what else was within the group's reach? In the hills just east of Damascus, in places where fighting now raged, lay the underground storage bunkers and production halls the CIA's "chemist" spy had helped commission some fifteen years earlier. There, too, were the mixing trucks designed to turn binary sarin into its lethal, final form. How hard would it be for al-Nusra to blast its way into one of the hidden sites and run off with the ingredients for a massive terrorist strike against the West—one that could potentially surpass the September 11, 2001, attacks on New York and Washington in the numbers of dead and injured?

"It was like watching a freight train coming," said a former intelligence official who attended many of the classified briefing sessions on Syria in Weber's office. "The real nightmare scenario for us then was al-Nusra. Already they were knocking over convoys, garrisons, storage depots. You had the potential for a bunch of very bad stuff getting out and ending up in places where it could have an impact on the world stage. They might not even know what they have, and just get lucky. Then it's 'Hold on, look what we've got.' "

Weber was convinced that the theft would be deliberate. Baghdadi possessed the capability and the will to pull off such an act. Sooner or later, the allure of the weapons would prove irresistible.

"Here was a well-organized al-Qaeda affiliate, capable of striking right in the very heart of Damascus," Weber said, recalling his thinking on that May morning as the reports of the twin bombing trickled in. "I thought, *My God. This is a nightmare.*"

—

The dream was nearly as old as al-Qaeda itself. It was the subject of fervent discussion and wistful scheming long before Osama bin Laden and his followers thought of the idea of flying airliners into buildings. Bin Laden once went so far as to declare the acquisition of nuclear, biological, and chemical weapons a sacred quest: "a religious duty," he said in 1998. He had tried multiple times and failed just as often. But if offered a chance to plunder Bashar al-Assad's chemical stockpile, there could be little doubt that al-Qaeda, or its jihadist rivals, would do it.

The diligence with which al-Qaeda pursued chemical weapons has been amply described, including in accounts by former members of the terrorist group. One of them, a Saudi-born operative named Aimen Dean, worked for a time in an Afghan training camp where different combinations of poisons were tried on rabbits, dogs, and other animals. The camp's chief "scientist," Abu Khabab al-Masri, had concluded that nuclear and biological terrorism were too technically challenging for amateurs. But chemical weapons were different. "They are within our reach," he told Dean.

One day Dean walked into al-Qaeda's crude lab as Masri was attempting an experiment with hydrogen cyanide gas, a substance that was used as a chemical weapon during World War I. As Dean watched, the gas was pumped into an aquarium in which Masri had placed a live rabbit.

"Within seconds the poor creature started furiously licking its lips," Dean later recalled. "Its breathing quickened and it started scratching furiously at the side of the tank before losing muscle control, rolling onto its back and convulsing. Finally, it was dead. The whole process had lasted a minute."

The experiment was impressive in a macabre way, and some of bin Laden's deputies began to see chemical weapons as a potential game-changer, although the group had not yet devised a method for dispersing them. Dean was sure his comrades would find one, and he became so troubled by the prospects of a large-scale chemical attack that he eventually left the group and became an informant for the British spy service MI6.

"The question that lurked at the back of my mind was how soon such a weapon might spread deadly gas in a cinema in London or in the Paris Metro," he later wrote.

It very nearly happened. A little more than a year after the group's September 11, 2001, attack, al-Qaeda developed a device for dispersing hydrogen cyanide, and its operatives were just weeks away from a planned mission to place it in the New York subway system, according to accounts by several former al-Qaeda members. The crude machine, dubbed *mubtakkar al-farid*—Arabic for "unique invention"—was operated remotely by cell phone and designed to release its lethal contents through a vent. A target date was set for early 2003.

Preparations for the attack were well under way when Ayman al-Zawahiri, then al-Qaeda's number two leader, got cold feet. At the time, the George W. Bush administration was inching closer to a threatened invasion of Iraq, and the Egyptian terrorist worried that a chemical attack in New York would become a pretext for war. Zawahiri postponed the attack, but by then it was probably too late anyway: Bahraini police, alerted by Britain's MI6 spy service and its secret informant, nabbed an al-Qaeda operative who was transporting blueprints for the *mubtakkar* on his laptop. Weeks later, the CIA built and tested a replica of the machine, and agency officials were so alarmed by the results that they brought the device to the White House to brief the president in person, according to author Ron Suskind, who first described the incident in his book *The One Percent Doctrine*.

"The prototype confirmed their worst fears," Suskind wrote of the intelligence agency's internal assessment. "In the world of terrorist weaponry, this was the equivalent of splitting the atom."

Al-Qaeda's Afghan laboratory was destroyed by U.S. troops in 2002, and many of its top weapons experts, including Masri, were later tracked and killed in CIA drone strikes. Whether the *mubtakkar* blueprints survived is unclear. But the jihadists' interest in chemical weapons most certainly did.

In the same period, in a mountain hideout on the border between Iraq and Iran, Jordanian terrorist Abu Musab al-Zarqawi and his disciples also carried out experiments using dogs and rabbits as test subjects, taking video of the grisly results. By late 2002 the militants were beginning to sketch out ideas and enlist recruits for a future chemical attack in Europe. Those plans were shoved aside when U.S. troops invaded Iraq and Zarqawi saw an opportunity to move to Baghdad to start an insurgency. He called his organization "al-Qaeda in Iraq." It would later call itself the Islamic State.

Like bin Laden and his followers, ISIS dreamed of a mass-casualty terrorist attack involving chemical weapons. In 2004, Zarqawi sent operatives to his native Jordan to carry out a plan to release a cloud of poison gas over the capital city, Amman. The bombmaker picked for the job had gathered the ingredients and chosen his target when Jordanian intelligence officials learned of the plot and killed or captured the ringleaders in a dramatic shootout. Later, after Zarqawi's death in 2006, his followers terrorized central Iraq with a string of chemical bombings that released chlorine, a common industrial chemical that can kill or injure if inhaled. In less than a year, U.S. officials recorded thirteen such attacks, including several that wounded American service members. In the deadliest single incident, in May 2007, a chlorine bomb detonated in a crowded marketplace in Diyala Province, leaving, between blast wounds and asphyxiation, thirty-two people dead and at least fifty injured.

Yet chlorine was a weak substitute for the poisons ISIS wanted most. To deliver a blow that would truly shock the world, Zarqawi's men needed something more powerful: a nerve agent. These could be obtained either by buying or stealing sarin or VX that had been made by someone else; or by acquiring enough real estate, equipment, and technical know-how to start a homegrown manufacturing operation.

For years, both routes remained beyond the terrorists' reach. In Syria's war-ravaged provinces, that was about to change.

2

"Something fell from the sky"

SARAQEB, SYRIA. APRIL 29, 2013

Just before the start of afternoon prayers, the Syrian guns fell eerily silent. Throughout the hot midday, as Saraqeb's residents sweltered in darkened houses, artillery shells shrieked and crashed as gunners demolished a row of apartment buildings near the highway, creating palls of smoke and dust on a day bereft of even the small mercy of a wind. And then, abruptly, the shelling stopped. Rebel lookouts peered warily from their posts and strained for the sounds of tanks on the move, but nothing stirred. Instead, from above the town came the faint whir of a lone helicopter, drifting down from the north, unhurried and very high, well beyond the reach of ground fire. From the barricades it appeared small and almost beautiful, a tiny pearl of reflected sunlight, floating above the ruins and squalor of an ordinary Syrian town under siege.

Then, as the rebels watched, something fell from the chopper and began hurtling toward the ground in a slow tumble, like a piece of furniture jettisoned at ten thousand feet. Some who saw it raised their cell phones to take video of the falling thing, not yet aware that they were witnessing a portent. For more than a year, the battle lines had whipsawed through Saraqeb, a northern city of thirty-four thousand that the rebels had seized, then lost, and then captured again. Entire families with small children lay entombed under the rubble of collapsed houses. Now something new was coming, and men watched and took their photos, murmuring an all-purpose supplication: *Allahu Akbar*. God is greater. And when the helicopter disgorged a second parcel, and a third, they prayed again.

Allahu Akbar. Allahu Akbar.

And then—nothing. The strange objects hit the ground in a straight line along Saraqeb's western fringe, yet none of them exploded. The first one crashed onto a deserted intersection and broke into pieces. The second thudded into a swampy field next to a retention pond. The third fell into a residential neighborhood of tidy middle-class homes and disappeared from sight. Although no one knew it yet, it had sliced through a grape arbor and landed smack in the middle of the walled courtyard of the house where Maryam al-Khatib, a fifty-two-year-old wife and mother, had huddled with her children to wait out the day's shelling.

The mistress of the house was a heavy woman with a round face and black hair cropped sensibly above the shoulders. When the fighting began, she had converted her basement into a makeshift bomb shelter for the extended family, stocking it with preserved vegetables she canned herself and whatever meager pickings could be found in the local markets. The house itself was encased inside a thick wall of rough-hewn limestone with a solid steel gate, painted bright blue and wreathed in Maryam's grapevines, guarding the entrance to the narrow alley that ran along the front of the house. It felt safe, as much as any dwelling in Saraqeb could be regarded as such, and on this day, the pause in the shelling had seemed to suggest that the immediate danger had passed. Maryam's husband, Ibrahim, a farmer and a devout man, decided to risk the four-block walk to the local mosque for prayers, leaving his wife and pregnant daughter-in-law, Ahlah, to begin to contemplate what to prepare for the evening meal.

A terrific thunderclap shook the dwelling, as though lightning had struck very close by. From the basement it felt as though the house itself had been hit; yet the walls still stood, and all seemed quiet above. Was it a dud rocket? Pieces from a falling airplane? Maryam crept up the stairs and saw, through a window, a pile of smoking rubble in her courtyard. The thing lay halfway between the steel gate and the rosebushes, having just missed the wooden toddler swing and the freshly jarred pickles Maryam had set out. She slipped on sandals, pulled her silk scarf over her head, and padded outside to investigate, with Ahlah trailing closely behind her.

The strange object that had fallen into Maryam's courtyard was not a bomb; it wasn't even metal. It appeared to be a crate of some kind, made of wood and wire and what might have been gypsum board, now smashed into thousands of chalky pieces. The impact had kicked up a cloud of dust, snapped off tree branches, and gouged a hole in the stone tiles, but otherwise it seemed to have caused little damage. As Maryam inspected the debris, she also noticed a small white canister, about the size of a coffee thermos but crushed nearly flat by the fall. There was a strange odor: pulverized cement mingled with something else, unpleasant but undefined, and Maryam felt her eyes starting to sting.

Just as she turned to go back inside, she was seized by a sudden, unimaginable pain, as though the upper half of her body were being crushed by an invisible vise. The breath of poison that had entered her lungs had already begun to do its work, hijacking her central nervous system and causing a million neurotransmitters to short-circuit in a single second. Tears and mucous began streaming in rivulets from her eyes and nose. There was a strange sensation—a feeling of being suffocated and intensely nauseous all at once, as though something big and dead had lodged itself in her stomach. Maryam fell heavily onto the stone floor, gasping, gray eyes wide with panic, unable to speak or cry out.

Only a few minutes had passed when Ibrahim, returning from prayers, rounded the corner to see neighbors and militiamen clustered around the blue gate. He pushed his way through the crowd and stepped into a vision of incomprehensible horror. Sprawled across the kitchen and living room was half his family: Maryam, Ahlah, three other children, and a sister-in-law, each gasping for breath, as though in the death grip of some invisible malevolence. The militiamen were organizing a relay, and Ibrahim rushed to help, grabbing his stricken loved ones by the arms and legs and hauling them to cars outside. It was clear already that Maryam was worse off than the others. Unable to speak, she looked up at her husband with frightened eyes, the lower half of her face obscured by a mask of white froth. The convulsions were now coming in waves.

Ibrahim was growing increasingly frantic. He ran into his son, Mohammad, who had been outside the house and saw what had happened.

"Something fell from the sky," Mohammad said.

The rebel soldiers raced through deserted streets to arrive at the makeshift medical clinic that had been set up as a triage station for wounded guerrillas. Inside, workers lifted Maryam and Ahlah onto examining tables while those with lesser injuries—a group that now included militiamen who had merely touched the victims—lay on the bare floor. An orderly splashed the women's faces with water while a pair of doctors scoured the clinic for vials of atropine, a drug kept on hand in Syrian villages to treat farm animals in cases of accidental pesticide exposure. A frantic rescue attempt lurched into gear, punctuated by desperate sounds: the retching and wheezing of the victims, pleading instructions from the doctors, cries and prayers from onlookers.

"Hold his legs! Come help me—anyone!" one of the doctors yelled as he tried to strap an oxygen mask to the face of a youth in camouflage who was gagging and flailing like a drowning man. A rough hand held the legs steady as a voice recited the prayer of the dying: "I bear witness," the voice said, "there is no god but God."

Others, sensing the magnitude of the events, again took out their phones to record the moment. They clustered around one of the doctors, a young man with a trim beard who ran through a list of symptoms that by now were obvious to everyone.

"We have all the indications of poison gas," the doctor was saying, spitting out a rapid-fire assessment as he put a bystander to work as a human IV pole. "The foaming, the tiny pupils, the suffocation, the seizures."

What kind of poison? No one knew. There was not much that the tiny clinic could do anyway. Behind the doctor, men took turns squeezing manual oxygen pumps and wiping foam from the faces of the injured. "We do not have antidotes for these kinds of weapons," the doctor said.

Minutes passed. Some of the victims with milder exposures were beginning to breathe quietly through their oxygen masks. But the doctors were growing increasingly alarmed over the condition of the pregnant Ahlah, and for Maryam, who was sinking in and out of consciousness. The older woman's breaths now came in shallow gasps, and her eyes, still wide open, with the same look of frozen terror, no longer moved at all, except for a steady, reflexive blinking.

The doctors squeezed more atropine into her IV tube and turned up the oxygen in her respirator, yet there was no change. She lay for an hour under a dirty blanket, her hair still tucked modestly under her floral head scarf, eyes fixed on the ceiling, making no sign or sound, but only blinking. Blinking. Blinking.

Twilight was approaching, and an anxious Ibrahim al-Khatib conferred with the doctors about what to do. They decided at last to gamble on what was clearly the victims' only remaining chance: a risky dash to the Turkish border. There was a hospital in Reyhanli, the nearest Turkish city, about ninety minutes away by car.

Maryam and Ahlah were gently lifted into ambulances, and Ibrahim climbed in next to his wife to begin the dangerous trek north. The drivers clung to back roads, where they were less likely to encounter patrols and checkpoints, and arrived just after dark at the slatted steel fence that marked the international boundary. At the border crossing, Turkish guards peered into the vehicles and conferred with one another. Minutes later, a supervisor delivered the heartbreaking news: The Turkish border authorities were not equipped to deal with a pair of sick women who had been contaminated with something no one could identify. There would be no entry into Turkey on this night.

Ibrahim refused to give up. The small caravan waited for an hour, and then two, as desperate calls were made to refugee groups on the Turkish side. At last, the guards relented. The gates opened, and the ambulances roared along the final five-mile stretch to Reyhanli and its Health Ministry State Hospital. It was now 10:15 p.m., and by that hour, the emergency room's staff had been alerted to the imminent arrival of poisoning victims and was ready for them. Ahlah was wheeled into the emergency room, where doctors began an infusion of antitoxins that would ultimately save her life and ensure the survival of her unborn child.

For Maryam al-Khatib, there would be no such attempt. Sometime during the journey's final leg, in the minutes between the border crossing and the arrival at the Turkish hospital, the blinking finally stopped. Of the Saraqeb townspeople sickened by the mysterious objects that fell from the sky on April 29, she was the only one to die.

A Turkish doctor noted Maryam's death at 10:45 p.m., of chemical poisoning. The nature of the poison, and who manufactured it, remained officially unknown.

Maryam al-Khatib had not yet died when news of the strange attack exploded across rebel-held northern Syria. Thousands of mobile phones lit up as a relay chain of social-media activists, rescue workers, students, and citizen-journalists leapt into action. The alert spread to local medical clinics and hospitals, including in the city of Aleppo, some thirty miles from Saraqeb, where a harried young physician in bloodstained scrubs paused to study the news.

Houssam Alnahhas was just twenty-five and technically not yet a doctor, though he had completed medical school and was in his final year as an intern when the civil war broke out. His lack of a certificate didn't much matter, because no amount of training could have prepared him for what he faced on his inaugural day in a war-zone trauma center. His first patient was a man with both legs blown off. The second had suffered a gruesome abdominal wound that left his intestines exposed. Alnahhas cleaned and patched as best he could and then moved on. Each day after that, he worked until the triage room emptied out, then flopped onto a hospital bed for a few hours of sleep before repeating the cycle. Despite perpetual dark circles under his eyes, he was a handsome youth, with thick black hair and scholarly glasses, and he stood out in the hospital's grim wards because of his irrepressible cheerfulness. Other doctors slept with pistols, not for self-defense but to avoid capture in case of an assault on the hospital. Not Alnahhas. "We're not going to die," he said. "We have something else to do."

In the Aleppo of 2013, that optimism was ever harder to sustain. Syria's largest city had been spared the worst of the violence in the civil war's first year, but then, in mid-2012, thousands of rebel militiamen poured in from the north and south in an attempt to capture the city. The army mounted a fierce counterattack, backed by helicopters and artillery, and over the next four years this ancient, culturally vibrant metropolis of 2.5 million was slowly ground into rubble, neighborhood by neighborhood and block by block.

In its effort to dislodge the rebels and their supporters, the Syrian army attacked residential neighborhoods with ballistic missiles and then with barrel bombs, a type of crude munition dropped by helicopter that consisted of an empty canister packed with explosives. Iran, Syria's closest ally, sent reinforcements in 2013 in the person of Major General Qasem Soleimani, the legendary commander of Iran's elite Quds Force, who proceeded to direct a new force of about four thousand Hezbollah militiamen from neighboring Lebanon. Then, when the rebels still refused to give up, the Syrians began to experiment with new kinds of weapons, looking for ways to frighten the resisters and drive them from their barricades.

There had been a half-dozen reports of poison-gas attacks by mid-2013, and the stories were usually vague and unconfirmed. But to Alnahhas they were profoundly troubling. Syrians died every day from bullets, blast wounds, and shrapnel injuries, but to exterminate human beings with chemicals, as though they were fleas or cockroaches—this, to the young doctor, was a different order of savagery.

His first awareness of such cases had come from his own mother. His parents lived in a government-controlled Damascus suburb, about two hundred miles south of Aleppo, and one day, after a bombing of nearby rebel strongholds, the wind had carried an odd smell, and people in the neighborhood immediately began experiencing strange symptoms: uncontrollable tearing, coughing, and a tightness in the chest. Alnahhas's mom phoned her physician son to ask for his opinion.

"What do you think is happening?" she wondered.

Alnahhas wasn't sure, so he began to research. The symptoms seemed to match those of people exposed to certain pesticides, called organophosphates. Maybe the fighting had ruptured tanks of farm chemicals.

But other reports followed, from different parts of the country, and the young doctor's interest grew into an obsession. If the government was using some sort of poison gas against civilians, people had to be warned. Doctors and hospitals had to prepare, so they could treat the injured and also avoid being contaminated themselves. And somehow, proof of this newest atrocity would have to reach the outside world.

Alnahhas bombarded colleagues with his findings and theories. After a while, among the medical workers and activists, he acquired a reputation as a kind of one-man clearinghouse for information about chemical weapons. He also picked up a new nickname: Hazem al-Kimawi, or in English, "Chemical Hazem." It fit. Since childhood, friends and relatives had called him "Hazem," which in Arabic means strong-willed.

But getting others to share his passion wasn't easy in the early days of the war. It was hard enough dealing with the daily traumas of life in northern Syria without worrying about a handful of mysterious deaths in far-flung villages. Besides, within the community of medical workers and relief agencies, there were doubts that the reports were real. The U.S. president, Barack Obama, had warned Syria's government of consequences if chemical weapons were used—he had called it a "red line." Surely even Bashar al-Assad would not be so foolish as to gas his own citizens and risk inviting a military strike by the Americans.

And yet, here was a new report of civilians being stricken by an invisible toxin. As he always did, "Chemical Hazem" gathered as much information as he could, and he tried to make sense of the strange details, especially the small canister, encased in a boxlike object dropped from a helicopter. At least two amateur investigators from within the broader network of activists hurried to Saraqeb to see what they could find. One of them got extraordinarily lucky. He was led by local residents to the swampy spot near a pond where one of the devices still lay, unexploded. It was gingerly picked up, examined, and placed in a plastic bag. The thing resembled a tear-gas grenade, with an inscription in English imprinted on the metal lid. The liquid contents were still inside.

The investigators also managed to track down Maryam al-Khatib's husband, Ibrahim. They accompanied him into his empty house and took video as he kicked at the broken patio tile, marking the spot where the deadly parcel had fallen into his courtyard.

The man was grief and fury combined. He had not been allowed to bury his wife, or even to claim her body, since Turkish authorities had ordained that Maryam's remains be quarantined because of the risk of spreading toxins.

"What is the world waiting for?" Ibrahim asked, his voice cracking with emotion. "Tell Obama to draw his red line here! It has been crossed twenty times over, and he cannot say a single word."

"What about the European nations? What about their 'human

rights'?" he continued. "Have we heard from a single Arab leader? Or a king? Or a president? The world sees that we are exterminated, with every type of weapon, and it does nothing."

It was wrenching to watch, and it was also evidence. The investigators had hit the jackpot in Saraqeb, successfully acquiring eyewitness testimony, soil samples, and—most extraordinarily—an unexploded bomb. As a precaution, the material was divided, to be carried to Turkey in separate cars, in case one of them was stopped.

Several days passed, and no word reached Aleppo on whether the investigators had made it safely across the border. Finally, Alnahhas began to pick up fragments of a story about one of the young volunteers who had transported the evidence from Saraqeb. The youth apparently had nearly made it to Turkey when his car was stopped. The border region was regularly patrolled by the *shabiha,* the pro-government thugs who functioned as a self-appointed home guard in Syria's contested provinces. According to the story, the militiamen had pulled the driver out of his car and, without provocation, shot him dead in the street. The fate of the evidence trove he carried was unknown.

Alnahhas was shaken. The young volunteer had taken great risks and achieved a remarkable success, apparently all for naught. By now, the hard-won evidence of the crime had surely disappeared, and that meant, as far as Syria's rulers were concerned, that there had been no crime at all.

But proof did still exist, though no one in Aleppo knew it.

It existed because Ibrahim al-Khatib, in his frantic bid to save his family, crossed into Turkey seeking medical help. Maryam died in a Turkish hospital, and under Turkish rules her body would remain there indefinitely, in the hospital's morgue. Thanks to Maryam and her family, there remained within reach a vitally important clue:

A corpse.

On the morning of July 5, just over two months after Maryam's death, the lights flickered on in the small chamber that serves as the Reyhanli hospital's autopsy room and morgue. Seven men in green scrubs and surgical masks filed into the room toting boxes and plastic bags and clustered around the bank of refrigerated drawers where the bodies were kept. Four of the men were doctors and hospital administrators from the town, but the other three were visitors, part of a delegation that had arrived from the Netherlands the day before. These began to quietly unpack their gear: sealed laboratory tubes and cups, marker pens, recording equipment, clipboards, and a small bottle of Vicks VapoRub. A small dab of the latter, smeared around the nose, would help offset the unpleasant odors that were likely to accompany the morning's work.

A Turkish doctor stepped forward to open one of the metal drawers, and the tray was pulled back in a rush of cold, dank air. A large body bag of dark blue plastic was lifted by the straps and lowered with effort onto a stainless-steel autopsy table. Carefully, the flaps of the bag were peeled back, exposing the face of the dead woman the visitors had traveled halfway around the world to see. She was middle-aged and obese, with matted black hair and arms crossed at the waist, and she was naked except for a hospital bracelet and a bloodstained sheet that had been draped modestly over her torso. After two months in the morgue, the dead woman's facial features had tightened into a grimace, and her skin was a mottle of unnatural hues: reds, oranges, and violets. The body itself was as rigid as a plank, because Turkish officials, unsure of how or when the corpse might be required in the future, had decided that it should be frozen solid. To get at whatever secrets the body might contain, Maryam al-Khatib would first have to be thawed out.

The autopsy thus began with warm water and a simple spray hose, of the kind found in most kitchens. The Turkish doctors took turns spraying the corpse, while the visitors—an Indian physician, a German, and a Serb—documented each step with video and still cameras as well as a voice recorder, into which the Indian man murmured a running commentary. Nothing was missed, because the foreigners, part of a special team of experts appointed by the United Nations, had been dispatched to Turkey not only to gather evidence, but also to create a careful record so there could be no question in the future of tampering or contamination.

So they watched, took notes, and snapped their photos. And they waited, patiently, for Maryam's defrosting to be complete.

—

The discovery of the body had been a godsend, though the man who arranged for the autopsy on this July morning would never have called it that. UN team leader Åke Sellström believed in science, above all. During four decades of professional work, science had been both a calling and a way of imposing order on a chaotic universe. On more than a few occasions it also served as a kind of refuge, a means of preserving distance between himself and the unsettling moral and political undercurrents that so often accompanied the work in his most unusual of occupations.

A tall, convivial Swede with an impish smile, Sellström had acquired, at the age of sixty-four, a reputation as one of the world's foremost authorities on tracking illicit WMD. The role had come to him by chance—"a slip on a banana peel," as he would say—while he was pursuing what otherwise might have been a quiet career as a researcher and medical professor. A leading specialist on the neurological effects of chemical agents, he was recruited in the mid-1990s to provide technical help for UN weapons experts investigating Iraq's chemical weapons program following the first Gulf War. Within months he was personally leading inspection teams in and out of Iraq, an assignment that would continue intermittently over several years. Investigations of this type often required searching for clues in unsavory places: in secret laboratories and underground bunkers; in dictators' palaces and in garbage dumps; in hospitals and graveyards where one might go to obtain the blood and tissue of the wounded and the dead. But Sellström exuded a kind of scientific gravitas and personal propriety that—together with his citizenship in neutral Sweden—lent additional credibility to his findings, however controversial they might be. With friends and colleagues he could be graciously charming, with a playful, self-deprecating wit that made him a popular manager and leader. But on the hunt, Sellström was every bit the dispassionate academic, as cool and unflinching as a surgeon's blade.

"I need a good standard—a scientific standard, that you can live with and die with," Sellström would say simply, in explaining his approach to the job. "Then I just do the best that I can to come to the truth. It's up to others to decide what happens next."

His Syrian assignment had proven more difficult than most. Three months earlier, Sellström had been asked by the UN secretary-general to investigate what was in essence a mass murder: dozens of killings, all reportedly involving some kind of poison gas, in scattered attacks in cities and towns across Syria. Yet he had not been allowed within miles of any of the crime scenes. The Syrians had agreed to the probe—had asked the United Nations for it, in fact—after a mysterious incident on March 19 in which a foul-smelling cloud drifted across a defensive position manned by pro-government forces in the village of Khan al-Assal, on the southern outskirts of Aleppo. The gas killed sixteen soldiers and ten civilians and left a trail of dead farm animals, and Damascus had blamed the antigovernment rebels, mainly on the grounds that most of the dead had been loyalist troops. But within hours of Syria's request, Britain, France, and Qatar had demanded that the probe be expanded to include other alleged gas attacks, ones that appeared to target rebel-held neighborhoods. Syria, which until now had steadfastly denied even possessing chemical weapons, was not about to allow a broad search, so it refused to let the inspectors in. As weeks passed with no change in the Syrian position, Sellström began to imagine the possibility of failure. Unless the Syrians could be persuaded to grant access, his investigation would probably never get off the ground.

There was another potentially worrisome outcome, too, although it went mostly unmentioned. If by chance the Syrians completely relented—if Sellström and his experts were allowed to conduct a proper investigation, without restrictions—there was a high probability that they would find evidence of a war crime. Then what? Sellström viewed chemical weapons as uniquely repugnant, and he believed that anyone using them should be held accountable for their actions. But he was also a pacifist at heart, a despiser of war who, as a youth, registered as a conscientious objector and accepted a civilian assignment when his time came to serve in the Swedish armed forces. The terms of the United Nations' agreement with Damascus barred Sellström's investigators from explicitly identifying a guilty party in any of the chemical attacks, but if the evidence clearly pointed to Syria, there would be consequences. Air strikes, no doubt. A major escalation of the war, perhaps. Syria's civilian population could be afflicted with new miseries that surpassed those they had suffered before the inspectors arrived.

Sellström had seen it happen before, and he had learned painfully that the "victories" in his line of work were never entirely clean.

During his time in Iraq in the early 1990s, he had helped uncover evidence—essentially through a confession, extracted through careful questioning—of a clandestine Iraqi program to manufacture VX, the deadliest known nerve agent. But Sellström also grew worried that Iraq's stonewalling of UN inspection teams was pushing the region toward a new military confrontation. In 1998, Sellström broke diplomatic protocol to make a direct appeal to Iraqi foreign minister Tariq Aziz, urging him to cooperate with the inspectors for the good of his country. "Throw us out and we'll have another war," he warned. Days later, the UN team pulled out, and on December 16, 1998, U.S. and British warplanes and ships unleashed a four-day barrage of bombs and missiles, killing an estimated 1,400 Iraqis, including civilians whose houses were destroyed when a few of the missiles veered off course.

Four years later, the Swede was tapped again as a consultant when UN inspectors investigated claims that Iraqi dictator Saddam Hussein was continuing to make weapons of mass destruction—WMD—in secret. UN teams roamed the country for four months, searching for hidden weapons factories and mobile laboratories that had been described in vivid detail by Iraqi defectors. None were found, and yet the inspectors pressed on with their work, intent on settling the weapons questions once and for all. They were still interviewing Iraqi scientists in March 2003 when a warning was passed from Washington that all foreigners should quickly leave the country. Days later, on March 20, the George W. Bush administration ordered the opening salvos of Operation Iraqi Freedom, the massive military intervention aimed at halting an Iraqi weapons program that, as subsequent investigations would later confirm, no longer existed.

After that, Sellström decided to return to Sweden. He continued to do occasional consulting work on arms control for the UN Secretariat, but mainly settled into a life of teaching university classes and enjoying his summer cottage on Sweden's rocky western coast. And yet, when Angela Kane, the UN high representative for disarmament affairs, telephoned him in late March 2013 to ask if he would accept a special assignment in Syria—one that would again require him to search for evidence that could tip the balance toward war or peace—he did not hesitate.

"What have you said yes to now?" his wife demanded after he hung up the phone.

"I'll been gone two or three weeks," he replied. "We prepare for a week or two, then we go into the country for a week, and then we write the report. That's it."

But three months passed, and there was no report, and only a fading hope that the investigation would happen at all. As the weeks dragged by, Sellström's team busied itself by studying the available evidence, including journalists' accounts and amateur videos of the dozen incidents in which chemical weapons were allegedly used. They met with Syrian defectors and intelligence operatives who had visited border towns and returned with physical evidence—hair and blood samples, mainly—that had made it across the border, hand-carried by Syrian rebel groups and activists who were only too happy to furnish "proof" of Assad's atrocities. But such samples were generally regarded as useless, because the providers could never satisfy the rigorous standards required of a UN scientific investigation. The kind of evidence Sellström needed to establish the facts did not exist except in Syria, and the Swede was not allowed to go there.

Then in June, Sellström and his deputies met with activists who described the case of a woman who had been poisoned in Syria but had died on the Turkish side of the border. They traveled to the Turkish capital to meet with government health officials, asking them about the disposition of the woman's corpse and whether they might be able to see it. Yes, the Reyhanli hospital still had the body in its morgue, where it had remained under Turkish control since the hour of the woman's death, Sellström was told. And yes, the UN team's medical professionals were welcome to have a look.

"That's when we realized we had something important," Sellström later recalled. "There was a body. And now there was a possibility for an autopsy."

There were gains to be made beyond collecting physical evidence. The Syrian government had managed to avoid a serious reckoning over chemical weapons attacks by simply refusing to let inspectors into the country. Now, with the discovery of Maryam's body in Turkey, the UN team would soon know which chemical was dropped over a house in Saraqeb on that afternoon in late April. Depending on the quality of the specimens collected, the experts might also learn how the poison was made, and perhaps who made it.

For the Syrians, any hope of influencing the outcome of the investigation—by asserting an alternative hypothesis, perhaps, or offering evidence that the rebels were equally guilty of chemical weapons offenses—lay in cooperating with Sellström's team.

Syria had no choice now but to let the inspectors in.

The body in the Reyhanli morgue slowly warmed into something that more closely resembled Maryam al-Khatib in life. The limbs regained their suppleness. The reds and purples faded, so that the skin took on the color of yellow alabaster. The men in the surgical masks could begin their work.

Dozens of plastic vials had been laid out in rows, and, one by one, each was filled with pieces of dissected tissue and labeled by hand: *Brain. Lung. Liver. Kidney.* The Turks had performed an earlier autopsy, and so, to rule out the possibility of tampering, the team filled additional vials with cuttings of skin, hair, and muscle taken from the body at random places. Later, these would be used to establish a DNA profile, against which every other bit of harvested tissue would be matched.

When all was finished, the vials were sealed with tamper-proof tape and divided into sets for testing at multiple independent laboratories, one in Turkey and others in Switzerland and Holland. Maryam al-Khatib, having provided testimony about the means of her own murder, was returned to her body bag and refrigerated drawer, and the door was shut.

Several days after the UN team had returned to the Netherlands, the lab results began trickling in. The Turkish facility lacked the necessary equipment to test for traces of a chemical nerve agent, so its report was inconclusive. But the analyses from each of the European labs contained the same striking result. In the tissues collected from the brain, skin, and other organs, the tests found a number of chemical by-products—residues, essentially—that occur when human cells are exposed to a nerve agent. And in the lung samples, there existed small amounts of a compound denoted on the lab sheets simply as "GB," the code name created by U.S. scientists in the late 1940s for the exceptionally lethal poison developed by Nazi Germany just before the start of World War II. Two months after her death, Maryam's lungs still contained tiny droplets of pure, military-grade sarin.

Who made the poison, and who ordered its use? There were dozens of unanswered questions, including a puzzling discovery of an unexpected element in the sarin, a chemical compound often found in explosives. It was called hexamine, and its presence in the sarin baffled the investigators at the laboratory that conducted the analysis.

A fuller accounting was likely still weeks, perhaps months, away, but Åke Sellström and his "good standard" had yielded results. Now his team could turn its attention to Syria itself, and to all the evidence—mystifying, heartbreaking, infuriating—that was still to be found there.

The more urgent Syrian threat—the one that kept Andrew Weber awake at night—grew more ominous by the day. Each morning, the color-coded map delivered to Weber's Pentagon office showed a further narrowing of the slender margin between security and disaster.

East of Aleppo, the al-Qaeda-allied group al-Nusra Front had captured a town called al-Safira, home to a major armaments works and a known storage depot for Syria's chemical weapons. Government troops had tried to clear out the bunker ahead of the rebel assault, but whether they fully succeeded was unclear. Meanwhile, in the far north, a different al-Qaeda offshoot that now called itself the Islamic State had captured a key air base after a ferocious battle at a place called al-Menagh. The little-known group now straddled the major supply route from Turkey to Islamist strongholds to the south and east. The story of the maps was regularly reinforced by dire warnings from Washington's closest allies in the region, the Israelis and the Jordanians. Syria's chemical weapons were at risk, and the risk was growing.

Weber studied the maps and watched, with a mixture of anxiousness and frustration, as civilian and military leaders debated wildly different, and ultimately ineffective, strategies for dealing with the threat. He had been present when President Obama delivered a fateful warning to his Syrian counterpart to keep his nerve agents under lock and key. He had sat through multiple Pentagon meetings in which military experts swore that they could take out Assad's chemical arsenal with a few bombs and missiles.

Weber was horrified. Even an extremely successful strike would fail to destroy all the chemicals. Indeed, it would probably just spread them, in the form of a poison plume wafting across neighborhoods crowded with women and children.

"For one hundred years," Weber said, "when people talked about chemical weapons deaths in Syria, we would be blamed."

The only truly safe thing to do was take the chemicals out, somehow. It had been done before. When the Soviet Union collapsed, thousands of weapons had been at risk of being lost or stolen, including entire warehouses stacked to the roof with bombs filled with sarin and VX. Within the upper echelons of the White House and Pentagon were numerous officials who had made their bones helping the former Soviet republics remove or destroy old WMD stockpiles. These included Ash Carter, the Pentagon's deputy secretary of defense, and Laura Holgate, the senior director on WMD terrorism at the White House National Security Council, and also Weber, who had distinguished himself among the weapons hunters as a man with a remarkable knack for getting bad stuff out of bad places.

Weber cemented his reputation in the early 1990s when he was a thirtysomething WMD specialist assigned to the U.S. embassy in Almaty, Kazakhstan. A Russian-speaker with a disarming smile and a try-anything approach to strange foods, liquors, and customs, Weber bonded easily with a cast of post-Soviet characters that included retired army generals, weapons scientists, and hard-drinking apparatchiks. With interlocutors such as these, he helped arrange the removal of a dangerous cache of nuclear material from the former Soviet republic of Georgia, as well as the purchase of an entire squadron of nuclear-capable Russian MiG-29 fighters that had been marooned in Moldova after the Soviet Union collapsed. After learning that Iran was seeking to buy the planes, Weber helped pay off the Moldovans, dismantle the jets, and quietly ship all twenty-one of them to an air base in Ohio before the rest of the world knew anything about it.

But Weber's most celebrated achievement occurred in Kazakhstan itself, and would become known to history as Project Sapphire. It started in 1994 when a Kazakh businessman approached Weber to ask if the Americans were interested in a large stash of uranium metal that had been orphaned at one of his factories amid the chaos that followed the Soviet Union's dissolution. The businessman traveled with Weber to an industrial complex near the Kazakh-Russian border and, after disarming the security system—a single padlock—ushered his visitor into a cavernous building where the uranium was kept. Inside, on makeshift tables perched on a dirt floor, were hundreds of steel buckets containing uranium fuel rods, all of them enriched to "weapons grade"—pure enough to make them immediately suitable for use in atomic weapons. The buckets had been spaced about ten feet apart because of fears that the uranium's radiation might trigger an accidental nuclear chain reaction.

Alarmed at the discovery of bomb-ready nuclear fuel in such a vulnerable place, the Clinton administration quietly cut a deal with Kazakhstan to purchase and extract the entire cache. A team of Americans was dispatched to Kazakhstan in a C-5 Galaxy cargo plane to begin the physical removal. Then, with Weber looking on, the U.S. experts packed the uranium into shipping containers, loaded it into trucks, and raced back to the plane. The 448-crate shipment that arrived at a Delaware air base on November 22, 1994, was calculated to contain 1,300 pounds of weapons-grade uranium, enough for about two dozen nuclear bombs.

Weber later returned to Washington and another "loose nukes" job, this time as a policy adviser for the federal government's ambitious Cooperative Threat Reduction program, which worked directly with Russia and other former Soviet republics to secure or dismantle Cold War–era nuclear, chemical, and biological weapons stockpiles and research facilities. It was in this capacity that he first encountered a young U.S. senator from Illinois named Barack Obama. The future president had campaigned for the Senate as a harsh critic of the 2003 U.S. invasion of Iraq and the flawed prewar intelligence about Iraqi weapons of mass destruction. Yet, soon after arriving in Washington, Obama chose weapons proliferation as one of his signature issues. In August 2005, he signed up for a congressional fact-finding trip to former Soviet nuclear and biological weapons facilities in Russia and Ukraine, accompanied by Senator Richard Lugar, an Indiana Republican and one of the Senate's leading champions of arms control. Weber was brought along as a kind of expert tour guide, and he was struck at once by Obama's nimble mind, thoughtful questions, and quick mastery of the subject matter. Having encountered numerous other U.S. lawmakers during similar trips over the years, he had not expected to be impressed.

"The guy was brilliant. He was fun. And he had this insatiable intellectual curiosity," Weber recalled years afterward. "He was on the visit to learn. It felt like I was being interrogated, because he had a million questions."

Many of those questions came as Obama and Weber walked together through sprawling factories and decaying, poorly guarded laboratories that once produced components for nuclear and biological weapons. Obama's eyes widened when, during a tour of a biological facility in the Ukrainian capital of Kyiv, a worker opened a small refrigerator to reveal row after row of test tubes containing the bacteria strains that cause anthrax and the plague—the seed stock for germ warfare.

"Hey, where's Lugar? Doesn't he want to see this?" said Obama, looking around. At the back of the room, the smiling, silver-maned Indianan had contented himself simply to watch. Lugar, who had personally witnessed the dismantling of numerous Cold War–era WMD stockpiles as one of the original founders of the Cooperative Threat Reduction program, had seen it all before.

"Been there, done that," Lugar replied.

Weber had seen it all, too. But something about the young Illinois senator, as he stood mesmerized by the latent terror contained inside a single vial of plague bacteria, made a lasting impression. Three years later, Weber would sign up as a volunteer campaign worker for Obama during his run for the White House. And in turn, the victorious Obama would personally recommend Weber for a new role as a lead adviser on weapons of mass destruction to the president's secretary of defense.

The new president quickly made WMD a top priority for the White House. Weber had not yet moved in to his new office when Obama, in one of his first foreign policy initiatives after becoming president, traveled to Prague, the Czech capital, in April 2009 to announce a global campaign to halt the spread of WMD and to commit his administration to seeking the eventual elimination of nuclear arms. Weber cheered from the Pentagon the following year when Obama signed a major agreement with Russia setting new limits on the number of deployed nuclear weapons and delivery systems in both countries. But before the end of the president's first term, progress on achieving Obama's ambitious goals appeared to stall. After Vladimir Putin's election to a new term as Russia's president in 2012, Moscow ended its participation in joint U.S.-Russian stockpile security projects. North Korea and Iran, defying warnings from Washington, dramatically cranked up their production of enriched uranium and nuclear-capable missiles.

Then, out of nowhere, trouble erupted in a place that scarcely registered on the Pentagon's list of potential hot spots. Beginning in early 2012 few national security crises consumed more hours, or evoked as many waking nightmares, as the prospect of 1,300 tons of lethal chemicals changing hands in Syria, suddenly the most dangerous country on Earth.

When the Syrian uprising began, the problem of the country's massive chemical arsenal seemed relatively simple: if the government in Damascus were to suddenly collapse—as had already happened in Egypt and Tunisia, the first countries caught up in the Arab Spring—Syria's weapons facilities might be left temporarily unguarded.

In those early days, conventional wisdom held that President Bashar al-Assad would be quickly swept from power. Indeed, there were fears within the White House that Syria's dictator might fall before the Obama administration had a chance to position itself publicly as a supporter of Syria's pro-democracy movement. Barack Obama took to the podium in August 2011 to declare to the world that the "time has come for President Assad to step aside." Those words would have enormous, unforeseen consequences in the months and years that followed.

Around the time of the speech, as the protest movement coalesced into a fighting force of army deserters and citizen-soldiers, the administration began to prepare a formal list of instructions for the rebels on what to do should they encounter one of Assad's chemical weapons depots.

"No shooting," the rebels were admonished, in case any were unaware of the potential consequences of puncturing a tank filled with sarin. "Don't touch the material."

In meetings in Paris and Geneva, U.S. diplomats followed up on those warnings by eliciting commitments from opposition leaders:

they were to place the stockpile under international supervision as soon as they gained power. That meant joining the Chemical Weapons Convention—Syria was among a handful of countries that had refused to sign—and submitting to oversight by the world's chemical weapons watchdog, the Organization for the Prohibition of Chemical Weapons, or OPCW.

The rebels were willing, agreeing to everything asked of them. But as the war progressed, the notion of a peaceful transfer of Assad's arsenal began to seem hopelessly naïve.

One problem was the rebels themselves. By 2012 it was clear there was no such thing as a rebel army. The opposition movement was headed by political leaders-in-exile with tenuous ties to the militias on the ground. And those militias were a confusing, ever-changing crazy quilt of armed groups, ranging from small, disciplined units of ex-Syrian soldiers, to neighborhood patrols of untrained students and shopkeepers, to criminal gangs. By mid-2012, a new element emerged: the jihadists. A few of these were bona fide terrorists whom Assad had cynically released from prison to support his claim that his government was battling dangerous extremists, not democratic reformers. Others were foreign activists and mercenaries with ties to the international Muslim Brotherhood or other Islamist organizations. Among the hundreds of rebel factions, the Islamists soon stood out. They were by far the wealthiest, thanks to generous donors and sponsors in the Persian Gulf. They also possessed ample fighting experience, an endless supply of weapons, and a radically different notion of what a liberated Syria should look like.

The other problem was Syria's president. Intelligence analysts everywhere predicted that Bashar al-Assad, a onetime ophthalmologist who was said to dislike the sight of blood, would fall quickly, perhaps forced into exile or even killed by his own intelligence services. But Assad had other ideas. The second son of strongman president Hafez al-Assad proved to be every bit as ruthless as his notoriously cruel father, and he resolved to avoid the fate of other Middle Eastern autocrats who had been swept from power by the Arab Spring. He met protesters' chants with batons and bullets, and then with tanks, determined to crush the uprising even at the cost of destroying Syrian cities. He was backed by frightened ethnic and sectarian minorities who saw their own futures at risk, and by brutal security forces who would not hesitate to slaughter Syrians, including fellow soldiers who refused to carry out orders to kill. "Assad, or we burn the country" was the popular slogan scrawled on the walls of bombed-out apartment buildings by loyalists.

More importantly, Assad, unlike the vanquished leaders of Egypt and Libya, enjoyed unwavering support from two foreign powers that viewed his regime's survival as a matter of vital self-interest. Russia, anxious to preserve its warm-water naval base at the seaport of Tartus, provided Damascus with an endless supply of helicopters, warplanes, and tanks. Iran sent guns, generals, and ground troops to Syria to prop up its most important foreign ally, and it would drain its treasury to keep Assad's economy moving and thus preserve Iran's all-important land corridor to the Mediterranean coast. This blank-check commitment from powerful allies became the secret to Assad's success. As the rebels and their supporters would painfully learn, Assad and his benefactors were always prepared to match them killing for killing, gun for gun, and battle for battle—and with enough added muscle to ensure that the regime never lost control over Damascus or Syria's other major cities. Assad's survival as leader was thus guaranteed, at least until his security forces wearied of the slaughter, or until another, stronger country chose to intervene by committing its own battalions to fighting in Syria's war.

So the bloodletting continued, eventually settling into a grinding stalemate in which neither side could fully prevail. And as the violence deepened, so did Western fears about the fate of Syria's chemical stockpile. There now were at least a half-dozen scenarios for how things could go badly off the rails. In addition to the threat from the Islamists, there was a concern that Assad might use his weapons against his own people. Or he might simply choose to hand them over to Hezbollah, the Iranian-backed militant group, to use against Israel. Thousands of Lebanese Hezbollah fighters already were in Syria to fight the rebels, and some of them bivouacked at military bases where Assad kept his poisons.

The threat became a recurring theme at White House intelligence briefings. Obama sat through hours of intense discussions, often personally quizzing CIA officials about what was happening and what could be done. Among the president's aides there was a collective realization that a mass-casualty attack involving Syria's chemicals—say, in Tel Aviv, New York, or London—would inalterably change the course of the Obama presidency.

The U.S. government was hardly alone in its concern. In Jordan, King Abdullah II quietly convened meetings of key NATO allies to brainstorm ways to quickly secure any chemical weapons facilities that might be overrun. Israeli officials rushed thousands of gas masks and medical kits to distribution centers in northern Israel out of fear that Hezbollah might acquire a few sarin-filled artillery shells and decide to lob them across the border. During one visit to Israel by Pentagon officials, Prime Minister Benjamin Netanyahu became visibly agitated when the subject of Syria's chemical arsenal came up.

"Think outside the box!" Netanyahu urged, leaping out of his chair. He began to toss around ideas in scattershot fashion. What if American, Israeli, and British commandos parachuted into Syria to seize control of the weapons depots? Or what if they planted land mines around the storage bunkers to discourage outsiders from breaking in? None of the ideas struck the Americans as plausible, and none were seriously pursued.

It was Netanyahu's government that supplied the intelligence behind Obama's "red line" warning, a phrase that would dog the forty-fourth U.S. president for the rest of his term in office. In July 2012, Israeli spy agencies began picking up signs of a general mobilization of Syria's chemical warfare units. The "mixing" trucks—the cleverly disguised vehicles that combine precursor chemicals to make binary sarin—came out of their depots, and soon they were being spotted by satellites at different bases. The poisons themselves also were being hauled out of bunkers by newly activated chemical-weapons brigades. Citing evidence that was never made public, Israeli analysts concluded that Assad was preparing to transfer at least some of his stockpile to Hezbollah, the Iran-backed militant group that had publicly committed itself to the destruction of the Jewish state. Ominously, the activity coincided with a curious statement by Syria's Foreign Ministry that appeared to acknowledge the existence of a chemical stockpile—something Syria had never done. A spokesman warned that Damascus possessed special weapons that, while currently "in storage and under security," might be deployed if Syria was "exposed to external aggression." Was Assad hinting of a pending attack against Israel or another neighbor?

The White House was not about to wait for answers. The administration immediately dispatched key aides and diplomats to warn Syria against either using or transferring its weapons. Deputy Secretary of State William J. Burns delivered the message in private to Syrian foreign minister Walid Muallem. The same warning was relayed at least twice to the Russian Foreign Ministry in Moscow, and also, through diplomatic back channels, to Iran.

To make the point absolutely clear, both Obama and Secretary of State Hillary Rodham Clinton issued at least four public statements threatening consequences if Syria used, or even prepared to use, its nerve agents. In late July 2012, Obama told a Veterans of Foreign Wars gathering that Syria would be "held accountable by the international community and the United States" if the country's chemical weapons came out of their bunkers. A month later, on August 20, Obama couched the same warning in a loaded—and his aides would later concede, ill-considered—turn of phrase. Asked about Syria's chemicals at the tail end of a news conference about health care, he described the use of chemical weapons as a "red line."

"We have been very clear to the Assad regime, but also to other players on the ground, that a red line for us is we start seeing a whole bunch of chemical weapons moving around or being utilized," Obama said, answering a reporter's question at a White House press briefing. "That would change my calculus. That would change my equation."

The comment was not part of a prepared statement, nor was it meant to signal a policy change. It was an unscripted, off-the-cuff repetition of the same warning Obama had delivered three weeks earlier. Still, some aides immediately cringed, sensing that the tough-sounding words conveyed more than the president had intended.

"In the course of a presidency, a U.S. president says millions of words in public," Ben Rhodes, Obama's deputy national security adviser for communications, would later write. "You never know which of them end up cementing a certain impression."

This phrase was one that would stick.

The full political impact of Obama's words was not yet clear when the president repeated the warning at a December 4, 2012, speech at the National Defense University on Washington's Anacostia River waterfront. This time, Andrew Weber was in the audience as Obama, addressing the Syrian president by name, said, "You will be held accountable."

"I want to make it absolutely clear to Assad and those under his command: The world is watching," Obama said.

The warning worked, for a time. The movement of heavy equipment abruptly halted. Months would pass before intelligence agencies discovered that Syria had used the lull to reimagine how its most prized weapons would be used: not in warheads delivered by missiles, but in tear-gas grenades and small artillery rockets. Useless on a battlefield, such small-bore delivery systems were ideal for clearing out villages and urban tenements where the rebels and their families tended to live.

Such weapons also were perfect instruments for terrorism, as Weber well understood. On many a morning, huddled with senior deputies in his office, the Pentagon official would lose himself in thought as he studied again the Syrian maps with the pinpoints in black denoting the locations of chemical facilities. Then, one day, he uttered aloud a question that reframed the discussion about Syria's weapons, effectively reducing the problem to a single, practical figure:

"How many trucks?" Weber asked, addressing everyone and no one in particular. "How many trucks would it take?"

Weber and a small network of military planners began to work through the logistics of how, if given a chance, they could haul away Syria's weapons and destroy them. The math was simple enough. Moving 1,300 tons of chemical weapons along with Syria's specialized munitions and equipment would require about two hundred armored tankers and tractor-trailers, an armada of vehicles stretching more than two miles. In the most optimistic case—meaning safe passage, so the convoy did not have to fight its way in and out—the mission would require an army of extras: scores of technicians in hazmat gear, plus scientists, engineers, medics, and mechanics, and enough soldiers, guards, and guns to offer protection from terrorists and other actors who might view such a caravan as an irresistible target.

It all seemed preposterous. But Weber had at least part of the answer.

As for where those two hundred trucks would go, and what would happen to their toxic contents, no one had a clue.

3

The Machine

On a blustery late December morning just three weeks after Barack Obama's speech, a small van with military tags approached the front gate of the Edgewood Chemical Biological Center in northern Maryland and slowed to let the armed sentry peer inside. After a quick check of papers and a snappy salute, the van pulled forward, and the lanky two-star general in the backseat took a first long look at the restricted Army research facility he had driven two hours, in the middle of the holidays, to see.

The base seemed a bit remote, which for Jay Santee was saying something. As a young lieutenant colonel, he had commanded an Air Force missile-tracking station in central Alaska, some eighty miles from a town of any size, in a place where bears outnumbered humans. Now he was staring at woods and empty fields, and a few sights that were downright odd. Near the entrance where other military bases might park a tank or a fighter jet, Edgewood displayed a pair of old trucks with giant, chimney-like spouts jutting from their backs. These belonged to a unit that makes what the Army calls "chemical obscurants" for the battlefield; their military specialty was literally blowing smoke. Other relics of Edgewood's colorful past were sealed off behind strands of razor wire and yellow hazmat signs. Here were the shuttered, rust-caked laboratory buildings in which America's now-outlawed chemical weapons were once made and tested.

"I never heard of the place," Santee admitted afterward. He was there, in the dead week between Christmas and New Year's, at the behest of Defense Department officials who had moved with sudden urgency to arrange a meeting with someone who, it was said, might have answers to the Pentagon's pressing questions about Syria. The man they were seeing was something of a legend, and to call him a polarizing figure was to understate the case. Beloved by subordinates, Timothy Blades was regarded by some in Washington as a character: stubborn, arrogant, and, most annoyingly, given to displays of disdain toward senior military officers and civilian managers who technically outranked him. There were some who called Blades a "chemical cowboy," a term not meant as a compliment. Yet it was indisputable that Blades and his team had amassed a remarkable record of achievement. In the world of chemical weapons, they were the "fixers," the ones who were called in for dirty jobs that no one else wanted to handle. Over the years, the man in charge had managed to carve out a small fiefdom of his own, tucked away on a corner of the Edgewood base, off a narrow road marked by street signs as "Blades Boulevard."

The idea of visiting Edgewood had come from Richard Falkenrath, a former official in the George W. Bush administration who had landed a spot on a Pentagon advisory panel that deals with WMD threats. Falkenrath had been asked to look at the Defense Department's preparations for dealing with a possible crisis in Syria, and he perceived a serious gap in the Pentagon's capabilities. Beyond the brainstorming about trucks, there was no firm plan for what to do with Syria's weapons if they were suddenly acquired. If Bashar al-Assad were assassinated or overthrown, the United States would seek to negotiate the removal of the weapons from Syria, surely, but then what? Where would all those sarin-filled trucks actually go? No one knew.

Santee had been puzzling over the same problem since arriving at his new post at Fort Belvoir, Virgina, that fall. The newly minted major general was now deputy director of something called DTRA, a two-thousand-employee organization on a large campus in a sprawling suburb of Washington, D.C. Pronounced *DIT-rah,* the Defense Threat Reduction Agency housed a mishmash of counter-WMD programs that had been cobbled together for convenience. Before Santee arrived, many of DTRA's senior military leaders had been reserve officers or soon-to-be-retirees finishing out their careers. But Santee was different. A gregarious and energetic fifty-four-year-old, Santee was an Air Force Academy graduate who flew combat missions on radar-jamming EF-111 Raven aircraft during Operation Desert Storm. He had no WMD expertise, but he had a knack for assembling talented teams and encouraging creativity in tackling difficult problems. A small group under Santee's command had already been put in charge of coming up with possible options for dealing with Syria's weapons, but the work had barely gotten under way, and the early results had not been encouraging.

The dearth of palatable choices became apparent when Falkenrath sat down with Santee in mid-December 2012 to review the list of disposal alternatives DTRA had come up with so far. The leading candidate was a vague proposal to mount mobile incinerators on the back of special trucks and destroy the weapons by burning them, presumably somewhere in Syria. Falkenrath was horrified. After the first Gulf War, U.S. officials had tried to incinerate Iraq's leftover chemicals in open pits, and the result had been an environmental disaster and a costly cleanup.

"The answers were lousy," Falkenrath recalled afterward. The truth was, he said, if U.S. forces were to suddenly find themselves in possession of Syria's entire chemical arsenal, "we simply didn't know what would happen next."

In the suddenly expanded search for alternatives, Edgewood emerged as a good place to look, and so Falkenrath and Santee gathered a small entourage to meet Blades and his team. They arrived on the morning of December 28, 2012, and filed into the rambling, single-story building that served as command center for Blades's all-civilian group, which called itself CBARR, short for Chemical Biological Application and Risk Reduction. They were greeted at the entrance by a life-sized mannequin wearing chemical protection gear, then made their way to a large conference room where Blades and a few of his staff were already waiting with a mixture of anticipation and puzzlement, not being entirely sure why a high-ranking delegation from Washington had decided to interrupt their Christmas holidays.

Falkenrath began speaking and, without mentioning a particular country, began to describe a hypothetical problem that the Pentagon might soon be asked to solve. If U.S. forces suddenly came into possession of a large quantity of chemical weapons—say, of nerve agents, mostly in bulk-liquid form—was there a kind of incinerator that could be set up quickly to destroy the poisons without creating an environmental mess?

It was implicitly clear that the topic of discussion was Syria. Several members of the CBARR team sketched out the possible options, and then all eyes turned to Blades. The team leader was slouched slightly, as was his habit. He had been listening quietly, with a look of bemused skepticism he normally wore when explaining chemistry to military officers and bureaucrats.

"An incinerator won't work," Blades said gruffly.

Santee had been taking notes, and he now turned to study the speaker. Blades was middle-aged, with a ruddy complexion and graying, short-cropped hair. It was sometimes said that he looked like Hollywood actor Philip Seymour Hoffman, though Santee didn't see the resemblance. The CBARR chief was sturdily built, with a slightly stocky frame that might have belonged to a dairy farmer—an occupation that Blades had in fact envisioned for himself as a youth, before a series of chance events landed him a job as a twenty-year-old local hire in one of Edgewood's chemical munitions facilities. He dressed and spoke like a construction foreman, serving up blunt-force opinions generously seasoned with expletives and delivered with a slight eastern Maryland twang. He seemed to wear his rough-hewn manner with a kind of cheerful defiance, as a man accustomed to scrapping and winning in an arena in which his competitors all possessed more medals, fancier titles, and bigger budgets than he had. It was part of the Blades lore that he had never completed college but had pulled himself up through hard work, native talent, and sheer competence, and now ran his own organization with considerable independence. Over a nearly four-decade career he had personally handled and destroyed every type of chemical weapon in the U.S. arsenal, and most of those manufactured by the former countries of the Soviet bloc and its Arab allies. And he had the scars—in his case, literal, disfiguring scars—to prove it.

Blades was by now proceeding to list the difficulties with incinerators. The main problem was time: it would take too long—years, probably—to properly build, staff, and operate even a small one.

Fortunately, he said, there was another method for destroying chemical weapons, one he had frequently used himself. It involved a product that was within that very conference room, in plastic bottles dispersed around the table.

Water.

"The only way you're going to do this, with the kind of time frame and mobility you're talking about," Blades said, "is with hydrolysis."

It is a simple fact of chemistry that the main ingredients in sarin, mustard, and VX combine easily with water. Under the process called hydrolysis, liquid poisons are pumped through a kind of mechanical blender and injected with streams of plain, hot water. The result is a highly efficient, irreversible chemical reaction that neutralizes most nerve agents as well as blister agents like sulfur mustard, in small batches as well as larger ones. Best of all, the mechanical elements were relatively inexpensive and easy to obtain, and the whole system could be set up and torn down relatively quickly.

Blades described how he and his team had used the technique in the past. They had designed and built small hydrolysis systems to destroy beer-keg-sized containers of leftover chemical weapons in Iraq, and assisted in developing a much larger one to eliminate a million-gallon stockpile of Cold War–era sulfur mustard at Edgewood. The process created by-products that were themselves corrosive and needed special handling, but these wastes were no more dangerous than the acids and caustic bleaches hauled on American highways and rail lines every day. If the Pentagon's goal was to build a system that was portable and fast, with a minimal risk of contamination, hydrolysis was the only way to go.

From the visitors in the room came nods of appreciation. Falkenrath had never heard of hydrolysis and was struck by the beautiful simplicity of it. Add hot water to binary sarin and it breaks down? Seriously? As for the Edgewood team, Blades and his crew were as refreshing as a sea breeze in summer. *These are highly operational, no-nonsense guys,* Falkenrath thought. Unlike the dry academics and PowerPoint warriors who usually dominated such discussions back in Washington, these men had actually done the work before and they had succeeded, including in difficult environments such as Iraq. As for Blades, he thought, the CBARR chief was exactly the man he had hoped to find: the kind of real "outsider who could swipe away the cobwebs."

Santee also decided that he liked the plainspoken Blades and admired his confident, can-do style. During a break, the two men bumped into each other in the men's room and, for an awkward moment, stood next to each other at adjacent urinals. The general broke the silence.

"Tim, the way you describe it, it doesn't seem like it's that difficult," Santee said.

"Yeah, we can probably do this," came the reply. "I don't know exactly how, but we'll find a way."

"It's a big job, but you just take it apart," Santee said. "You do it in pieces."

Blades was quiet, clearly thinking.

"Yeah," he said finally. "We can do this."

Hours later, Santee and Falkenrath were both sending glowing accounts of the meeting to colleagues and bosses in Washington. Falkenrath emailed Ashton Carter, then the deputy secretary of defense, to request an in-person briefing. Then he phoned Andy Weber at his house in Arlington, Virginia, to give him a rundown.

"These guys think they can deploy a mobile system that can render that stuff as harmless as Coca-Cola," Falkenrath told Weber, with slight exaggeration. "We need this capability."

At Edgewood, meanwhile, Blades and his team were already beginning to think about how to design a hydrolysis machine that would meet the Pentagon's unusual specifications. The device must be portable, which meant building something that was small and self-contained. It would have to be simple enough to operate in a challenging environment, yet sturdy enough to be shipped overseas and plopped onto an airfield or military base, perhaps in Syria itself.

The first crude design was scrawled on a napkin by Blades, who handed his sketch and notes to his small team of mechanical engineers and electricians to begin working out the dimensions and specifications for a prototype. A month later, Blades found himself at the Pentagon clutching a copy of the completed blueprints. In a presentation to Weber and a handful of advisers, he ticked through a list of features of the proposed device, which had been given a suitably wonkish name: the Field Deployable Hydrolysis System, or FDHS. Eventually, a Pentagon wag, noting similarities between CBARR's invention and the mixers used by bartenders to make frozen cocktails, came up with a nickname that stuck: the Margarita Machine.

The officials around the table had a slew of questions. How quickly could the Edgewood team make one of the machines? And how much would the system cost?

Blades was ready with answers. It would make sense to build three of the devices, two of which would be kept on standby for immediate deployment, and a third reserved for use in the event one of the others broke down, he said. Since some of the more specialized components were already in storage in government warehouses, Blades figured he could have a working prototype ready by midsummer for a total price, including parts, man-hours, and overtime, of about $3 million.

Three million dollars? For a sarin-destroying device that could be shipped anywhere in the world at a moment's notice? Weber was impressed. He wasn't yet convinced that Blades's invention was the final answer, but it made sense to have such machines in the Pentagon's inventory, regardless of whether they were ever used in Syria, he thought. And the cost, by Defense Department standards, was almost laughably small. An expenditure of that size could be approved internally without a special authorization from Congress.

Weber spoke up.

"What do you need to go forward with this?" he asked the CBARR chief.

Blades didn't miss a beat. "I think a memo from the assistant secretary of defense for nuclear, chemical, and biological defense programs would be sufficient," he said.

That would be Weber himself, of course. The Pentagon official turned to one of his aides.

"Spend the money," Weber said.

In eastern Aleppo, a short walk from the hospital where the young doctor Houssam Alnahhas worked, there stood a small mosque that had somehow managed to keep its doors open despite the daily bombings and street battles that convulsed Syria's largest city. One day in June 2013, a handful of worshippers who had gathered for afternoon prayers suddenly fell to the ground, as though stricken by some invisible hand.

Ambulances arrived to pick up the victims, but by the time the medics arrived at Alnahhas's hospital, they, too, had apparently fallen ill, some of them collapsing in the emergency room. Waiting-room visitors and passersby gathered to watch, then backed away, with some younger ones breaking into a run. Hospital orderlies and nurses simply froze. Clearly some kind of toxin was at work, but no one knew what it was, or what to do.

Alnahhas watched the commotion and smiled to himself. It was only a drill—a test he had set up himself. The worshippers and ambulance teams had been friends, and off-duty hospital guards played the victims. They had performed perfectly, helping underscore a point that "Chemical Hazem" had been trying for weeks to make: a big chemical attack was coming, and Aleppo's medical workers were nowhere near ready for it.

Alnahhas spent many hours gathering details about known gas attacks. One of them had occurred in an Aleppo suburb barely ten miles away, and some of the injured had been treated at a teaching hospital where he had once studied. The doctors there lacked medicines for treating nerve-agent victims, and they had failed to grasp the risk of cross contamination when hospital workers came into contact with patients who had been exposed to sarin. It had been an unalloyed disaster, and there was no reason to think that other hospitals would have fared better. Syria's medical corps possessed neither the equipment nor the training for dealing with a chemical attack, and no one, it seemed, was doing anything about it. When Alnahhas approached European experts and relief agencies to ask for advice, the responses had been all but useless.

"You should just run away," one official advised him.

The only available remedy was to help his medical comrades prepare themselves. So Alnahhas arranged for the fake chemical attack and then set up a decontamination tent outside the hospital entrance. Using reference materials he had found online, he demonstrated proper techniques for dousing off newly arriving patients and reviewed the steps for preventing secondary contamination, since merely touching tainted clothing or skin is enough to harm or even kill.

Alnahhas typed up guidelines for treating victims of chemical weapons and emailed copies to everyone he could think of, including friends in relief agencies across the border in Jordan and Turkey. Although the feedback was positive, some colleagues questioned the drill's underlying premise, still skeptical that real nerve agents were being used against civilians in Syria.

"Great training," one of them told Alnahhas, "but I hoped it would be about something else."

Yet "Chemical Hazem" was sure of it. A bigger attack was coming. To him, it was the inevitable next phase of a war that was constantly inventing hellish new ways to torment the country's civilian population.

Alnahhas had witnessed the cruel progression with his own eyes, and the experience had changed him. In the early months of the uprising he had vowed to steer clear of politics to concentrate on finishing his medical studies. That ended when police in Aleppo began the practice of regularly bursting into the hospital to search for patients who had been injured during antigovernment demonstrations. Those who were dragged away were often never seen again. Alnahhas and a few fellow medical students decided then to create a kind of invisible clinic, one that treated the wounded privately, away from the hospital, or when necessary concocted cover stories for patients so their injuries appeared to have resulted from falls or car accidents. That went fine for a few months, but then one day three of his friends were stopped by soldiers at a checkpoint, in a car that happened to be filled with medical supplies. The authorities guessed what they were up to and decided to make an example of them. Days later the car turned up outside the hospital with the bodies of the three men inside. They had been tortured and shot, and their bodies set on fire. Someone had placed the youths' medical ID cards on top of each corpse.

That was the day Alnahhas officially became an activist. When students and neighborhood residents rallied the next day near the spot where the bodies were found, he felt suddenly compelled to speak up. "This is a new start for us," Alnahhas told the crowd.

"If they died for you," he said, "then it is our honor to die for you as well."

His words were soon put to the test. One evening, as he and a friend drove their car across one of the city's countless unmarked boundaries in a quest for food, they were stopped by a patrol of pro-government militiamen. The gunmen searched their car, taking great interest in the young men's medical ID cards and Alnahhas's small notebook, which contained a list of medical supplies. As the two friends sat frightened in their car, Alnahhas's companion turned to him and asked quietly, "Do you think it's our time to be burned?"

The two were arrested and taken to a holding cell, where Alnahhas was forced to lie on his back with his hands tied while guards took turns beating him. After that he was led to an ordinary cell, a single room about the size of a small studio apartment that already was packed with fifty-two other inmates. Others in the prison quickly learned that Alnahhas was a doctor, and after that he was constantly sought after for medical advice, including on one occasion by the prison's warden. The guards had been beating an inmate in one of the interrogation rooms when the man suddenly began vomiting uncontrollably. Alnahhas was summoned, and after a quick check he discovered that the man had severe head injuries, perhaps a fractured skull.

"He is probably suffering from internal bleeding in his brain," Alnahhas told the guards. "If you don't take him to a hospital he will die."

One of the guards gave the victim a kick.

"Go to hell," he said. The man died the next day.

Miraculously, just a few days after that, Alnahhas found himself back in his childhood home near Damascus. His father, who owned a small business, had learned of his son's arrest and gathered up some money to pay the necessary bribes to secure his release. The young doctor sat in his old bedroom for several weeks until he could take it no longer. He had to get back to Aleppo. He woke up early one morning to try to sneak out of the house, but found that his parents had anticipated his plan and hidden the house keys. His rummaging awakened his sleeping family, and Alnahhas was forced to endure what was perhaps the worst torture of all: his mother's anguished, tearful pleas for him to stay home. At one point she snatched a kitchen knife and tried to force him to take it.

"Kill me before you go," she said. "I cannot tolerate living every minute of my life waiting for someone to call me and say, 'Houssam is dead.'"

Alnahhas would not be dissuaded. He left Damascus and made his way across the rebel lines. Soon he was back in eastern Aleppo and in his own hospital, where there were more broken bodies to mend and preparations still to complete. One June day, around the time of the chemical weapons drill, he received with delight a large parcel containing chemical-protection gear, donated by a foreign relief organization. He opened the boxes and found gas masks—but only sixteen of them.

It was barely a start. Aleppo had no testing kits for deadly chemicals, and the supply of lifesaving atropine was barely enough to treat a hundred people, in a city of 2.5 million.

Alnahhas asked for more masks, and never stopped hoping that an adequate supply might already be on its way.

In Washington, the Obama administration also had gathered extensive detail about the strange, grenade-sized sarin bombs that had gone off in Saraqeb and other towns. By April, a CIA review had concluded that the attacks almost certainly involved small quantities of nerve agent, and that Assad's forces were responsible. Finally, on June 13, 2013, deputy national security adviser Ben Rhodes released a lengthy public statement outlining the evidence. Assad had used chemical weapons, including sarin, "on a small scale against the opposition multiple times over the past year," it said. One hundred to one hundred and fifty people had died, and while that number was tiny compared to the ninety thousand who had been killed by then in Syria's war, the "use of chemical weapons violates international norms and crosses clear red lines," the statement said. Additional forensic evidence was being gathered, and all of it would be shared with Åke Sellström, the Swedish scientist who was preparing to enter Syria at the head of a UN fact-finding mission, Rhodes wrote.

But now that Obama had acknowledged Assad's trampling of his red line, what would he do about it? The president had repeatedly warned of consequences, but Rhodes was vague, saying only that Assad should know that his actions "have led us to increase the scope and scale of assistance that we provide to the opposition."

In briefings and writings afterward, Rhodes would offer a few hints about what those words meant. It was difficult, because the details were highly classified. "Legally, we couldn't say what the support was," Rhodes would later write. "All I could say were things like, 'This is going to be different.'" In 2012, then–secretary of state Hillary

Rodham Clinton and CIA director David Petraeus had urged Obama to authorize a program of covert lethal assistance for Syria's rebels. At that time, Obama had declined, worried that the United States was being dragged into yet another unpopular Middle East war. But now, confronted with evidence of chemical attacks against Syrian civilians, Obama gave his approval. He signed a secret document known as a confidential "finding," essentially a legal memorandum authorizing covert action. The CIA would now have authority to deliver training and lethal military equipment—guns, ammunition, and more—to certain carefully vetted opposition groups.

The operation, called "Timber Sycamore," started slowly, as the CIA struggled to find, within the hundreds of rebel militias in Syria, a few groups it regarded as trustworthy and capable partners. But within a few months it launched a massive train-and-equip mission that ultimately involved thousands of Syrian opposition fighters operating out of bases in Turkey and Jordan. At a total cost of well above $1 billion, it was one of the largest U.S. covert aid programs of the last half century. In time it would change the trajectory of the war, at least for a while.

The White House simultaneously considered a number of plans that involved going after Assad personally. The plans did not anticipate assassinating Assad—the killing of a foreign leader by the U.S. intelligence services is forbidden by law—but they would be designed to deliver a very personal message.

"What if, all of a sudden, Assad's presidential helicopter disappears? Or what if his private study blows up one day when he's not there?" said a former senior U.S. official familiar with the internal debate over the plans. "Some of us felt, 'Let's take a shot at something he really cares about and demonstrate that he's within our reach. Maybe that will motivate him to come to the negotiating table.'"

Obama listened to the proposals but was deeply skeptical. What if something went wrong, and members of the president's family were killed? Or Assad himself? What would Syria do then, and how would the United States respond? The discussions generally came around to what officials described as Obama's chief fear: getting drawn by mishap into another open-ended Middle Eastern war.

"How does it end?" Obama would repeatedly ask, according to the former aides. Ultimately, he declined to give the authorization.

In the Syria of mid-2013, opposition groups could only dream of a foreign intervention so dramatic that it could tip the war in their favor. Throughout much of the country that summer, progress by Syria's moderate rebels appeared to have stalled. In the north, government troops reclaimed Aleppo neighborhoods that had been captured by the Syrian Free Army the previous year. In the east, a rebel coalition seized Raqqa—the first Syrian provincial capital to fall to the opposition—only to be driven back by ISIS fighters who would soon claim the city as the headquarters of their new caliphate. A far bigger blow was the loss of al-Qusayr, a strategic crossroads near the Lebanese border that straddled a major supply route. In April, a force of Syrian soldiers and Hezbollah fighters advanced on the town under the command of Qasem Soleimani, the charismatic Iranian general who had arrived in Syria that spring to help rally Assad's beleaguered troops. With Soleimani personally directing strategy, the pro-government forces captured the local airport, laid siege to the town, and began a weeks-long assault that routed the rebels there, killing or capturing two-thirds of the two thousand defenders.

With the loss at al-Qusayr, rebel morale plummeted. Neighborhoods that supported the rebellion were being systemically besieged and starved. A campaign of psychological warfare had been launched against opposition strongholds to terrorize civilians and force them to flee. At first the tool of choice was the barrel bomb, the crude explosive device dropped from helicopters to incinerate entire apartment blocks. And now, a new horror, sarin gas, had been added to the mix.

At talks in Ankara and other Turkish cities, the rebels' desperation was becoming ever more apparent. Opposition leaders continued to hold regular meetings with U.S. officials, especially Robert Ford, the U.S. ambassador to Syria, and a young Arab-American diplomat named Wa'el Alzayat. The Damascus-born Alzayat spoke fluent Arabic and was called upon to serve as a liaison to the rebels, and occasionally an impromptu translator when the conversations with other U.S. officials became difficult. Having met with the rebel leaders since the earliest days of the uprising, he was a witness to their growing frustration and ever more urgent demands for help—not just guns or training, but American firepower.

"Early on, a lot of them really did not want direct U.S. military intervention, because they didn't want the war to seem like some kind of American enterprise," Alzayat said. "But that changed. First, they asked us to arm the opposition. Then they wanted a 'no-fly' zone. And then it was MANPADS," the shoulder-fired surface-to-air missiles capable of bringing down an enemy helicopter, or—as U.S. officials feared—a passenger jet.

By 2013, there was a new "ask."

" 'We need military intervention by you,' " Alzayat recalled one of the rebel spokesmen saying.

Ford tried to lower expectations, advising the rebels to put away any notions of U.S. tanks rolling down the streets of Damascus. "The American cavalry will not come," he said.

Yet in 2013, many of the rebels continued to cling to a small hope that Washington might still come to their rescue. If Syria's president persisted in using chemical weapons, the Americans might view the conflict in a different way. Obama himself had said so—he had said the use of chemical weapons would "change my calculus."

He had called it a "red line."

In late June, just ahead of the Pentagon's deadline, Tim Blades's Margarita Machine was ready.

The public unveiling took place on a warm Thursday, on a day when much of official Washington was preparing to decamp to beach houses and lake cottages for the Independence Day holiday week. Edgewood had planned an elaborate ceremony by the base's usual standards, with photographers and exhibits and a large tent set up with dozens of chairs on risers for the small throng of generals, contractors, and other dignitaries who were expected to attend. Beyond this gathering, awareness of the device was nonexistent. The event would not merit a single line in the local newspapers, and no TV crew would make the drive to the out-of-the-way Army base to see a strange-looking mechanical contraption that, at that moment, had no official purpose.

Among those who did make the trip was Santee, the Air Force major general and DTRA deputy director. Having been present at the inception exactly six months earlier, he was not about to miss the official rollout, though he wasn't sure exactly what to expect. He ducked into the tent, and there it was, lit up like a shiny new truck in an automobile showroom.

Beautiful, Santee thought.

Viewed from inside the confines of the tent, the CBARR team's invention looked surprisingly large, with a vertical section on the left side that was the height of three men. On closer inspection, the ingeniousness of the design became clear. The entire device was contained within two boxlike rectangular frames that fit together to form an upright letter L. Separately, each of the frames was built to fit snugly inside a standard twenty-foot shipping container. The vertical section contained a titanium reactor vessel that stood nearly two stories tall. To its right, in the second rectangular box, was the "mixer"—a Rube Goldberg assemblage of brightly colored pumps, tanks, and valves, all interconnected by hoses and metal pipes. Each component had at least one "twin" of the same color, so that any single part could be taken offline and replaced without shutting down the entire system. With its rows of identical, interconnected parts in red, blue, and yellow, the thing looked like a Tinkertoy project constructed by giants.

Later, some of the visitors were treated to a live demonstration, in which plain water was substituted for the poisons that would normally flow through the tanks and valves. With the flick of a switch, the pumps and generators roared to life while workers in protective suits swarmed over the equipment checking gauges and connections. Inside the tent, the effect was like being in a laundromat with a dozen commercial washers and driers all starting up in unison.

The sensation was even more exhilarating for seasoned Pentagon hands such as Santee, who understood the minor miracle that had just occurred. Normally, it would take several years—perhaps even a decade—for a new piece of military hardware to make the journey from raw idea to finished design to working prototype. Here, it had happened in six months, with all the work performed by government employees, at a cost that was in line with the initial estimate. It was almost unheard of.

It was also, very possibly, a meaningless success. In Syria, the civil war ground on. The Pentagon had by now authorized the manufacture of seven of the devices, but no one knew when, if ever, they might be used.

The man most responsible for the machines had already decided that the answer was probably "never." Tim Blades was fiercely proud of what his team had accomplished, but in his nearly forty years at Edgewood, he had seen many a good project stall and wither. Sometimes the fault was bureaucratic, and other times the moment simply passed. It wasn't personal. It was government work.

Yet this time, the prospect of seeing the machines gathering dust in an Edgewood warehouse truly bothered him. He said so to his wife one evening in late summer 2013, a few weeks before events in Syria upturned his world.

"We paid a lot of money to build seven of these things," he said, recalling his words to Karen Blades years afterward, "and we're never going to use them.

"But then, bam. Was I ever wrong."

4

"Help, please—they're dying!"

BEIRUT, LEBANON. AUGUST 18, 2013

Six weeks after the autopsy in Turkey, Åke Sellström stood outside Beirut's Phoenicia Hotel and studied the boxy SUV that was to be his lifeline during the treacherous descent into Syria. The mission was finally on, but the mere act of traveling to Damascus, as the Swedish scientist discovered, was complicated and dangerous. All commercial flights into the capital had been halted because of the civil war, so the United Nations had obtained seven Toyota Land Cruisers for an arduous overland trek that was to take Sellström and his twenty-member team of inspectors and assistants through the narrow passes of the Anti-Lebanon Mountains along the border, and then down into Syria and its landscape of shifting battle lines. Those vehicles now sat in a gleaming white row outside the hotel, each as bright as a spotlight in the morning sun, with "UN" painted in giant black letters on the sides and rear. Whether the markings made them safer, or simply a more obvious target, was an issue that had been intensely debated but never entirely resolved.

Just since June, UN relief convoys and aid workers in Syria had been targeted nearly a dozen times. In the past two weeks, one UN worker had been killed by unknown assailants in Damascus, and another had been pulled from his truck near Aleppo, robbed at gunpoint, and then shot in the back. On cable news shows that week, analysts had speculated about whether Sellström and his team were more likely to be blown up or ambushed, or simply locked away in a Syrian prison. To provide a measure of protection against such threats, UN headquarters had opted for armor-plated vehicles, which meant that the SUVs' side panels could absorb small-arms fire without damage to the passenger cabin. But it was commonly known that multiple shots fired at the windows would eventually cause the glass to weaken and shatter. And if the attack involved something larger than an AK-47 round, all bets were off. A large IED, for example—the preferred weapon of some of Syria's jihadist rebel groups—could crush a 5,800-pound armored Land Cruiser like a soda can.

To keep the jitters at bay, Sellström and his deputies kept the team busy with checklists and rehearsals in the hours before the planned departure. Responsibility for the mission's safety had been entrusted to a forty-three-year-old Canadian named Diarmuid O'Donovan, a former navy officer and security expert from the Yukon who had spent part of his childhood in an Inuit outpost north of the Arctic Circle. A veteran of previous UN missions in Haiti and Afghanistan, O'Donovan had earned a reputation for extraordinary coolness under fire, and an oddsmaker's gift for being able to mentally calculate the relative risks and potential rewards in any given situation. As many in the group had never been in a war zone, he schooled the team on what to do if their vehicle's tires were shot out, or if one of the SUVs became suddenly disabled or was separated from the rest of the column. In the final minutes before leaving the hotel, O'Donovan gathered everyone in the lobby for a final review. With his confident, soft-spoken manner, trim salt-and-pepper beard, and sturdy outdoorsman's frame, the Canadian could lower the temperature just by walking into a room. But some of his charges were rattled anyway.

"Be aware. Don't get lost in your thoughts," O'Donovan said. "Stay focused."

In reality, O'Donovan was more anxious than he let on. It was naïve, in his view, to think that the Syrians would grant Sellström's team the kind of access necessary for conducting a meaningful investigation. And he was sober about the prospects for safely getting all twenty team members into Syria and back home again. The Syrians claimed to control the highways, but beyond the streets of the capital, they clearly did not.

"It was going to be a very hard mission," he would later say. "I couldn't say with conviction that we could do it without coming under fire. Or with everyone coming back."

At just past 10 a.m., the UN convoy, now with an escort of armed Lebanese, was finally ready, and the vehicles departed the hotel and headed southeast. After an hour, the high-rises and expressways of metropolitan Beirut gave way to the olive groves and beet fields of the Beqaa Valley, and then to craggy hills as the team neared the Syrian frontier. Past the Lebanese border town of Masnaa, the vehicles squeezed through a gauntlet of shops and roadside stands clotted with Syrian day-shoppers engaged in frenzied haggling over prices for cigarettes, toys, cell phones, and canned food. The buying and selling continued right up to the border itself, and then halted as cleanly as though the two countries were separated by an invisible wall. Here, one by one, the SUVs slipped across the boundary and into one of the most desolate, inhospitable places many in the group had ever seen. This was no-man's-land, a narrow buffer zone of steep gorges and arid, boulder-strewn hills. The place was eerily empty, cleared long ago of human inhabitants, and forsaken by most other life-forms except vipers and lizards. From this point onward, Sellström and his team would be on their own.

From his perch in the rear vehicle, O'Donovan scanned the canyons ahead for signs of trouble. The day was airless and oppressively hot, and the SUVs ahead wore a coating of yellow dust, which, since midmorning, hung in the air like a fine mist. If there was to be an ambush, it could well happen here. Abandoned cars littered the roadside, each of them a potential hiding place for a bomb. The assailants might be any of a dozen rebel groups unhappy to see a UN delegation arriving in the country as official guests of the regime. Or they might be Assad loyalists carrying out an official order to squash the investigation before it could get started. If the convoy survived the passage through the canyons, the next hurdle would be the Syrian military detachment and whatever welcome the regime had prepared at the checkpoint just over the hills. The government's real intentions, good or ill, would become clear very soon.

The UN caravan passed the surreal sight of a Dunkin' Donuts shop, now abandoned and desolate, as the eerie emptiness of the border zone finally gave way to derelict roadside stalls and duty-free stores. Then, at last, the checkpoint came into view, and behind it, a fortress-like customs office, with its giant sign welcoming visitors to the Syrian Arab Republic. A gaggle of soldiers, looking young and very nervous, fingered their weapons as Sellström and the other team leaders climbed out of their vehicles. The Syrians had been watching the convoy's approach and now came out to meet it.

Damascus had sent a mid-level uniformed officer to receive the UN visitors, and by all appearances his job was to drag out the entry procedure as long as possible. Sellström and his Canadian deputy, chemist and Armed Forces veteran Scott Cairns, were escorted into a VIP lounge and parked on chairs in front of a gigantic portrait of dictator Bashar al-Assad framed in white roses. Someone snapped a photograph as Sellström, looking tired but dapper in his denim work shirt and neckerchief, managed a weak smile. The team leaders were served tea in glass cups and kept busy with small talk and visa checks, while outside, other members of the welcoming party were slowly pulling apart every duffel bag, knapsack, and pallet in the UN vehicles, as if on a hunt for hidden contraband. Cairns, the de facto chief of staff for the mission, had instructed the team to politely defer to the Syrians on any reasonable request. But Cairns's own patience was tested when the searchers announced that a banned item had been discovered: Sellström's satellite phones. The devices had been brought along to ensure that the team could reach headquarters at any hour of day to pass along sensitive messages or to seek help in the case of an emergency.

A Syrian officer examined the phones with a scowl. Such items were banned in Syria, he said, and they would have to be either sent back to Lebanon or confiscated.

Cairns protested. The phones were essential for the mission, end of story. The team could not do its job without them.

More scowls. The Syrians retreated to make calls and confer among themselves. A half hour passed, then an hour. Was this how the Syrians planned to torpedo the mission?

Sellström decided to try a firm approach. The Syrian officer in charge was too junior to make any weighty decisions on his own, so the Swedish scientist tried a tactic that was guaranteed to rattle him: he threatened to make trouble with the man's boss.

"We were invited here by *your* foreign minister," Sellström said sternly. "If we are not allowed to bring these to Damascus, I will not enter the country."

The Syrian was clearly nervous. More minutes ticked past, and then, finally, he relented. The phones would be allowed to accompany the caravan into the country, although the Syrians insisted on physically transporting them in one of their escort vehicles. They would be returned to Sellström in Damascus.

The team leader had prevailed in his first showdown with his Syrian hosts. The tests that followed would be harder.

The reports from the UN advance team had described Damascus as a bastion of relative safety, as the capital so far had largely escaped the ravages that gutted other Syrian cities. In August 2013, however, the reports were no longer entirely accurate.

In central Damascus the Syrian authorities had carved out a security corridor, similar to Baghdad's Green Zone, with multiple roadblocks and checkpoints to prevent attacks on key government installations. On one end was the city's luxurious Four Seasons Hotel, an opulent, eighteen-story tower visible throughout Damascus and noted for its palm-fringed swimming pool. Since the start of the civil war, the building had served as headquarters for UN relief agencies, as its steel perimeter fence offered a measure of protection from car bombs. Anchoring the security zone's opposite end, about a mile to the west, was the Sheraton Hotel, the preferred meeting place for Syrian government ministers. The territory in between had been among the safest places in the country, but more recently, it was now being targeted. Rebel militias had seized several close-in suburbs in a district known locally as Ghouta, a swath of former agricultural land that forms a partial belt around central Damascus, extending clockwise from the east to the southwest. Some of the fighters had advanced within mortar range of the government's inner sanctum and regularly lobbed shells into it, occasionally scoring a lucky shot. As Sellström and other team members rolled into Damascus on the afternoon of August 18, gray talons of smoke and dust arced over the rooftops, evidence of the day's strikes. Other reminders of the fighting—the blackened frames of abandoned automobiles, rubble piles that were once houses—flashed into view and then receded as the caravan wound through the ancient city's narrow streets. For the next weeks, or however long the mission lasted, Sellström and his team would be living and working in an active war zone.

That the UN delegation was present in Syria at all was a tribute to the negotiating skills of the Swedish scientist and a handful of UN diplomats. As predicted, the autopsy in Turkey had increased the pressure on Damascus to allow a limited probe into the allegations of chemical weapons use. In late July, Sellström traveled to Syria with Angela Kane, a German national and a notoriously tough negotiator who headed the UN Office of Disarmament Affairs, to work out access and schedules. But the talks nearly collapsed when the Syrians repeatedly insisted on limiting the probe's scope to a single event: the March 19 incident in the village of Khan al-Assal, in which most of the dead had been Syrian soldiers killed when poison gas drifted through their defensive position. The United Nations insisted on investigating at least two other alleged attacks, with UN officials free to choose the locations.

At one point, Sellström decided to try a little personal diplomacy by going out for a meal with the two top officials on the Syrian side. Over a Chinese dinner, he tried to convince his counterparts of his ability to serve as an impartial judge, free of Western bias. As evidence, he talked about his aversion to militarism as a young man, and how he attained conscientious objector's status to avoid serving in the Swedish army.

The Syrians appeared mystified by the complexities of military service in democratic Sweden. Young Swedes could opt out of the army on moral grounds?

"We don't have those kinds of problems in Syria," one of them finally said.

But soon afterward, the Syrians relented, accepting the UN proposal of a three-site investigation—Khan al-Assal plus two others.

Now came the moment when Syria's true intentions would become clear. Sellström had arrived in Damascus carrying a list of three Syrian villages where his investigators intended to collect samples and conduct their interviews. His success now hinged on Syria's willingness to honor its commitments by ensuring that the UN investigators could make it to the sites and back again, with evidence and all team members intact.

Early on the morning after their arrival, Sellström and the rest of the UN team made the trek across the secure zone to the Sheraton Hotel and a first meeting with Syrian officials to work out the logistics for the inspections. The delegation had barely arrived when a loud blast shook the lobby. A mortar shell had exploded just beyond the hotel driveway, shattering glass and showering the building's facade with shrapnel. Security chief Diarmuid O'Donovan, who had seen many a mortar attack in Afghanistan, calmly shooed the UN team away from the windows, but some of the Syrians were visibly rattled. It had been an uncomfortably close call.

The morning's schedule resumed minutes later with an opening session in a large conference room, with the Syrians seated on one side of a long table and the UN officials on the other. The cast of Syrian officials would shift slightly over the days that followed, but it was quickly clear that two men had been pushed forward to serve as the primary interlocutors on chemical weapons. One was the balding, bespectacled deputy foreign minister, Faisal Mekdad, an urbane and well-read diplomat who spoke flawless English. The other, more colorful negotiator was an air force brigadier named Hassan al-Sharif. Sharif was overweight and perpetually rumpled in his ill-fitting civilian suit, and his most distinguishing physical traits were his bushy mustache and equally bushy, wonderfully expressive eyebrows. Sharif appeared to understand English but spoke it only rarely and haltingly, yet he possessed an uncanny ability, using eyebrows alone, to convey the entire gamut of human emotion, from rapturous delight to bitter disdain. He was, as one of Sellström's aides quipped, "a man of few words but much eyebrow."

The initial gathering at the Sheraton was meant to be a technical discussion of the arrangements for the site visits, but it soon became clear that the hosts had a different objective in mind. The Syrians had prepared a series of elaborate briefings that dragged on for hours, including a mind-numbing presentation on the fundamental science behind chemical weapons—all couched in theoretical terms, since Damascus continued to deny having chemical weapons at all. Sellström's aides finally got their turn, and they proceeded to lay out objectives and requirements for the visit. But then it was back to the Syrians and more pointless lecturing. The pattern continued throughout the first day and into the next.

"They kept explaining very basic concepts, in very slow order, just to waste our time," said one team member who sat through the meetings. "The whole thing was about running out the clock."

Scott Cairns, Sellström's chief deputy, repeatedly tried to redirect the conversation by asking about details of the reported chemical attacks the UN delegation had come to investigate. Grasping for any means to draw the Syrians into a candid discussion, he asked whether the alleged attacks might have involved stolen munitions.

"Is it possible that 'terrorists,' as you call these people, took something from your stockpiles of chemical weapons?" Cairns asked.

There was an awkward pause. "We don't have a chemical weapons program," one of the Syrians finally replied.

By the third day, it was clear that the Syrians had no intention of arranging site visits or doing anything else to aid the investigation. Sellström's frustration finally reached the breaking point. If the Syrians were planning to do nothing but lecture, it was time to quit.

"We are going nowhere," Sellström said aloud after one of the sessions ended. "If you don't start cooperating, we will just leave, and the blame will be on your side."

On the night of August 20, Sellström gathered his team around a large table in a Four Seasons Hotel ballroom that had become the UN command center. After a discussion the group decided to make one last attempt at a breakthrough—a final offer, consisting of a list of interviews and evidence that Sellström considered essential for a successful mission. The Syrians would probably say no, effectively signaling the end of the mission, the group reasoned. But at least they would have tried.

It was now late, so Sellström adjourned the meeting and everyone shuffled off to their rooms. Within the UN delegation there was a dawning realization that it might be their last night in Damascus.

Scott Cairns could not sleep.

Since the departure from Beirut, the day-to-day responsibility for managing the mission had fallen on the shoulders of Sellström's chief of staff, and it had taken a physical toll. The tedium of the negotiations had put everyone's nerves on edge, but Cairns bore the additional burden of ensuring that every member of the delegation was kept alive and safe in this most unpredictable of settings. He could not escape feeling personally accountable, not only to the team members, but also to their spouses, parents, and children back home. There was a constant worry that something bad was about to happen, and it literally kept him up at night.

The very grimness of Damascus also had its own peculiar effect on the psyche. Unlike his countryman O'Donovan, Cairns had not previously served in a place where outgoing artillery fire was part of the local ambience. The tall, boyishly handsome Canadian had spent much of his military career as a chemical weapons specialist at a base in a remote corner of southern Alberta Province, making small batches of nerve agents used to test protective gear. Eager for a change of scenery, he had taken a position in 2008 as an inspector for the Organization for the Prohibition of Chemical Weapons in The Hague, the Dutch capital. Much of the job consisted of traveling in and out of Russia for routine inspections certifying Moscow's destruction of the country's Soviet-era chemical stockpile. Syria, by contrast, was anything but routine. The pressures of the mission were compounded by the country itself, with its jarring extremes: opulent wealth next door to destruction and ruin; his five-star hotel with its swimming pool and marble terraces, and the elderly women in tattered abayas taking advantage of a quiet morning to scurry off to the corner market; the lovely nighttime vistas of Damascus with its thousands of shimmering lights, and the certain knowledge that people were suffering and dying in darkened suburbs within sight of the hotel.

Cairns was lying awake in his bed with the curtains open around 2:30 a.m. when he became aware of a new sensation: flashes of light, like distant fireworks, and the muffled booms of explosions. He rose, looked out the window, and saw what seemed to him to be a full-blown artillery barrage.

The firing was coming from the hills just to the north, and the projectiles—bright streaks against the black sky—were arcing over central Damascus and landing a few miles to the east. There were at least a dozen explosions in an attack that seemed to go on for more than an hour. A long pause followed, and then a shift in direction, with the tracers passing over the hotel toward the southwest. Someone in the city's suburbs was getting pounded, Cairns thought.

By the time the firing ended it was nearly dawn, and Cairns could see black smoke in the direction of the Ghouta suburbs to the east, no more than five miles away. As the light grew stronger, he noticed something odd about the smoke plumes. Instead of rising, they were flat and low to the ground.

Something about the strange smoke compelled him to take a photograph.

Others in the UN party had also been awakened by the attack, or by text alerts that began firing off as the sun rose. Team leader Åke Sellström rolled out of bed early and instinctively tuned his television to a cable news station. A habitual exerciser when on the road, he had just started his morning routine of sit-ups and push-ups when something on the television brought him to a dead stop. There was major breaking news coming out of Damascus—this same Damascus—about a horrendous attack with massive numbers of casualties somewhere in the capital's outskirts.

The images that flickered across Sellström's screen in the moments that followed were almost beyond comprehension. There were dozens and dozens of victims, lying dead in rows on the floor. Many of the victims were children and toddlers, some of them still in their pajamas. Curiously, none had visible injuries or wounds, but nearly all were soaking wet, as though they had been doused with water. In repose, they looked like drowning victims pulled from a capsized passenger ship.

Far worse were the images of the injured. These lay on a floor as well, as rescue workers frantically poured water on their faces, the only treatment that seemed to be available to them. The camera zoomed in on a tiny girl who lay gasping softly, like a fish unable to breathe and too far gone to struggle, while a man gently dabbed at a clot of foam that had formed over her mouth and nose. Near her, a boy of perhaps seven or eight was twitching violently, his small arms flailing as though trying to beat back an invisible foe.

The newscasters were speculating about poison gas, but Sellström, one of the world's leading researchers on the physiological effects of nerve agents, could see the symptoms with his own eyes and knew very well what had happened.

Someone had launched a major chemical weapons attack on the Ghouta suburbs. They had killed and injured scores of civilians, and perhaps more. Indeed, the toll would prove to be staggeringly large: at least 1,400 dead, including more than four hundred children.

And it happened at the precise moment when a body of UN experts was present in Syria to document the deed.

Kassem Eid heard the incoming rockets as well. Or, more accurately, he *felt* them.

The early morning of August 21 found the twenty-seven-year-old Syrian lying on a friend's sofa in Moadamiyeh, a rebel-held neighborhood in western Ghouta district, a few miles southwest of central Damascus. It was the wee hours, and, like Scott Cairns, Eid had struggled to fall asleep. He and some friends had spent the previous evening doing what they did most every night in this third year of the Syrian uprising: scrounging for bits of food and looking for a place to charge their cell phones. Having wearied of those tasks, they had returned to the apartment where Eid, the son of Palestinian refugees and a rebel sympathizer, had stayed intermittently since the day his family's house was destroyed in fighting. It had been a warm night, and an unusually noisy one. Syrian artillery had been mostly quiet for a change, but then, from the nearby al-Mazzeh military airport, came the wailing of sirens, eerie and mysterious, and continuing off and on for hours. Eid peered from an open window onto the darkened street below but saw nothing. He lay down again. It was too hot to sleep.

At just after 5 a.m., a new sound entered his consciousness. It was a loud whooshing, like that of an artillery rocket passing overhead, but there was no explosion. Instead, from nearby came a loud thud and a jarring sensation, as though someone had dropped a sandbag from a high window just outside the building. Then there was a second thud, and a third.

Eid lay quietly for a moment, thinking that the Syrians had perhaps acquired some dud rockets. All at once he became aware of a burning sensation, a stinging in his eyes that quickly moved to his throat. He leapt up from the couch.

"Wake up!" he screamed to the sleeping household. "It's a chemical attack!"

Three of Eid's friends were asleep in the apartment, and within seconds the four young men were staggering around the living room coughing and gasping for air. Eid splashed water on his face and struggled to find his clothes. His chest felt as though someone had grabbed him from behind and was squeezing the life out of him. Somehow, he was breathing.

There was a sudden pounding at the front door. On the other side was a young mother Eid recognized from the building carrying her two children, ages six and four, under her arms. Both were unconscious and drooling a kind of white froth.

"Help, please! They're dying!" she said.

The men grabbed the children and started down the apartment building's staircase, with the mother trailing behind them. Reaching the ground level, they stumbled out onto the street and into a scene of unimaginable horror. Dozens of gas victims—men, women, and children—sprawled on the concrete in the dim light. Some writhed in agony. Others lay still, apparently dead. Nearby apartment buildings disgorged still more victims, along with knots of screaming, wailing survivors. Eid was struck by the preponderance of the very young among the dead and dying. Then he realized why: In war-ravaged Moadamiyeh, most families had adopted the practice of bunking the mothers and children in basement apartments, which offered more protection from artillery and aerial bombs. But poison gas is heavier than air, and so the greatest numbers of casualties would naturally occur on the lowest floors. The men behind the attack would certainly have grasped that fact as well.

For a long moment Eid stood and watched, unsure of what to do. Then he noticed a small figure on the ground a few dozen yards away, separated from the other victims. He walked closer and saw that it was a small boy, lying facedown. He rolled the child onto his back and looked into a pair of brown eyes that would haunt him for the rest of his life. Years later, he would struggle to describe the desperation he felt at that moment.

"The sight of his face made me forget every horror I had seen in the past three years," he wrote in a memoir about his experiences in Syria. "All I could focus on was the innocent face of this boy, stained with grotesque shades of red, yellow and blue. His eyes returned an empty, glassy stare."

The child was still alive, though his labored breathing made an awful rasping sound. Eid stripped off the boy's shirt and began massaging his chest to keep him breathing. Without pausing to think of the risk, he pressed his mouth against the boy's froth-covered face and tried to force a few breaths of air into his lungs. He then scooped up the youth and ran to jump onto a truck that was headed for a local hospital. The vehicle was packed with victims, but Eid squeezed into a spot in the back and cradled the boy in his arms for the duration of the trip.

"I held him," he wrote, "and cried."

The raspy breathing continued all the way to the hospital. But by the time the truck arrived, the trace of poison Eid had ingested while attempting to resuscitate the boy had taken its toll. He managed to lift the young body, which felt so much heavier now, and placed it gently on the ground.

It was the last thing Eid remembered before losing consciousness. He never learned what happened to the boy he had tried to save.

5

"No one is coming out alive"

WASHINGTON, D.C. AUGUST 21, 2013

By the time Tony Blinken arrived at the White House early on the morning of August 21, the grim images were playing in an endless loop on every cable news channel.

"Breaking overnight: more bloodshed and disturbing news in Syria's civil war," the anchor on CNN's morning show was saying. Video supplied by activists had shown the scores of dead bodies in a Damascus suburb, victims apparently of some kind of poison gas. Nothing had been officially confirmed, but the news network's early morning commentators speculated that there would be "pressure on the White House."

Blinken, President Barack Obama's principal deputy national security adviser, was already sure of that. He walked next door to the office of Susan Rice, the chief national security adviser and his boss.

"We've got a real issue here," he said.

The two went together to the Oval Office, where Obama was preparing to receive his daily intelligence briefing. Blinken and Rice sat in, as they normally did. By that hour the CIA already had picked up multiple strands of evidence pointing to the use of a nerve agent, but it was early. No one could yet say with certainty who was behind it. Obama listened, his expression grave.

"He was immediately seized with it," Blinken recalled.

The president moved quickly after that. Although much of the staff was away on late-summer vacations, Obama wanted all his key advisers at an emergency meeting in the White House Situation Room the following morning. That was Thursday, August 22, and by then the intelligence from Syria was clearer. The nerve agent was almost certainly sarin, and the casualties numbered in the thousands, with hundreds dead. Electronic eavesdropping—snippets of conversations between Syrian military officials—strongly pointed to the Assad regime as the culprit.

Everyone at the meeting was polled on their views about the proper U.S. response. The consensus in the room overwhelmingly favored a military strike, soon. A few expressed misgivings about the risk of an escalation leading to war, yet there was unanimous support for starting preparations for bombing Syria.

"There was a sense that America was about to go over another Middle East waterfall," one of the participants said afterward.

But first there was work to be done. Obama wanted an ironclad evidentiary case to present to the American public, to avoid the intelligence debacles that preceded the 2003 Iraq war. White House lawyers would have to construct legal arguments to justify the attack. The Pentagon needed to hone their list of potential Syrian targets.

The president ordered the planning to move forward, intending, his aides later said, to launch the attack within days.

But there was a hitch: Åke Sellström.

Damascus was now firmly in the White House's crosshairs, but a team of UN inspectors stood in the way. When the missiles flew, they would be at risk. They might be inadvertently injured or killed. Or they could become hostages of a suddenly vengeful Assad. As the plans for Syria were finalized and debated, aides said, Obama would return to the professor again and again.

Åke Sellström must leave Damascus, now.

Back in Syria, the canny Swede had begun taking matters into his own hands. Sellström suspected that an air strike was coming, judging from TV reports. But he had no interest in departing Syria until his work was done. Without waiting for approval from his UN bosses, he launched a very public campaign to pressure Assad to let him investigate the horrific events in the Ghouta suburbs. The instructions from New York had been to avoid interviews and to keep his opinions private. But Sellström could not help himself. *This is so horrible, we need to do something,* he thought.

UN officials could only watch with chagrin as Sellström strolled up to a bank of microphones at his Damascus hotel to make an unscripted appeal: Governments around the world should demand an immediate UN investigation of the crime. If enough countries filed formal petitions with Ban Ki-moon, he said, the UN chief would be obliged to respond.

"Write or call the secretary-general," Sellström urged. Weeks later, he would learn that some thirty-five countries had taken up his advice.

A more intensive lobbying campaign was just getting under way in private meeting rooms in Damascus as Sellström prodded the Syrians to allow an immediate fact-finding trip to Ghouta. Joined again by Angela Kane, the German diplomat and UN disarmament official who raced back to Syria still wearing the floppy hat from a friend's wedding ceremony, Sellström tried to convince Syrian officials that it was in their interest to allow his team to conduct an investigation. Damascus was insisting to the world that it had nothing to do with the attack. So why not allow the UN experts to make an impartial assessment?

The Syrian response was an ever-shifting series of excuses, most of them related to practical difficulties involved in escorting UN officials through neighborhoods that were disputed or under rebel control. At one point, Sellström cornered Sharif, the bushy-eyebrowed Syrian general, and implored, "You have to let us in!"

Sharif gave him a doubtful look.

"Impossible," he said. "There's a war going on. You can't go there."

"Okay, then let us meet with people who are fleeing the area," Sellström said, tacking slightly. "We can talk to the people as they're coming out and try to investigate that way."

The eyebrows arched slightly, then lowered.

"It's of no use to you," Sharif said calmly. "No one is coming out alive."

The young doctor known as "Chemical Hazem" was taking a catnap in an empty office when word arrived in Aleppo of the massive attack near Damascus. He had worked the overnight shift and had only slept a couple of hours when the hospital's chief physician roused him.

"Wake up!" his boss said. "There's been a big chemical attack."

Alnahhas quickly started up his computer to check the news. Within seconds, the awful images from Ghouta were streaming across his screen. *This is exactly what I predicted might happen,* he thought.

As he searched for more details, Alnahhas's Skype account began to light up. On the line was a doctor from a hospital in east Ghouta. Alnahhas had never spoken with the man before, but he was frantic and looking for expert help. No one in Ghouta had been trained to treat victims of a poison-gas attack, he said, and now his hospital was overwhelmed with them. There were hundreds of sick and dying, and more arriving. Nurses and hospital orderlies were collapsing as they worked.

Alnahhas had his guidance documents ready and began to calmly read, as the Ghouta doctor jotted notes. He described decontamination techniques, such as how a mixture of chlorine and water could be used to remove sarin from exposed skin. He ticked off a list of medicines to be used and the proper doses. He detailed the kinds of protective clothing that could prevent secondary contamination of medical workers.

The doctor thanked him and ended the call. But then a second doctor called. And a third.

Alnahhas continued to take calls throughout the day, but the more advice he meted out, the more futile it all seemed. There simply weren't enough medicines. There were no decontamination areas for washing down victims. There were no masks or protective gowns for staff.

What was clear, even over Skype, was that the number of victims was massive, and many were dying who might have been saved.

During a pause later in the day, Alnahhas stopped to think about what would happen if a similar attack occurred in his corner of Aleppo, a place he believed was ready for a chemical attack, largely because of his efforts.

"We had been working hard on preparations for handling up to a hundred victims," he said. "Here we were looking at thousands. By the time it was over there were maybe twelve thousand exposed and fifteen hundred dead. And there was nothing we could do."

—

The job of trying to extract Åke Sellström from Syria fell most heavily on Samantha Power. The new U.S. ambassador to the United Nations was a forty-two-year-old Irish-American academic who had been on the job less than three weeks when the crisis erupted. Before joining the White House as an adviser to Obama during his first presidential term, Power had built a career as a human rights policy expert arguing for a forceful intervention on moral grounds to stop the slaughter of innocents. Her Pulitzer prize–winning book, *"A Problem from Hell,"* was a powerful critique of past U.S. administrations that had been bystanders to acts of genocide. Now her president was preparing to do something about a mass killing in Syria, and her job was to press the UN bureaucracy to remove an impediment to U.S. military action.

"Sam, I need you to get those UN inspectors out of Syria," Obama told Power in a meeting in the White House Situation Room. "That UN mission needs to be shut down now."

Power was more than ready to do her part. She had been on maternity leave after the birth of her second child when Obama made his "red line" remarks and had not been involved in the debate that erupted, but Power now stood firmly with the majority of advisers who favored immediate air strikes. She also shared the president's essential view about the Sellström mission: however well-intentioned at the outset, it was at this juncture a pointless bureaucratic exercise that now stood in the way of a serious response to the Syrian crisis. The White House had supported the appointment of Sellström, but opinions had shifted in the wake of the poison-gas attacks. U.S. analysts were sure that Assad would try to turn Sellström's presence in Syria to his advantage, even if only as a means to stall for time while covering up evidence of the crime. Moreover, the mission's original goal—to determine whether chemical weapons had been used in Syria—now seemed preposterously out of date. Neither the Russians nor the Syrians denied that Ghouta's dead had been killed by nerve agents. The key remaining issue was culpability, and that was the one question that the United Nations had explicitly agreed not to answer.

Power called Ban Ki-moon, the UN secretary-general, to ask him to pull the plug.

"This is a moot mission," she said. "The UN is being manipulated."

Others in the administration made similar calls, including Obama himself. Reaching Ban by phone while the UN leader was enjoying a late-summer holiday, he argued for Sellström's evacuation in a tone so insistent that it jostled the genteel South Korean's sense of diplomatic propriety, aides later said.

"You need to pack it up," Obama said.

But persuading UN leaders proved to be a harder sell than the White House anticipated. Although Ban was repulsed by the images of the dead in Ghouta, he believed the United Nations was in the business of preventing conflicts, not starting new ones. Delaying an air strike by even a day or two meant more time to find a diplomatic alternative, one that could prevent still more Syrians from being killed. The last thing the UN chief wanted was to be seen as tacitly enabling a military response.

What's more, Ban did not share the Americans' skepticism about the value of having a team of international weapons experts on the ground in Ghouta. There were, indeed, good reasons for skepticism about the early allegations of guilt. Ban and his aides already were hearing from dozens of perplexed diplomats who found the timing of the Syrian attacks extremely suspicious. Why on earth would Syria's president order a massive chemical attack on multiple Damascus neighborhoods, at the precise moment when an international team of chemical weapons experts was present in the capital? Was it not possible that another party—the list of possible suspects ranged from the rebels themselves to one of Syria's neighbors—was trying to provoke a crisis in hopes of forcing the United States to intervene militarily in Syria? A deliberate, methodical investigation by Sellström's fact-finders could deliver the kind of unimpeachable evidence that could serve as the proper basis for a truly international response. If Sellström could convince the Syrians to let him visit the crime scene, surely he would deserve a few days to complete the work.

"We cannot *not* proceed," the UN chief told Power in one of their phone calls.

This was not the response Obama was seeking. The refusal to evacuate Sellström became a source of daily frustration for the U.S. president, who perceived that the passing of time would only present more obstacles to a military strike.

"But for the ongoing presence of the inspectors, we would have struck," probably as early as Sunday, August 25, four days after the Ghouta attack, Power said. "There's no question. A hundred percent."

As they waited, the evidence pointing to Assad continued to mount. By that Sunday, Obama had learned classified details of the attack that would not be described publicly for another week. U.S. spy satellites had detected the rocket launches coming from government-controlled areas on the morning of August 21, and spotted preparations by Syrian chemical weapons units as early as August 18. From electronic eavesdropping and other highly sensitive sources, U.S. officials learned that Assad had delegated authority over his chemical weapons to his generals, who prized them as effective tools for driving rebels out of their urban strongholds. The Syrian army commander who ordered the attack had been preparing to launch an armored assault against Ghouta neighborhoods that same day, and he had apparently wanted to soften up his targets. There was no evidence that the commander considered the UN inspectors or U.S. "red lines," or was even aware of them.

The eavesdropping did reveal that the Syrian military was surprised by the outcome. The army had never used sarin on such a scale, and in intercepted phone calls, officers fretted about the high numbers of casualties, fearing that it would cause trouble for their bosses.

In the following days, Britain and France also released intelligence findings conclusively linking Assad to the attack. Two of Syria's neighbors, Turkey and Israel, did the same. Of the major powers, only Russia adopted Syria's official explanation of the gas attack as a "false flag" operation carried out by rebels and their foreign backers in an effort to draw the United States into the civil war.

"No one doubts that poison gas was used in Syria," Russian president Vladimir Putin wrote in an unusual *New York Times* op-ed in which he pleaded against a U.S. air strike against Russia's closest Middle Eastern ally, "but there is every reason to believe it was used not by the Syrian Army, but by opposition forces, to provoke intervention by their powerful foreign patrons, who would be siding with the fundamentalists."

The jihadist wave in Syria was the true menace, one that "threatens us all," he wrote.

Included in the essay was a warning that some interpreted as Putin's "red line," though it did not carry an explicit military threat. Noting that international law prohibits foreign military intervention—with exceptions only for self-defense or when authorized by the UN Security Council—Putin declared that the missile strike contemplated by the Obama administration would be not just unwise, but illegal. Such a use of military force would be "unacceptable under the United Nations Charter," he wrote, "and would constitute an act of aggression."

Yet in the West Wing, the preparations for war continued to move forward. Over the next week, the Pentagon finalized a list of potential targets: about fifty sites, to be struck by Tomahawk cruise missiles fired from a small fleet of destroyers in the eastern Mediterranean. The vessels were already in position, their missiles ready in their tubes. All they awaited was the president's order to launch.

Other American officials were preparing, too.

Tim Blades was flying home from an overseas business trip when he happened to catch a news report about the Syria massacre on an airport lounge television. The man behind the Pentagon's Margarita Machine had a hunch that life for him and his Edgewood team was about to change. He phoned one of his deputies to say so.

"It looks like this thing is going to start up," Blades said.

He watched the screen as the awful images of dying Syrian toddlers and children played in an endless loop. Blades had four children back in Maryland. He also had firsthand knowledge of what it felt like to be locked in sarin's deadly embrace. In all of America, only a handful of people could say that.

There had been two near-fatal encounters, about three years apart, when Blades was in his early twenties. The first, in 1975, involved a sarin precursor ingredient known as hydrofluoric acid, or HF, an extremely toxic compound that is sometimes called "the Bone Seeker." The nickname derives from the acid's chemical affinity for calcium; even in tiny quantities, it eats through layers of skin and muscle to begin dissolving away the living bone. Minor exposures can result in gruesome tissue damage, or death.

In Blades's case, it was four drops of liquid—merely, precisely, four—that escaped from a hose and landed on his bare arm as the young chemist's assistant was disconnecting a canister in one of the Edgewood labs. He was barely twenty, but he knew immediately that he was in trouble. A quick plunging of his arm into water did nothing to relieve the searing pain or stop the HF from burrowing into his flesh. An Army doctor administered an injection to try to slow the acid's advance, but the only "cure" was radical excision: a hasty operation to cut away the skin, blood vessels, and muscle around the exposed area before the acid could reach the bone. Blades was rushed to a nearby hospital for immediate surgery.

He was in the emergency room when his mother arrived. She had never known exactly what her son did at the highly secretive Army facility, and now she looked at Blades with a mix of bewilderment and horror.

"What are you doing that you're ending up like this?" she asked. "Is this really what you want to do?"

"Yeah, Mom," the twenty-year-old replied. "I know what it looks like. But it's going to get better."

Blades did get better, but the wound required skin grafts and two weeks of hospitalization. He was off the job for nearly two months.

The second time, the culprit was actual sarin. Three years had passed, and Blades was now an experienced technician and part of a three-man team checking leaky welds on beer-keg-size containers filled with nerve agent. All three were wearing respirators and working in a sealed room, accessible only through a pair of airlocks. There was a puddle of liquid on the floor—from a water spill, the men thought—and one of the workers reached down with a paper test strip in his ungloved hand to make sure it was harmless. The paper instantly turned brown. It was sarin.

"That ain't water, dude," Blades said to his partner. "You need to clean yourself up."

Panicking, the man tore through both airlocks and into the unprotected office space where they all worked. As he ran, he left behind a trail of sarin from the puddle he had just tracked through.

The other two team members emerged from the airlocks and proceeded to take off their protective gear, not knowing that their offices were now contaminated.

Blades became instantly aware of a strange sensation. He donned his respirator again, but it was too late. He had been exposed—"bitten," as Edgewood's workers say.

"My nose was running, and it kept getting worse and worse—I mean gushing, like someone had flipped a switch," Blades said. Then his vision began to narrow, and he felt intense pressure, as though someone had lowered a Volkswagen Beetle onto his chest. Finally came the sensation that Blades calls the "dead cat": extreme nausea coupled with a feeling of something big and rotten stuck inside his abdomen. Blades began gagging into his respirator.

That's four symptoms, he thought to himself. *I'm screwed.*

In fact, he was lucky. Alarms were now ringing throughout the building, and the base's medical clinic prepared itself to receive patients suffering from a condition the doctors had seen before and knew how to treat. Within hours he was recuperating at an Army hospital in Fort Meade, Maryland.

He returned to his job at Edgewood a bit wiser, and with a story that would be amusingly told to friends and colleagues for years to come. But the pain and fear he felt that day would stick with him as well. Decades later he could vividly recall every minute and each distinct sensation from his encounter with sarin: the extreme agony. The feeling of suffocation. The utter helplessness.

Now that same suffering had been intentionally inflicted upon entire communities in the suburbs of Damascus. The number of dead, dying, and injured exceeded the population of Blades's childhood hometown. For many of these victims, there would be scant medical care, and perhaps none at all.

The terrible images flickered again on the airport television monitor. From his phone call home, Blades knew that his Edgewood team was watching, too. It was all that anyone could talk about.

Surely there would be a use for their machines now, Blades thought.

"Someone is going to have to help them get rid of that stuff," he said.

In a most insidious way, Syria was readying itself as well. First came the bombardment: a thunderous, days-long artillery barrage on the same Ghouta neighborhoods that had been hit by poison gas. Whatever evidence Sellström's team had hoped to collect, there would now be less of it.

Assad's second act went largely unnoticed in the West. It began on a morning immediately after the chemical attack, when a fleet of buses pulled up outside the infamous Adra Prison, home to thousands of Syrian political prisoners who lived in vermin-infested squalor just to the northeast of central Damascus. Hundreds of inmates were roused from crowded cells and ordered to line up. Among those staggering to his feet was a reed-thin thirty-six-year-old named Mazen al-Hamada. A petroleum engineer in normal times, Hamada had been arrested the previous year while attempting to deliver packages of baby formula to a family in one of the capital's besieged suburbs. In the months since then, he had been beaten, burned with cigarettes, hanged from the ceiling by handcuffs, and tortured by means of having a metal clamp placed around his penis. Now, without explanation, he was forced onto a bus along with hundreds of other inmates and driven in the direction of Damascus, their ultimate destination still a mystery.

The buses arrived at the al-Mazzeh military airfield, one of the Syrian Air Force's premier bases and the one closest to Moadamiyeh, the suburb that was hit by poison gas on August 21. Guards ordered Hamada and the other inmates out of the buses into a metal-roofed aircraft hangar, where all were told to sit on the ground. For hour after hour they sat. The guards mostly milled around outside, talking, only rarely venturing into the hangar. They seemed to be expecting something.

Night fell, and the inmates still sat. Hamada and the others—he counted about nine hundred prisoners—then waited through a second day in their metal box, which the scorching August sun had converted into a virtual oven. Then a third day passed. The men collectively settled into a kind of routine, taking turns queueing up to use an outdoor latrine that had been set up for the inmates, or to get a drink of water or piece of bread. The men had stripped to their underwear in the relentless heat, and they passed the time just talking: about the heat, their past lives, their families, their injuries and illnesses. And they speculated among themselves, in quiet tones, about the possible reasons for their sudden transfer from a hellish prison to an equally miserable existence in the middle of a Syrian airfield.

Finally a new group of detainees arrived, with fresh news from the outside. There had been a series of massive attacks with chemical weapons in the villages around the capital, the newcomers said. Many had died, and the world had pointed an accusing finger at Assad.

Was it true? Adra Prison had always been awash in rumors, many of them outlandish and surely false.

Hamada could no longer contain his curiosity. Mustering his courage, he walked up to one of the guards, a man who struck him as less menacing than the others, and stammered through a pair of questions.

"What's going on?" he asked. "Why did you bring us here?"

Yes, the stories about a chemical attack were true, the guard said. Then, smiling as though he had just thought of an uproarious joke, he explained to Hamada how the inmates' new quarters and the deaths in Ghouta were directly related.

"America wants to strike," the guard said. "They're sure to come after the military airports. And if they drop their bombs here, they'll kill all you prisoners. We'll be rid of you, and we can say that it was the Americans who killed you."

Hamada nodded and turned back to join the others. He was satisfied. The Americans were coming for Assad and the hated regime, perhaps. *Inshallah*—God willing—they would destroy them both. The fact that he and other inmates might also be destroyed didn't seem so important.

"In prison, we always knew that the regime might kill us," Hamada said afterward, recalling his feelings that day. "If you believe that you could die at any time, it doesn't really matter what the circumstances are.

"If it's to be in an air strike, okay," he said. "It doesn't change anything."

Hamada found his spot in the crowded, sweltering hangar, sat on the floor, and waited.

6

"We go in again"

DAMASCUS. AUGUST 25, 2013

On the fifth day, the Syrians relented.

After vigorous prodding by UN diplomats and quiet cajoling by the Russians—and with the passing of a few more hours of heavy shelling in the suburbs—Bashar al-Assad was ready to deal. In the end, he did not so much agree to a UN investigation of the killings in Ghouta as he resolved not to stand directly in the way.

By the dictator's orders there would be a cease-fire on the government side for five hours on Monday, August 26, and on each of the following three days. Armed Syrian escorts would guarantee the UN team's safety as far as no-man's-land, the invisible boundary marking the outer limits of government control. Everything else—including cease-fire terms with the opposition and arrangements for safe passage through a patchwork of fiefdoms held by competing rebel and Islamist factions—would be left up to Åke Sellström.

On Sunday night, the eve of the first site visit, Sellström called his team together in the Four Seasons ballroom that had served as the command center during the Syrian trip. Everyone sat around a long table as the Swede began to talk about what the group might face in Ghouta and how they should prepare themselves. In a single day, the mission had radically changed. It had started as a search for fleeting evidence and survivors from incidents that occurred months ago.

Now they would be entering an active war zone, without weapons, and visiting a crime scene in which the victims were still fresh and the murder instrument very possibly still present. They would see things they might wish they could unsee, and the emotional and psychological weight of those experiences could linger for years, Sellström warned. On top of all that, the journey itself would be physically—perhaps even mortally—dangerous.

Because of those risks, rules and procedures would now change, he continued. Until that moment, Sellström had adopted a kind of leadership-by-consensus approach to the mission. From now on it would be military-style discipline, he said. Lives could depend on it.

"Once we step into those cars, I want you to immediately do as I say," he said.

As those tough messages settled in, Sellström scanned the faces around the table for signs of discomfort. If someone looked unduly frightened, it would be safer for the group if they remained behind.

The room was silent. There were twenty in the core group, not counting drivers and escorts. Three were medical professionals from the World Health Organization whose past jobs had included fighting jungle diseases in the tropics. Three others were security experts, though they carried no weapons. Two were medics and four were translators, and the rest were civilian weapons inspectors of the OPCW. They hailed from sixteen different countries, from Canada and Western Europe to Africa and the Middle East. Three were women, including one of the OPCW inspectors, a German national. Most had never done anything remotely resembling the task at hand.

"Everyone is here by their free will. You don't have to go," Sellström said. He waited a long moment and looked away to allow those with cold feet to make a graceful exit.

No one moved.

At 1 p.m. Damascus time—the agreed start of the cease-fire—the UN team was ready. Five white SUVs with giant "UN" markings set out from the Four Seasons Hotel garage and onto a nearly empty highway headed toward the southwest.

Sellström had chosen as his first stop the town of Moadamiyeh.

The distance from the hotel was only seven miles by car, and the detailed security plan for the mission predicted a journey of less than thirty minutes. But nothing on this day would go according to plan.

A contingent of armed Syrians traveled with the convoy during its first leg, from central Damascus to the last government outpost just beyond the al-Mazzeh air base where Hamada and his fellow prisoners were being held. At the checkpoint, the UN team parked one of the Toyotas, intending to keep it in reserve in case one of the others broke down. This having been accomplished, the Syrian escorts peeled off. The four remaining SUVs, each carrying a complement of inspectors, support staff, two-way radios, and sampling gear, continued south toward Moadamiyeh and the rebel lines.

Sellström was now completely on his own. The last vestiges of government-controlled Damascus quickly faded as the convoy passed into a buffer zone of bombed-out houses and vacant apartment buildings. The Swede, riding in the second car, watched from a rear seat as the highway went from empty to desolate, with few signs of life, human or animal, on either side. The vehicles advanced slowly and in silence, interrupted only by the occasional crackling of the radios.

Everyone understood that this was the point of maximum danger, but the actual degree of risk had been impossible to calculate. Surely it was high. While Assad had acquiesced to inspections, there were many in the army and intelligence services who would be only too happy to see Sellström fail. Some might even be willing to intervene to ensure that his inspectors saw none of the evidence they hoped to collect. On the rebel side, things were scarcely better. While some groups welcomed the investigation, others were openly scornful of a UN mission that was constrained from actually blaming anyone for the crimes they uncovered. One of the major rebel alliances had just warned Sellström—in an open letter that addressed the scientist by name—that he was at risk of being viewed as an Assad collaborator. Unless a credible investigation was launched immediately, the letter warned, the rebels would "officially consider your team persona non grata."

The truth was, the man in charge of the mission wasn't sure what to make of the evidence he had seen so far. The timing of the attack was peculiar, indeed; an impartial judge would have to consider the possibility that the chemical attack was a provocation aimed at drawing the United States into Syria's civil war. At the same time, Sellström understood the technical complexities of chemical warfare far better than most. Making liter-sized batches of high-quality nerve agent was not amateurs' work. Nor was the feat of delivering sarin by rocket to multiple neighborhoods on a single night. If Sellström ever needed a "good standard" for judgment, it was now.

Two men riding in the lead vehicle had a different set of worries. Diarmuid O'Donovan, the Canadian navy veteran and security chief for the mission, was the man most responsible for ensuring that everyone in the team returned home safely. He was joined by Mohammed al-Khafagi, an Egyptian national who was the closest thing to a local security expert, having been assigned by the UN to protect its relief organizations based in Damascus. The latter's presence in the lead SUV was essential: since Khafagi's regular job required him to be in frequent contact with opposition groups, it had fallen to him to make all the arrangements with rebel leaders, including setting up a rendezvous with a guide who would escort the team to their ultimate destination. He had done so, but all the conversations had occurred by phone or Skype. Khafagi had never personally met the opposition leaders who had promised to take the UN team under their protection in Moadamiyeh. Whether these men had the means or even the intention of keeping their promise, the group would soon find out.

At last the team came to a small bridge where the road crossed a dry streambed. On the other side, somewhere, were the rebels, including the guide who was supposed to meet them. The vehicles stopped just before the bridge as O'Donovan and Khafagi scanned the buildings on the far side for a sign of their contact. Nothing stirred. The lack of movement was eerie, even ominous. Had something happened?

It would be too risky to cross into rebel territory without a guide. O'Donovan directed the vehicles onto a side street, where they all pulled over and waited while Khafagi tried to raise his rebel contacts on the phone. As they were sitting, O'Donovan looked up to see people. Lots of them.

A mob.

As quick as a dam burst, the convoy was surrounded by scores of protesters. They had emerged from the nearby buildings as though on cue, and now they were surrounding the vehicles on all sides. Some carried signs and portraits of Bashar al-Assad—a clear indication that this was no spontaneous demonstration. O'Donovan and Khafagi looked at each other, unsure of what to do.

"They're not happy about us crossing," Khafagi said. "To them, the people on the other side are enemies."

Khafagi ordered the driver to slowly ease away. As the vehicles moved, angry faces pressed against the windows, young and old, male and female, shabby and well groomed, shouting in Arabic.

And then it stopped. As the vehicles pulled away, the crowd quickly dissipated. In minutes the four vehicles were alone again in the empty street, as though the protest had never happened.

The sudden appearance of the mob had surely been a message, and if so, it was an effective one. Khafagi resumed punching numbers into his phone, but no one was answering. The vehicles halted again. Armor-plated and buttoned up as they were, the investigators were reasonably safe, but with each passing moment, O'Donovan felt increasingly uneasy. He didn't like sitting still. If they didn't start moving soon, someone else would "discover" them, perhaps to deliver more than just a scare.

Hallo? Hallo? Khafagi was finally speaking with someone. Everything was fine, the voice on the other end said. The rebel escorts were waiting for the convoy on the other side of the bridge. Look now, the speaker said, and you should already be able to see your guide: a man on a bicycle.

Khafagi and O'Donovan again scanned the street beyond the streambed but saw no one. Still, reassured by the phone call, they decided to move forward. The vehicles maneuvered to get back into formation to move toward the bridge. O'Donovan fixed his gaze on the far side. Where was that guide?

POP. Something struck the Toyota's armored frame on the passenger side. The sound was like that of a small rock smacking against metal at high speed.

POP. A second impact. O'Donovan was certain now. These weren't rocks. He looked at Khafagi.

"Yes, we're being shot at," the Egyptian announced to the car. "Be calm."

It was too late for calm. More bullets hit the SUV, puncturing two tires. From one of the rear vehicles, the agitated voice of another security adviser came over the radio.

"Shots fired! Shots fired!" the man shouted.

O'Donovan pressed the talk button.

"Stay calm and stay in the car," he said to the convoy, his voice low and firm.

At that moment came a loud cracking sound as a bullet slammed into a side window inches from Khafagi's head. Then the windshield took a direct hit. The bulletproof glass was holding up so far, but each impact left a spiderweb of tiny lines that were now starting to spread.

Still another round slapped the window near Khafagi. This was beyond serious, O'Donovan thought. Another shot or two and the glass would almost certainly fail.

"We've run out our safety line on this one," he said to his partner. Then, picking up the radio, he ordered the drivers to fall back.

"We're moving back to the rally point," he said.

The convoy reversed course and roared off in the direction of Damascus. O'Donovan's badly damaged vehicle, with its blown tires, limped along on its reinforced rims, but all four vehicles made it to the army outpost. Then they stopped to regroup.

Khafagi and O'Donovan got out of their SUV and walked to Sellström's car in their body armor and helmets. The Swede rolled down his window. The others thought the leader seemed anxious but not panicky. Khafagi was the most familiar with the local terrain, so Sellström turned to him with his most pressing question:

"What do we do, Mohammed?" he asked.

Khafagi didn't hesitate.

"We go in again," he said.

"What?" Sellström was incredulous.

"If we don't go today, we'll never go," the Egyptian said. "They will know that they can frighten us, and your mission will be over."

O'Donovan reflected for a moment, then nodded his approval. The team still had a spare vehicle at the checkpoint, left behind for just such a purpose. Whoever fired the shots must have intended only to intimidate, otherwise a more powerful weapon would have been used. Going back would be risky, but those dangers would have to be weighed against what seemed to be a genuine opportunity: a chance to accomplish what they had come to Syria to do.

Sellström sat quietly, thinking. Then he reached for his phone. He was being asked to send his team back down a road where a waiting sniper was merely the only threat of which they were absolutely certain. The scientist needed to do everything he could to minimize the risk or, at the very least, to increase the odds of success when, and if, the inspectors reached their destination. One of the calls he placed was to his Syrian hosts, to ask for more time. The team was allotted just five hours to travel to west Ghouta, conduct interviews, gather physical evidence, and return to home base. Now nearly half of that time had been lost. The cease-fire must be extended, he demanded.

"I will not risk my team going in for just two hours," Sellström said. "We need more time if we're to get something done."

More minutes passed. Finally, the phone rang, and Sellström received the reply he had been waiting for.

"You have all the time you want," the scientist was told.

Sellström called his team together to share the news.

"Okay," he said, "we go in."

Moments later, the Toyotas lined up again for a fresh attempt to cross into rebel territory. This one would look markedly different: rather than cautiously feeling their way through no-man's-land, they would dash across it like inmates on a prison break.

Khafagi grabbed a spare armored jacket and, scooting down into his seat, used his feet to press it against the windshield. Team members in the other cars did the same. When everyone was ready, the SUV passed through the checkpoint and then tore down the narrow road with as much speed as the drivers could muster. The vehicles shot across the bridge and did not slow until all four were well on the other side.

This time, no shots were fired. O'Donovan, exhaling, surveyed the road ahead and there, appearing in the middle of the highway like some kind of apparition, was the guide. He was an older man, wizened and gaunt, and he was astride a rickety green bicycle that looked even more ancient than its rider. But there was no question: this was their escort.

The man acknowledged the lead vehicle with a nod, then turned and began to pedal. The SUVs trailed after him in a row, a curious procession moving through deserted streets at the pace of a casual walk.

The bicyclist turned down a narrow street lined on both sides by tall apartment buildings. Then, in the middle of a block of seemingly abandoned buildings, he stopped, looked around, and dismounted.

The UN team, believing that this was at last the site of the rebels' underground hospital, prepared to get out of their vehicles. But before they could unstrap themselves, another throng had started to gather around the convoy. Just as had happened hours earlier, people of all ages and sizes began streaming out of nearby buildings and onto the street. This was no angry mob, however; unlike the protesters earlier in the day, these Syrians appeared positively jubilant. Older women ululated. Younger ones threw flowers. Children ran between the parked SUVs, shouting.

Sellström, watching the crowd gather from his backseat perch, was so touched by the emotional welcome that he felt himself choke up. As he would learn, the UN convoy was the first tangible sign of outside help that the town had seen.

"It was like the Beatles had come," he recalled afterward. "We were heroes to them because we were the first ones to show up in almost a year."

But others in the crowd appeared more subdued. As O'Donovan and Scott Cairns, the deputy leader, climbed out of their vehicles, it quickly became obvious that many were hoping for aid of a different kind. The Assad government had blocked all deliveries of food and medical supplies into Moadamiyeh for months, and famine had settled over the town like a slow-moving pestilence. The children and toddlers scampering around the UN vehicles were thin and appeared malnourished. The sour odor of rotting garbage permeated the place.

But nothing could have captured the town's desperation as much as the scene that unfolded next. From out of the crowd, a man emerged, cradling something in his bony arms. The man appeared to be elderly—in Moadamiyeh, it was hard to tell—and from a distance, it looked as though he were holding a doll, or perhaps a sleeping toddler. Tiny legs and a mop of tangled light brown hair hung limply as the man walked closer. But this was no doll. It was a girl, perhaps as old as twelve or thirteen, judging from her facial features. Her stunted little body was frighteningly thin, like one of the living skeletons from photos of liberated Auschwitz in 1945. Her dark eyes seemed to float about randomly, without seeing.

The man approached Cairns and O'Donovan and began to speak in Arabic, a language that neither understood well. But the nature of his request was soon plain enough. He was not begging for food or asking for medicine. He wanted the foreigners to take the girl.

"He was holding this bundle of sticks, and trying to give her to us," Cairns would later say in describing the moment to friends. "And we couldn't do a thing."

Years later, he remembered every moment of the encounter: the old man, the twig-like limbs, the mass of light brown curls, the vacant eyes.

"I will always have that picture seared into my brain," Cairns said.

The UN team's security men could not focus on the hungry and sick. Surveying the crowd, they were struck by the number of armed irregulars milling about, watching the inspectors unload their gear with casual interest. Some appeared to be part of a semiofficial protection force for the visitors, while others looked on with expressions that ranged from curious to scornful. Few wore anything approaching a uniform, so it was hard to tell who was who. All carried assault rifles, at a minimum.

The weaponry added an air of volatility to the gathering. Mohammed al-Khafagi, who had been around Syria long enough to be attuned to the possibility of a hostage taking, decided he should try to mitigate the odds. At one point he pulled Sellström aside and whispered that, as a precaution, the two of them should pretend to swap roles: Khafagi would make a show of issuing orders while Sellström stayed in the background, hopefully out of harm's way.

"Yes, boss," Sellström, catching on quickly, said aloud. It made sense. While most of the townspeople seemed genuinely ecstatic about the UN team's arrival, there had been warnings about possibly hostile elements within the rebel alliance. Even in a favorable environment such as this one, an accidental gunshot or a tussle between rival militias could provoke a crisis, as quick as a heartbeat.

It very nearly happened just that way.

Out of nowhere, a rust-colored truck whipped around the corner and screeched to a halt a dozen feet from where the UN vehicles were parked. Khafagi, looking up, saw the threat right away: it was a "technical," an improvised fighting vehicle of the kind popularized by insurgent groups in East Africa and around the world, consisting of a small pickup with a very large gun mounted on the back. Manning the weapon was a bearded figure clad fully in black. He was shouting something.

Khafagi struggled to make out the words, but the man's intentions became fearfully clear when he swung the gun around to point the barrel directly at the nearest UN vehicle. The Egyptian security expert knew the weapon by sight: this was no ordinary machine gun, but a mounted 20mm cannon with a bandolier of shells, each nearly the size of a beer bottle. A 20mm round could slice through the Toyotas' armor plating as though it were cardboard.

Before anyone in the convoy could move, other militiamen in the street began converging on the technical to try to wave the intruder off. Some stood directly between the UN vehicles and the gunner while others tried to calm the man down using words and gestures. The confrontation took on a fraternal tone, as though the Moadamiyeh men were talking a drunken buddy out of starting a bar fight. Khafagi's impression—later confirmed—was that the man in the technical was from a different militia that had not been consulted about the UN team's visit and was not in favor of it.

The gunman finally relaxed his grip on his weapon. As soon as he did so, the others swarmed over him like ants on a dead beetle. He was whisked away, and the UN team never learned his fate.

The excitement having passed, it was time to start gathering evidence. The team divided itself into two groups. Half would head off with local guides to look at impact craters where the rockets had struck and collect soil samples and any fragments from the weapons that they could find. The rest would descend into the rebels' underground hospital to interview victims and take blood samples.

Sellström, as a medical professor, was part of the latter group, and followed the others into the apartment building that sheltered the makeshift clinic. He had barely entered the building when his phone rang. One of the UN team's Syrian hosts was calling from Damascus with an important update.

Those additional hours you were promised for the investigation? That's not happening after all, the official said.

"We can't give you any more time," the caller said.

The cease-fire would end precisely at the five-hour mark, as originally promised. Nearly three hours had already passed, and the collection of evidence had not even begun.

The physical effects of Kassem Eid's encounter with sarin had mostly worn off twenty-four hours after the terrifying attack on his Moadamiyeh neighborhood.

Eid awakened to find himself on the floor of a basement clinic surrounded by dozens of other victims, many of them dead. A stranger splashed water in his face, another jabbed him with a needle, and in a few minutes he felt his strength returning. His eyes burned and his chest still hurt, but he was soon well enough to stand. At that moment, in a clinic packed with dead and dying neighbors, he understood that his life had inalterably changed. Until then, the former University of Damascus student and hotel worker had watched mainly from the sidelines as friends and schoolmates had taken up arms in Syria's civil war. Most had enlisted with one of the rebel factions, though a few had decided to stick with Assad. Now it was Eid's turn to join the fight.

The five days that followed brought a succession of novel encounters and experiences, including at least two more brushes with death. Eid was nearly killed when an artillery shell—part of the Syrian government's bombardment of the suburbs—struck the building where he and other sarin victims were being treated. He took part in his first firefight as he joined a small band of rebels trying to halt a Syrian troop column that was advancing on the town. After a quick tutorial from a friend, he aimed an assault rifle at a cluster of soldiers in the street and squeezed the trigger. When one of the soldiers fell, he felt a rush of euphoria that morphed quickly into something that felt more like regret.

"I couldn't tell if I was proud or sad," he recalled afterward. "I had ended someone's life."

Between firefights, he found a useful role for himself as an intermediary between the town's rebels and foreigners of all descriptions, from journalists to government officials. Eid spoke excellent English, and he had a functioning cell phone, whenever he could find enough electricity to charge it, and he became an indispensable source of news about conditions behind the rebel lines.

Among the dozens of callers in the days after the poison-gas attack was Wa'el Alzayat, the Syrian-American who served as a State Department liaison to the Syrian opposition. Alzayat and a colleague had been working the phones in a search for witnesses to the events in Ghouta, and after punching in a Skype number they found themselves speaking with one.

"What are you seeing right now?" Alzayat asked.

"I'm standing next to fifty dead bodies," Eid told him.

The two communicated regularly after that.

Then, on August 26, a member of Moadamiyeh's rebel council called Eid to ask if he could help with a different kind of mission. Because of Eid's English skills, the council member wanted to know if Eid would be willing to help serve as a guide and translator to UN officials who were investigating the gas attack. Eid agreed, and that afternoon he had watched as the four white SUVs rolled into town to gather evidence. He was standing a few feet away when the angry technical driver nearly rammed the convoy, and he understood more than most present just how much danger the foreigners were in. "The gunman had lost two of his brothers and he was angry," Eid said. "He was literally about to shoot."

The UN inspectors remained remarkably calm, which impressed Eid. Later, as he helped escort the officials through the medical clinic and into the neighborhoods where the rockets had fallen, he watched with admiration as they carefully and methodically went about their work, usually with stoicism but occasionally betraying their emotions when confronted with the suffering of small children. Some of the inspectors carried chocolates, which they tried to give away before realizing how trifling the gifts seemed in the face of so much real hunger.

Eid watched as one of the inspectors fought to restrain tears. "We're sorry we can't bring you food," the man said in English after handing out the last of his supply of chocolates to a cluster of small faces.

Every turn of a corner brought fresh scenes of destruction and deprivation. The victims of the chemical attack were only one facet of a sprawling humanitarian disaster. In the underground clinic that served as an emergency room and field hospital for injured and wounded, the triage center was an unfinished room with a dirt floor. It was packed with people afflicted with broken and crushed limbs, concussions, and gruesome cuts and wounds from bullets and shrapnel. Patients lay on stretchers on the bare floor, some moaning, others silent. The dank cellar exuded a sickening musk: blood and human waste. Dirt and cordite.

The victims of poisoning lay in more sanitary rooms in an adjoining basement separated by a door. Here the foreigners divided themselves into groups of two to collect biological samples—blood, urine, and hair—and to take witness statements on video. One of the pairs, an Italian with a bushy beard and a tall man with a Canadian accent, started their work at the bedside of a young man who appeared to be about Eid's age. The victim tried to answer the questions, but whenever he spoke about his ordeal, he started to shake. Another victim went into convulsions as he was being interviewed.

Eid watched as another of the foreigners—an older man with graying, short-cropped hair—got into a heated discussion with someone on his cell phone.

"We need more time!" the man kept repeating, as though there could ever be time enough to fully process all they had seen.

In a strange way, seeing the foreigners at work made Eid feel hopeful. Here, at last, someone from the outside world had come to Moadamiyeh to bear witness. It was a small thing, perhaps. But for the first time, a delegation representing all nations of the earth had looked into the faces of Assad's victims. It was possible now to watch these inspectors—these twenty brave men and women who persisted despite threats, and even after coming under fire—and imagine a future day when the dead of Ghouta would have their justice.

"They were professionals," Eid said, recalling his impressions that August afternoon. "They were investigating a crime scene, in the middle of a war—a war in which there was no accountability. And they were trying their best."

Two days later, on August 28, Åke Sellström was ready to try again. The target this time was a cluster of Ghouta villages on the east side of Damascus. Getting to them meant navigating the same obstacles they encountered in the earlier mission, plus one more: the jihadis. Parts of the eastern suburbs were firmly under the control of Islamist extremists.

With more time to reflect, the Swede might have talked himself out of it. The UN team's visit to Moadamiyeh had ended successfully, if frantically—the four SUVs had barely made their exit when the bombardment started up again—and the inspectors had collected environmental samples and blood from survivors. There was enough raw evidence to keep the labs in Holland busy, and presumably enough to demonstrate to the world the nature of the crime committed in the Damascus suburbs. But Sellström felt compelled to press on. The attacks east of Damascus had been bigger and deadlier, and it seemed important to make an appearance there. Moreover, according to rebel sources, remains of some of the rockets used in the attack still lay where they fell. If an actual warhead could be recovered, there might be priceless evidence still inside.

The inspectors gave themselves an extra day to make preparations, including confirming and reconfirming arrangements with rebel contacts who would serve as escorts on the other side of no-man's-land. They also decided, after an intense discussion, that Sellström should stay behind at the Damascus command center. Since the poison-gas attack, the scientist was attracting ever-larger crowds of journalists and amateur bloggers wherever he showed up, and it was becoming a distraction and possible encumbrance to the mission. Reluctantly, he agreed to remain at the hotel.

By early afternoon on Wednesday, everything was ready. The booming of the artillery batteries in the Damascus hills ended abruptly with the start of the cease-fire, and the convoy began its eastern trek through a city that had again grown suddenly, and uneasily, quiet. Once more, the SUVs rolled through a no-man's-land of abandoned neighborhoods and then crossed into rebel-controlled territory on their way to the appointed rendezvous spot. And once again, they arrived to find the place deserted. This time, as O'Donovan scanned the street ahead of him, he saw something that made his blood freeze: wires, running at odd intervals across the pavement. Roadside bombs.

It got worse. He now noticed a row of Claymore antipersonnel mines studded along the edge of the highway like lethal dominoes, each pointed in the direction of the SUVs. His eyes followed the wires to a command detonator clearly visible amid the roadside detritus. It was the classic setup for an ambush, no doubt with a complement of snipers' nests in the taller buildings on either side. Could the UN convoy be the intended target? O'Donovan wasn't eager to find out.

"Let's hold here," O'Donovan instructed the driver, who veered into an alley, trailed closely by the other vehicles, and waited as the team leaders discussed what to do.

The rebel contact was quickly raised by phone and a strangely intense negotiation ensued. As it turned out, the Islamist militia leader on the other end of the call also feared being lured into a trap. The UN column would have to advance farther, the rebel chieftain said, to guarantee against the possibility that the newcomers were being followed.

O'Donovan wasn't having any of it. "Your guy has to make himself visible," he insisted.

At last a dust-caked vehicle roared up from the rebel side and whipped around in front of the alley, its driver beckoning to the waiting SUVs to follow him. They did, and as they bumped along, O'Donovan noticed something striking about the rebel car: it was an armored Toyota Land Cruiser, just like the one he was riding in. Then he looked closer and was sure: it was one of his Toyota Land Cruisers. The vehicle was identical to the ones purchased by the United Nations for use in Syria. An SUV exactly like the one in front of him had gone missing after a carjacking by unknown militants several months earlier. And now, here it was. Should he say something? O'Donovan considered the matter, but minutes later the convoy pulled in to a staging area packed with menacing-looking fighters wearing thick beards and tactical vests. Maybe a missing SUV was part of the cost of doing business, he thought.

Compared to Moadamiyeh and its deprivations, the villages of eastern Ghouta were better off, at least on the surface. The inspectors conducted their interviews with survivors in the well-lit wards of a proper medical clinic staffed by doctors and nurses. But the stories they collected were no less harrowing. A week had passed since the attack, and of the victims who remained hospitalized, many were children whose ordeals included not only exposure to nerve agents but also the loss of siblings and parents. One boy, a twelve-year-old with close-cropped hair and an otherworldly sense of calm, told of losing his entire family to poison gas. In another section of the same ward, a young girl described losing consciousness during the attack and waking up later in a dentist's office that had been converted into a makeshift emergency room. She still had no idea what had happened to her parents.

Meanwhile, in a neighborhood a few hundred yards from the clinic, other members of the UN team were on the cusp of a discovery. Two impact craters, one on a rooftop and another in a field, still contained large rocket fragments, including crumpled sections of the original warheads that would have delivered the poisons. The rocket that landed in the field had hit soft earth, and its shaft and engine were still partially buried and clearly undisturbed. Wearing protective suits and masks, the inspectors picked up some of the metal pieces and placed them in evidence bags and used special swabs to collect environmental samples from rocket parts that were too heavy to carry.

From the evidence, UN experts were able to reconstruct the particulars of the unusual rockets that struck the eastern Ghouta neighborhood in the early hours of August 21. The designer of the rocket had crafted the nearly seven-foot-long device with the obvious intention of delivering a large quantity of liquid over a long distance without losing any of the contents. The warhead itself was a fat cylinder built to hold about fifteen gallons, or roughly the volume of a laundry tub. A small fuse at the tip would ensure that the warhead ruptured and released its payload upon impact but did not explode or burn.

Days before the Sellström team entered the Ghouta suburbs, multiple governments and dozens of professional experts had already concluded from video footage that the victims had been exposed to a nerve agent, most likely sarin. Now the inspectors possessed in their evidence kit actual samples of the liquid, recovered from the remains of rockets used in the attack. Their findings, when analyzed days later by a pair of independent laboratories, banished any lingering doubts. It was sarin, in high-quality form.

Once again, it contained traces of an unusual additive: hexamine, also discovered during the investigation of the Saraqeb attack that killed Maryam al-Khatib. It was a uniquely Syrian formulation, and now it had been incontrovertibly linked to the attack on Ghouta.

Where had the rockets come from? On the rooftop in east Ghouta, the investigators discovered two holes that had been created during the impact: one of them through the roof itself, and another at a spot where the rocket had penetrated an outer wall. Just by lining up the two holes, the inspectors could roughly deduce the flight path.

A more precise calculation could be obtained from the other impact site, in the open field. Suppose someone shot an arrow that flew in a high arc and came down to stick in the ground tip-first; by following the line of the shaft, you could calculate where the archer stood when he snapped the bowstring. This rocket's nose was buried in the ground, with the tail jutting into the air at an angle. The UN inspectors would later state in their official report that the flight had "an azimuth of 105 degrees, in an East/Southeast trajectory." In other words, the rocket was launched in an area northwest of Ghouta. Government territory.

No one had asked Åke Sellström to reach a verdict on who was behind the killings in the Damascus suburbs. The Syrians had specifically demanded that he refrain from doing so. But the scientist, adhering to his "good standard," had managed to level an accusation without uttering a word. His discovery was indeed an arrow, one that pointed directly at Syrian army units in the pay of Bashar al-Assad.

7

"The eye of a hurricane"

DAMASCUS. AUGUST 29, 2013

A storm was coming. The ordinary citizens of Damascus could sense its approach and began to prepare. Across the capital, markets and cafés that had remained open and lively throughout the war began to shut down. Well-to-do businessmen and bureaucrats who could afford to escape slipped away to villas in the country and along the coast. Local workers for the international aid agencies found extra cash in their pay envelopes—enough, it was hoped, to survive the tribulations that would surely befall the city after America's missiles struck.

Åke Sellström and his team, returning to their hotel after three days of evidence collection, noticed the change and perceived that it was partly about them. It had been a safe bet that no U.S. missiles would fly while UN fact-finders remained in the field. But the mission was now over, and the Syrian government knew better than anyone what was in the boxes and bags that the inspectors had brought with them from Ghouta. Soon the rest of the world would know, too, and all that evidence, along with the UN officials themselves—the last physical hindrance to a military strike on Damascus—would be on its way out of the country.

Unless, of course, Syria could find a way to stop it.

Sellström and his aides huddled in the command center, debating what to do. Inside the Four Seasons ballroom, the mood was darker than it had been at any point since the mission began. To a person, the team was physically and emotionally spent. For three days they had been transported into a world of unimaginable suffering, to reconstruct in gruesome detail what was surely one of the century's most insidious war crimes. Each night they tramped through the Four Seasons' chandeliered lobby with the dust from Ghouta still on their shoes, filing past exquisitely arranged trays of tropical fruit that would have triggered a riot in any of Moadamiyeh's famine-stricken neighborhoods. When they first arrived in Damascus, the hotel had seemed like a gilded cocoon, one with a spa and a well-stocked bar. Now it just felt uncomfortably ostentatious, and exposed. Other UN agencies in the hotel were complaining that Sellström's team had made the Four Seasons unsafe for all of them. Some talked about temporarily moving into the hotel's underground parking garage until the confrontation over chemical weapons had passed. Everyone in the UN contingent sensed that something bad was about to happen.

"It was like we were all in the eye of a hurricane," one UN official present at the time recalled afterward. "You could feel it. You could feel the weight in the air."

As Sellström's aides sat to assess their prospects, they saw threats everywhere. By all accounts, an American air strike was imminent, perhaps just hours away. Each minute in Syria increased the risk of being physically harmed in the attack or caught up in the turbulence that would surely follow it. Even more worrisome was the very real prospect that the dictator Bashar al-Assad would intervene to ensure that the team's evidence kits never left Syria. His secret police might decide to raid their hotel rooms on a trumped-up charge and seize everything. Or—far more likely, in the opinion of Sellström's security advisers—the UN team would come under attack on some desolate stretch of highway during the journey back to Beirut. The regime would almost certainly blame the rebels, and there would be no witnesses around to refute the claim.

They were all but powerless to improve the odds for their own safety. So the inspectors decided to do what they could to ensure the survival of the evidence they had collected.

That night, Sellström took a careful inventory of everything the team had brought back from Ghouta. All the physical evidence—the rocket fragments and soil samples in plastic bags and boxes; the blood and urine specimens in small coolers—had been cataloged and placed under tamper-proof seals. Now these were divided up among the inspectors to be stashed away, as best as they could manage, in their individual rooms.

As an insurance plan, it was admittedly modest. But if a missile struck the hotel, some rooms might be spared serious damage, even if others were destroyed. If Syria's secret police raided the hotel in the middle of the night, they would know the kind of evidence they were looking for, but not the amount. Or where it all was kept.

By the time the sun rose over central Damascus in the morning, some of the Ghouta evidence might well be confiscated or destroyed. But Sellström had done what he could to ensure that at least some of it would survive.

But the missiles weren't coming. Not yet.

Obama's plan for a quick air strike was running into obstacles on multiple fronts. As the president waited for the inspectors to finally leave, powerful voices around him were urging caution. On the day of Sellström's visit to east Ghouta, Obama received a letter from congressional leaders warning him against taking any military action against Syria without first seeking legislative approval. "Engaging our military in Syria when no direct threat to the United States exists . . . would violate the separation of powers" provisions of the U.S. Constitution, the letter admonished. Later that day, one of Obama's closest foreign allies, German chancellor Angela Merkel, offered sobering advice, telling the Democrat that he risked being "left on a limb" unless he slowed down and let the UN investigation take its course. Deputy national security adviser Ben Rhodes, who listened in on the call, said afterward that the president's confidence seemed to melt away.

"It was the first time I saw him look uneasy about acting in Syria," Rhodes later wrote.

But it was another ally, Great Britain, that delivered the biggest blow. British prime minister David Cameron was an early supporter of military action, and his government began making preparations to participate with the United States and France in a three-nation air strike against Damascus. But privately, Cameron was telling the White House he needed a delay of a few days so he could organize a vote in Britain's parliament supporting a military intervention. For the Tory leader, the vote was more than a mere formality. Many in the United Kingdom still resented their government's decision to follow the United States into a war against Iraq, and Cameron wanted political cover before committing British forces to another open-ended engagement in the Middle East. It was not to be. Despite a last-minute scramble by Cameron and a public appeal to Britons to uphold the international norm against the use of chemical weapons, the authorization measure fell short by thirteen votes. Britain was officially out of the coalition.

To the White House, the British vote was like a bucket of ice water on hot coals. Obama's aides were incredulous, and also unnerved. "It spooked everyone," recalled a participant in that week's West Wing meetings.

The next day, August 30, the White House released an unclassified summary of the U.S. intelligence community's assessment of the Ghouta attack, asserting "with high confidence that the Syrian government carried out a chemical weapons attack" that killed 1,429 people outside Damascus. The document's publication appeared to presage the launch of missiles as early as that weekend. Yet instead of ordering a strike, Obama stepped out of the White House that afternoon for what would become the most widely chronicled walk of his presidency. Under a late-summer sky studded with fair-weather clouds, he and his chief of staff, Denis McDonough, went for a long stroll through the White House's gently rolling South Lawn, meandering through the ceremonial gardens and groves of magnolias and ancient oaks. Through the countless hours of debates in the Situation Room, McDonough had been a lone voice urging restraint. "What would come next?" he would ask, according to Rhodes's account. "What if we bombed Syria and Assad responded by using more chemical weapons? Would we put in ground troops to secure those stockpiles?"

Somewhere along the way, Obama arrived at a decision. When he returned forty-five minutes later, he announced to his staff that he would seek a formal authorization from Congress before launching the air strike.

His decision meant a delay of several days, certainly, and perhaps even weeks. But philosophically it hewed closer to the ideals of a younger Barack Obama, who, as a senator and presidential candidate, argued for restraint in the use of military force. "We've had enough of presidents who put tough talk ahead of real diplomacy," candidate Obama had said in a 2007 campaign speech on the Iraq war. Despite the shift, as his advisers huddled through the weekend to retool the White House's Syria strategy, Obama continued to argue that a military strike was necessary. After the "red line" threats, he said, U.S. credibility was at stake. The laws and treaties prohibiting the use of chemical weapons were worth defending.

To a person, Obama's national security advisers agreed with the decision to go to Congress, as several would later recall in written accounts of the weekend's meetings on Syria. The only significant dispute was over whether Congress would go along with Obama's plan. To many senior aides, it was a no-brainer: of course lawmakers would want a hand in punishing Assad for the horrifying deaths of children and other innocents that Americans had witnessed on their television screens. Most Democrats would fall in line behind their party's leader, and Republicans—traditionally the more hawkish party—could scarcely object to a limited strike against a Syrian dictator who allied himself with Iran and allowed his country to serve as a transit hub for jihadists who killed U.S. soldiers in Iraq.

Against this consensus view, only Susan Rice, Obama's national security adviser, sounded a note of dissent. Counting on lawmakers to take a principled stand was a fool's bet, she said.

"Congress," Rice told the president, "is never going to give you this authority."

Within a few hours of Obama's South Lawn stroll, Ban Ki-moon telephoned Samantha Power with an important update from Syria. Sellström had finished his work, the secretary-general said, and within hours his team would be on its way out of the country, along with a trove of evidence. The UN chief offered no opinion on air strikes, but he made it clear that the biggest single obstacle to Obama's military plans would soon be out of the way.

This was hardly news to a White House that was obsessively tracking Sellström's movements. But Power was genuinely relieved to hear from Ban himself that the inspectors were leaving. "It would give

President Obama the peace of mind he had been seeking to launch the planned air strikes," she later wrote, strikes she believed were now only hours away.

Power did not yet know that Obama had decided to go to Congress, so Ban remained in the dark as well. Believing an attack was now imminent, the secretary-general summoned a handful of trusted aides to his east Manhattan residence on Sunday morning to wait for news. Susana Malcorra, Ban's Argentine-born chef de cabinet, and UN undersecretary-general for political affairs Jeffrey Feltman sat on sofas in Ban's living room thinking they were about to learn that an attack was underway—that it was "officially D-Day," as one of the participants wryly remarked. Ban placed a speakerphone on the mantel above the fireplace. Within a few minutes, the phone rang. It was Samantha Power.

"Mr. Secretary-General, I just want to inform you . . . ," Power began. In a businesslike tone, she told Ban that air strikes were off the table, for now. The conversation was over in less than two minutes.

Ban's relief was palpable. Never one to relish confrontation, the secretary-general had been torn between his perceived obligations as UN leader, on one hand, and the nearly irresistible pressure from the United States and other Western governments on the other. He never wavered on whether Sellström should be allowed to continue his investigation, aides later said, but he had been personally repulsed by the images of the dead at Ghouta, and he hated being seen as a one-man obstacle by those who believed that punishing Assad was the only moral response.

"He felt the pressure very, very deeply," said a close adviser who was beside Ban during those days in late August. "Member states will do what they're going to do, but our argument was that there was unfinished business: we had an opportunity to try to find the truth. But it was a very hard place to be."

In Washington, Obama was in an even tougher bind. White House aides had begun canvassing lawmakers to gauge support for a possible Syrian air strike, and the early results were astonishing. The appetite for a U.S. military intervention wasn't just soft. It was practically nonexistent.

Within the president's own party, few were willing to commit to a yes vote for a military strike. Even Democrats who had publicly condemned the poison-gas attacks now said they feared going against the wishes of constituents overwhelmingly opposed to any action that might draw the United States into another Middle Eastern war. One Democratic House member said she had kept a tally of nearly 2,500 calls from voters in her district who telephoned to sound off about a possible U.S. air strike. Opponents of military action were leading by a margin of forty to one, she reported.

Among Republicans, some of the opposition to the president's plan appeared to be nakedly partisan. Republicans had demanded that the White House seek Congress's consent for a military strike, yet when Obama tried to comply, GOP leaders turned him down anyway. Mitch McConnell, the Republican majority leader in the U.S. Senate, gave a speech on the Senate floor blasting Obama's plan to bomb Syrian military sites over Assad's use of chemical weapons. Four years later, McConnell would praise Obama's Republican successor for attacking Syrian air bases under nearly identical circumstances, and without waiting for congressional approval.

But other Republicans were simply reflecting the opinions of their constituents, who, by and large, were just as opposed to military intervention as their neighbors in more left-leaning districts. Samantha Power, who was enlisted to help with the congressional lobbying effort, was advised by an Arkansas Republican to forget about looking for support for military action, even in his most military-friendly state. "I can't find anyone in Arkansas supportive of this, and I've been everywhere," Power was told.

In the months and years that followed, analysts and opinion writers would spill barrels of ink dissecting U.S. decision-making on Syria, and most especially the Obama administration's failure to back up its "red line" threat with military action in the waning days of August 2013. Some would criticize the White House for squandering an opportunity for decisive action in the immediate aftermath of the Ghouta attack, when public outrage was highest. Others would blame the fecklessness and hypocrisy of a Congress that had become so risk-averse and so riven by partisanship that it was no longer capable of leading. Still others would conclude that the primary fault lay with the president himself, for uttering the words "red line" in the first place.

But there was another reason, underlying all the others, for the collapse of the Obama administration's plan to punish Assad over his use of chemical weapons. When it came to Syria, Americans by historic margins simply did not wish to get involved. Pollsters who rushed out to test the public's mood in late August 2013 found Americans to be beyond apathetic. U.S. troops were still being killed in Afghanistan, in a conflict that was now the longest in the country's history. The last U.S. troops had departed Iraq just two years ago, in 2011, the same year that Arab Spring uprisings began sweeping the Middle East. Americans deeply opposed any U.S. military involvement in Syria, regardless of the reason, and no matter how limited. One opinion poll conducted in the immediate aftermath of the Ghouta attacks found that only 25 percent of Americans favored bombing Syria, even if the evidence pointed to Assad as the culprit behind the gruesome images they had witnessed on television that week. Another survey two weeks later found opposition to a proposed air strike at over 51 percent, a measure of reluctance for military intervention that surpassed anything the pollsters had seen in twenty years.

There were plenty of reasons for the country's wariness. The wars in Afghanistan and Iraq had been grinding, brutal campaigns with few obvious victories, against enemies whose preferred weapons were suicide vests and roadside bombs that blew up GIs in their Humvees by remote control. The early euphoria over the so-called Arab Spring revolutions had long since given way to despair as Americans witnessed the rise of a Muslim Brotherhood government in Egypt and the ascendance in liberated Libya of Islamist militias who murdered a U.S. ambassador and burned and sacked the consulate at Benghazi. The world had not yet seen the Syrian conflict's most calamitous effects: the millions of refugees and the rise of a terrorist caliphate in the heart of the Middle East. But in the summer of 2013, most Americans had seen enough. Once, in the previous decade, they had believed a U.S. president who sold them on the idea of a war to prevent the use of weapons of mass destruction. However noble the cause this time, Americans weren't buying it.

Obama tried once more to sway public opinion. In the days following McConnell's remarks, he had released the classified report showing why U.S. intelligence officials believed Assad was behind the gassing of Syrian civilians. Now he appeared on national television to deliver a speech explaining his reasons for going to Congress as well as his continuing conviction that military action was necessary—that "this menace must be confronted."

Yet it was becoming clear that the authorization vote in Congress was still doomed. An unofficial head count by White House aides suggested that the nay votes could outnumber yeas by as much as four to one.

If Obama lost, the political embarrassment would be but one dimension of a far-reaching policy disaster. White House aides had been so convinced of congressional support for a military strike that they had barely considered what might happen if the lobbying effort failed. If Congress refused to go along with its Syria plan, the White House would be out of options. Assad would face no serious consequences for using poison gas to kill 1,400 of his citizens. And the rest of the world would witness the humbling of a U.S. president who could manage to rally neither the United Nations nor his own Congress to do something about the slaughter. Other tyrants and strongmen, from Iran to North Korea to Venezuela, would certainly take note.

As White House aides debated what to do, one possible alternative—a way to salvage at least a partial win—had failed to gain traction. During the initial debate over the outreach to Congress, Samantha Power, on a video conference screen from New York, wondered aloud about whether the threat of force might be leveraged to achieve the ultimate objective: eliminating Assad's arsenal of poisons.

"Why not try to secure the dismantlement of the chemical weapons stockpile program?" Power asked. While she supported the air strike, it was clear that with bombs alone "we're not going to do anything to fundamentally put a dent in his stockpile."

The suggestion hung over the room for a brief moment, but then the discussion moved on. The idea that Assad might voluntarily surrender his most important strategic weapon seemed too far-fetched to warrant serious debate, and Obama was still intent on pushing the authorization measure through Congress.

"People were so sure that we were going to get the congressional authorization, we didn't have a Plan B," she said. "As it became chillingly clear that we weren't going to get the authorization, we were naked. I mean, we were so naked."

—

Dawn broke on Saturday, August 31, to find the Four Seasons Hotel and the rest of central Damascus still standing. But the evidence that had been carefully stashed in the inspectors' rooms had been cleaned out. Every scrap of it.

The UN team was gone as well. Åke Sellström surprised his Syrian hosts by departing hours ahead of schedule. Instead of lining up outside the hotel at 8:30 that morning, the inspectors quietly loaded their gear into the Toyota Land Cruisers and took off for Lebanon in a sprint at 5 a.m., a full hour before sunrise. Secured inside the vehicles—there were six of them now, minus the one that had been shot up—were dozens of bags and boxes representing the entirety of their collection effort in Ghouta. Also in the SUVs, looking slightly dazed and sleep-deprived, were two Syrian officials: Brigadier General Hassan al-Sharif—the "man of much eyebrow," as the inspectors jokingly dubbed him—and one of his deputies. They had been brought along to serve as Syrian guarantors against any tampering or mishandling of the evidence. It had also occurred to UN security chief Diarmuid O'Donovan that the presence of Syrian military officers in the convoy might lessen the chances of an ambush along the road to Lebanon. But given the team's experiences of the past week, it was a small comfort, at best.

O'Donovan judged that the early departure would give the team a good head start. If they were lucky, they might make it all the way to Lebanon before the Syrians could scramble their scattered assets to try to stop them. Sure enough, the vehicles, racing along on empty highways, covered the forty miles to the border crossing without mishap, in record time.

It wasn't over yet. Sellström, sitting in the backseat of one of the SUVs, felt his shoulder muscles tense as the lights of the Syrian checkpoint came into view. The Toyotas queued up for passport inspection, and one by one, each approached the guard station. Then, one by one, the SUVs were waved through.

They were officially out of Syrian territory. It had been easy. Almost too easy.

Minutes later the convoy began the ascent through the rocky gorges of no-man's-land. They drove along in silence through canyons still dim in the early light, and then at last the red-tiled roofs of the Lebanese frontier town of Masnaa came into view. Sellström felt himself beginning to relax. *We managed it,* he thought to himself. *We did our job, and nobody got hurt.*

Then he saw the faces of the Lebanese security officials who had come to meet the convoy. Something was wrong.

"There is a threat against you from Hezbollah," the chief security officer told Sellström, gravely. Lebanese intelligence had learned of a serious plot by the powerful Shiite militant group to target the UN convoy after it crossed into the country from Syria. The timing and location of the planned attack were unclear, the official said, but the mission was in imminent danger.

So this is how it's going to be, Sellström thought. Assad allowed the UN team to slip out of Damascus with its trove of evidence, knowing that Hezbollah—a group closely allied with Syria as well as Iran—was poised to strike outside the country, where his government could not be directly blamed. How would they accomplish it? An ambush somewhere along the highway? A bombing at the hotel, perhaps, or at the airport?

The Lebanese security men were not in a mood to speculate. They rushed everyone back into their SUVs as a black armored escort vehicle took its place at the head of the column.

"Your presence is a threat to Lebanon," the security chief explained to Sellström. "We have to rush you to the airport. We cannot stop anywhere."

Then they took off. The team later recalled the wild dash across Lebanon as the most harrowing journey of the entire expedition. The convoy raced along narrow mountain highways and careened through village streets with horns blaring. Special-forces officers leaned out of the windows of the lead vehicle, waving guns and shouting at motorists to get out of the way. In Beirut's outskirts they zagged in and out of traffic, forcing other cars onto the shoulder. They continued to roar along at the same breakneck pace up to the moment the convoy reached the Beirut–Rafic Hariri International Airport and deposited its frazzled passengers at the door of a private departure lounge. Outside on the tarmac, just a few steps away, a chartered German jet stood waiting for them.

There was a nervous pause as officials scrambled to obtain a Dutch visa for the two Syrians. But with all passports finally stamped, the UN team was hustled onto the plane for the flight to Holland. Only after the jet reached an altitude of twenty thousand feet—beyond the range of most shoulder-fired antiaircraft missiles—did Sellström and his deputies finally allow themselves to breathe.

The Swede had been thoroughly wrung out by the ordeal, and he looked exhausted. But he was happy. In his carry-on bag he had a new souvenir: a Syrian flag, signed by each member of this makeshift inspection squad. Below his seat, in the cargo hold, were crates containing the evidence they had collected: the sealed boxes, coolers, and plastic bags, all ready for forensic analysis at labs in Holland and Switzerland.

Sellström's entry into Syria had been clouded by skepticism, with members of his own team counted among the legions of doubters. Now, as he departed the country, the UN mission was being heralded in Western capitals as an astonishing success. Despite obstacles, official resistance, and even violence—both threatened and real—he had accomplished what he had set out to do, and much more.

The evidence in the cargo hold presented the world's nations with a choice: it would test whether international standards of accountability on chemical weapons were empty promises or solid, tangible things. Sellström's own "good standard," meanwhile—his dogged pursuit of the truth, against political and emotional crosswinds, and in spite of Syrian interference, manipulation, and deceit—had been abundantly met.

When it was clear that the UN team's departure would not immediately bring about a missile strike, Damascus also drew a collective sigh of relief. The cafés and nightclubs slowly reopened, and the lights flickered on again in the tonier neighborhoods in the hills above the old city.

Kassem Eid, the Syrian youth who had survived the poison-gas attack at Moadamiyeh, scoured Western news sites for hints about coming military strikes and any word of progress from the UN investigation he had helped facilitate earlier in the week. That Saturday he happened to catch streaming video of President Barack Obama's Syria speech. As he watched, his mood shifted from elation to bewilderment. Were the Americans bombing, or not?

The U.S. president started by outright blaming Syria's government for the "murder" of more than a thousand people with poison gas in the Damascus suburbs. He called the act an "assault on human dignity" that risked "making a mockery of the global prohibition on the use of chemical weapons." And he pledged that the U.S. military would soon respond.

"After careful deliberation, I have decided that the United States should take military action against Syrian regime targets," Obama said. The strike would be limited, but the U.S. leader said he was "confident we can hold the Assad regime accountable for their use of chemical weapons, deter this kind of behavior, and degrade their capacity to carry it out."

Bravo, Eid thought.

But a minute later, Obama seemed to put his plan on hold. He announced a kind of procedural detour, saying he would first seek the backing of Congress before launching any missiles. There was no urgency in bombing Syria, so he would wait for the lawmakers—now on vacation, apparently—to return to Washington, and he would allow the UN investigators more time to continue their work. The United States would eventually move to confront Syria's murderous dictator and defend international norms, he said, both for the sake of U.S. national security and because "it's who we are, as a country." But it wouldn't do anything quite yet.

Since the morning of the poison-gas attack, Eid had told friends that Western countries would now be compelled to come to the aid of the rebels. The coming air strike would certainly target Syria's helicopters and fighter jets, and without them, the government's remaining strongholds would be quickly overrun. Assad and his hated regime would collapse like a house of twigs.

Now Eid felt his certitude starting to fray. Days earlier, Britain's prime minister had placed his bet on his country's parliament, and he had lost. David Cameron had seemed disappointed, but was he really? Maybe this was the plan all along.

Eid resolved to remain optimistic, telling himself that America's elected representatives would not merely back the president but would go even further, authorizing a larger and grander intervention. But as the days passed with no word of a congressional vote, it became harder to keep up the pretense.

"I began to doubt," he said.

Mazen al-Hamada, languishing with hundreds of other prisoners in the aircraft hangar outside Damascus, heard nothing of Obama's speech, so he continued to wait.

He tried to keep track of time, but it was difficult. Maybe a week had elapsed; perhaps it was more. The hours passed with a dull rhythm, consisting of a slow progression from the miseries of the daytime, when the August sun transformed the metal hangar into a convection oven, to the miseries of the night, when Hamada and the other inmates tried to sleep on the hard ground without mattresses, pillows, or blankets. During the in-between hours, Hamada would become more acutely aware of a thousand pains from months of beatings and torture in prison, and of the more constant pain of hunger.

But there were small mercies, for which he was thankful. Because the inmates were placed in the hangar to be slaughtered, no one bothered with interrogations or torture. Massed together in a single room, the prisoners were relatively free to speak to one another and share information about missing loved ones and friends. They talked endlessly to pass the time and, when they could, tried to help the more seriously injured among them. Over the months, the population at Adra Prison had become a repository of knowledge on how to treat maladies ranging from puncture wounds to broken limbs, without drugs or medical instruments. Sometimes, on the bare tarmac under the hangar roof, they would even attempt a kind of crude surgery when no other options were available.

"There was one man whose leg was really swollen from infection," Hamada remembered. "We literally used our hands and fingernails to open his wound to let out the pus and inflammation."

Sometimes at night, as Hamada tried to fall sleep, he would think about his past life. He thought about his brothers and his parents, wondering if they were still alive, and if they had ever been told what had happened to him. He stared up at the ceiling and wondered what it would be like if a missile, launched perhaps from a ship or submarine hundreds of miles away, suddenly came crashing through the thin aluminum. Would he hear its approach in those final seconds? Would there be a flash of pain, or just instant, unfeeling oblivion? What would happen to his body? Would there be enough left of him to identify and bury? In any case, could a fate such as that be any worse than the one he was enduring now?

Hamada was still wrestling with those questions when, one morning, he heard the distinct roar of multiple diesel engines. Minutes later he and his friends were roused by the guards and told to queue up to leave the hangar. Outside, waiting in the midmorning glare, were a dozen prison buses. The inmates quietly climbed aboard, and an hour later they were back in their cells at Adra Prison.

The prisoners speculated among themselves about what had happened. Had the air strike been called off? Had the Americans discovered the men's presence at the military base and decided to send their missiles elsewhere?

Hamada was never able to learn the answer.

"No one said a thing to us," he said. "They just put us in the buses and sent us back to prison. No explanation."

8

The Deal

GENEVA, SWITZERLAND. SEPTEMBER 14, 2013

The middle-aged man in the skimpy Speedo bathing suit seemed to have no inkling that he was being watched. It was a chilly September morning in Geneva, the kind of day that normally entices few guests at the InterContinental Hotel to go sunbathing, and the man appeared to have the hotel's giant outdoor pool to himself. He lay for a while on a lounge chair, then began to swim laps, oblivious to the stares of the plainclothes security men who stood by the pool's entrance with submachine guns barely concealed under their jackets. The swimmer continued at a leisurely pace, showing no awareness of the well-dressed dignitaries gathered around a table on the pool terrace just a few steps away, and no sign that he recognized the famously stentorian voice of the tall, silver-maned gentleman at the head of the table who was doing most of the talking.

"Sergey, you have to do this," the tall man, easily recognized by other hotel guests as U.S. secretary of state John F. Kerry, was heard imploring a bespectacled Russian diplomat seated to his left.

A quieter conversation ensued, with some at the table glancing distractedly at the swimmer, who had unknowingly become part of the backdrop for high-stakes diplomacy on the hotel patio. A few minutes later, the booming baritone rose again above the splashing in the pool, this time with a tinge of what sounded like exasperation.

"If they're truly bad guys, I don't care how you kill them," Kerry was saying loudly. "Just don't use chemical weapons!"

In the time it took for the swimmer to finish his laps and towel off, the poolside haggling had ended, and the outlines of a historic diplomatic accord had come into view. Kerry and his Russian counterpart, Foreign Minister Sergey Lavrov, concluding a three-day negotiating marathon in the Swiss Alpine city, had settled on a collective response to the chemical weapons attacks in Syria. The final details were hammered out under a parasol on a hotel pool deck perfumed by catalpa trees with a faint undertone of chlorine.

The solution proposed—and the speed with which it came together—were unlike anything seen in modern diplomacy. Under the plan, there would be no air strikes against Syria, at least for now, and no immediate attempts to push for a vote in the UN Security Council authorizing the use of force against Syria's government. But there would be a reckoning of sorts over the crimes committed at Ghouta. With Russia and the United States serving as guarantors, Bashar al-Assad would be compelled to surrender his entire chemical arsenal, a weapons system that served for decades as Syria's main strategic deterrent against archrival Israel. The dictator would have just seven days to reveal the location of every production facility and storage depot for chemical weapons and to produce an inventory accounting for every ounce of sarin, VX, and sulfur mustard in the country's possession, along with the precursor chemicals and the warheads, bombs, and shells used to deliver them. Then he would watch as all of it was collected and eliminated. Under the terms of the deal, it would happen at blazing speed, with the entire arsenal, including delivery systems and production lines, destroyed within nine months.

For Damascus, the capitulation came with a side serving of humiliation. Besides being a strategic asset, Syria's chemical stockpile also was a closely guarded state secret, and one that carried the additional stigma of being banned under international law. Assad had never acknowledged possessing nerve agents. Now he was confessing, renouncing, and surrendering, all at once. It could be likened to asking Israel—an undeclared nuclear weapons state that does not officially acknowledge the existence of its estimated eighty to four hundred nuclear bombs and missiles—to suddenly pull back the curtain on its entire nuclear arsenal and then invite outsiders to come in and trash everything: the missiles, the warheads, even its heavily guarded nuclear reactor.

But for Assad, and for Russia, this was the price for forestalling a U.S. air strike and postponing the collapse of Assad's regime, even if just for a little while. And Assad was willing to pay.

For the Obama administration, it was the political equivalent of a Houdini act: the White House had somehow managed to simultaneously delay a military strike and avoid the humiliation of its failure to win congressional support for one.

The idea of a grand U.S.-Russian bargain to eliminate Syria's weapons stockpile had been floating around for months, in very different settings. Richard Lugar, the Indiana senator and arms-control advocate, publicly proposed such a deal during a visit to Moscow in July 2012, and Andy Weber mentioned it afterward in Pentagon meetings. The idea piqued the interest of then–deputy secretary of defense Ash Carter, who, like Weber, had worked with Russians in the 1990s to secure Soviet-era nuclear and chemical weapons. After that, U.S. and Russian diplomats and military officials kicked the idea around in a series of private meetings in Moscow and Washington, without reaching any firm conclusions.

Meanwhile, the same thought had occurred to the Israeli government. Immediately following the Ghouta attack, Israeli minister of intelligence Yuval Steinitz summoned Russia's ambassador to his office to ask about Syria's weapons. This is becoming an embarrassment for you, Steinitz said, referring to Syria's latest international outrage, according to a participant in the meeting. Why don't you force Syria to get rid of them? A few days after that, an Israeli businessman conveyed the idea privately to a White House official as the Obama administration was struggling to line up votes for its planned air strike.

Yet to many U.S. officials who were aware of the proposal, it seemed like a fantasy. And so it remained, up to the moment that Syria's biggest champion, Vladimir Putin, decided that this most improbable of ideas might have merit.

On September 6, Syria's weapons came up during a brief exchange between Putin and Obama at the G20 summit in the Russian city of St. Petersburg. The two leaders met privately, without senior aides present, but afterward Obama told advisers that he had suggested the two countries find a way to work together. Putin, clearly anxious to stave off a possible U.S. air strike, appeared to listen.

You shouldn't do this, the Russian leader had said, referring to the planned attack on Syria.

I've been trying to talk to you about the chemical weapons issue since you were reelected, Obama said. If you would solve this problem, I wouldn't have to strike.

Putin made no commitments, but said he would "have Lavrov call," according to Obama's account of the discussion.

Three days later, Secretary Kerry was holding a press conference in London when a reporter asked a theoretical question: What could Syria possibly do to avoid a U.S. military strike? Kerry's answer was equally theoretical: Assad could save himself only if he were to voluntarily give up his entire arsenal.

"He could turn over every single bit of his chemical weapons to the international community in the next week. Turn it over, all of it, without delay, and allow a full and total accounting for that," Kerry said. "But he's not about to do it."

That afternoon, during the flight back to Washington, his press spokeswoman went to considerable effort to tamp down suggestions that Kerry had been hinting about a strategy change. "This is not a change in policy," the official insisted to reporters traveling with the secretary of state.

But Russian diplomats who watched the exchange saw an opening. Before Kerry's flight landed at Joint Base Andrews in the Washington suburbs, a call from Moscow came through on the plane's secure line. It was Lavrov, the Russian foreign minister and Kerry's friend and occasional diplomatic sparring partner.

"I saw your comments," Lavrov began. There was a strong chance, he said, that Syria was prepared to accept America's terms.

Just seventy-two hours later, Kerry and Lavrov would be on their way to Geneva to test, over three days of talks, whether the "impossible" notion of a Syrian disarmament could be transformed into something real.

To prepare for the talks, calls went out to lawyers, intelligence analysts, weapons experts, and Syria specialists spread across a half-dozen agencies, with instructions to be ready to travel to Switzerland within twenty-four hours. The initial instructions were vague, as there was no real precedent for what the experts were being asked to do. The word from Moscow was that Assad had privately consented to signing on to the Chemical Weapons Convention, and the act of signing would trigger a number of legal obligations, including a requirement to declare and destroy any weapons Syria possessed and to submit to international inspections by the convention's enforcement body, the Organization for the Prohibition of Chemical Weapons, or OPCW. Beyond that, no one knew what to expect, or how the meeting's lofty goals might be accomplished.

On the first day in Geneva, Kerry and Lavrov gathered everyone into a large room in the InterContinental Hotel and divided the technical experts into two working groups: one for legal issues, and the other to tackle the logistical challenges involved in destroying Syria's chemical stockpile. But the U.S. representatives quickly ran into a problem: there were no Russians on the other side with whom to negotiate. Lavrov had arrived in Geneva with a small handful of deputies, and only then discovered that his side was outnumbered and overmatched. More aides were summoned from Moscow, but these began to trickle in only after the talks were well into the second day.

The Americans took advantage of the extra twenty-four hours to fine-tune their strategy. It was a safe bet that the Russians would press for as many delays as possible, so the Americans prepared to battle against any stalling that might allow Syria to drag out the disarmament process in the hope that the rest of the world would eventually lose interest. Robert Mikulak, the Obama administration's ambassador to the OPCW, had begun drafting the text of a resolution that could be endorsed by the organization's executive council, legally committing Syria to eliminate its weapons on an aggressive timetable. Rebecca Hersman, the Pentagon's chief representative and a deputy assistant secretary in charge of WMD policy, sat down with him to help. Diplomats rehearsed their arguments for what everyone assumed would be a grinding, line-by-line slugfest over how, and how quickly, Syria's chemical weapons would be destroyed.

But when the talks began in earnest on the second day, the Americans found many of their Russian counterparts—a mix of uniformed military officers and civilian technocrats—to be curiously quiescent. There was little quibbling over the essential facts of Syria's weapons program, and surprisingly little pushback on proposed schedules and time lines for the destruction. The Russians, as a group, showed scant enthusiasm for the task at hand, but they marched in lockstep to the cadence set by Lavrov and other senior Kremlin officials. Moscow appeared to want a deal, and they would do their part to deliver one.

In the logistics working group, the leader for the U.S. side, Thomas Countryman, the State Department's top nonproliferation official, decided that the Russians and Americans should start by mutually agreeing on the size of the problem: how many tons of chemical weapons the Assad regime actually possessed. A U.S. official gave a rough sketch, describing the CIA's current thinking about the quantity of poisons in Syria's stockpile, and where they were kept. Then it was the Russians' turn, and the Americans waited to hear what Syria's closest military ally—one that had helped equip Assad's army and frequently visited its military bases—had to say. The official from Moscow blandly offered a substantially smaller figure, but then quickly assented to the American view. "That's more than we thought, but maybe you're right," the Russian said through an interpreter. Months later, evidence from Syria would show the CIA's estimates to be remarkably accurate, though the Americans could never be certain about what new facilities and weapons, if any, Assad had created in the years since the death of the CIA's "chemist" spy.

A simple compromise settled the potentially contentious question of how quickly Syria's arsenal would be destroyed. After considering competing suggestions of six months and twelve months, the experts split the difference and decided that the stockpile should be eliminated by the end of June, just over nine months away. Even at the compromise date, the pace required to meet the deadline was, as Countryman later acknowledged, "on the border between feasible and insane."

Significant clashes did erupt over how Syria's chemicals should be eliminated. Countryman's negotiators tried to prod the Russians into agreeing to do the physical collecting and destroying of Syria's poisons on their own, with international oversight. The idea made logical sense: the Russians, as Assad's trusted ally, would have easier access to Syria's weapons factories. Moreover, Moscow already had a navy base in Syria, in the port city of Tartus, and it would be relatively easy to load the chemicals onto a navy vessel and ship them across the Black

Sea to Russia, where they could be destroyed in any of six modern plants built over the past decade to eliminate Russia's Soviet-era chemical stockpile. In addition, after some quick digging through intelligence files, Countryman's team had discovered that the Russian army once fielded an entire brigade devoted solely to neutralizing chemical weapons, using a fleet of specialized vehicles that could destroy sarin and other nerve agents on the spot. Why not take those vehicles out of storage and put them to use in Syria? the Russians were asked.

The experts from the Kremlin refused. It was impossible for Russia to accept Syria's weapons, they said, because importing toxic chemicals was illegal under the country's laws. Whether the claim was technically true or not, it struck the Americans as a dubious excuse, since Russia's strongman president could surely grant himself an exemption if he wanted to. As for the brigade and its specialized vehicles, the Russians initially seemed baffled. But the Americans persisted and supplied additional details, until at last a different answer was relayed back from Moscow. "That brigade has been abandoned for years," was the reply.

When it was the United States' turn to present ideas, the most important task fell to Jeff Harris, a mechanical engineer who worked with Tim Blades. Harris had flown in from the Edgewood Army base near Baltimore to brief the Russians on the Americans' new invention. At that moment, six of the new Margarita Machines sat in a warehouse in Maryland, ready to go.

The first mentions of the Pentagon's new Field Deployable Hydrolysis System had elicited puzzled expressions and even scoffs from the Kremlin's experts in Geneva. "Totally impossible" was the Russian verdict in one of the early high-level sessions. But when it was time for Harris's presentation, the men in uniform crowded into a conference room for a chance to see what the fuss was about. Speaking through an interpreter and using a colored diagram as a prop, Harris stood before a row of stern-faced Russians and began to describe the device's modular features, and how the machine could be quickly taken apart, transported in standard shipping containers, and set up almost anywhere: on an airfield tarmac, on a harbor pier, or wherever there was a flat piece of turf and a convenient water source. Using the schematic, he traced the flow of liquid nerve agents through the machine and into the maze of pipes and valves where the toxic molecules would be bombarded with a stream of scalding water. Then he showed how the neutralized leftovers were pumped into a wastewater tank to be taken away for treatment elsewhere.

Among the Russians, one retired general appeared to follow the presentation with particular interest. When Harris finished speaking, the man—a former operator of chemical weapons destruction plants in Russia and a venerated member of the delegation, judging from the deference the others accorded him—peppered the American with technical questions. When he had carefully gone through all these, he sat back, apparently satisfied.

"This will work," he said in English.

With that, the talks seemed to turn a corner. Later that night, the sides were close enough to a deal to start putting the text on paper. It fell to Countryman's group to write a new draft of the proposed agreement, filling in the blanks with specific details they had worked out with the Russians. It was nearly 11 p.m. when Countryman surveyed his exhausted team. "Who's going to help me write this up?" he asked.

An Air Force colonel named John Cinnamon raised his hand. Cinnamon, known to his friends as "Toast," was one of Major General Jay Santee's lead planners on Syria with the Pentagon's Defense Threat Reduction Agency, or DTRA. He followed Countryman to his room and the two began to write, with Cinnamon punching in the words on Countryman's laptop. After a few frustrating minutes, they changed seats.

"Move over. I type faster than you do," said Countryman, taking the keyboard. "Okay, John, what are we going to write here?"

Countryman typed:

"The parties agree to set the following target dates: Completion of initial OPCW on-site inspections by November. Destruction of production and mixing/filling equipment by November. Complete elimination of all chemical weapons material and equipment in the first half of 2014."

Cinnamon thought the time lines were optimistic—"pie in the sky," he later said. But the two men finished the revisions and passed the document along to Kerry's aides. The next morning, September 14, Kerry and Lavrov sat by the hotel pool to give the draft a final review. The two men argued briefly over one remaining sticking point: whether the agreement should be backed by a UN Security

Council resolution, to ensure compliance by a Syrian government that, after all, was not even present at the talks in Geneva. Lavrov at first resisted the idea of a UN pact, but then, once again, the Russians acquiesced. The four-page framework, with timetables and deadlines just as Countryman and Cinnamon had typed them the night before, was signed by the two diplomats that afternoon. Thirteen days later, a pair of resolutions adding legal underpinnings to the Geneva agreement were approved in near-simultaneous decisions by the United Nations and the OPCW.

Through it all, the Russians remained oddly indifferent about many particulars of the disarmament agreement, according to officials who were present in Geneva. Rebecca Hersman, the Defense Department's point person at the talks, later recalled her uneasiness at seeing Moscow's representatives swallow one extremely challenging deadline after another, without protest. As the negotiations progressed, it was the American side—and often Hersman herself—who began pushing the negotiators for more realistic timetables. As she watched the Russians, Hersman perceived a sinister strategy at work: Moscow, she believed, was quietly seeking to engineer a failure.

"We were all for doing it fast," Hersman said afterward. "But if you set a time line that you physically can't achieve, and the whole thing fails, then the Russians get what they want: nothing."

Even a casual observer at the Geneva talks might have believed he was witnessing a boondoggle in the making. An untested sarin-destruction machine, built to fit in a tin can? An inspection force, still to be determined, roaming around the Syrian countryside looking for hidden weapons in the middle of a civil war? It all must have struck Kremlin analysts as absurdly optimistic: another exuberant American expedition to the Middle East that would surely break up after a few weeks of crashing against Syria's unforgiving shoals. When it did fail, the Russians could say that they had tried. Meanwhile, any lingering enthusiasm for a U.S. air strike would have passed.

"I think the Russians really believed we couldn't do it," Hersman said. "They believed it would fall apart, and then they would have the best of both worlds. The failure would be on the Americans. And they would have succeeded in backing off the aircraft carriers."

In fact, it was the Russians who miscalculated, Hersman said.

"They woefully underestimated us," she said.

—

The victory celebration in Geneva ended almost before it started. Within hours, the Obama administration's relief over finding a face-saving way out of the crisis had given way to new worries over how to make the accord work.

Colonel John "Toast" Cinnamon called his boss at DTRA, Santee, to break the news. After months of continuous thinking and hypothesizing about Syria's chemical weapons, the agency now was faced with having to turn paper plans into reality.

"We're now committed to doing all this stuff," Cinnamon said.

"Ummm. Okay, John," came the reply. "I guess we have our work cut out for us."

Rebecca Hersman flew back to Washington and was quickly summoned to brief Chuck Hagel, the defense secretary, in his Pentagon office. The former senator and one-time infantry squad leader in Vietnam appeared skeptical, and his scowl deepened as Hersman described the time lines for dismantling Syria's chemical weapons complex. Seriously? he asked.

"It just sounds impossible," Hagel said.

"I don't know about 'impossible,' " she said. "Maybe 'really, really hard.' "

One of those hard tasks was to figure out how to dispose of all those weapons—1,300 tons' worth, in all, of sulfur mustard, sarin, and ready-to-mix precursors, according to the official Syrian tally delivered to UN officials. Some related items could be safely destroyed in Syria, such as production equipment and unfilled chemical warheads and shells. But the rest had to be removed and neutralized elsewhere. Tim Blades and his six brand-new hydrolysis machines stood ready to help, in theory, but there was as yet no place to put the devices and no plan for how to extract the chemicals from the country.

Moscow's willingness to contribute to the execution of the agreement, meanwhile, was close to nil. That became abundantly clear when, just over a week after the Kerry-Lavrov agreement, Hersman and other U.S. officials traveled to The Hague to attend a technical meeting with Kremlin counterparts at the Russian embassy. The aim of the meeting was to put flesh on Geneva's still-skeletal framework. But in The Hague, away from TV cameras and absent Cabinet-level supervision, the pretense of cooperation dried up like a puddle after a desert rain. Instead of trading suggestions on how to get the job done, the Russian officials refused to answer even basic questions about their capabilities and possible contributions. The meeting dragged on past the lunch hour, but the Russians offered no food or refreshment, and they eventually resorted to hurling personal insults at Hersman whenever she tried to speak.

"It was six hours of just 'no, no, no, no,'" Hersman would later say of the embassy gathering. "It was one potshot after another, disputing whatever we said we knew, or what we believed was feasible."

Washington and Moscow might honor their political agreement on Syria, but hopes for a genuine technical partnership on disarming the country effectively died that day, Hersman said.

Yet Moscow had contributed something of inestimable value: it had forced its reluctant Syrian ally to comply, to give up its most strategically important weapons while the rest of the world watched.

Exactly how Moscow managed to extract such a capitulation from Assad was never precisely known, but the pressure must have been considerable. Lavrov offered a hint one day, some months later, while he and Kerry were embroiled in one of their many arguments over Syria. At one point, Kerry scolded his Russian counterpart for failing to chastise Assad over some infraction.

"Damn it, you know how to make the Syrian government behave. Why aren't you doing it?" Kerry asked Lavrov. "When it came to the chemical weapons, you were able to turn them around in twenty-four hours."

Lavrov returned his friend's earnest gaze and uttered a single word in reply:

"Less."

9

"No one is coming to help you"

SEPTEMBER 16, 2013

Two days after the Geneva agreement, Åke Sellström strode into the UN headquarters building in New York in his best suit and blue tie and clutching a copy of his still-secret findings under one arm. The report with its extensive laboratory analysis had been rushed together in thirteen days after his team's return from Syria, and the strain of the past month showed on his face. He looked tired and grim as he stood next to Ban Ki-moon while the UN chief read a brief statement before television cameras.

"The findings are beyond doubt, and beyond the pale," Ban said. "This is a war crime . . . the worst use of weapons of mass destruction in the twenty-first century."

The report's broad conclusions were already publicly known. Innocent civilians in the Damascus suburbs had been attacked with sarin. The government of Syria had subsequently acknowledged possessing chemical weapons and expressed a willingness to give them up. Yet both Bashar al-Assad and Vladimir Putin vehemently denied any Syrian involvement in the events of August 21, and many other countries were opting to reserve judgment, not wishing to take sides in an intelligence dispute between Russia and the West.

But here was Sellström, weighing in with evidence that he and his team had collected on the ground, at great personal risk, while the crime scene was still fresh. His report, with its lab results and calculations published for the world to see, was more than a confirmation that a crime had been committed at Ghouta. It was an indictment. The document did not explicitly name a suspect, but it contained within its thirty-eight pages of detailed forensic analysis an assertion of guilt that was plain to anyone, except perhaps the most imaginative conspiracists or the willfully blind.

Before his appearance for the TV cameras, Sellström was given a chance to describe his findings in an off-the-record briefing to UN Security Council members. There, Vitaly Churkin, Moscow's UN ambassador, questioned the Swede's scientific methods and belittled his conclusions. If the Syrian army truly was behind the attack, surely at least one of the rockets would have struck a rebel military outpost instead of falling in a residential district crowded with families. He later left the briefing to say to waiting reporters, "We need not jump to any conclusions."

If the interrogation was meant to rattle Sellström, it did not work. In a voice as steady as a bank examiner's, the scientist took his audience on a virtual tour of the crime scene, explaining in particular detail the evidence that pointed to a culprit.

He described the fragments of M-14 artillery rockets recovered in Moadamiyeh, still bearing the manufacturer's markings in Russian, and the pattern of impact craters that pointed to the use of a multibarrel, 140mm rocket launcher. Syria was known to have Russian-made rockets and launchers of precisely those dimensions in its inventory.

Sellström cited findings from his trajectory analysis, showing how the projectiles all came in from the northwest. Government forces occupied the territory northwest of Ghouta on the morning of the attack.

Finally, there was the sarin itself. While the chemical degrades when directly exposed to the elements, tests of the rocket fragments and soil samples collected by Sellström's team still contained small amounts of pure sarin. And in nearly every case where sarin was found, the lab workers also detected traces of the additive called hexamine. What seemed at first to be a curious anomaly now appeared to be a unique feature of Syria's manufacturing process; no other country was known to use hexamine in its sarin recipe. Finding hexamine was the closest thing to finding Syrian fingerprints on the murder weapon.

Sellström carefully stayed within UN rules. He never explicitly named Syria as the guilty party, instead laying out the facts that pointed inescapably in one direction. Could someone else have been behind the attacks on August 21? Perhaps. But the perpetrators would have to have managed a trifecta of nearly impossible feats. First, they would have to steal Syrian-made liquid sarin—one of the government's most closely guarded assets—along with the modified rockets and multibarrel launchers used to fire them off. They would have to possess the skills and expertise needed to properly mix the chemicals, and then pour the finished sarin into the rockets, using highly specialized equipment, without getting themselves killed. And they would have to somehow launch the rockets from government-held territory and escape again without being detected.

Several who watched Sellström's presentation said afterward that it was masterful. In a building where countries are accustomed to projecting their own versions of reality—sometimes to advance an agenda, in other cases to perpetuate a carefully constructed political fiction—Sellström maintained an almost old-fashioned fidelity to facts, to science, and to his own "good standard." He didn't tell his audience what to think but, according to a close aide, he wanted to make it very hard for others to twist his words and distort his conclusions.

"In his mind, there should be no opportunity for people to read into the report their own narrative, or to just read something that wasn't there," the aide said. "His goal was to clear away as much ambiguity as possible and to rely on the facts to craft a report that was unassailable.

"That," the aide said, "was his armor."

The report was later expanded to include a forensic analysis of earlier attacks, at Saraqeb and other Syrian towns. But Sellström's work was essentially finished. Some members of his team were already back at their homes and regular jobs. A few of the inspectors for the Organization for the Prohibition of Chemical Weapons, including Sellström's deputy Scott Cairns, would soon be on their way to Syria to help with the disarmament mission.

Sellström was working on revisions to the report on the brisk October morning when a spokesman for the Norwegian Nobel Committee announced an unusual winner for that year's Peace Prize. The 2013 recipient was not an individual but rather an organization: the

OPCW, cited by the committee for its "extensive efforts to eliminate chemical weapons." Later, members of the Norwegian committee would privately explain that they had been inspired by the bravery of the Sellström mission, which had made its dramatic exit from Syria just as the judges were finalizing their selections. OPCW inspectors made up two-thirds of Sellström's on-the-ground team.

Immediately, Sellström's phone began buzzing with calls from journalists in his native Sweden.

Congratulations, the callers said.

Sellström had to explain, somewhat awkwardly, that he wasn't part of the OPCW, so he had not won anything. He had only been the leader of the mission.

"No, I didn't get it," Sellström said.

Several of the Swedish journalists expressed sympathy, and some seemed mildly insulted that their countryman had not been named among the winners. Sellström shrugged it off. He had been given an important job and had accomplished it with his dignity intact. He had succeeded in alerting the world to a threat that had been the subject of his life's work—something more important to him than a medal.

"What I had really done," he said, "was to help put this issue on the front pages of newspapers all over the world."

Among the last to learn of the deal to destroy Bashar al-Assad's chemical arsenal were the people who had suffered the most from it. Far from being excited, many felt angry and betrayed. Years later, some of those who had survived the attacks at Ghouta would remember the day of the U.S.-Russia agreement as the moment that all hope died.

The news came to Kassem Eid, the young Syrian who inhaled poison gas during the attack on southwestern Ghouta, as he was waiting out the day's artillery barrage with friends in a basement bomb shelter. Having succeeded in charging his cell phone, Eid was scouring Internet sites for war news when he noticed that Barack Obama had again delivered a televised speech about Syria. He clicked on the link to watch the video and simultaneously translate the U.S. president's words into Arabic for his friends who gathered around to listen.

Obama started by explaining why he remained reluctant in principle to intervene in Syria's conflict, however outrageous Assad's conduct might be. "We cannot resolve someone else's civil war through force, particularly after a decade of war in Iraq and Afghanistan," he said. And yet, just as in his earlier speeches, he argued that Assad's gassing of civilians was a special case: a uniquely grave offense that threatened the civilized order and put all countries at risk. Obama said that a targeted military strike against Assad remained warranted because it would serve notice to all dictators to "think twice before using chemical weapons."

But something had happened to stay the president's hand. Because of the diplomatic breakthrough with Russia—which itself was due in part to the threat of military force—there was an opportunity now to achieve something of lasting value by eliminating the chemical menace altogether, Obama said.

"Any agreement must verify that the Assad regime keeps its commitments," Obama said. "But this initiative has the potential to remove the threat of chemical weapons without the use of force."

Here, Eid stopped. The U.S. military strike was not happening. He turned and left the room without finishing his translation.

"I didn't have the heart to look my friends in the eye and tell them that the United States had caved in," he later wrote. Oblivious to the crashing of artillery shells outside, he walked out of the building and began to run, cursing and sobbing.

There had been a brief moment in the waning days of summer 2013 in which both Syria's government and the rebels believed that a U.S. strike was imminent. To Eid, as for many in the opposition, it was impossible to believe that Obama could fail to respond to Assad's heedless trampling of his red line. The United States might not enter the war on the rebels' side, but it would surely punish Assad, in a manner that could potentially tip the balance in the opposition's favor. At the very least, the hated planes and helicopters responsible for so much of the country's suffering would be destroyed or chased from the sky.

The signing of the Geneva agreement crushed those hopes. If America would not strike even when its own honor was at stake, the rebels were truly on their own.

It was then, Eid later remembered, that many in the rebel movement began to look elsewhere for help. The most extreme voices within Syria's Islamist camp—groups such as al-Nusra Front and the Islamic State—had long argued that the Western powers could not be trusted. Beginning that fall, both groups witnessed a surge in recruitment unlike anything seen since the start of the war. In just three months, the larger one, ISIS, had taken control of Raqqa, Syria's sixth-largest city, and was preparing to march across northern Iraq.

"For these groups, the 'red line' had become a recruitment tool," Eid said. "It allowed the jihadists to tell people: 'The West doesn't care about you. It's all lies. No one is coming to help you.' "

Houssam Alnahhas, the young physician in Aleppo known as "Chemical Hazem," had seen some of these Islamists at his hospital. At first they came around looking for medical treatment for their wounded. Sometimes the medical staff would try to engage the bearded visitors in conversation, pressing them on why they wanted to replace a secular dictatorship with a religious one.

After the sarin attack, Alnahhas was too absorbed in his work to pay attention to politics. He also had fallen in love. A young woman named Yasmin worked in the hospital pharmacy, and the two had grown close. During air raids, or when helicopters hovered low over the building, the young doctor and his new friend would run to find one another. Often they huddled together under a hospital bed until the danger had passed. "Either we survive together, or die together," Alnahhas said. During a quiet interval he traveled to Yasmin's childhood home to tell her parents that he intended to marry her.

Alnahhas meanwhile had begun looking for a safer setting for his chemical-weapons training program, and he eventually found one, in Bab al-Hawa, a town in a relatively quiet district near the Turkish border. The couple was beginning to think about a future family, and Aleppo, with its daily aerial bombings and legions of Islamist fighters, was far too dangerous. Both also perceived that the uprising itself had changed. The young men and women who had inspired them with their brave protests in 2011 were mostly gone now, replaced by a new breed of radicalized, hate-filled killers like the young Islamist soldier who taunted Alnahhas one day as he awaited treatment at the Aleppo hospital.

"You relied on the West, but they will not help you, and we will continue to die," the youth said. "For me, my life is already destroyed. So what do I have to lose?"

Alnahhas ignored the taunts, just as he tuned out the predictions of aid workers who tried to convince him that the chemical weapons threat was now finished. Each day, the triage center at the border hospital overflowed with men, women, and children suffering from every imaginable variety of injury and wound. Syria's northern cities were being systematically depopulated, and the fleeing survivors spoke of acts of brutality that defied comprehension. Alnahhas patched up bodies, and, during free moments, he got on his computer to ask for more protective gowns and masks.

This wasn't over. Not even close.

PART II

10

"An elephant with a tick on its back"

PORTSMOUTH, VIRGINIA. DECEMBER 4, 2013

On a gray morning in early December, Tim Blades pulled his rental car onto the General Dynamics wharf at Portsmouth, Virginia, and paused to take in the swirl of activity around him. Orange forklifts zipped around like a swarm of metallic beetles, hauling crates from a line of trucks that stretched out to the highway. The dockside flickered with the blue light of welders' torches as platoons of workers in yellow vests—stevedores, carpenters, electricians, mechanics, plumbers—scurried about on myriad errands. A light breeze carried a musk of diesel, paint, and brackish water, along with the steady thrumming of air compressors.

Looming above it all was a vessel nearly as big as a battleship, with a towering superstructure and a mast soaring 150 feet into the air on the bow side. At the stern, a ramp had been lowered to allow trucks to pass directly into a cavernous maw wide enough to accommodate two M1 Abrams battle tanks traveling abreast. This ship, the MV *Cape Ray,* was to become the receptacle for Syria's chemical weapons and also, by unfathomable chance, Blades's new home.

Nearly three months had passed since the deal was struck in Geneva, and there were still many unknowns. While dozens of international inspectors were already on the ground in Syria, not a drop of poison had departed Bashar al-Assad's bunkers. No one knew when the chemicals would come out, or how or where the *Cape Ray* would receive them. And above all, no one knew whether the current plan—to destroy Assad's nerve agents on the heaving deck of a seagoing cargo ship—would work.

There were plenty of reasons why such an idea had not merited consideration. A modest spill could kill and injure crew members and leave the survivors with a contaminated vessel and no easy means of escape. A more serious accident could dump hundreds of tons of deadly poisons into the ocean. Almost no one at the Pentagon had liked the idea, for these reasons and others. At a White House national security meeting just weeks earlier, the notion of trying to destroy chemical weapons at sea was ridiculed as "harebrained." Even for Blades and his team, it had been viewed as an option of last resort. "It was not 'Plan A,' or even 'Plan B,'" a Pentagon manager who worked closely with Blades acknowledged afterward. "It was more like 'Plan Z.'"

Blades was responsible for the operation aboard the ship, and he would shoulder the greatest share of the blame for anything that went wrong. A state trooper's son from rural Maryland, he had never spent time on a ship. And he had never faced a challenge as complicated or as risky as the one he was now taking on. Yet when Blades stepped onto the *Cape Ray*'s main deck, it was as though he were walking into one of his machine shops back at home base. Neither excited nor flustered, he displayed the same mix of cantankerousness and swagger that made him a revered figure at Edgewood and a frequent source of exasperation among his Pentagon overseers.

"He was typical Tim: very confident, a little crotchety," said one Defense Department official who sat through many meetings with Blades as the *Cape Ray* was being outfitted. A recurring argument that erupted during those days, the official said, usually started with Blades expressing certitude over his team's ability to perform a task, followed quickly by annoyance when others questioned him.

"Don't worry about *how* I'm going to do it," Blades would say. "I can do it."

"You can't just say that," came the inevitable reply. "You have to tell us how."

"Don't worry about it," Blades would say. He nearly always had the last word.

In his mind, Blades was not being blithely dismissive of the risks.

He had complete faith in the Edgewood-engineered hardware that was being brought onto the ship. And he believed in the competence of the men—most of them handpicked, from his staff at Edgewood—who would be operating the machines.

On that chilly day in December, Blades walked the decks, took measurements, and drew and redrew the diagram he kept in his mind for how each step in the destruction process would proceed. There were critical elements of the mission, he knew, that could not be controlled through planning or sheer force of will. Only later would he come to fully appreciate how untamable they were. One was the ship. The other was the sea.

DTRA, the Pentagon agency in charge of countering WMD threats, had spent months developing options for how to deal with Syria's chemical weapons in a sudden crisis. The planning effort had lurched into high gear after the August 21 chemical attack at Ghouta and accelerated further with the announcement of high-level U.S.-Russian talks in Geneva. But almost no one had foreseen a day when Bashar al-Assad would voluntarily surrender his weapons and allow foreigners to take them all away at once. Now that it was happening, the Pentagon's experts were scrambling to figure out where the chemicals would go.

Thanks to earlier decisions by Andrew Weber, Major General Jay Santee, and others, the United States had its Margarita Machine—the mobile contraption that could be dispatched almost anywhere in the world to neutralize liquid nerve agents. Once it was clear that Moscow would not lift a finger to accept chemical weapons from its Syrian ally, U.S. officials began scouring the globe for countries willing to take the chemicals or serve as hosts for a temporary destruction facility where Tim Blades could operate his machines. They started off in mid-September with a short list that shrank steadily in the weeks that followed.

Jordan, Syria's neighbor and a close U.S. ally, initially seemed like a logical choice, but U.S. and Israeli officials worried that a chemical weapons facility in the Hashemite kingdom might be vulnerable to terrorists slipping across the border from Syria or Iraq. Moreover, Jordan's monarch, King Abdullah II, was already struggling with the political and economic fallout from a mammoth refugee crisis—more than a million Syrians had fled into Jordan to escape the war, increasing the country's population by 15 percent in two years—and officials feared that talk of bringing chemical weapons into the country would send protesters into the streets. Jordan was quietly dropped from the list before any formal request was made.

A few contenders emerged among America's NATO allies, all of them professed supporters of the deal to eliminate Syria's stockpile. France and Belgium were both home to specialized hazardous-waste incinerators designed to destroy liquid toxins ranging from battery acid to old pesticides. The Belgians even operated a plant that was built specifically to destroy chemical weapons, chiefly World War I–vintage phosgene and sulfur mustard found in old artillery shells. Some of these still turn up during spring plowing on fields that were once the battlefields of the Great War. The Belgian facility happened to be located just outside Ypres, the city in western Flanders that gained unwanted fame in 1915 as the place where modern chemical weapons were first used in battle.

In mid-October, Weber led a delegation to Paris and Brussels to see if either country might be persuaded to accept the deadly chemicals that made up the core of Syria's stockpile. The French flatly declined. The Belgian reply was a quick tutorial in the country's absurdly complex regulatory process. Even if the country's politicians went along with the plan, the Belgians explained, it would likely take many months, and probably years, just to secure all the necessary permits from the many overlapping federal and provincial jurisdictions. Weber and the other officials returned home disappointed but hardly surprised. It was difficult to imagine their own government—the owner of multiple state-of-the-art incinerators, built for the express purpose of destroying chemical weapons—mustering the political support for bringing foreign-made sarin into the country.

There was, however, one country in 2013 that appeared willing to take the risk. Albania, the tiny Balkan country on the eastern Adriatic coast, possessed a number of features that allowed it to catapult to the top of the Americans' list. It was staunchly pro-Western and a recipient of significant sums of U.S. foreign assistance cash. It already had a small chemical weapons destruction facility, built with U.S. aid money, to destroy munitions left over from the country's communist

Beginning in the 1980s, Syria's government built a vast research and production complex for a class of highly lethal chemical weapons called nerve agents. Starting with relatively crude machinery, as pictured here, the complex produced hundreds of tons of binary sarin and VX. *Author's collection*

Houssam Alnahhas holds a young patient at an Aleppo hospital. The Syrian medical intern became an activist after three medical workers were murdered when police caught them delivering life-saving supplies. *Courtesy of Houssam Alnahhas*

Below: Alnahhas, in civilian clothes, poses with Syrian medical workers in newly donated chemical protection gear. Alnahhas helped organize training for Syrian doctors, fearing that a major chemical attack was coming. *Courtesy of Houssam Alnahhas*

By 2013, jihadist militants such as the al-Qaeda-allied al-Nusra Front, shown here, had emerged as the strongest fighters on the rebel side, able to capture military bases and perhaps, the United States feared, Syria's chemical arsenal. *Middle East Media Research Institute*

Andrew C. Weber, pictured with President Barack Obama in 2012, was a Defense Department official responsible for defending against WMD threats when the Syrian civil war broke out. He pushed his staff to begin planning how to remove and eliminate Syria's weapons if given the chance. *Andrew Weber*

Air Force major general Jay Santee, deputy director of the Pentagon's Defense Threat Reduction Agency, helped lead the search for technology that could destroy Syria's chemical weapons. *Defense Department photo*

Tim Blades, civilian leader of a small chem-bio defense unit in Edgewood, Maryland, spent decades helping to destroy America's chemical weapons. His team came up with a novel machine that used water and pressure to destroy liquid nerve agents. *Joby Warrick*

The Field Deployable Hydrolysis System, dubbed the Margarita Machine, was designed, built, and tested in less than five months. *Joby Warrick*

Åke Sellström, a Swedish scientist and a top chemical weapons expert, was tapped by the United Nations to lead a team to investigate early reports that chemical weapons were being used in Syria's civil war. *Henry Arvidsson / OPCW*

Below: Sellström's inspection team was in Damascus waiting to begin its work when a massive sarin attack occurred on the outskirts of the capital. The attack on the Ghouta suburbs on August 21, 2013, killed an estimated 1,400 people in the deadliest use of such weapons in a quarter century. *Sameer al-Doumy*

Below: Sellström's inspectors drove into an ambush as they traveled to Ghouta to gather evidence. One vehicle was disabled by gunshots, but Sellström ordered the others to press ahead. Team members determined that the artillery rockets contained sarin gas, and a subsequent investigation concluded they were fired from government territory. *Author's collection*

President Barack Obama confers with national security advisers in August 2013 to debate the U.S. response to Syria's chemical attack. Obama's plan for an immediate air strike was delayed in part because of worries about UN inspectors still on the ground. *Official White House photo by Pete Souza*

Russian foreign minister Sergey Lavrov (center, seated), and U.S. secretary of state John F. Kerry (left, seated) haggle over final details of a deal to remove and destroy Syria's chemical arsenal. The deal delayed an attack on Moscow's closest Middle East ally while offering the West a strategic win. *State Department photo*

With no country willing to host a destruction facility for Syria's weapons, the Pentagon was forced to consider eliminating them at sea. Officials searching for a suitable platform eventually settled on the MV *Cape Ray*. Mississippi native Rick Jordan was picked as the ship's captain. Before departing Norfolk, he steered the ship into a gale to see if the chemical-destruction equipment could withstand the stress of rough seas. *Defense Department photo*

To oversee the dismantling of Syria's stockpile, the United Nations chose Sigrid Kaag, a veteran UN manager and mother of four from the Netherlands. Kaag had no background in chemical weapons, but she was judged to possess the diplomatic skills and personal toughness to keep the operation on track. *Arenda Oomen, Royal House, Netherlands Government Information Service*

After gaining access to Syria's secret weapons facilities, inspectors found chemical "mixing" trucks like this one. Ordinary looking from the outside, it contained mobile equipment for loading sarin into bombs. *Author's collection*

An inspector with the Organization for the Prohibition of Chemical Weapons examines storage tanks filled with binary sarin. *Author's collection*

Under the disarmament deal, Syria promised to scrap not only its weapons but also production equipment such as the vessel being destroyed here. An exemption spared Syria's military research labs. *Author's collection*

A trailer filled with Syrian weapons is driven onto the *Cape Ray* at the port of Gioia Tauro, Italy. The Italian government agreed to allow the use of the port for one day, so that hundreds of tons of lethal Syrian chemicals could be transferred to the American ship. *Defense Department photo*

The *Cape Ray* heads into the open Mediterranean to begin its mission. More than six hundred tons of Syrian chemicals would be destroyed on its decks in less than six weeks. *Defense Department photo*

One of the Edgewood team's crew members makes adjustments to the Margarita Machine as the mission is getting underway. With a flotilla of activists pursuing the ship, the *Cape Ray* was surrounded by naval destroyers to prevent intrusions. *Defense Department photo*

Iraqi Kurdish fighters examine the debris after a failed ISIS suicide attack using chlorine gas in January 2015. Unable to steal chemical weapons from Syria, the terrorist group attempted to make its own. *Kurdish Regional Government of Iraq*

Samantha Power, President Obama's ambassador to the UN, chats with John Kerry and Sergey Lavrov in 2015. Power nudged the Russians into allowing a UN panel to formally assess blame for the Syrian chemical attacks. Moscow ultimately used its UN veto to halt the panel's work. *State Department photo*

White House envoy to the anti-ISIS coalition Brett McGurk confers with U.S. Joint Chiefs chairman General Joseph Dunford in 2017. One of a few senior advisers to serve under Obama and Donald Trump, McGurk resigned his post to protest a decision to unilaterally withdraw all U.S. forces from Syria. *Defense Department photo*

A soldier photographs the remains of a Syrian military laboratory after the facility was flattened by a U.S.-French missile strike in April 2018. Trump ordered the strike following reports that Syria had again used chemical weapons, killing civilians at Douma, a Damascus suburb. A later investigation confirmed the use of chlorine gas at Douma but found no traces of sarin or other nerve agents. *Omar Sanadiki, Reuters*

past. And at that moment, newly elected prime minister Edi Rama had a special reason for wanting to curry favor with Washington: Albania was applying for membership in NATO, and it needed U.S. support. Rama had numerous friends and acquaintances within the Obama administration, including Tom Countryman, the State Department's top arms-control official, and they began privately encouraging the Albanian leader to consider hosting a temporary chemical weapons destruction facility somewhere along the coast. Rama was potentially willing, so Weber quickly assembled another delegation and flew to the Albanian capital, Tirana, to meet with government officials and scout for possible sites. They found a small navy base just north of the port city of Durrës that checked every box: flat, isolated, and easily accessible to Mediterranean shipping, with a ready supply of water for chemical processing.

"It's perfect," Weber told his superiors at the Pentagon.

As a sweetener for the would-be host country, Weber began pitching the idea of a U.S.-funded permanent waste incinerator for Albania, one that could destroy the by-products from Tim Blades's machines while also giving the country a state-of-the-art disposal facility that would allow it to clean up its own toxic waste sites and perhaps those of others in the neighborhood. Rama would be doing the Americans a favor while also creating a new industry for Albania that could generate much-needed revenue for decades to come.

While Weber was negotiating, Santee's planners at DTRA continued to explore other options, just in case Albania fell through. Santee's deputy, John "Toast" Cinnamon, led a small cadre of Syria specialists who did much of the researching, compiling, winnowing, and vetting. The group was mainly young and mainly made up of women, including two officers, Army major and microbiologist Tina Schoenberger and Air Force lieutenant colonel and pilot Jannell MacAulay, and a Yale University–trained biologist named Julia Brown. The most junior member of the group, international relations specialist Chelsea Goldstein, was a petite twenty-five-year-old who looked so young that, when a cookie-sale notice was posted near her desk during one of her first weeks on the job, several DTRA coworkers mistook her for a Girl Scout.

Most of the women had no experience with chemical weapons, but collectively they showed a remarkable talent for turning complex projects into manageable to-do lists. Throughout the fall, they chased down and analyzed alternative methods and sites for destroying Syria's arsenal. Some were fanciful, such as a proposal to drop Blades and his machines onto a desert island somewhere in the Pacific. But one idea began to look increasingly plausible the more the women studied it: if all else failed, it might be possible to neutralize the weapons on a ship.

Their boss, Santee, was intrigued. He had no idea whether the idea was feasible, but it seemed worth exploring.

"Build a plan and show me," Santee ordered. "Tell me how you would do it."

Schoenberger rounded up maritime experts and began touring shipyards to look at vessels and gather information. She was able to narrow her search to a class of large seagoing cargo ships known as "ro-ros"—short for "roll-on, roll-off"—that are used to haul large equipment, from oil rigs to helicopters and Humvees. The U.S. government's Maritime Administration keeps nearly three dozen ro-ros on standby in ports around the country as part of a ready-reserve fleet that can be activated quickly in case of war. Of all the ships they visited over the following weeks, one of them stood out: the Motor Vessel *Cape Ray*.

The big gray ship was in mothballs at Portsmouth harbor when the visitors came calling. Built by Japan in 1977, it spent half its life in the Saudi Arabian fleet hauling oil-drilling equipment before being purchased by the U.S. government shortly after the first Gulf War. A ghosted image of a palm tree and Arabian scimitar could still be seen on the boat's superstructure, an artifact of an earlier paint job, when the ship was known as the MV *Saudi Makkah*. It was moderately large by the standards of modern container ships, at just over a hundred feet wide at the beam, with four decks running the full length of its 647-foot hull. Its distinctive, drawbridge-like ramp jutted high above the stern when the boat was in motion, then lowered at port to allow trucks and other large vehicles to drive directly onto the ship.

But the features that caught the visitors' attention were not visible from the outside. The *Cape Ray*'s main trailer deck—essentially the floor just below the top deck—was unusually spacious, with just enough headroom to accommodate Blades's twenty-foot-tall machines. Below the waterline, the ship was also equipped with a variable-pitch propeller and retractable fins called stabilizers that emerge from the hull to reduce the ship's roll in heavy seas. Both helped keep things relatively calm inside the ship during voyages, something the Pentagon's experts judged would be an asset for a vessel carrying tons of deadly liquids.

Blades traveled to Portsmouth to look at the ship as well. Back in their offices, his team began trading figures with DTRA's experts to determine whether a floating platform the size of the *Cape Ray* could meet the basic requirements. Was it big enough to hold not only Blades's machines but also the Syrian weapons and hundreds of additional tanks and barrels filled with chemicals and waste products from the neutralization operation? Was there adequate ventilation? Could the ship supply enough water, electric power, and living quarters for the workers and crew?

The answers were surprisingly positive. There were even security advantages to confining the chemicals, workers, and equipment within a single, self-contained structure. Moored in a protected harbor or anchored just offshore, a boat would be less vulnerable to intrusion or attack.

Others at the Pentagon didn't see it that way. The ship idea was regularly mocked whenever it came up at meetings. "A bunch of Army guys on a boat!" was a common scoff. Schoenberger felt slightly embarrassed when she finally sat down with Santee to present her findings.

"Sir, it looks like this could work," she said.

"All right," replied Santee, who believed in keeping all doors open. "Keep going."

The women continued their research, and by mid-October, as Weber was touring potential sites in Albania, they helped produce a nineteen-page technical study titled "Field Deployable Hydrolysis System: Ship-board Option." The report concluded that a vessel such as the *Cape Ray* could be a viable alternative and would require a comparatively small investment in time and money—about six months and just over $100 million, from start to finish. With added safety features and ample protective gear for the crew, a ship could have "an equally low likelihood of accidents as compared to land-based destruction," the report said.

It hardly mattered, though, because the Albania option was moving forward at full speed. Rama, the Albanian prime minister, appeared to fully embrace the plan in secret talks with the Obama administration, and he appointed senior aides to work directly with the Americans in hashing out the details. Andrew Weber's vision of a permanent incinerator in the Balkans—one that could destroy not only old weapons but also chemical hazards of every kind—was beginning to take shape.

Then came the leak. On October 31, a U.S. news site posted an online article describing the plan to destroy Syria's chemical weapons in Albania. A few days later, the story was spreading through the Albanian press and drawing angry denunciations from the country's main opposition party. On November 12, a few hundred demonstrators gathered outside the U.S. embassy in Tirana, some of them wearing gas masks and carrying banners that read, "We are not a bin for chemical weapons!" By November 14, thousands were marching through the streets in multiple Albanian cities. Huge crowds shut down traffic around Albania's parliament and government buildings, chanting "No! No! No!"

It was more than Albania's new leader could bear. Rama, who had campaigned for prime minister on a pledge to clean up the environment, broke the news in a phone call to Secretary of State John F. Kerry as Countryman, the State Department's top arms-control official, listened in.

"I really wanted to do this. I know it's important," Rama said. He walked to an open window in his office and held the phone receiver next to it. The two U.S. officials in Washington could hear the chanting crowd coming through the speaker all the way from Tirana.

"I just can't," Rama said.

The Albania proposal died hard. Weber continued to wage a lonely fight for the Balkans incinerator, clashing at times with other Defense Department officials and even some of his subordinates, who quietly sent a copy of the DTRA's boat study to the White House. The matter was finally decided when the Obama administration's National Security Council convened to review the options for dealing with Syria's chemical stockpile. By November 15, only one remained.

The decision was relayed to Santee and passed along to his staff. Chelsea Goldstein, the youngest member of the group, burst into the office to share the news with the others.

"We're going with the ship!" she said.

It was such an astonishing turn of events that the women were briefly dumbstruck.

"We all stood there, looking at each other," remembered Julia Brown, the biologist. "Then it was, 'Oh my God. We're actually going to have to do this. We actually have to build a chemical weapons destruction facility on a ship.' "

Nearly a week passed before news of the decision was relayed to Tim Blades. By then, November was nearly over, and the Pentagon was clamoring to have the *Cape Ray* fully outfitted and ready to sail by January 1, just over a month later.

"Enjoy your Thanksgiving," Blades told his employees that week, "because this is it. We're rolling."

Not even Blades imagined how quickly it would all come together. The wheels of the Defense Department's giant logistics machine began to turn, oiled by millions of newly appropriated dollars, and within days an armada of supply trucks and contractor vans was speeding toward Portsmouth. Regulatory approvals that normally require months to complete rocketed through the Pentagon's bureaucracy in days. The ship itself underwent an astonishing, bow-to-stern transformation in less time than it takes to frame a suburban house.

By design the *Cape Ray* was meant to function as a kind of mobile parking lot, with a static cargo of vehicles and parts, overseen by a crew of twenty-five to thirty civilian mariners splitting duties over two twelve-hour shifts. Now it was being remade into a seaborne industrial facility with a workforce of nearly 140 people, all of whom would need a place to sleep, eat, bathe, and do laundry. Construction crews and technicians assembled a "hotel" of boxlike sleeping pods, mess halls, kitchen units, walk-in refrigerators, and bathrooms, all welded to the ship's uppermost spar deck. They built a helicopter pad and a medical clinic with special gear for treating toxic exposures. They installed a laboratory for testing chemicals, and osmosis machines for converting seawater into fresh water. They configured cargo decks to securely hold more than three hundred tanker-truck-sized containers of toxic chemicals and waste products without anything breaking loose or tipping over in rough seas. Finally, they converted the main trailer deck into a giant, hermetically sealed biohazard unit, with a tent of thick plastic covering Blades's hydrolysis machines, and a separate, negative-pressure ventilation system for the entire deck to lower the risk of contaminating the rest of the ship in the event of an accident. Working straight through the Christmas holidays, they finished primary construction by New Year's Eve.

Santee dispatched several deputies, including some of the women who worked for Cinnamon, to stay at Portsmouth so they could quickly smooth out any kinks in the supply chain. Blades and his engineers bounced between Edgewood and the dockyards to supervise the assembly of their machines and the installation of a small control room with TV monitors. During one of the early visits, Blades paid a courtesy call to the *Cape Ray*'s captain, a gregarious fifty-four-year-old Mississippi native named Rick Jordan who had arrived just two days earlier from commanding a different ship in the port of New Orleans. It was a less-than-memorable first meeting, as Jordan was preoccupied with getting his own crew organized. But during the long days of meetings that followed, Blades and Jordan discovered that they had several things in common. They were close in age and nearing the pinnacle of their respective careers—meaning that both men knew their jobs and were not particularly concerned about promotions or how others viewed them. Both were blunt-spoken, supremely confident, and remarkably optimistic, yet also pragmatic. But what truly bonded them was their shared, eye-rolling disdain for bureaucracy and their absolute dedication to seeing the mission through.

Jordan was on the *Cape Ray* because he wanted to be there. A veteran sea captain who had commanded cargo ships on multiple missions to the Middle East and South Asia since the mid-1990s, he had heard about the mission through friends and decided to volunteer because it sounded like an interesting challenge. There also was a personal connection: one of his great-grandfathers was a Syrian named Khalil who immigrated to the United States and landed at Ellis Island. Jordan thought of his relatives when he saw the images of dying children in the Damascus suburbs. Here was a chance to do something, even if his job was only to pilot the boat that destroyed the chemicals so other Syrian children would not suffer the same awful fate.

After a few days in Portsmouth, Jordan had seen enough of Blades and his crew to conclude that he had made the right decision. Like Jordan, most were from backwater towns in Maryland or the rural South. As a group they were quietly competent, as solid and sure as a stone bridge.

These are my kind of people, Jordan thought.

Yet they were different, in fundamental ways, from the seamen under Jordan's command. Merchant mariners and Army weapons experts may come to admire one another, but they inhabit entirely different worlds. They even speak different languages.

In the weeks that followed, those differences threatened to scuttle the *Cape Ray*'s voyage before it even began.

In more than twenty-five years as a mariner, Chris Myers, the *Cape Ray*'s chief engineer, had never seen anything like the Margarita Machine. He stood on the main trailer deck and watched as men in hard hats made adjustments to a pair of devices that looked like something from a mad scientist's workbench. Wires and hoses snaked across the steel floor in every direction, along and around rows of barrels and tanks festooned with colorful hazard labels. From the upper and lower decks came jarring sounds: the metallic banging, grinding, and screeching of a ship being altered into something that had never existed before.

Myers, a solidly built Virginian who had earned his officer's ranks after years of laboring in the sweaty engine rooms of cargo ships, was fascinated. He also was a little nervous.

"It was like a huge science experiment," Myers recalled thinking at the time. "And it was being put together so fast. How was this going to work?"

Myers would strike up conversations with the men from Edgewood who were in charge of the giant machines. They were friendly and smart, but as they readily admitted, they knew almost nothing about ships, and they were having to feel their way through challenges they had never encountered before. They had lots of questions, and Myers had one in particular of his own. A ship at sea is a thing in constant motion. When its two giant diesel engines fired up, every metal surface and part of the ship would be subjected to continuous vibrations. Moreover, even in moderate seas, a ship's movements can mimic those of a roller coaster: alternately pitching left and right, up and down, forward and backward. Every pipe connection and welded joint would be repeatedly twisted, squeezed, and pulled. Could Edgewood's machines survive those kinds of stresses without spewing their toxic contents all over the ship?

The initial answers were not convincing. The engineers were trying to figure it out, but on the fly, with the ship's departure date hurtling toward them.

"If you were to take your time and do this normally, how long would this whole evolution take?" Myers asked one day.

"A couple of years," came the reply. It was a reasonable estimate for time required to design, engineer, test, license, and build new technology for the military.

Now it was all being jammed into a span of less than two months.

Mind-blowing, Myers thought.

Jordan was beginning to feel uneasy as well. He grew especially agitated one day when one of his officers passed along a startling request from the ship's land-based guests: Was it okay if they cut a few holes in the deck for their wires and hoses?

"You can't just go around cutting holes in ships!" Jordan spluttered. "This kind of thing goes back to the *Titanic*!"

Blades's team was frustrated, too. Often, the information they received from the mariners turned out to be technically accurate but not quite the full story.

Was it possible to use the ship's elevators to move waste-storage tanks to the lower decks? Yes, it was possible, Blades and his deputies were told. But only later did Blades learn that the tanks, once filled with waste, would be too heavy for the elevators, so the lifts were useless. Another question: Could Blades use forklifts to move barrels of chemicals around? Yes, technically speaking, came the reply. But the forklifts could not always be operated while the ship was underway, which was precisely when Blades needed them.

Blades made a more consequential discovery when his chemists back at Edgewood began running tests to simulate conditions aboard the *Cape Ray*. Under plans drawn up by the Pentagon, his hydrolysis machines would be used to destroy three of the most dangerous substances from Syria. Two of them, sulfur mustard and the sarin precursor DF, were well understood and reasonably straightforward.

The third, a VX precursor dubbed "B-solution," was more volatile and required particular care. Indeed, as the Edgewood scientists conducted their experiments, they discovered that B-solution had a distressing tendency, in certain conditions, to catch fire.

A chemical fire involving a nerve agent could be disastrous if it happened in a regular laboratory. On a ship, it could be catastrophic. Blades was compelled to call Santee at his Fort Belvoir, Virginia, office to break the news. The VX precursor was simply too dangerous to be processed aboard the *Cape Ray*.

The normally cool-running Air Force general was exasperated. The *Cape Ray* was just weeks away from its departure date.

"You should have known that!" Santee said. "Now what are we going to do?"

"I'll come up with something," Blades replied. Days later, Blades, with help from other U.S. officials, worked out a deal in which Britain's Ministry of Defence agreed to accept the troublesome chemical. Many months later, the VX precursor was quietly dropped off at a British port. Eventually it was incinerated by a commercial disposal company equipped to handle toxins of the same sort.

But the biggest blow to the mission came from outside Portsmouth. In mid-December, as Blades and Jordan were busily hacking their way through thickets of technical glitches, a small delegation of naval architects and maritime experts arrived from Washington for a close-up examination of the *Cape Ray*. A few days later, on December 20, an electronic copy of their findings landed simultaneously in Santee's inbox and those of a dozen other officials from Edgewood to the Pentagon. The delegation's report was essentially a disaster warning, rendered in language so dire as to be almost biblical.

The report's authors pointed out that Blades's machines were not designed for use on a ship, so they could easily fail, perhaps catastrophically, if subjected to the physical stresses of a sea voyage. If defense officials persisted with their plan to destroy Syria's chemical weapons aboard the *Cape Ray*, the report said, there was a "high potential" for an accident or disaster, one that could wreck the ship, kill and injure crew members, and spill lethal poisons into the environment.

The report ticked through a frightening list of possible disasters and noted that, because of the ship's extremely hazardous cargo, survivors of the initial accident might not be immediately rescued. "In the event of a disaster or spillage, a helicopter medivac or other response mechanisms may be impossible," it concluded. Even if the ship made it to a port, it said, no rescue team would be willing to board a vessel that was contaminated with lethal chemicals.

And the risks extended beyond the ship and its crew, the Navy experts said. From the moment Blades's hydrolysis machines started running, there would be a "high potential" for leaks or spills of chemical weapons as well as toxic waste products, they concluded. Poisonous liquids and gases could end up flowing everywhere: up through the ship's air intake vents, down into the bilge system, or "overboard, into the ocean."

It was a stunning setback, delivered just weeks before the ship's scheduled departure. In Portsmouth, Edgewood, and Fort Belvoir, in offices that were already thinning out for the Christmas holidays, the report was studied and carefully parsed. Its pages contained no specific recommendations or suggested remedies, but only a general assertion that any complex, inherently risky system designed for use on land would become far more hazardous at sea. The same sentiment had been expressed in a more informal manner by a senior Pentagon official who met with Jordan and Blades soon after the *Cape Ray* was selected for the mission. "A ship is like an elephant," the officer had said. "If you put a tick on its back, it just doesn't like it. It's always flexing."

"Basically," Jordan said, summarizing the report's conclusions in his soft Mississippi drawl, "it says we're all going to die."

The *Cape Ray* had taken a broadside. But by the time the experts' report landed on December 20, the ship was also the only available option, in all the world, for destroying Syria's chemical weapons. There was no other choice, and at this late hour, there would be no turning back.

Santee, who was on a business trip when the report came out, spent hours on a conference call with the report's authors while sitting in a McDonald's parking lot, pressing the maritime experts to list any practical improvements that would make the ship safer. None were offered, and Santee began to see the document as the equivalent of a yellow caution flag in car racing: the warnings should be taken seriously, but they should not be allowed to paralyze the mission.

"It's just FUD," Santee said, using a Pentagon acronym for a disabling case of the jitters. "It's Fear, Uncertainty, and Doubt."

Blades, though exceedingly annoyed, pushed his engineers to rework their plans to try to anticipate every possible mishap or unlucky turn. Blueprints were redrawn, and then altered again. Rigid lines and pipes were replaced with flexible hoses that could twist and bend with the ship. Essential equipment was welded into place, and then the welds reinforced. Official inspectors from the Army and Coast Guard examined the hydrolysis machines and the ship itself and certified both as fit for duty.

The work continued straight through Christmas. Then, on December 27, Blades and Jordan gathered their respective crews for three days of training, with each group sharing the fundamentals of their craft with the other. On one day, the chemical experts from Edgewood learned how to be sailors, undergoing drills on the use of lifeboats and what to do if there was a fire aboard the ship. Then mariners sat through tutorials on basic chemistry, including a graphic presentation on hydrofluoric acid, or HF, the "bone seeker" that bores through skin and muscle to attack the calcium in human bones. Afterward, Jordan watched to see if any of his rank-and-file crew members—many of whom had believed they were signing up for an ordinary voyage—would drop out after learning the hazards that would be present on the *Cape Ray* in tanker-sized quantities. None did.

With the training and reengineering now completed, it was time for a test drive. Jordan had already taken the *Cape Ray,* minus most of the Edgewood workers, on a brief spin off the coast of Norfolk so his sailors could get a feel for the ship. Now the full complement of chemists, machines, and mariners would head out into the North Atlantic for a three-day sea trial that, by design, would subject people and equipment to conditions as bad or worse than any they would face at sea. On a bright but bitterly cold morning, Jordan eased the ship through the Norfolk Harbor Channel and into the Chesapeake Bay. Then he turned to starboard and steered toward Cape Hatteras—and straight into a gale.

Many in the Edgewood contingent had never been at sea, and the mood was festive as the ship rounded Cape Henry at the Chesapeake's southeastern tip and passed into the open Atlantic. A few hours later, several of the chemists and engineers were in their boxlike control room when they noticed, to their amusement, that their rolling desk chairs were beginning to move beneath them. As the sea swells grew larger and farther apart, the ship rolled with them, sending the chairs skittering toward one end of the room and then to the other, like loose marbles in a child's wagon.

Then the fun was over. One by one, the grins disappeared, replaced by expressions of vague concern. Faces took on a greenish pallor, and men began to slip out of the room. Some disappeared into the latrine. Others prostrated themselves on the freezing deck or hugged the taffrail, with their heads hanging over the ship's stern.

"Most of us wished for death," one of the Edgewood crew members said afterward. "I had never gotten seasick before in my life. It was just awful."

The misery stretched on through a rough first day. Crew members who were still on their feet put the hydrolysis machines through a series of drills, testing the reactors and pumps using water instead of liquid poisons. The gale grew stronger, and Jordan nudged the boat into a beam sea, crashing into the waves at right angles to put the machines and pipes through as much stress as the North Atlantic could muster on a blustery winter day. The *Cape Ray*'s decks pitched and rolled, and men groaned and embraced toilet seats, buckets, or whatever they could find. At last Jordan, satisfied, ordered his mariners to extend the ship's stabilizer fins. The seesawing diminished at once, and the helmsman swung the ship's bow toward calmer waters. Still, the seasickness would not fully release its grip on some passengers until the vessel returned to Portsmouth three days later.

Back at the General Dynamics wharf, engineers scurried across every inch of the ship and scoured the hydrolysis machines for evidence of cracks or leaks. A few welding joints had to be repaired, but on the machines themselves not a single flaw was found. The equipment had held firm.

The Edgewood team had not been so lucky. Blades had somehow managed to avoid becoming ill himself, but he had seen some of his strongest men stricken to the point of helplessness. Some of them would understandably want to quit.

His workers had other ideas. Once ashore, they filed into the local pharmacies and snapped up seasickness medicines and remedies by the cartonful. Then they proceeded to pack for the Mediterranean. Each had signed up for the mission as a volunteer, and now, even after the ordeal of the sea trial, not one of them dropped out. Their departure was three weeks away.

11

"A technical delay"

LATAKIA, SYRIA. DECEMBER 28, 2013

Just after dusk, Sigrid Kaag slipped out onto a balcony of her seaside hotel and stood silhouetted for a long moment against the Mediterranean, now as gray and flat as a tombstone in the evening gloom. The lights around Latakia harbor flickered on, illuminating a line of quays that were nearly empty, to Kaag's dismay. Tall and slender, with blond hair cut to the shoulder, the Dutch diplomat headed the international operation to extract hundreds of tons of deadly chemicals from this very port. Yet in three months the Syrians had delivered nothing, and their failure threatened to derail Kaag's mission, and perhaps her career. There were mortal risks, too, and a sinking feeling among Kaag's advisers that their luck was running out.

Northeast of Latakia, an Islamist army was massing for an offensive aimed at capturing the ancient city and its harbor. Snipers stalked the highway to Damascus. Syrian officials whispered warnings about car-bomb plots, some of them explicitly targeting the mission's leader. Kaag's face betrayed strain as she stood, her back to the sea, to explain her team's faltering progress in a video message. "A technical delay has been encountered," she began solemnly.

Until her arrival in Syria, Kaag had no experience with chemical weapons, and her selection to lead the disarmament mission had been surprising and, in some quarters, controversial. Kaag and her team had silenced critics by achieving one difficult milestone after another, nearly always on time and with a minimum of fuss. And then, nearly everything about the mission seemed to go bad all at once.

A freak autumn snowstorm had closed the mountain passes to the west for nearly a week, blocking needed supplies coming into the country from Lebanon. Flatbed trucks arriving for transport duty were found to be missing steering wheels and other key parts. Procurement offices struggled to find adequate numbers of storage tanks, cranes, and forklifts. Rebel armies meanwhile were suddenly on the march in the north and east, harassing military convoys and advancing to within striking distance of the weapons depots themselves. And the Syrians, pliant at first, now balked at minor requests while bombarding Kaag with a never-ending list of demands: more armor, more heavy equipment, more time.

Most stressful of all were the demands from Kaag's employer, the UN Security Council. The entire council had voted in favor of the disarmament effort, despite deep skepticism over the mission's chances, and the members had insisted on monthly, in-person status reports from the leader. Kaag, typically outfitted in brightly colored blazers and scarves, had managed until now to be upbeat. She described steady progress by her international team of diplomats, inspectors, and weapons experts, who had collectively managed to gain access to dozens of sensitive weapons sites across Syria, and to supervise the dismantling of production equipment. Whenever she spoke, because she cared passionately about the subject, Kaag tried to inject a few personal observations about the plight of Syrian civilians, gently admonishing the world body to apply the same level of diplomatic energy to ending the war as it did to eliminating a weapons stockpile. "The tragedy continues unabated," she would say.

Her optimism worked for a time. But now, with deadlines slipping and the Syrians in a defiant mood, the skeptics were back. Some governments were privately suggesting that the whole project should be declared a failure, potentially opening the door again to alternative methods for disarming Bashar al-Assad.

Kaag was not giving up, regardless of how bleak things looked. So on December 28, 2013, she stood before the camera at the entrance to the nearly empty harbor—a place that should have been bustling with trucks and ships preparing to haul Syria's chemicals out to sea—and tried to put the best face on a dreary situation.

There were legitimate reasons for the delay, and Kaag listed some of them: security crises, technical breakdowns, and logistical snafus. "We continue, however," she said brightly, "to intensify all efforts to achieve measurable progress to realize the goal of the removal and elimination of chemical weapons from the Syrian Arab Republic."

Kaag avoided any mention of another factor in the mission's faltering progress, though she spoke about it privately in conversations with aides and friends. At her meetings at the UN Security Council, in Damascus, and in scattered foreign capitals—her regular circuit encompassed Washington, Moscow, Ankara, and Tehran—she could see more clearly the geopolitical chess game underway in Syria. Each of the major powers was seeking to shape events in Syria to suit its own interests, and each suspected that others were exploiting the chemical weapons crisis to gain an advantage. Was Russia stalling for time so it could rearm its ally for a crushing blow against the rebels? Were Western governments planting spies inside the inspection force and secretly plotting to overthrow Syria's leader, as they had done earlier to Libya's Muammar Gaddafi? Why were the Iranians and their Hezbollah allies turning up at so many of the military bases where the weapons were stored?

All these countries had been involved at some level in the decision to dismantle Syria's stockpile. Yet months after the deal was struck, it seemed to Kaag that the actual removal of the weapons had receded in priority in many capitals, if indeed it mattered at all. And thus, when the mission ran into problems in the waning weeks of 2013, many on the Security Council appeared unsurprised. Indeed, some seemed almost relieved.

"The fact is," Kaag would later say, "almost no one connected to this mission truly wanted it to succeed."

The Geneva accord that led to the creation of Kaag's small inspection force consisted of a disarmament pledge and a set of ambitious deadlines, and not much else. All the particulars had to be figured out on the fly, including the establishment of the hastily assembled team of weapons experts, technicians, and diplomats that Kaag now led. Until August 2013, no one had imagined the need for an international inspection force that could parachute into a war zone and oversee the dismantling of an entire weapons program while under fire.

The only organization remotely qualified was the Organization for the Prohibition of Chemical Weapons—the group that had won the Nobel Prize shortly after Åke Sellström's mission—but the OPCW was hardly built for such a purpose. The Hague-based organization employed a cadre of about two hundred experts who typically traveled abroad to carry out routine, prearranged inspections of commercial chemical plants and facilities where Cold War–era munitions were being destroyed. With an annual budget of less than $80 million, it lacked the resources, equipment, or infrastructure to sustain a months-long deployment overseas. When the crisis erupted in Syria, some of the OPCW's own executives expressed doubts about whether the organization was up to the task.

Some top UN officials believed that the leadership role was rightly theirs; a job as big as the disarmament of Syria required the United Nations' vastly larger budgets and resources, presumably with technical help from OPCW inspectors and other experts who would be placed under their command. But the OPCW had no interest in taking orders from New York. The agency's forward-thinking director-general, Turkish diplomat Ahmet Üzümcü, had followed the events in Syria with keen interest, and he had begun quietly training inspectors and gathering equipment for a possible emergency deployment. He would need help—money and vehicles, perhaps—but he was adamantly opposed to placing his workforce under the authority of the United Nations, which, by reputation, was slow-moving, excessively bureaucratic, and hamstrung by arcane rules and complex lines of command.

The two organizations arrived at a compromise: an OPCW-UN hybrid created exclusively for the dismantlement of Syria's weapons complex. The new entity would come to be known as the "OPCW-UN Joint Mission," or simply the "Joint Mission." It relied on the United Nations for money, equipment, and diplomatic support, while the OPCW provided the expertise and most of the inspection manpower. Its leadership would consist of one senior deputy from each of the organizations and an independent "special coordinator" who would be in charge of it all, reporting directly to the UN Security Council.

Picking the "special coordinator" to head the mission fell to Ban Ki-moon's staff, who came up with an inspired choice. Sigrid Agnes Maria Kaag, fifty-one, was regarded within New York headquarters as a doer: a tough, pragmatic, and unflinching veteran of humanitarian crises throughout the developing world. The daughter of a classical pianist and a schoolteacher from the suburbs of Utrecht in central Holland, Kaag was married to a Palestinian dentist and kept a primary residence with her four children in Jerusalem. Fluent in five other languages besides Arabic, she had a working knowledge of Syria from her past humanitarian work with Palestinian refugees there. Once, during a visit to a refugee camp near Damascus in the late 1990s, she had met Asma al-Assad, the stylish, British-born wife of Bashar al-Assad, who was then being groomed as the successor to his strongman father, President Hafez al-Assad. At the time, the country's heir apparent was seeking to cultivate an image as a Western-educated reformer who supported humanitarian causes and had little in common with the elder Assad, who had famously slaughtered up to twenty-five thousand of his countrymen while crushing a popular uprising in the city of Hama in the 1980s. By the time of Kaag's next encounter with Syria's first family in 2013, the son's death toll exceeded the father's by at least threefold.

Among those pushing the Dutchwoman's candidacy was Susana Malcorra, Ban's Argentinian chief of staff, who perceived in Kaag an "it" factor closely tied to her femininity. Kaag was physically striking: tall and lithe, with blue eyes and golden blond hair and a stylishness that stood out amid the gray and navy pinstripes in the UN executive office suites. She also was intelligent, articulate, and graceful, and she was deeply grounded in the nuances and sensitivities of Arab political culture. All these qualities would be assets in dealing with the testosterone-fueled world of Syria's military establishment, Malcorra felt.

"The fact that she's a woman would make a big difference," Malcorra said, explaining her thinking at the time. "It was everything: her background. Her style. Her ability to be so calm and so much in command, and at the same time to have a softer side that allows her to be practical, to multitask, to be—well, nice."

Kaag was preparing to board a plane for an aid donors' conference in Turkey when the job offer came. She had just been turned down for a different leadership position, and this sounded like an interesting opportunity. The job was supposed to last only a few months, and she would be doing the UN Secretariat a favor while leading one of the world body's highest-priority missions.

"I thought, *Okay, I can do this,*" she later recalled. "But I didn't know what I was saying yes to."

A week after the initial phone call, the appointment was approved by the UN Security Council. Kaag received instructions in the form of a vague, three-page letter from Secretary-General Ban. Days later she was on her way, to lead a team she had not yet met, in a country at war, to attempt a task that had never been tried, using methods that, in some cases, had not been invented.

She immediately traveled to Damascus, and on October 22, her first full day in Syria, she strode into the Foreign Ministry building to formally present her credentials. Meeting privately with Syrian foreign minister Walid Muallem and his top deputies, she politely and firmly laid out her goals for the mission, shifting with ease from English to Arabic and back again. Her job, she explained, was to help the Syrians fulfill their promise to quickly eliminate their chemical weapons stockpile. That was it. Having accomplished it, she and her team would go home.

"We have one shared goal, which is elimination of the program," said Kaag, looking businesslike in a simple black dress, her hair tied in a matching bow. Getting rid of the chemical weapons, she added, would be "a benefit to all, and particularly the Syrian people."

That afternoon, she unpacked her bags in a room at the Four Seasons Hotel, which had already become headquarters for the OPCW inspectors who had arrived in the country three weeks earlier. Except for official travel and a few holidays with her husband and children, this would be her home for the next nine months.

Kaag took an instant liking to her two deputies. The leader of the OPCW contingent was Julian Tangaere, a New Zealander and an experienced weapons inspector beloved by his OPCW comrades. The former manager of a remote research station in Antarctica, Tangaere was the solidly built son of a Maori tribesman who wore a distinctive Maori tattoo that ran from his elbow to his shoulder and conveyed the entirety of his tribe's history. The senior UN deputy was Abdullah Fadil, a Canadian of Somali descent who had helped manage humanitarian and peacekeeping operations in Africa, the Middle East, and the Balkans. Under their leadership the inspectors had gotten off to a running start, but the progress was limited to one facet of the mission: verifying Syria's declared stockpile and disabling the production equipment. It was not yet clear how the chemicals themselves would be physically removed, where they would go, or how they would be safeguarded along the way. The OPCW's experts knew their job, but the agency lacked the resources, the expertise, or even a good plan for eliminating 1,300 tons of deadly chemicals.

"It was like bringing a patient to a nonexistent hospital," Kaag would later say of the state of affairs in mid-October. "Or like trying to take a trip when there's no plane, no crew, and no one who even knows how to fly."

In the early days of the Joint Mission, Bashar al-Assad made a convincing show of cooperating with the United Nations and the international inspection force. In interviews, his aides even tried to spin the disarmament plan as something the dictator had always wanted to do. When Russian president Vladimir Putin first phoned Assad to broach the idea of dismantling his chemical stockpile, the Syrian leader agreed right away, in one of the "most quick decisions" of his presidency, deputy foreign minister Faisal Mekdad later said. It was a striking reframing of the arm-twisting Sergey Lavrov had implied in his conversation with John Kerry.

"I am ready, because I don't need these kinds of weapons," Mekdad quoted his boss as saying.

Syria's more cooperative attitude was apparent from the moment the inspectors sat down with their Syrian counterparts in a Sheraton Hotel conference room on October 2. Barely a month earlier, Åke Sellström had sat at the same table and faced a row of grim-faced diplomats and military officers who openly lied about Syria's weapons and threw up an endless array of excuses and obstacles. Now the same grim-faced diplomats and military officers were ready with records and practical suggestions about gaining access to secret stockpiles that, just two weeks earlier, did not officially exist.

After a strictly business opening session, the Syrian side of the table even began to relax a little. During breaks, the guests and hosts exchanged pleasantries over coffee, and a few shared cigarettes and even a chuckle or two. Tangaere's deputy Jerry Smith, the Joint Mission's head of field operations who helped lead some of the early meetings, saw it as a good omen; any warmth generated here might help prevent a freeze later on when the tasks grew harder.

Three days in, the planning was going so smoothly that Smith took a moment to congratulate the group on getting along so well.

"This is a bit like a date, isn't it?" he asked, as one of the participants later recalled. "When we met each other, we were all a bit uncertain. Now we've done this, and we've done that, and it's like we're dancing and it's all good. What are we going to do next?"

An awkward moment passed as the question was translated. Then one of the Syrians spoke up in perfect English.

"Now we kiss?" he said.

The room exploded with laughter.

The next day, October 6, the inspectors were ready for their first look at one of Syria's weapons facilities. They set out at dawn in a small convoy of UN armored cars, in what was essentially a trial run, testing whether unarmed inspectors could cross contested terrain, then return to base without losing weapons or people. The consensus view in early October 2013 was "not likely." There were thousands of ways the mission could fail, and of those, a good many involved violent attacks against the inspectors.

"If they're planning to whack us," one of the inspection leaders added, "you have to figure it would be on the first day."

Diarmuid O'Donovan, the security chief from the Sellström mission, was back in Syria to help safeguard the small advance team of weapons experts, and he had pressed the Syrians to provide a proper military escort for the day's expedition. Instead, at the arranged rendezvous point on the Damascus outskirts, the inspectors were met by an ancient, Soviet-era armored patrol car known as the BRDM-2, a kind of sawed-off tank on wheels, built to operate on land or in the water. With its metal hatches and rear propeller, it bore a vague resemblance to the amphibious "Ducks" built by the Pentagon during World War II and later used commercially to haul tourists around European and North American cities. The UN vehicles and Syrian police escorts all lined up behind the armored car, and the procession began moving slowly—very slowly. The BRDM-2 struggled to make thirty miles an hour on the open highway, and it was loud. O'Donovan had hoped for a serious military presence. What he got instead was a large, imposing, noisy convoy moving at the speed of a farm tractor. A would-be assailant wouldn't need binoculars to see them coming.

"This doesn't work," O'Donovan said. But there was no choice. The convoy rumbled along like a heavily armed funeral procession, taking forty-five minutes to cover a twenty-mile stretch of highway.

The caravan was approaching Adra, a dusty industrial town famous for its massive prison, when the BRDM-2 pulled off the main highway and onto a smaller road that wound along a rocky ridge. The vehicles passed through a security gate and then descended into a small gorge surrounded by hills. There were people milling about, and a pair of odd-looking trucks next to a few dozen large metallic objects arranged in a row on the ground. On a ridge to the left was an artillery placement with a large self-propelled gun, its barrel pointed toward rebel lines to the southeast. On the right, cut into the hillside itself, was the entranceway to a secret production center. The portal was carefully constructed to be invisible to passersby on the highway and extremely difficult to spot from the air. It was sealed by a blast-proof door of steel and concrete that now stood wide open.

In official UN records, this was "Site 7," one of the biggest and most modern of Syria's chemical production facilities. But some inspectors, noting the resemblance to the secret mountain laboratory in the movie *Austin Powers,* gave it a different nickname: "Dr. Evil's Lair."

The Syrians at Site 7 were clearly ready for their visitors. They were a mix of military men and technicians, none of whom wore masks or any other kind of safety equipment. One of them, a site manager in civilian clothes, stepped forward to greet the foreigners who had come to destroy his workplace. Polite but reserved, and shadowed by an army colonel who provided translation, he beckoned the newcomers to follow him on a tour unlike anything the inspectors had ever witnessed.

The line of metal objects turned out to be, on a closer look, empty five-hundred-pound aerial bombs and Scud warheads, numbering perhaps two dozen in all. All were designed to carry chemical weapons, with valves and internal chambers that would be filled with liquid poisons just prior to use. Syrians had brought them outdoors and placed them in a row to be destroyed. Behind the munitions were the two trucks the inspectors had noticed earlier. From a distance these resembled ordinary tractor-trailers; on the outside, each was fitted with commercial license plates and a soft tarpaulin cover that featured the logo of a Hungarian company. But the Syrians had removed the tarp to reveal the ruse: the trucks were mobile filling stations for chemical weapons, with specialized tanks and nozzles for injecting sarin into bombs and warheads. Before the invasion of Iraq in 2003, the George W. Bush administration had claimed that Saddam Hussein had built mobile "labs"—a claim sourced to an Iraqi informant code-named "Curveball," who, as it was later discovered, tricked U.S. and German intelligence agencies with made-up stories and phony drawings and diagrams. Syria, it was now clear, possessed the real thing.

But the most impressive sights awaited the team inside the hillside bunker. Behind the blast door, the inspectors entered dimly lit rooms where the poisons were stored. One chamber held thirty-two gray tanks on metal stilts, each containing about five hundred gallons of the liquid chemical known as DF, or methylphosphonyl difluoride, the primary precursor for sarin. In other rooms the Syrians had stacked barrel after barrel of isopropyl alcohol, dry salts, and other ingredients used in nerve agents. Another door opened to a large production hall, lined with reactor vessels and stainless-steel tanks where the precursors were mixed to produce lethal sarin. The larger tanks appeared new and still bore labels from the German companies that made them. Even in low lighting, the room sparkled.

"There was all this beautiful, gleaming equipment," one of the team members said afterward. "It was high-precision production. Even the welding was high-quality. You could see some of the chemists having a bit of a tear in the eye about having to cut it all up."

Having finished the touring, the inspectors were ready to go to work. The terms of the UN agreement with Damascus held that the Syrians were to dismantle and destroy their chemical weapons infrastructure while outside experts looked on. But it was quickly clear that things weren't going to be so simple. Each tank of sarin precursor needed to be packed up and hauled out of the country, and no one knew how that would happen, or where the chemicals would go. Decisions about hardware—machines and equipment used in making and handling chemical weapons—were caught up in endless haggling as the Syrians fought to preserve costly items such as ventilation systems that legitimately could be used again at universities or hospitals rather than being simply destroyed. But the Syrians lost far more of these arguments than they won. The visitors walked through the bunkers' corridors and liberally marked with spray paint every piece of hardware that they judged needed to be cut up, smashed, or filled with concrete. In the end, almost nothing was excluded, including the tunnels and bunkers themselves.

The easiest decision was to eliminate the empty bombs and warheads. Yet even that chore turned out to be more complicated than the inspectors at Site 7 imagined.

Team leader Jerry Smith was considering the row of munitions when he perceived an opportunity. What if the Syrians could be persuaded to truly embrace disarmament—to see it not as an obligation but as something good for the country? An image of Syrians enthusiastically smashing their own weapons stockpile might do wonders for the country's image and show the world that the disarmament plan was really working. Smith remembered how Iraqi chemical bombs had been crushed by a tank under UN oversight after the first Gulf War. Why not try something like that here?

He called some of the Syrians together and tried to explain the concept of a photo op.

"Nothing could be more photogenic than having something drive over those things," Smith told the officials, gesturing toward the bombs, as witnesses to the exchange later recalled. "You have an opportunity to demonstrate that you're off and running."

There was a large bulldozer inside the compound, and the Syrians started it up while a TV crew from the state-run news service recorded the moment on video. The sixteen-ton earthmover roared across the dirt lot and, belching diesel fumes, proceeded to roll across the row of empty bombs with its steel treads.

Afterward, the inspectors and Syrians looked at the bombs, then at each other. The munitions were all intact. The bulldozer had barely scratched them.

A T-72 tank, a late addition to the security detail, arrived at the compound as the inspection was underway, and the local Syrian officials decided to enlist the crew in the destruction effort. The Soviet-made behemoth lumbered down the path, and the shells disappeared beneath giant metal treads for the second time. The result was almost identical. A couple of bombs popped open, but the rest were unscathed.

Smith was incredulous. "These bombs are really tough!" he said to the Syrian colonel.

The man smiled and thumped his chest.

"Made in Syria!" he crowed.

Back at their hotel that night, the inspectors placed an order for plasma torches.

The honeymoon in Damascus lasted a remarkable two weeks. In fourteen days, the Joint Mission team managed to conduct initial inspections at three-fourths of Syria's declared chemical weapons sites, and they oversaw the destruction of production equipment at nearly half of them. UN officials in their internal emails were still calling it "Mission Impossible," but in the early going, the task seemed feasible, if not exactly easy.

The inspectors had plenty of help. The Syrians, led by the suddenly ingratiating and energetic Brigadier General Hassan al-Sharif, were surprisingly eager partners—almost too eager, at times. Once, when Joint Mission leaders expressed concern about a fresh outbreak of fighting near a weapons depot they were about to visit, Sharif responded by ordering a massive artillery bombardment on nearby rebel positions, in an apparent attempt to calm things down until the inspections were over.

Diarmuid O'Donovan was horrified.

"They just launched a barrage around that site because we were worried about getting out there," the security chief told Julian Tangaere. The two went to Sharif to dissuade him from using the inspectors as an excuse for carrying out future attacks.

Sharif shrugged. "We can do this another way," he said.

Still, as the inspections progressed, the teams found themselves moving ever closer to the front lines, and sometimes through them. From mid-October onward, barely a day passed without some kind of disturbance or close scrape to keep adrenaline levels high.

With so much ground to cover, Tangaere opted to divide the inspectors into two groups, keeping half in Damascus while sending the rest to Homs, an industrial city a hundred miles north of Damascus and an early epicenter of the Arab Spring uprising. The city itself was under a Stalingrad-like siege, with thousands of civilians trapped in ruined houses with little food or water while Syrian troops backed by Iranian and Hezbollah fighters waged a brutal, block-by-block campaign against remaining pockets of Free Syrian Army resistance. Famed journalist Marie Colvin had been killed there a few months earlier in a government rocket attack while covering the siege. East of Homs lay a different kind of danger: a half-dozen of Syria's chemical weapons facilities were scattered across a landscape littered with the blackened hulks of vehicles from previous military convoys that had traveled down the same roads.

Any trip to the region would be a roll of the dice, so Tangaere decided to reduce the risk by billeting the Homs team near the city to limit their time on the Homs–Damascus highway. The Syrians offered an abandoned villa in a government-controlled neighborhood on the outskirts of the city and provided a cook and a company of soldiers who formed a protective cordon around the house. Three Kalashnikov assault rifles were left in the villa in case the inspectors found themselves in a fight for their lives.

Even here, life settled into a kind of routine. When not working, the inspectors slept on inflatable mattresses, ate Syrian food, talked endlessly, and occasionally trained. Each was given a whistle to wear, to make it easier to find one another if they had to scatter at night. One day the group's military veterans staged a demonstration on how to dismantle and reassemble the assault rifles the Syrians had left with them, and then they put on a contest. The surprise winner—the fastest hand at rebuilding the rifle by far—was Christopher J. Kennedy, an American with no military training at all.

The work at Homs consisted of white-knuckle forays into the battle-scarred countryside to visit hidden weapons depots while jittery Syrian soldiers looked on. The inspectors wandered through rundown storage bunkers, some of them so old that the garlicy odor of sulfur mustard could be detected from outside—a sure sign that the containers for the poisons had started to leak. They toured gleaming production centers, marking the machines and tanks with spray paint. They peered into empty warehouses, including one that had been long since abandoned and was being used by a local tanner to cure sheep pelts. On the road they would sometimes pause in their vehicles to listen to the low roar of artillery shells passing overhead, or to watch helicopters returning to base from bombing runs over Homs's embattled neighborhoods. At night, after a meal cooked on hot stoves, they sat on the villa's rooftop terrace to watch the tracer fire and listened to the sounds of fighting in the old city, perhaps two miles away.

The flashes and booms could almost pass for a distant thunderstorm. But O'Donovan was acutely aware that people were dying not far from where he sat. One night he watched the flickering lights with Scott Cairns as the two talked quietly about the war and the surreal part they had been asked to play.

"This is not a place I ever expected to be," O'Donovan said.

Cairns shrugged.

"If not you, who?" he asked.

Though it was rarely discussed aloud, the job had exacted an emotional toll, similar to that borne by aid workers and journalists in countries afflicted by famine or violence. They were Europeans and North Americans, mostly, well fed and relatively comfortable, yet surrounded at all times by suffering and misery. Most were convinced that their work had merit: removing Bashar al-Assad's arsenal of poisons would doubtlessly make the world safer, and it would free the country of a uniquely cruel and dangerous weapon that could inflict death on a massive scale. Yet Syrians continued to die anyway, by the thousands. And there was nothing that any one of them could do about it.

Still, there were deadlines to meet, and by the end of October, they had achieved the first of the mission's primary milestones. Sigrid Kaag prepared to fly to New York to brief the UN Security Council in person, while her aides dashed out a statement for her to deliver.

"The Joint Mission is now satisfied that it has verified—and seen destroyed—all of Syria's declared critical production and mixing [and] filling equipment," it said.

Only the chemical stockpile remained inside the dictator's bunkers, just as dangerous, and nearly as vulnerable, as before.

12

Ghost Armies

In the same week the weapons inspectors arrived in Damascus, an Iraqi army helicopter with four crewmen aboard left its base to investigate reports of a strange military encampment in the desert near Baiji. The town in north central Iraq, about 120 miles up the Tigris River from Baghdad, is close to Tikrit, the birthplace of Saddam Hussein, in a neighborhood known as a haven for armed gangs of all kinds. One of these gangs had apparently settled in the arid hills outside town, and it had exchanged gunfire with an Iraqi army patrol. A chopper and crew—pilot, copilot, crew chief, and gunner—were dispatched to look for the militants and then to give chase.

The pilot skimmed the tops of date-palm groves and followed newly planted barley fields along the lush corridor of green where the Tigris snakes through the desert. Then he headed out over the wastelands to begin the search, the gunner scanning the terrain from the open side door. They spotted something in a cleft in the hills, and as they flew closer, they discovered a small vale that had been turned into a military encampment of astonishing size. This was no band of renegades. It was a small army, with vehicles, tents, heavy weapons, and a mountain of supplies. Before the crew could react, a swarm of machine-gun rounds ripped through the helicopter's unarmored floor. The aircraft went down in a spiral and crashed hard, killing all four crew members.

The incident received scant notice in the U.S. capital, where a partisan squabble over health care had triggered a budgetary crisis and a shutdown of the federal government. But within a small cadre of officials monitoring Iraq's growing Islamist insurgency, the helicopter's fiery demise flashed like an alarm. The Islamic State of Iraq and al-Sham—now widely known as ISIS—had smashed through yet another threshold on its path to becoming a true regional menace. In the week that followed, the group downed two more Iraqi helicopters, evidence of its vastly enhanced firepower.

Among those studying the reports was a State Department policy expert and diplomatic troubleshooter named Brett McGurk. At age forty, McGurk already was regarded as one of Washington's most experienced and capable Iraq hands. He served as a legal counsel to the U.S.-led Coalition Provisional Authority beginning in early 2004, eight months after the 2003 invasion, and he helped draft Iraq's interim constitution. After returning to Washington, he served as a senior adviser on Iraq for the George W. Bush White House, earning distinction as a leading architect of the 2007 "surge" policy that brought stability to Iraq after a brutal, three-year insurgency. He was then tapped by President Barack Obama to help untangle various diplomatic disputes with Iraq, becoming one of a small handful of political appointees to serve under Bush and Obama. Tall and athletic with square-jawed good looks, he impressed superiors with his ability to perceive root causes of complex problems and then to work smartly and diligently to overcome them.

At the time of the helicopter crash, McGurk was just two months into a job that came with an unobstructed view of Iraq's rapidly deteriorating security environment. His post as the State Department's deputy assistant secretary for Iraq and Iran meant frequent travel to Baghdad, as well as to provincial capitals around the country. He read classified reports and interviewed U.S. and Iraqi security officials, each of them adding fine detail to a narrative that was becoming startlingly clear: Iraq's most notorious terrorist group was back from the dead.

McGurk was still new to the country when al-Qaeda in Iraq, the bloodthirsty sect founded by Jordanian terrorist Abu Musab al-Zarqawi, rose to prominence. Zarqawi and his fanatical followers beheaded captives, bombed marketplaces, and assassinated Shiites in a savage campaign that brought the country to the brink of civil war by 2006. U.S. forces killed Zarqawi that summer, and by 2009 his organization—rebranded as the Islamic State of Iraq—was effectively finished, broken into fragments by the combined pressures of the U.S. troop surge, improved counterterrorism tactics, and a grassroots revolt by Iraqi tribal leaders, known as the Anbar Awakening. But Zarqawi's old gang wasn't beaten. The United States pulled out of Iraq in 2011, the same year that civil war broke out in Syria. New leader Abu Bakr al-Baghdadi began rebuilding his organization in Iraq and, sensing an opportunity, dispatched some of his best warriors and generals across the Syrian border to establish a presence there. By 2013, the outpost had grown into a terrorist army with thousands of new followers and an endless supply of weapons. Brought back to life in Syria, the Islamists returned to Iraq to reinfect their original hosts.

Alarmed by ISIS's growing strength, McGurk sent urgent cables to the White House and State Department, describing the terrorists' takeover of border crossings and their formation of training camps in the desert.

The Iraq-Syria border is being erased, he wrote.

Then, a few weeks after the downing of the helicopters, he strode into the U.S. Capitol to repeat the warning before a congressional committee.

"We face a real problem," McGurk said in testimony before a panel of the House Committee on Foreign Affairs. U.S. spy agencies were seeing new terrorist enclaves spring up in the desert, and they were sharing the intelligence with the Iraqis. But Baghdad possessed neither the high-flying aircraft needed to conduct surveillance nor the armored attack helicopters to flush the terrorists from their hideouts. "When they fly an unarmored helicopter to these camps, the helicopters are getting shot down," he said. "Pilots that we have trained are being killed."

The response to McGurk's warnings was a collective shrug. There was little sympathy in Washington for Iraq's prime minister, Nouri al-Maliki, who, after being elected with U.S. support, presided over a government most notable for its corruption, incompetence, and official repression of the country's Sunni minority. If there was an armed resistance in western Iraq's Sunni heartland, Maliki had surely brought it upon himself. Moreover, any impulse for helping the Iraqi strongman had died away because of Maliki's penchant for insulting and irritating his U.S. benefactors. He quietly cultivated ties with

Iran, America's archfoe, while publicly pushing for the removal of every U.S. soldier from his country, on the fastest possible timetable. And yet when the old Zarqawi insurgency sputtered back to life in 2013, Maliki traveled to Washington, hat in hand, to ask for more U.S. military aid.

The Obama administration agreed to provide Maliki with more aircraft, but officials made clear in interviews that they believed Iraq's chief affliction was bad governance.

"Part of solving the security situation is solving the political situation," a State Department official told the *Washington Post* as Maliki was leaving town.

If the White House response was tepid, Congress's was downright icy. After McGurk finished laying out the details of Iraq's insurgency threat, conservative lawmakers questioned why Americans should ever again commit themselves to—as one senior committee member put it—"pouring more money down the rat hole."

"Why do we care anymore about whether or not al-Qaeda is operating and killing some of their soldiers?" Representative Dana Rohrabacher, a California Republican and one of the committee's most outspoken Maliki critics, demanded of McGurk. "They don't care for us. They're not grateful for what we have already done."

McGurk politely persisted. The new incarnation of the Zarqawi network was even more dangerous than before, he said. In Syria, ISIS had transformed itself from a local insurgency to an international cause. The group now had a larger mission, one that appealed to radicalized Muslim youths around the world, and it was able to connect with a global audience using social-media platforms that had not yet existed when Zarqawi was alive. The group was unleashing suicide bombers in waves, in Iraq and Syria, and the violence was beginning to rile up dormant Shiite militias, some of them armed and funded by Iran. The region appeared to be hurtling toward a cataclysm.

"You have a youthful population, you have an underemployed population, and they are watching the conflict unfold on YouTube," McGurk told the committee. "And that is having a militarizing, radicalizing effect."

After the hearing, McGurk did what he could to help the Iraqis deal with the threat on their border. With his behind-the-scenes encouragement, the Obama administration diverted one of its Global

Hawk surveillance drones to northwestern Iraq, while supplying the Maliki government with new Hellfire missiles that could be launched from its helicopters. The drone went on the hunt for secret ISIS bases in the Iraqi desert, and it found them—five of them.

By this time ISIS was also on its way to controlling a major Syrian city—Raqqa, a provincial capital of a quarter-million inhabitants on the banks of the Euphrates River—and it was sending columns of raiders into western Iraq. McGurk watched and waited, certain that Zarqawi's old terrorist network was getting ready for a big move.

In Damascus, the start of 2014 was marked by an eerie calm. Since the summer's chemical attacks, the army, newly reinforced by Iranian regulars and Hezbollah militants, had reestablished control over the capital's close-in suburbs, so the daily mortar barrages in the central district largely ceased. No longer subjected to loud, random explosions outside their hotel, the Joint Mission team was instead left to contemplate quiet warnings from intelligence agencies about threats to their safety. One of these arrived on January 2, 2014, five days after Sigrid Kaag posted her video message at Latakia harbor.

"Extremists linked to al-Qaeda intend to attack foreigners involved in the chemical weapons work at the Four Seasons Hotel," the warning read. A second report, also in January, included the first mention of a serious Islamist plot to steal the weapons themselves. According to the report, al-Qaeda leader Ayman al-Zawahiri had dispatched emissaries to Syria to study how the chemicals were being moved. The terrorist group was working with its al-Nusra ally and explicitly "talking about acquiring" nerve agents, an official briefed on the intelligence later said.

The reports were specific and vague at the same time, and there was nothing Kaag and her team could do but hunker down inside the Four Seasons and its fragile security perimeter. Already, except for official inspections, the team largely confined itself to two floors of the hotel, which were sealed off from the others and accessible only through a special elevator and doors equipped with fingerprint scanners. Not even the hotel's waiters were permitted in the Joint Mission's rooms. Kaag regularly used the hotel fitness center and occasionally held court over glasses of wine in the lobby bar. But otherwise, "entertainment" consisted of movie nights in one of the hotel suites, or sloppy karaoke contests fueled by bottles of anise-flavored raki.

The business that brought the inspectors to Syria appeared to be at a standstill. Since the successes of October, the disarmament mission had devolved into a dreary exercise in transportation logistics. Everything that had seemed simple at first had become mind-numbingly complex. Some of the tanks that held Syria's binary sarin turned out, upon inspection, to be old and too fragile for transporting, so new ones had to be purchased, imported, and hauled overland through contested territory, and the chemicals siphoned off by workers in protective suits. Just moving the tanks in their bunkers required special cranes and forklifts, and a fleet of tractors to shuttle the gear around. After all that was accomplished, the Syrians became obsessively worried—with justification—about the possibility that the rebels might puncture one of the chemical tanks with a bullet or a well-aimed rocket-propelled grenade, releasing the toxic contents. Hassan al-Sharif, the bushy-eyebrowed Syrian brigadier, traveled to The Hague to appeal to UN officials for armored trucks so the chemicals could be hauled safely to the port at Latakia. When that request was refused—Western countries were not about to supply militarily useful vehicles to the Syrian army—he insisted instead on a supply of bulletproof covers or "jackets" that could be fitted over Syria's existing trucks. No such armored jackets existed, so they would have to be custom-made, at UN expense, in a process that would take months. The December 31, 2013, goal for removing the chemicals from Syria was officially doomed, and the overall deadline—the complete elimination of Syria's weapons stockpile and production facilities by June 30, 2014—now looked very much in doubt.

When progress with the Syrians appeared to stall completely, Kaag and her deputies would drive across Damascus to seek help from the only two countries that possessed the clout to change Assad's behavior. Kaag became a regular visitor to the Iranian embassy, where the bearded ambassador would offer a sympathetic ear and trays of roasted pistachios, only to complain afterward that Kaag's dress was too short and that she had allowed too much of her blond hair to spill out from under the head covering that she dutifully wore.

The Russian embassy was farther away, outside the Damascus

Green Zone, in a neighborhood that still received occasional incoming fire from rebel skirmishers. The main embassy building was protected behind a fortress-like barrier: a high cement wall at the ground level, topped by a steel fence crowned with concertina wire. The compound was regularly struck by stray shells and bullets, yet the Russians routinely refused to allow Kaag's vehicle inside, forcing her to park on the street and scurry through a maze of sandbags and two sets of outer gates to gain entrance. During one visit a mortar exploded a few yards from the sandbagged footpath, forcing everyone to dive for cover. Kaag, more annoyed than shaken, brushed herself off and pushed on.

The visits were usually worth the trouble. Russian ambassador Azamat Kulmuhametov was the dean of the diplomatic corps in Syria and a man with unrivaled connections among the country's elites. A fluent Arabic speaker with polished manners and a trim mustache that matched his flint-gray hair, Kulmuhametov had served multiple postings in Syria since the 1970s, and he had known Bashar al-Assad as a boy. He listened to his visitor's complaints with a world-weary air.

"I'll see what I can do," he said.

Exactly what he did was never clear. But suddenly, days after the missed December 31 deadline, Syria announced that it was beginning to move some of its chemicals to the port at Latakia.

The change was so abrupt that the Joint Mission team had to rush to finalize arrangements for a pickup. The *Cape Ray* was still being loaded and tested in southern Virginia, nearly six thousand miles away. But a fleet of volunteer ships from a half-dozen countries lay moored off the Syrian coast, waiting with impatience and trepidation for just this signal to come ashore.

On the morning of January 7, the frigate HDMS *Esbern Snare,* a top-of-the-line combat ship of the Danish Royal Navy, shut off its main engines and slipped into Latakia harbor, its gun crews out of sight but ready. Thrusters churning, the ship swung into position inside the breakwater about a hundred yards from the docks, a distance equally suitable for observing the shoreline or for concentrating firepower, depending on how things went.

On the bridge, the frigate's skipper, Captain Torben Mikkelsen, a wiry, sun-creased fifty-year-old wearing a camouflage uniform and stubbly gray beard, picked up his field glasses for another sweep of the port. It was an eerie sight: a large, modern harbor, as desolate as a ghost town. Nothing moved, from the marina and palm-lined beaches to the north to the rusting cranes and container yards to the south. The docks and piers stood empty, except for a few dozen soldiers positioned at intervals on the breakwater and along the wharf. Farther back, Mikkelsen could see a small tent partly obscured by sandbags, and behind it, rows of trucks bearing deadly cargo. It was Monday and the first day that Syrian chemical weapons would be passed into international hands, and the trailers were carrying tons of ready-to-mix precursors for VX.

Mikkelsen was no chemist, but he knew enough about nerve agents to do some quick calculations. The trucks represented enough killing power in theory to wipe out most of Scandinavia.

"Inside those containers," he said to his crew, "is the death-dose equivalent for twenty-one million people."

The Danish captain was the commanding officer of the small flotilla of ships, mostly from Denmark and Norway, that would do the actual extraction of Syria's chemical weapons. A larger maritime task force that included British and Chinese vessels and a smoke-belching Russian battle cruiser waited offshore to help protect the chemicals at sea. Mikkelsen's command included the Danish-owned *Ark Futura* and the Norwegian freighter *Taiko,* the two commercial cargo ships that would carry the weapons out of Syria; and a military escort that consisted of his heavily armed flagship, the *Esbern Snare,* and the Norwegian navy frigate *Helge Ingstad*. A pair of British frigates would join the convoy at various times as added protection against an array of threats, among which the chemicals themselves were perhaps the least significant. As recently as late summer, fierce fighting had erupted in the hills just to the east of Latakia's airport. Intelligence reports from Syria carried daily reminders of the Islamist rebels' intense interest in the chemical cargo that was beginning to move around the country and would soon be concentrated in a single spot inside Latakia harbor.

Mikkelsen considered his choices carefully. The Syrian government had invited his ships to come ashore, and as a sovereign state, even in wartime, Syria was officially in charge of providing security for the port. A guns-drawn, "ring of steel" entry into Latakia might make his crews feel safer, he thought, but it would probably be seen by the hosts as offensive. The captain opted instead for the middle ground: a small, understated landing party consisting of a few special-forces operators in an inflatable craft called a RHIB, followed by the *Ark Futura,* which would be shadowed closely by his fully equipped, missile-toting frigate. As added protection, Mikkelsen's crews rigged the cargo ship's mooring lines with explosive charges so the vessel could spring away in an instant if militants tried to fight their way aboard. From the shore, the enhanced security measures would remain all but invisible. Even the flotilla's canine crew member—the merchant ship had a bomb-sniffing dog named Coyote who was on hand to inspect the incoming cargo—would be kept out of sight to avoid offending the port's Muslim dockworkers.

As he waited to give the order to go ashore, Mikkelsen's mind was preoccupied with another worry: What would happen to his freighters and their cargo the next day and the following week? If the loading of the chemicals progressed flawlessly, his ships would sail out of Latakia harbor with a cargo of lethal poisons and literally nowhere to go. At some future point there would have to be a rendezvous between the *Ark Futura* and the MV *Cape Ray*. But two enormous obstacles stood in the way of that meeting of ships. And at that moment, neither Mikkelsen nor anyone else could see a way around them.

The first barrier: the rendezvous point did not yet exist. It was too risky to transfer chemicals from one vessel to another on the open sea, so the meeting would have to take place in a harbor, with both ships secured to a dock. UN officials had been pressing countries around the globe to offer up a commercial seaport or navy base, but their efforts had failed. The reluctance was easy to understand: an accidental spill or an act of sabotage could threaten local populations and the environment and would likely shut down commerce for weeks or even months. Few countries would willingly take on that kind of risk.

The other obstacle was equally daunting. Under the disarmament agreement, the transfer between ships could happen only once. The *Ark Futura* could return to Latakia as often as needed to pick up more chemical weapons as Syria delivered them to the port. But the ship could not discharge its cargo to the *Cape Ray* until it had everything—until the entire 1,300-ton stockpile had been hauled from its bunkers and loaded onto the Danish freighter or its sister ship, the *Taiko*. From the minute the freighters picked up the first load of chemicals, they would effectively remain in limbo at sea until their entire mission was finished.

The cargo ships could not go home. They could not seek refuge at another port. Their only option was to wander around like oceanic nomads until Syria had delivered the last of its weapons. And no one knew when that would be.

There also were real safety concerns. One late-winter morning as the *Taiko* was tied to Latakia's docks, rebel fighters launched a fresh offensive that seemed to target the harbor itself. One stray shell landed in the water a few hundred feet from the *Taiko,* creating a geyser of seawater but causing no harm. On another occasion, the *Ark Futura*'s crew spent a frightful morning searching for a hidden bomb—a false alarm, happily—and days later they doused a deck fire that broke out near containers filled with mustard gas.

But the most dramatic incident occurred on a winter's evening when the cargo ships lay anchored with their Danish and Norwegian escorts off the Syrian coast. Just after 3 a.m., the radar operator on the Norwegian frigate *Helge Ingstad* spotted a pair of small boats on radar, heading in the convoy's direction. The sea was dead calm and lit by a gibbous moon, and the night watch on the bridge could soon make out a pair of dark shapes moving toward him across water as flat as a sheet of foil. The strange vessels looked like a pair of Syrian fishing boats out for a midnight trawl, except their hulls were painted black and their running lights were turned off. And they appeared to be on a collision course with the cargo ship *Taiko.*

The *Helge Ingstad*'s skipper, Commander Per Rostad, signaled the intruders on his radio's emergency frequency. There was no reply.

Onward the boats came, with the cargo ship directly in their path. Worried that a suicide attack was under way, Rostad ordered his crew to send up a warning flare. When the mysterious boats still refused to change course, he fired a flash grenade in the direction of the closest ship, then a second grenade, and a third. Nothing worked.

At last he called for the *Helge Ingstad*'s 76mm deck gun to be swung around. Rostad was seconds away from giving the order to shoot when the oncoming boats suddenly veered off. They sped away in the darkness, fading from view as quickly as they had appeared.

As he watched their departure, Rostad heard a strange chanting sound, coming over the same radio frequency he had used to try to warn away the boats. It was a *nasheed,* an a cappella song in Arabic. Nasheeds are frequently used by ISIS and other Islamist extremists as background music for propaganda videos celebrating their attacks.

After it was over, Mikkelsen speculated that the strange vessels might have been merely smugglers who inadvertently wandered into the convoy's position. Contraband runners were a common sight off the coast of Syria, where luxury goods and even ordinary commodities such as cigarettes were in short supply because of Western trade embargoes.

Rostad was skeptical. The boats had ignored repeated warnings and acted with a brazenness not usually associated with black marketeers.

"The boats may have been loaded with explosives," Rostad later said. "Had they made their way alongside the *Taiko,* things could have gone really badly."

Whatever the intentions, the encounter raised fresh doubts about whether cargo ships filled with deadly chemicals should be allowed to wander the seas indefinitely, even with military escorts. Mikkelsen became so concerned that he pressed UN officials repeatedly on the matter, urging them to wait until there was a clear destination—until they had found a willing port for the transfer between the *Ark Futura* and the *Cape Ray*—before sending ships into Latakia to pick up chemicals. He received in reply only vague assurances, followed by, on January 6, an order to prepare to sail to Latakia.

The next morning, January 7, Mikkelsen put his careful plan in motion. The inflatable RHIB with its special-forces troops rounded the breakwater and entered Latakia harbor, followed by the *Ark Futura* and then his own ship, the *Esbern Snare,* with the Danish captain standing in the bridge, watching closely to see how the thing would go.

As the ships arrived at Latakia harbor, a handful of Syrian officials and invited guests from the Joint Mission took seats behind a sandbag wall to enjoy the view. It was a seasonably cool day, but fair, and a slight breeze tugged at the canopy that had been set up to shield the spectators from the sun and from any snipers who might be lurking in the apartment buildings near the quay. Brigadier General Hassan al-Sharif puffed quietly on a cigar, his eyebrows furrowed as he studied the approaching vessels. Near him, another of the Syrians, an older man wearing a civilian coat and eyeglasses, was complaining aloud about the sacrifices his country was being forced to make.

"They were good weapons," the official said in forlorn English, nodding toward the chemical-laden trucks lined up near the docks.

The small Joint Mission contingent under the tent was headed by Jerry Smith, the British weapons expert who led the first inspection, to the underground bunker dubbed "Dr. Evil's Lair." He sipped tea and watched with the others as a large merchant ship with a bright blue hull—the name painted on the bow in white letters was *Ark Futura*—maneuvered its way toward the quay, trailed by a navy ship with angular features that gave it a vaguely futuristic look. Dockworkers lashed the cargo vessel to bollards on its starboard side, and when it was secure, a huge metal ramp was slowly lowered until one end lay flat against the concrete wharf.

The *Ark Futura*'s crew had kept mostly out of sight as the ship came ashore. But now, Smith spotted a lone figure walking down the ramp. He was a Danish special-forces operator, judging from the man's insignia and tactical garb. He was perhaps thirty, lean and muscular, and he wore a pair of wraparound sunglasses and a shoulder holster for his side arm. He stood at the bottom of the ramp, alone, with his hands on his hips. Other than the pistol, he was unarmed.

The Syrians just gaped, as though an alien spacecraft had landed. No one in the tent had known how the morning was supposed to proceed, and no one moved or spoke for a long moment. Finally, Smith decided to approach the Dane.

"Hello," he said in English. "Welcome to Syria!"

"Thanks!" the man replied.

The visitor strode over to the tent to introduce himself to Sharif. As he made small talk with the Syrians, other workers in orange jumpsuits emerged from the *Ark Futura* and began to set up equipment, including what appeared to be a mobile X-ray scanner.

The Danes proceeded to explain how the transfer would work. It was simple, they said: Each of the Syrian trucks would pass through the X-ray machine, then drive directly onto the *Ark Futura,* where Danish workers in protective gear would unload their cargo. Then they would drive out again. When the last truck was empty, the ship and its escorts would turn around and head back to sea.

Smith was surprised and a bit uneasy. The Syrians were being allowed to drive directly onto the ship? Was that safe? He took one of the Danish officers aside for a private chat with the Joint Mission team.

"Are you sure about this?" he asked. "The Syrians will be driving onto what is effectively sovereign Danish territory. What if one of the drivers claims asylum or something?"

The Dane smiled. "It's okay. They can drive on," he said.

Minutes later, the first of the Syrian vehicles—a red semitruck hauling VX precursors inside a beige trailer—fired up its engine and began moving toward the *Ark Futura.* After it passed through the mobile scanner, one of the Danes suddenly yelled out something. The X-ray team had spotted something inside the truck.

"Is there a gun in the cab?" one of the technicians demanded. The image on the X-ray monitor showed a long metal object behind the driver's seat. It appeared to be an assault rifle.

Other drivers had come out of their vehicles when the disturbance began, and one of Brigadier General Sharif's aides now turned to address them.

"Okay, who else left a rifle in their truck?" he asked in Arabic.

About half the men raised their hands. Most had brought a gun along to defend themselves in case of an ambush along the road to Latakia.

"Sorry," the first driver said as he retrieved his rifle from the cab. Minutes later, the line of trucks was moving again, past the scanner and onto the ship.

In just a few hours, it was done. After the last truck departed, the *Ark Futura*'s mariners secured the chemical containers to the deck with thick straps to prevent them from moving around. Then they raised the loading ramp and pushed off, as the Syrians and inspectors watched from shore.

The RHIB and its crew were hoisted onto the *Esbern Snare,* which now pointed its bow toward the harbor entrance. The frigate and its commander guided the small procession through Syrian waters and then out into the open sea, to wait.

On January 27, nearly three weeks after the *Ark Futura* left Latakia, the MV *Cape Ray* was finally ready to sail.

There were, predictably, a few last-minute snafus. As the ship was preparing to depart, coastal Virginia was plunged in a deep freeze as a historic polar vortex event drove temperatures into the teens for days.

"Conditions this morning are TERRIBLE," one of the *Cape Ray*'s portside managers wrote in a status report on January 22. "Entire spar deck is black ice with two inches of icy snow on top. Welders knocked off at 0200 this morning. Temporary shelters we built for them have blown away with the wind. Temps in the teens, roads bad and wind still howling. Other than that, everything is swell."

It got worse. As the cold snap lingered, the ship's newly installed PVC pipes exploded, sending freezing water gushing onto the deck. It was only water—the hydrolysis machines were empty and unplugged at the time—but the ship's crew now faced days of cleanup and rebuilding. Jordan, as captain, proposed setting sail quickly to bring the *Cape Ray* into warmer Gulf Stream waters, but the damage was too extensive, and there was thawing out to do before repairs could even start.

The prospect of a delayed departure triggered another round of fretting at the Pentagon and National Security Council. President Barack Obama was personally informed of the setback during a White House meeting with his defense advisers. His response, relayed back to the *Cape Ray* team in a single terse sentence, brought both relief and—for those unaccustomed to having their work scrutinized by the U.S. commander in chief—a small thrill.

"We briefed POTUS on this tonight," the message read, using the acronym for president of the United States, "and there is no pressure."

There was genuinely no rush. After the *Ark Futura* picked up its first load, progress stalled again, with only one other small consignment of chemicals arriving in the port that month. Each day brought fresh reports from Damascus about problems and delays. The *Cape Ray*'s managers had expected to begin destroying Syria's weapons in late January. Now the date was being pushed back until late February at the earliest, and perhaps significantly later than that. Tim Blades's crew would likely face weeks of idle time once their ship finally reached its destination. "Which is faster—snails, or movement of Syrian chemicals?" one U.S. official wrote in a January progress report from The Hague.

The lack of movement allowed more time to work out a few lingering issues with the ship that had not been fully resolved. One was the question of who was in charge. A ship can have only a single captain, but besides Jordan, there were two others who shared responsibility for what happened on the *Cape Ray:* Tim Blades, whose chemical weapons destruction operation was the sole reason for the voyage; and a Navy captain named Richard Dromerhauser, who was assigned by the Pentagon to serve as commodore, the officer in charge of the overall mission aboard the ship. Dromerhauser had no chemical weapons background, but he was a U.S. Naval Academy graduate with a distinguished career that included command of a $2 billion Navy destroyer, the USS *Fitzgerald,* in the Pacific. At age forty-six, he had a graying crew cut and still retained the powerful physique of the rugby player he had been as a Navy cadet. But despite his rank and intimidating appearance, Dromerhauser had an easygoing personality and a playful sense of humor that made him easy to like. (Dromerhauser had received parting instructions from his own superiors, distilled into a single phrase and conveyed with utmost sincerity: "Don't spill a drop.") The three men came up with a cooperative arrangement in which each would be responsible for his own department—Jordan as the boat's skipper, Blades as director of operations, and Dromerhauser as mission manager—and they would consult collectively on the most consequential matters.

It would be a problem for the *Cape Ray,* though, if the Syrian delays stretched on indefinitely. Jordan's and Blades's crews had both signed up for what they believed would be a ninety-day assignment. That was enough time in theory to pick up Syria's chemicals—at a port still to be determined—and destroy them all before returning to Portsmouth again. Now no one knew when the physical dismantling of the weapons would start. The Pentagon had arranged for the *Cape Ray* to wait out the delays at a U.S. Navy base in Rota, Spain, a sun-drenched city of palm trees and white sandy beaches just west of Gibraltar. There are worse places in the world to get stuck, but many in the crew had families, and an extended delay would mean hardships and, no doubt, many resignations.

Already, some of Jordan's mariners were talking openly of quitting rather than sitting on an idled ship for weeks, or perhaps months, Jordan told Blades.

"Holding folks this long will be asking quite a bit from them," he said.

For the moment, though, some on the ship actually looked forward to having a little time to thaw out and recuperate after the ordeals of the past two months. Besides the beaches, there were golf courses near Rota, and spectacular Spanish castles and ancient forts.

"I plan to become a bullfighter," Dromerhauser quipped.

A few last crates of fresh food were loaded onto the ship, and the navigator ran final calculations for the voyage, setting a course toward Gibraltar, exactly seven days and twenty-one hours away, at an average speed of eighteen knots. The crew carried out final safety drills, including checks on the ship's small supply of rifles, handguns, and ammunition, which Jordan kept locked in a safe near the bridge, in case of encroaching pirates or terrorists.

Families came to the port for farewells. Blades's young son, who had become unusually anxious about his father's voyage, came aboard with his mom, clutching a blanket and some handwritten notes to leave in Blades's cabin. Jordan, ever the gracious host, took the child on a captain's tour of the ship, from the galley and officers' quarters to the helmsman's station on the bridge. The boy departed with a *Cape Ray* hat, a commemorative coin, and an ear-to-ear grin.

Then they were off. The January freeze had loosened its grip, so the *Cape Ray* started its diesels and left Portsmouth harbor with a moderate southwesterly breeze at its stern. Jordan extended the ship's stabilizer fins to smooth out the bumps, and the crews sat down for a pancake breakfast as the ship headed east to catch the Gulf Stream.

Jordan had received an important letter just before the departure, and he took advantage of the relative quiet to share it with others. It was a personal note from Defense Secretary Chuck Hagel, addressed to "Captain Jordan and the crew of the MV Cape Ray."

"You are about to accomplish something no one has tried," Hagel wrote. "You will be destroying at sea one of the world's largest stockpiles of chemical weapons and helping make a safer world."

Hagel acknowledged the mission's difficulty and its many risks, but said: "You are ready."

"Take care of yourselves," he wrote. "God bless you all."

13

"A perfect loophole"

KAFR ZITA, SYRIA. APRIL 2014

We've been spotted.

Houssam Alnahhas watched the helicopter nervously from his car seat, not yet sure if he should be worried. For a time the pilot seemed to wander aimlessly, cutting lazy circles over the rooftops of the farming village Kafr Zita, as though looking for something. Now the chopper was almost directly overhead, trailing the car in which the young doctor known as "Chemical Hazem" was traveling. It was midafternoon and the vehicle was moving on a narrow lane just outside the town, flanked only by empty fields and olive groves. There were no other possible targets in sight.

No doubt about it: the helicopter was coming for them.

Alnahhas glanced at his two companions, a pharmacist and another doctor, both of them looking equally grave. The thrumming of the chopper's engine was growing steadily louder, even through rolled-up car windows.

"This is for us," Alnahhas said quietly.

The three men sat upright in their seats, waiting. Alnahhas's thoughts turned briefly to his family back in Damascus. He thought of his mother. Yasmin, the girl from the Aleppo hospital, who was now his fiancée. He thought about the sealed bags hidden in the ice chest in the back of the car, and of the precious evidence inside them—evidence that he had risked his life to obtain.

The car was still moving, now in the very shadow of the helicopter overhead. As he tried to contemplate what would happen next, a new thought flashed through Alnahhas's brain:

Was it worth it?

It was crazy to think that Bashar al-Assad would use chemical weapons again. The leader of Syria would not be so foolish—especially now, with teams of international experts actively roaming the country—as to commit an act that might again put his government in peril. But Alnahhas had remained convinced that it would eventually happen. The war's momentum had unexpectedly shifted in the rebels' favor; Assad would surely find clever new ways to break the opposition's morale and terrorize their families.

Eight months after the last big chemical attack, the young physician had become one of his country's most vocal advocates for preparing for the next one. His training classes for medical workers had expanded into an education task force and early warning network that operated out of a hospital on the Turkish border and extended deep into the Syrian countryside. But interest and funding were running out, and so were the justifications for keeping the program going.

"There *is* no more sarin," a doctor friend argued one day. "We have other problems to deal with. Why spend more money preparing for something that's already gone?"

But just as Alnahhas predicted, shifting fortunes in the war prompted a return to old behaviors. From the countryside north of the city of Hama came reports about a new kind of barrel bomb loaded with toxic chemicals instead of the usual explosives. In the village of Kafr Zita, someone had captured the attack on cell-phone video. It depicted an explosion and a cloud of yellow-green smoke that smelled like bleach and drifted along the ground like valley fog. More than one hundred people in the cloud's path were immediately sickened, and three later died.

Yellow-green smoke? Was Assad now using chlorine, the common industrial chemical used in water-treatment plants and swimming pools? Alnahhas talked it over with two hospital friends. Why not find out for themselves?

"Here's our chance," Alnahhas said. "Let's go there."

He was still organizing the trip when news arrived of a similar attack in the village of Talmenes, about thirty miles from Kafr Zita. This time some of the victims turned up at Alnahhas's own hospital. Seizing the chance to get started with their investigation, the three friends began collecting evidence—hair and blood samples as well as stories: one account after another of a sickening gas that smelled like strong bleach.

One question remained: How could he find physical proof at the sites themselves? It is commonly known that chlorine dissipates quickly. It is detectable for a few hours, or perhaps a day or two, and then vanishes. Where might traces of the gas still linger after an attack, and how could he preserve the evidence if he found it?

Alnahhas made several calls to overseas experts for advice. Eventually he connected with a retired British army colonel who was willing and able to help. Hamish de Bretton-Gordon knew something about defending against a chemical attack, having commanded WMD response units in the United Kingdom and in NATO. By chance, he and Alnahhas had crossed paths: after leaving the army in 2011, de Bretton-Gordon had served for a time as an adviser to relief organizations in Syria. He had briefly worked as an instructor, offering guidance to Alnahhas and the group he founded on how to prepare for a chemical attack.

The young doctor reached the retired officer at his home in southwest England. Of course he would help, de Bretton-Gordon said. In fact, the colonel even offered to travel to Turkey to help test any of the evidence Alnahhas happened to find.

De Bretton-Gordon had been following the strange reports of new chemical attacks in Syria, and he had a theory. If Assad was indeed using chlorine as a weapon, the colonel reasoned, then Syria was playing a cruel and cynical game. Assad was making a public show of giving up his arsenal of deadly nerve agents, but his soldiers had merely switched to a different kind of poison gas—this one a common industrial chemical that Syria was legally permitted to possess.

Chlorine is far less deadly than sarin, but it can be a weapon of terror just the same. It was the first lethal chemical weapon used by European armies in the trenches of World War I, before the discovery of frightful new substances such as mustard gas. Later, the drafters of chemical weapons treaties decided against including chlorine on their lists of banned substances, since it was impractical to ask countries to get rid of it. The use of any "asphyxiating" gas as a weapon was technically illegal, but no modern army had contemplated using chlorine on the battlefield in nearly a century. For Assad, though, the intended targets were not trenchworks or infantrymen. They were apartment buildings and bomb shelters filled with civilians. To be successful, the attack need not kill everyone. It just had to generate enough victims to cause panic and clear out rebel neighborhoods so Syrian troops could move in.

"It's brilliant," de Bretton-Gordon said. "Low-casualty, but psychologically effective."

The Syrians had found a perfect loophole. No one had asked Assad to give up his chlorine, and he had plenty of it, including thousands of canisters of Chinese-made stuff purchased from legitimate suppliers. If chlorine killed fewer people, it was actually a good thing. Fewer casualties meant fewer images of dead and dying children creating a spectacle on social media. Moreover, chlorine's rapid degradation would make it harder to prove that the chemical was ever used.

But evidence could be found, if a trained specialist managed to get to the crime scene quickly enough, and with the right tools. Anyone attempting to do so in this case would have to cross disputed terrain, patrolled by government helicopters, snipers, Islamist militants, and armed gangs.

Alnahhas was willing to risk it. On a morning in mid-April, he and his two friends met in southern Turkey and climbed into a car with an ice chest they had packed with empty laboratory vials and plastic bags. Then they drove into Syria to see what they could find.

The first to die had been the birds: the chickens and pigeons in their roosts, but also wild swallows and sparrows that were caught in the path of the poison cloud and fell to the ground in clumps of two or three. Next came the smaller mammals, the goats, sheep, and feral cats that lasted a few minutes or perhaps up to an hour. One family's cow lingered for eight hours, wheezing pitifully as she slowly drowned from a buildup of fluid in her lungs.

Alnahhas took photos of the animals, and of the ugly red gouge in the earth where a barrel bomb had landed just behind a farmer's house in Talmenes. He took a deep breath. The faint odor of bleach was still detectable a day after the attack.

The owner of the house had been taken to Alnahhas's hospital for treatment, so the young doctor had already recorded his story before starting his trip. The farmer had been home on the day of the attack, caring for his invalid wife and several grandchildren, when they heard the passing helicopter, followed by a whistling sound, like that of a falling bomb. But instead of an explosion there had been only a jarring thud. He tried to calm his family, telling them that the bomb had missed them.

"It was far away from us, so don't worry," the man said.

But then came an overpowering chemical smell, and the grandchildren began to cough and choke. In a panic, he rushed them into the bathroom, closed the door, and turned on the shower, forcing each child to stand under the water in the hope that it would dilute the effects of whatever poison they were breathing. Having accomplished that, he ran to help his wife, who was sixty-five and too frail to move on her own. The woman was struggling as though someone was suffocating her. By the time the family arrived at the local clinic, she was unconscious. Later, Alnahhas learned, the woman died.

Alnahhas left the farmer's house and continued to trace the cloud's path eastward. Where the chlorine plume had passed, there was a dead wake of scorched and shriveled plants, corroded metal, and strangely discolored fabrics. Eventually the trail led to a culvert in a nearby olive grove where families sometimes sought shelter during air raids. The poison had settled in this low spot, and two young children who were hiding there with their families became gravely ill from the fumes. Both later died.

In each of the stricken towns, Alnahhas and his friends easily found the remnants of the bombs themselves. Using the specimen kits they brought from Turkey, they recorded the exact locations with GPS equipment and scooped up metal fragments and a few tablespoons of soil, placing each sample in a separate plastic bag inside the ice chest. The steel tanks that held the poison were ripped open but mostly intact. Still visible on each were three characters engraved on the side of the metal casing: *CL2*. It was the chemical symbol for chlorine gas.

Alnahhas had arranged visits to medical clinics in both towns to collect statements and additional biological samples from health-care workers there. It was at the Kafr Zita hospital that Alnahhas first noticed the helicopter circling overhead. The doctor he had been interviewing at the time noticed it, too. Everyone became nervous, so the visit was cut short, and the three visitors returned to their car to begin the trek north.

If the helicopter was looking for something, it seemed to have found it. As Alnahhas's vehicle turned to head away from the village, the chopper did the same. Within minutes it was clear the pilot was following them, hovering just behind the car and matching its speed. But why? Alnahhas's mind raced through the events of the day. It had been impossible to collect evidence in secret, so there were ample opportunities for the regime's spies to spot three strangers taking photographs and picking up bomb fragments. In Kafr Zita they had been so close to the front lines at Hama that someone with binoculars could have watched them from the other side. It was easy to imagine how the three had been betrayed, just as it was easy now to imagine the helicopter gunner, somewhere above them, lining up his sights and preparing to pull the trigger.

But no shots were fired. A few excruciating moments passed, and then the helicopter simply veered away. Soon the car was alone on the narrow lane. One danger had passed, but snipers waited in the hills ahead. The driver hit the gas and the car roared through the olive trees, heading north.

Near the Turkish frontier, the three friends separated. According to the prearranged plan, Alnahhas, carrying the samples, crossed into Turkey alone near the city of Gaziantep. At the border, he thought again about the activist who had been snatched from his car in 2013 and shot dead in the street while transporting the same kind of evidence that Alnahhas now carried with him. But this crossing was uneventful, and no one bothered even to glance at the bulky ice chest. For the first time, Alnahhas allowed himself to relax. It had been one of the most frightening days he could remember, but he had made it.

"This is one of the best things I've done in my whole life," he thought.

Alnahhas sent a text message to de Bretton-Gordon to let him know of his success, and the next day the retired colonel was in a Gaziantep hotel waiting for him. The Englishman had brought along some equipment, and the two set up a testing station on the hotel's rooftop, while a journalist for the British newspaper *The Telegraph* looked on. De Bretton-Gordon slipped on plastic coveralls, gloves, and a mask and picked up the first of the sealed bags from the cooler. Inside was a plastic specimen cup containing a few grams of powdery soil Alnahhas had scooped from inside one of the impact craters at Kafr Zita.

After checking the wind direction, de Bretton-Gordon placed the cup inside a clear plastic bag that also contained a handheld detector. With gloved hands he opened the vial and waited a few seconds to allow the air trapped inside the container to mix with the clean air inside the bag. As he watched, the numbers on the detector's screen began to rise.

CL 0.3 ppm, it said. Three days after the attack, the tainted soil was still giving off measurable levels of the gas.

"We have found evidence of chlorine," de Bretton-Gordon announced.

But the few bags of soil tested on a hotel rooftop represented only a fraction of Alnahhas's trove. The young doctor carried other samples by car to Ankara, the Turkish capital, where European and American officials quietly accepted them for their own laboratory analysis. He transferred gigabytes of data—videotaped statements, photographs, lab reports—to a representative of the international chemical weapons watchdog, the OPCW. His offer of soil samples from the impact craters was politely declined; however careful he may have been, Alnahhas was regarded as an activist, and the OPCW could not rule out the possibility of tampering.

But the OPCW was facing growing international pressure to launch an independent investigation of multiple claims of chlorine bombs falling on villages in northern Syria. In May, its inspectors retraced Alnahhas's path to Kafr Zita, and in September, relying on video recordings, medical reports, and eyewitness testimony as the primary evidence, they released a report echoing his findings, concluding that the town had been struck by a pair of chlorine bombs. But the OPCW—like Åke Sellström's team before it—was barred from rendering a conclusion regarding who committed the crime.

—

For the Obama administration's top diplomat at the United Nations, each new chlorine attack was a screaming reminder of failure in Syria. Samantha Power kept close tabs on Assad's attempt at improvised chemical warfare and complained bitterly in private meetings at the White House and with UN colleagues in New York. If no one could act to stop the killings in Syria, she argued, then there should at least be accountability—justice, in some form, for the victims.

What Power wanted most was war-crimes charges brought against Assad in the International Criminal Court in The Hague, and she began to advocate for such a move. As always in diplomatic affairs, it was complicated. Syria was not a party to the statute that created the tribunal, so Assad could be referred to the ICC only by a decision of the UN Security Council. And Russia would always stand ready with its veto to prevent that from happening.

Then, in April 2014, amid news of the chlorine attacks, France began circulating a draft resolution calling for prosecution of Syria at The Hague on war-crimes charges, and Power threw her support behind the measure. It was always a long shot, and as the day for the formal vote drew closer, Russia's delegation warned other council members that it would not allow the measure to advance.

Power was undeterred; debating the doomed measure before the Security Council would at least offer an opportunity to shame the Russians publicly.

"This is a chance to get trained legal professionals to do forensic analysis," Power said. Russian officials constantly claimed at UN meetings that rebels were behind the chemical attacks, and so here was a chance to prove "beyond a reasonable doubt who's the perpetrator of these crimes," she said.

She decided to enlist a Syrian refugee to help her make the case for criminal charges. She found the perfect candidate, an articulate twenty-eight-year-old who had survived the sarin attack at Ghouta. It was Kassem Eid, who had assisted Åke Sellström's investigation of the attack and was now in the United States on a temporary visa.

Since the events in Ghouta, Eid had become something of a public figure. With his English skills and earnest manner, he had become an unofficial spokesman for the Syrian opposition, giving hundreds of interviews describing the plight of ordinary citizens in the besieged Damascus suburbs. He created a blog under the nom de guerre Qusai

Zakarya, and in November 2013 he went on a public hunger strike in which he posted daily video of himself on Skype as his body gradually weakened. On Christmas Day, the thirtieth day of his fast, leaders in his hometown of Moadamiyeh signed a truce that ended open resistance to the Syrian government. Eid was briefly detained and interrogated, and then, to his astonishment—and perhaps owing to his international celebrity—he was allowed to escape to Lebanon. With help from friends he purchased a plane ticket, and in March 2014 he landed at Dulles International Airport outside Washington, D.C., a place he knew only from movies and magazine articles.

Eid was instantly embraced by Syrian-American activists who made him a sought-after speaker at rallies and fundraisers, and even arranged for him to visit Washington to meet with policy experts at the State Department. Then, in May, he received a surprising message from the office of the U.S. mission to the United Nations in New York. It was Power, asking if the young Syrian would be her personal guest at a UN debate over possible war-crimes charges against Assad.

Eid agreed. On May 22, he walked into the famous chamber wearing a T-shirt featuring a two-finger "peace symbol" painted with the red, green, and white colors of the Syrian flag. He sat in the auditorium a few yards from Syria's UN ambassador, Bashar Jaafari, and watched the proceedings with a mixture of fascination and unease. A resolution calling for accountability for Assad was read aloud, and a vote was called. In a show of hands, the measure won overwhelming support, with a vote of 13–2. Yet it still lost. The two opponents, Russia and China, used their veto votes to kill the resolution.

Everyone knew that the outcome was preordained, but Power did all she could to make the occasion as excruciating as possible for the Russian delegation. She asked Eid to stand, and when he did, she read aloud from the Syrian man's own written account of his experiences during the ordeal in Ghouta, from the searing pain to the desperation he felt in trying to rescue the young boy he found lying in the street.

"Qusai's account of his experience in Moadamiyeh deserves to be heard," Power said, using Eid's nom de guerre. "It deserves to be examined by an independent court and, if crimes are proven, those responsible deserve to be held accountable. The vetoes cast today prevent that from happening."

Eid stood quietly through the speech. As grateful as he was for his words to be heard, he also found himself repelled by what he was witnessing. With a simple raise of the hand, Russia had been able to flick away any talk of accountability for the man who had killed so many of his neighbors and friends. Western countries protested, but their words alone would do nothing to end the suffering of ordinary Syrians.

"In that moment I really wanted to scream and say, 'Screw all of you—the whole world,'" he would later say. "It all seemed like a political game. Just one fancy, dressed-up person after another saying, 'We're sorry. We're helping. We're sending aid.'"

Power could sense the young man's ambivalence. She knew that Eid's anger was not limited to his own country's president. He also blamed the United States, and President Obama specifically, for failing to launch a military strike after the August 2013 attack that killed so many of his neighbors. Watching Eid as he stood silent before the Security Council in his T-shirt and jeans was as moving as anything Power had experienced since accepting the job in New York.

"The debates can seem clinical, but here was someone who had suffered, right there, looking at you," Power said. "At that moment you could really feel the stakes of the veto. You were vetoing his truth. His story."

There would be no accountability for Assad on this day. But Power was not about to give up.

14

Race to the Coast

ROTA, SPAIN. JUNE 4, 2014

For a man whose port window overlooked a Mediterranean paradise, Tim Blades was about as miserable as a human can be. The sunny beaches and golf courses of Rota, Spain, had bedazzled the *Cape Ray*'s crew after their chilly Atlantic crossing in late January, but that was seventeen weeks ago. Now each day's main preoccupation was identical to that of the day before: a tedious wait for news from Syria about when their mission would actually begin.

"Freakin' Groundhog Day," Blades spluttered to the *Cape Ray*'s captain, Rick Jordan, referring to the 1993 Bill Murray movie in which the lead character is doomed to relive the same day for eternity.

"It's a slam dunk we will be here at least another week," replied Jordan, who, despite his captain's accommodations and command perks, was just as frustrated as everyone else. "My best advice is to scream and kick now."

On this June morning, the reports were grim. For a brief period in early spring, the logjam over the movement of Syrian chemicals appeared to have broken, and a long procession of trucks hauling binary sarin and sulfur mustard began making its way to the port at Latakia. During those weeks, more than 90 percent of Syria's liquid stockpile was rushed to the docks and loaded onto the Danish and Norwegian ships. But then, just as suddenly, everything shut down again.

This time, it was the war that intervened. After months of bitter fighting in a mountainous region called Qalamoun, the Syrians and their Iranian allies had driven the rebels from a key stronghold and supply hub along the Lebanese border. Thousands of fighters, many of them members of Islamist brigades, streamed south to take up new positions in the rugged terrain west of Damascus. In their retreat, the militants overran one Syrian military base along the major M2 Highway, and completely surrounded a second one a few miles away. The first base had been cleared of chemical weapons a few weeks before the rebels arrived. The second one, called Sayqal, still held thousands of gallons of ready-to-mix binary sarin. It was the last known repository of nerve agents in the country, and now those weapons were effectively marooned. No trucks could approach the base because heavily armed Islamist fighters controlled the only access road.

Syria could not be declared free of chemical weapons until this last stash was cleared out. Until then, everything and everyone was in a state of suspended animation: the Syrian drivers in their newly armored trucks; Sigrid Kaag and her weapons inspectors, stuck in their Damascus hotel; the Danish and Norwegian naval crews, spinning circles in the eastern Mediterranean with cargo holds stacked to the roof with deadly chemicals; and the men of the *Cape Ray,* stranded in a Spanish naval town some 2,400 miles away, with little to do but wait and speculate gloomily about when they might get home again.

"The next time you see Maryland, the leaves will have changed," Jordan wrote to Blades in an email from his cabin.

"I'm as sad as my poor dog Buck," Blades replied.

The weeks in Rota had not been entirely idle. Jordan's ship hands—those who had not yet bailed out after their initial contracts expired—stayed busy cleaning decks, preparing food, and keeping the boat's twin diesel engines in running order. During off-hours they binged on the TV shows they had downloaded before the crossing—every episode of *Breaking Bad* and *Game of Thrones* was screened and rescreened in the break room—or took long walks along Rota's ten miles of white-sand beaches. When fresh provisions began to run low, the galley crew went scavenging for local eggs, milk, and vegetables. One such expedition netted sacks of Brussels sprouts, which would later become a source of alarm when someone remembered from training that DF, the sarin precursor, gave off an odor similar to roasted sprouts.

Blades's teams meanwhile put themselves through endless drills. They practiced cleaning up spills and putting out fires, and occasionally they switched on the pumps and generators for a full-blown test of the hydrolysis system. Since there still were no chemical weapons on the ship, they ran ordinary seawater through the Margarita Machine's hoses and pipes and collected the treated final product in tanks on the other side. ("Destroyed 1,279 gallons of water today," the night shift's supervisor noted dryly in his report on the day's exercises.)

More substantial issues emerged as the men waited. Blades learned to his chagrin that the tanks of toxic chemicals arriving at the Syrian port were slightly larger than the standard shipping containers he had expected. The difference per tank was small, but multiplied hundreds of times, it meant he had to rework all his calculations and rethink where to store all the liquid waste that would be created when his machines were running. The decks on the *Cape Ray* already were nearly full, and now he would have to find more room, somewhere.

Of potentially greater consequence were reports of a burgeoning protest movement targeting the ship itself. Pentagon officials had anticipated that environmental groups might object to the notion of destroying chemical weapons at sea, and Major General Jay Santee had tried to head off confrontations by inviting environmentalists and reporters to visit the ship and meet with the scientists and engineers behind the hydrolysis system. Still, opposition to the destruction plan was building in southern Europe, where Greek and Italian chapters of Greenpeace were beginning to mobilize to try to stop the *Cape Ray*. There was little for the ship's crew to do about it, but Jordan issued stern warnings to his mariners to avoid mentioning anything about the boat or its location on social media. "Loose tweets sink fleets," he wrote in an all-hands posting.

But the biggest adversary was the calendar. They were now starting their fifth month on the *Cape Ray*. The delays were no longer merely frustrating; they now posed a serious risk to the mission itself, as Blades saw it. Forget the United Nations' June 30 deadline for destroying Syria's stockpile. Of bigger practical concern now was the

June 28 start of the Muslim holy season of Ramadan, when the pace of work slows as faithful Muslims begin a month of fasting. If the last of the chemicals were not gone by then, it could be August or later before anything moved, Blades wrote in an email to one of his superiors in early June.

"Many of the original ship's crew have left and been replaced. Many of the military guys have left and been replaced. We continue to burn time, money, people, and good weather while we wait," he wrote. He would not ask his men to remain idle in Rota indefinitely, and if he sent them home, he said, "most folks will not want to come back."

In his reports to headquarters, Blades made at least a pretense of politeness. With crewmates he was less genteel.

"If we don't sail soon," he snapped one morning, "I'm gonna end up causing total mayhem."

A major focus of Blades's frustration was the decision to delay the destruction of any of the Syrian chemicals until the entire arsenal had been safely removed from the country. The policy had been set by the White House, and there was a clear logic behind it. For one thing, U.S. officials were intensely fearful that Syria might stop cooperating before the job was done. If the *Cape Ray* began destroying the chemicals that were already out of the country, Assad might decide that a 90 percent success was good enough. Syria would be left with a small but potent stockpile that would remain vulnerable to misuse or theft, and the West would have lost the leverage needed to force Damascus to surrender the remaining 10 percent. The other reason was purely practical: the United Nations was negotiating with Italy about the possible use of one of its southern harbors as the transshipment point, where barrels of liquid poisons could be moved from the Danish cargo ship *Ark Futura* to the *Cape Ray*. Getting the Italians to say yes on a single transfer of chemicals on their soil was proving to be extremely difficult. Multiple transshipments over several weeks were almost certainly out of the question.

Blades was beyond caring about the choreography of how the final barrels would be moved. The far greater danger, in his view, was the possible collapse of the program, which would mean that none of the chemicals would be destroyed. At that moment, there were grave doubts about whether the *Taiko*—one of the two cargo ships in the Danish-led convoy authorized to take on Syrian chemicals—could finish the task. An old vessel that was headed for the scrapyard later that summer, the *Taiko* could not legally operate at sea after June 30. Like its sister ship, the *Ark Futura,* its cargo decks already were nearly full, yet it could not discharge its load until the mission was over. Danish Commodore Torben Mikkelsen faced the prospect of having to return the *Taiko*'s entire haul to Latakia and scramble to find another cargo ship to take its place.

In emails and video conference calls, Blades pressed the Pentagon to reconsider its "100-percent" policy, but the reply was always the same: any deviation from the rule would have to come from the White House. And the White House wasn't budging.

Blades was disappointed but not entirely surprised. In his world, politicians always had the final say. Over his thirty years in government, there had been many moments when political considerations won out over the judgment of the technical professionals. At times, the results had been outright disastrous.

His early career was a series of jobs cleaning up the messes from the bad decisions of previous administrations. In the 1950s and '60s, political expediency had led to the wholesale dumping of U.S.-made chemical weapons in the ocean off Baltimore, and in swamps and creek beds around Edgewood, Maryland. The costs ultimately included an expensive, decades-long cleanup and criminal charges for a few of the decision-makers.

Years later, he watched in disbelief as the Clinton administration appeared to pick a fight with Iraq over that country's faltering cooperation with UN weapons investigators following the 1991 Gulf War. By the late 1990s, Blades had spent the equivalent of several years inside Iraq helping destroy old chemical munitions while pressing Iraqi scientists to fully account for their past weapons research. Occasionally the work would bog down for political or technical reasons, but Blades believed he had won the trust of his Iraqi counterparts and was making progress. It all ended in 1998 with Operation Desert Fox, when the United States led an international bombing campaign to punish Iraq for blocking access to certain suspected weapons sites. As a result of the air strikes, the weapons investigations were halted altogether.

"That's bull!" Blades yelled aloud at his TV when news broke of a wave of strikes against Iraq that December. "This wasn't driven by the UN. It was the politics of the United States!"

But his most profound disillusionment came five years later as a different U.S. administration was preparing to launch a military campaign against Iraq. The George W. Bush White House cited Iraq's weapons of mass destruction as one of the reasons for war, and in the months preceding the 2003 invasion, Blades found himself in meetings with intelligence experts discussing what passed for official evidence of a secret Iraqi WMD program. As one of only a few American experts with recent experience inside Iraq, Blades was asked to look at photographs of suspicious buildings and offer his opinion. Might these be secret weapons factories?

As it turned out, Blades had spent many hours inside each one of the facilities in the photographs, and he knew them intimately.

"Umm. No," he replied.

After that, Blades was no longer invited to the meetings. Weeks later, in February 2003, he again found himself staring at his TV in amazement as Secretary of State Colin Powell made the case for invasion before the UN Security Council. As a prime piece of evidence for a secret WMD program, Powell displayed an illustration of a strange-looking vehicle that was said to be an Iraqi mobile biological weapons laboratory. Blades had seen such vehicles during his time in Iraq. They were not weapons labs.

They fill helium balloons with those things, Blades thought to himself. *I can see where this is going, and there's nothing I can do about it.*

Months after the invasion, when the hunt for Iraq's elusive weapons was finally abandoned, Pentagon officials acknowledged the mistake. A talented, if unscrupulous, Iraqi informant had led the entire U.S. intelligence establishment astray. In fact, the strange vehicle in the diagram was designed for pumping helium into weather balloons, not for mixing anthrax bacteria for bombs.

Such experiences did little to abate Blades's natural cynicism, but they did make him less bashful about voicing his opinion, on matters large and small. While in Spain, for example, he harangued his bosses constantly over their refusal to allow his men to take short home breaks during the long weeks of waiting for the mission to start. The Defense Department insisted that the *Cape Ray* be fully manned at all times as a subtle means of keeping up the pressure on Assad. Blades thought the restriction was ridiculous, and one afternoon in mid-May he unloaded on the Pentagon's Andrew Weber in an angry phone call that could be heard from several cabins away.

"I can't keep them here if they're volunteers!" Blades shouted.

Weber was equally exasperated, and at one point retorted, "Who can tell you that they've got to stay?"

Blades paused for a moment. "You know, you've got a good point." He hung up the phone and then rang his assistant back in Maryland. "We're coming home," he said. Over the Pentagon's vehement objections, everyone on the Edgewood team got a plane ticket and a stretch of home leave ranging from a few days to two weeks.

Then they were back on the ship again, to find that nothing had changed during their absence. In Syria, the trucks sat idle, the weapons remained in their bunkers, and there was no sign anywhere of a change that would bring the mission to its conclusion.

Groundhog Day, Blades thought.

Another problem loomed for the *Cape Ray*'s crew members, one that was discussed only in hushed tones and restricted conversations. Some of Syria's chemical containers were leaking.

The flaw was discovered in April when a new shipment of DF—the precursor for sarin—arrived by truck at the port of Latakia. When Danish technicians screened the incoming cargo for harmful vapors, their handheld detectors began to squawk. Peering inside one of the Syrian semitrailers, the inspectors saw a tiny puddle on the trailer bed. A search of a second trailer produced the same result.

The leaks were attributed to a combination of heat—the hotter temperatures of the Mediterranean spring were causing pressure to rise inside the tanks—and faulty valves deemed liable to sudden failure. Syrians and Danes scrambled to find a solution, and within hours they had cleaned the spill and replaced the bad valves, wrapping them in Teflon tape as an additional precaution. The tanks were loaded onto the *Ark Futura,* but within days it was clear that other containers had problems as well. The conditions aboard the ship were not helping matters. Between the warming temperatures and the constant jostling and pitching of the ship, there was a growing risk of a catastrophic valve failure that could send liquid poisons gushing onto the ship's decks.

With one of his deputies, Blades arranged a visit to the fleet. Climbing onto the *Ark Futura,* Blades was able, for the first and only time during the mission, to make out the gray outlines of Syria just off the ship's bow.

On board, the visitors were struck by the fitness regimen of a Danish special-forces operator who happened to be training as they arrived. Wearing combat boots, running shorts, and a gas mask, the man ran up five flights of stairs, circled the deck, trotted downstairs, and then repeated the cycle again and again, pausing occasionally to squeeze out a set of chin-ups with a large barbell plate strapped to a chain around his neck. Blades and his deputy exchanged appreciative looks. No one would be stealing chemical weapons from *this* ship.

The Americans conducted a detailed examination of two of the Syrian tanks, scrutinizing the troublesome valves, making measurements, and taking photos. On one tank they could see corrosion in places where liquid had previously seeped through tiny openings in the exterior plumbing. The tank was old and likely nearing the end of its life span. Blades and his deputy dabbed a waxy coating over the valves to give them an additional seal. That was all they could do for now, so they thanked their hosts and prepared to return to the *Cape Ray.* As they left the ship hours later, Blade caught a glimpse of the Danish commando, still in his combat boots and gas mask, still running.

Back in his cabin, Blades mulled what had been learned. Age and corrosion were not the only problems. The ship's technicians had concluded, based on the pictures and measurements, that the location and fragility of the fixtures on the tanks made them susceptible to being sheared off during handling and transport. To the list of dozens of things that could potentially go wrong, the visit added one more.

The sudden military crisis that blocked the flow of chemical weapons to Latakia in the spring of 2014 occurred at a place so remote that most Syrian maps didn't mention it. There were no towns or settlements anywhere nearby, just a small military base with a pair of runways and a few aircraft hangars, surrounded by mile after mile of empty sand. Located off Highway 2, about halfway between Damascus and the Iraqi border, it was known to locals as Sayqal, or by its geographic name al-Sin, while Joint Mission maps designated it simply as "Site Two."

Site Two was flagged by the weapons inspectors as particularly important early on because it held an assortment of the deadliest materials in Syria's arsenal, including the ingredients for both binary sarin and VX. It contained nearly six thousand gallons of the sarin precursor DF, enough to fill a small swimming pool. One of the Joint Mission teams had toured the base briefly in October and taken an inventory, but that was before the facility had come under siege by a large Islamist army.

The Islamist militants had poured out of the mountains in early April, then regrouped to organize an offensive that routed Assad's troops across a broad front east of the capital. The dominant group in this mix of retreating militias was known as the Islamic Front. Its fighters overran the chemical weapons facility, near the town of Ad-Dumayr, that had been emptied out just a few weeks earlier under the supervision of international inspectors.

The rebel force pushed on and reached Sayqal. Site Two at that point was under the control of a small garrison of government troops left to defend its handful of Soviet-made fighter jets and very large quantity of chemical weapons. The rebels' attack was repelled, but the Islamists surrounded the base and settled in to prepare for a new assault.

At no time during Syria's civil war had an Islamist army come so close to taking control of a cache of nerve agents. Intelligence officials watched the developments warily, while diplomats and military experts tried to downplay the risks in interviews with journalists. If the attackers succeeded in taking the base, the experts speculated, they probably lacked the skill needed to combine the binary components without hurting themselves. But such pronouncements were less than reassuring.

"They [could] move it out or sell it," one diplomat conceded.

On many occasions over the past eight months, Syrian officials had blamed security concerns for their inability to grant access to facilities, or for the slow pace of the shipments of chemicals winding their way to the port at Latakia. Often the claims sounded less than genuine, prompting complaints from weapons inspectors that the Assad government was merely stalling.

This time, the security problem was all too real.

Back in Damascus, Sigrid Kaag and other Joint Mission officials shuttled between offices trying to engage Syrian officials in discussions over how to get the Site Two chemicals out of harm's way. Suggestions of an air evacuation of the chemicals were floated but quickly rejected; diplomats on both sides worried that a crash—whether accidental or by hostile fire—could result in an unthinkable calamity if the plane and its toxic cargo went down in a populated area. Then OPCW experts in The Hague prepared a matrix of emergency procedures that could be used if the base was at imminent risk of being overrun. Chemicals could be dumped or burned in a real crisis, though this was "NOT a particularly safe or environmentally friendly option" and was probably against rules of the Chemical Weapons Convention, the OPCW report said. There also were chemical concoctions on the market that could turn sarin precursors into a thick gel that would no longer be effective as a weapon.

The Syrians were not interested. On May 14, Kaag and her deputies sat with Hassan al-Sharif—the brigadier was now a newly minted major general—to plead their case, only to be met with firm refusals. "Sharif reemphasized that [Syria] will not consider airlifting any chemicals" and would not attempt to destroy them. Refusing to be rushed, the Syrians insisted that the chemicals eventually "will be moved using ground transport" when the roads were deemed safe. When and how that would happen was anyone's guess.

In early June, Kaag flew to New York to brief the UN Security Council on the standoff. There, she acknowledged Syria's legitimate concerns about what she called the "very volatile" situation at Sayqal. But she also made clear that the disarmament effort had reached a crisis point. Kaag had already given up hope of meeting the June 30 deadline for destroying the arsenal, and now other parts of the mission were at risk of falling apart. With little to do, many of the weapons inspectors on her staff had opted to return home, and only eight remained in Damascus. One of the two Scandinavian cargo ships in the eastern Mediterranean was preparing to head home, and the Danes were threatening to disband their maritime operation altogether if the situation remained frozen. In three weeks, Ramadan would begin.

"The deadline will not be met," Kaag said. "What is important, however, is that all the materials are brought out of harm's way [so] that destruction can start as soon as possible."

Even as she was speaking, the Syrian government's prospects in eastern Syria were beginning to brighten. On the day Kaag flew to New York, loyalist troops regained control of the two abandoned chemical weapons facilities, then began driving the Islamist rebels from their defensive lines near Sayqal. Military vehicles reappeared on the M2 highway, moving east. Yet Sharif, when pressed, refused to commit to moving any chemicals from Sayqal.

"Too much risk," Kaag was told.

"We know our obligations, and we'll do it our way, when we're good and ready," one inspector said, summarizing the prevailing view among the Syrians in late spring.

Kaag, more than ever, found herself in the center of the storm. Western leaders wanted to enlist her team in the investigation of the chlorine attacks, now occurring with alarming regularity in the countryside. Intelligence agencies from several governments—including the Americans, the British, and the Israelis—approached her deputies with alarming evidence of possible hidden weapons caches. There were photographs of suspicious storage facilities in the mountains near the military seaport at Tartus, and credible reports of ongoing chemical weapons research at the Damascus research complex known as CERS.

But Kaag would be not be distracted. While the issues were important, they were properly the domain of other agencies and different teams of investigators. Kaag had one mission—to oversee the removal and destruction of Syria's declared weapons stockpile—and she would see it through. And then the inspectors would go home.

"We will work within the parameters of what we've been asked to do," she said.

Even so, overcoming the last hurdle pushed Kaag's diplomatic skills to the limit. Until now she had been careful to avoid directly criticizing the Syrians in public settings, but it was time to present Sharif and his bosses with what amounted to an ultimatum. One version was delivered in private, and the other in a closed session of the OPCW's Executive Council in The Hague, with diplomats from Syria, Russia, and dozens of other countries looking on.

"It's now or never," Kaag said in the private session. "The excuses have to stop." If the weapons weren't removed by the end of June, she would have no choice but to report the failure to the Security Council and place the blame on Syria and its president.

At The Hague, her words were more formal, but the message was the same.

"It is no longer sufficient," she said at the June 17 meeting, "for Syria to point to security problems to explain their failure to remove the remaining chemicals."

Three days after the meeting in The Hague, Sharif informed Kaag's team that Site Two's chemicals were finally coming out.

Kaag relayed the news of the possible breakthrough to OPCW headquarters, and Director General Ahmet Üzümcü personally alerted the Danes and other key participants to the details. The operation was to take place amid heavy secrecy to minimize the chances of an attack, but word quickly spread to U.S. diplomats in a June 20 email under the subject line "URGENT."

"The removal of the chemicals from Site Two will take place on Monday, June 30 and Tuesday, July 1. There is to be one convoy with eight containers each day," the note said. The chemicals would be brought to a temporary holding facility in Damascus, then "properly packed and then moved to Latakia," it said.

The email was wrong. By the time it was written, a small convoy of trucks with distinctive armored jackets had already arrived at Sayqal to pick up a load of chemicals. The Syrians started the work without bothering to tell anyone, and they were moving quickly. The next day—a Saturday, June 21—the first batch of weapons was already heading east.

Kaag's team dashed off a secure cable to OPCW headquarters with the news.

The sudden departure prompted a wild scramble as weapons inspectors and maritime crews rushed through preparations to receive the weapons. Syria dispatched a second convoy to Sayqal hours after the first one had departed, and by early Sunday, the air base that held the last and worst elements of Assad's chemical arsenal was officially empty.

The Danish ship *Ark Futura* had set sail for Latakia overnight, and by eleven o'clock Sunday morning the big freighter was steaming into the harbor for the final pickup. That same morning, after some last-minute repacking and checks for leaks, the first four trucks carrying the contents of Sayqal's bunkers roared out of the Damascus compound and barreled north toward the port city under heavy guard. By Sunday afternoon, the bulk of the chemicals, including some six thousand gallons of binary sarin ingredients, sat in semitrailers lined up along one of Latakia's concrete wharfs. The rest would arrive the following morning.

That day was Monday, June 23. It was five days before the start of Ramadan and just a week before the final deadline for eliminating the Syrian stockpile.

The timing of the loading operation was kept secret, but early Monday, a sizable delegation of Syrian and Joint Mission officials gathered at the dock to watch the chemicals being wheeled aboard the ship. The morning was overcast and humid, with a light sea breeze that dulled the edges of Syria's early-summer heat. Sharif sat under his tent smoking his usual cigar. Kaag, Julian Tangaere, Abdullah Fadil, and a few others from the Joint Mission talked quietly and took photographs. When the loading was finished, they shook hands with the *Ark Futura*'s Danish crew and watched as the fully loaded freighter left the harbor and headed out to sea.

Back in The Hague, Ahmet Üzümcü, the OPCW chief, waited for confirmation of the *Ark Futura*'s departure before issuing a prepared statement announcing the successful evacuation of the last cache of weapons. He called the moment a "major landmark."

"Never before," Üzümcü said, "has an entire arsenal of a category of weapons of mass destruction been removed from a country experiencing a state of internal armed conflict."

As the statement was being transmitted, the Joint Mission's daily progress report was updated with a new figure—"100 percent."

"All removal operations for declared chemicals have been completed," the report said.

With the Danish ship retreating from sight, UN and OPCW staffs retired to a nearby hotel for a celebratory drink. There were hugs and a chorus of "well-dones," but the affair was subdued.

Kaag felt relieved, yet any deeper sense of satisfaction eluded her. A difficult task had been accomplished and, miraculously, no one on her team had been killed or injured. But ordinary Syrians had continued to die, and the dying would go on—perhaps not from sarin, but from bombs or bullets, or from malnutrition, or the effects of torture or disease. The Joint Mission had deprived Assad of a particularly egregious weapon, one that posed a threat not only to his citizens, but—in the hands of terrorists—to people everywhere. Yet the dictator surely possessed the capacity to make new poisons, and he showed no signs of being chastened or deterred.

In her moment of personal triumph, Kaag could not escape the feeling that the international community had let ordinary Syrians down. One day, as she was wrapping up her work, she sat with her old friend Lakhdar Brahimi, the Algerian diplomat who served as the United Nations' special envoy to Syria during her time in Damascus, to try to put it into words.

"I hope the people of Syria can forgive us," she told him. "We didn't change their lives."

The meeting of the ships took place at Gioia Tauro, an industrial seaport at the very tip of Italy's boot. The town, with its distinctive key-shaped harbor, is far removed, geographically and aesthetically, from Italy's tourist destinations. It is famous chiefly for its historical ties to organized crime, being a favorite European port of entry for traffickers in narcotics, weapons, and other contraband. The Italian mafia effectively controlled the port for decades, and the town council had to be dissolved twice because it had been infiltrated by the mob. In early 2014, the port made headlines when U.S. and Italian authorities interdicted a half-ton shipment of cocaine hidden in what appeared to be cans of pineapple slices and coconut milk on a ship from Guyana. Now it would have a new source of renown: for one day only, the port would play host to both the *Cape Ray* and Denmark's *Ark Futura* in one of the biggest international transfers of chemical weapons known to history.

The exchange almost didn't happen at all. The Italian government had agreed to make the port available, on the condition that the chemicals moved from ship to ship across a concrete wharf without touching actual Italian soil. But Gioia Tauro's harbor operator had its own list of demands. Since the port would have to be shut down during the transfer, it wanted a payment of millions of dollars to compensate for lost business. It also insisted that the United Nations purchase an unlimited-liability insurance policy generous enough to cover billions of dollars in potential losses and costs, should anything go wrong.

U.S. officials were incensed. An unlimited-liability policy would be obscenely expensive and, as far as the White House was concerned, a deal-breaker. Diplomats were dispatched to Italy's Ministry of Foreign Affairs to see if the port operator could be induced to back off on his demands.

As it had done so many times before, the Defense Department rallied, sending its teams of planners scouring the globe for possible fixes. Some of the Pentagon's investigators rang up insurance brokers to ask about cheaper alternatives. Others began scouting for an alternative harbor, chasing a small handful of prospects from coastal Croatia to the Azores in the mid-Atlantic, some two thousand miles farther west. The crisis was averted when the Italian port authority agreed at the last minute to accept a lesser, though still expensive, insurance policy.

Days later, the crew of the *Cape Ray,* roused suddenly from their forced Spanish holiday, stood on the main deck and gaped as their ship entered the Italian harbor with an escort of tugboats. The mammoth port was eerily empty, and even the streets leading to the harbor had been sealed off by police. From the ship it was as though the entire city had been evacuated ahead of a coming plague.

On July 3, the American and Danish ships docked next to one another under a trio of spindly gantry cranes, as a phalanx of stevedores, some of them wearing protective suits despite the intense morning heat, trotted out to begin the task of unloading and loading. One by one, the harbor cranes hoisted the rusting semitrailer containers from the *Ark Futura*'s upper deck and lowered them onto flatbed trucks, which then traveled along a hundred yards of dock before ascending the ramp leading into the *Cape Ray*'s cavernous hold. By late afternoon the transfer was complete. Both ships took on fuel, unlashed their mooring lines, and prepared to head out to sea. A cluster of news photographers and TV crews recorded the moment as the *Ark Futura* and its escorts cleared the harbor entrance and veered westward toward Gibraltar and, eventually, home. The *Cape Ray* looped around Sicily, skirting the narrow Strait of Messina to avoid possible encounters with protesters. Then it took a southeasterly bearing, toward the open waters of the central Mediterranean, to start the work that its crew had waited five months to do.

No one felt the weight of the moment as much as Tim Blades, who spent part of the first night of the outward voyage walking through the maze of tanks and trailers, testing straps, checking for leaks, and conferring with Jordan and Dromerhauser. With so much that *could* go wrong, Blades knew, it was inevitable that something *would*. When it did, because of the nature of the ship's cargo, there would be no safe harbor for the *Cape Ray*, anywhere in the world. Until the last ounce of poison was destroyed, there would be no home but the sea.

"So it begins," he told the others.

15

"The number we will never know . . ."

JULY 4, 2014

On the first full day of its mission—July 4, the American Independence Day—the *Cape Ray* vanished from public sight. The disappearing act was partly by design, as the ship's captain steered the vessel toward an open expanse of the Mediterranean where it could not easily be seen or tracked. But it also helped that monumental events had seized the attention of the world.

That same day, in the northern Iraqi city of Mosul, a cleric-turned-terrorist who called himself Abu Bakr al-Baghdadi climbed onto the podium of a historic mosque to announce the creation of a new country, a theocratic empire that stretched from central Syria to the outskirts of Baghdad, the Iraqi capital. He called it *ad-Dawlah al-Islamiyah,* or the Islamic State.

ISIS had come a long way since its attack on a Syrian helicopter base a year earlier. With tens of thousands of new followers—including disillusioned ex-members of Syria's secular opposition and thousands of foreign volunteers—the jihadists were now a powerful army with well-equipped divisions in two countries. Stronger by far than any of its rivals in the Syrian opposition, ISIS was the first to seize and hold large swaths of territory, having captured the provincial Syrian capital of Raqqa as well as the Iraqi city of Fallujah in early 2014. Under Baghdadi, ISIS fighters poured into Iraq that spring, routing local defenders in a string of stunning defeats across the west and north. By mid-June, the jihadist army controlled a third of Iraq's territory, including Mosul, Iraq's second-largest city. Baghdadi's holdings included not just real estate, but also oil fields, military bases, universities, and hundreds of millions of dollars in cash. Almost overnight, the Islamic State was transformed into the wealthiest and best-armed terrorist group of all time.

A triumphant Baghdadi marched into Mosul's iconic al-Nuri mosque to declare the start of a new Islamic caliphate, with himself as leader. The bearded, slightly pudgy cleric stood before his followers to congratulate them on the start of what he described as a new chapter in human history. Their conquests so far, he predicted, were only the start.

"You will conquer Rome," he said, "and own the world."

"Rome"—jihadist shorthand for the West—was not within Baghdadi's reach. But on the afternoon of July 4, the Islamic world, extending from the deserts of northwest Africa to the Persian Gulf and South Asia, seemed suddenly, startlingly vulnerable.

Brett McGurk had been in the northern Iraqi city of Erbil less than a month before Baghdadi's triumphant speech. The capital of northern Iraq's semiautonomous Kurdish enclave, the city is less than fifty miles from Mosul, and the Kurds were seeing worrying signs of a major new ISIS offensive in the making.

The Kurdistan regional government maintained an extensive intelligence network with outposts in towns and villages across Iraqi Kurdistan, from the Syrian and Turkish borders north and west, to Halabja, the city devastated by Saddam Hussein's 1988 chemical weapons attack, to the east. From these sources, the Kurds picked up the first signals of new columns of ISIS fighters advancing from Syria into Iraq in early June. Soon a larger ISIS force was rolling through villages in the north and massing on the outskirts of Mosul itself. McGurk, alarmed, immediately phoned Iraqi prime minister Nouri al-Maliki to see how his government was responding. The Kurdish authorities were worried about Mosul and even offered to send their vaunted Peshmerga fighters to reinforce the city's defenses east of the Euphrates River. Yet Maliki so far had declined.

"You have to let the Peshmerga into east Mosul," McGurk said to the prime minister, insisting that he accept the help from the Kurds.

"No need," Maliki replied. He explained that he had arranged for three additional Iraqi brigades to travel to Mosul to support the trained and capable army divisions already defending the city. The new troops should be in place within a week, he said.

The reinforcements never made it. On June 8, more than one hundred ISIS vehicles packed with jihadis roared into Mosul, setting off bombs and attacking police stations and army positions with help from sleeper cells inside the city. The Iraqi government sent an urgent request to the Kurds, but it was too late. By June 10, central Mosul had fallen, along with the city's airport. Two Iraqi army divisions and equal numbers of federal police—as many as sixty thousand in all—had melted away ahead of an advancing force of a few thousand jihadists.

McGurk spent the night writing urgent cables to President Barack Obama's national security advisers back in Washington, describing the threat in the direst terms. Having failed to win congressional or public support for an air strike on Damascus a year earlier, the White House had been leery of talk of committing U.S. forces to Iraq or Syria. But McGurk was insistent.

If we don't do something to combat it, Baghdad could fall, he warned. Across central Iraq, he said, there was "panic and a snowballing effect southward toward the Tigris valley."

McGurk jumped on a plane in Erbil and flew to the Iraqi capital, stopping along the way at a former U.S. air base to pick up American contractors left stranded in ISIS's path. He arrived in the capital to find the city awash in rumors and paralyzed by fear. A jihadist horde was sweeping southward, pausing only to slaughter the Iraqi soldiers and bureaucrats they managed to capture. The attackers were said to be closing in on the Baghdad airport, which was widely expected to fall.

For the first time, McGurk and the hundreds of other American officials and workers in the city perceived their own lives to be in danger. If the airport fell, their main escape from the city would be blocked.

The ISIS invaders eventually paused to regroup, and McGurk took advantage of the lull to board a plane to Washington. He landed hours later in a U.S. capital still struggling to comprehend an Iraqi meltdown that almost no one had believed was possible. Within the White House, Obama's advisers were divided about what to do. Some pressed for immediate military action, including air strikes to turn back ISIS's advancing columns. Others were convinced they were witnessing a Sunni uprising against the imperious Maliki, whose corruption and repressive policies had brought disaster upon himself and his country. In any case, it was feared, a U.S. military campaign that appeared intended to prop up Maliki might have little popular support with Iraqi Sunnis and Kurds. Iraq's survival, the advisers concluded, depended on a leadership change.

Quietly, McGurk and other U.S. officials encouraged parliamentary leaders to replace the strongman with a more unifying figure who could rally the country for a life-or-death struggle against the Islamists. Gradually, the effort worked. Maliki resigned in mid-August, and within days, the outlines of a counteroffensive began to take shape. Still, despite the political breakthrough in Iraq, some U.S. analysts in Washington began describing the ISIS takeover of parts of Iraq and Syria as a fait accompli, and possibly permanent. "We're going to have to find a way to negotiate with these guys," one Middle East expert told an astonished McGurk in the diplomat's Foggy Bottom office.

"No way!" McGurk shot back.

The world had not yet witnessed the atrocities for which ISIS would soon become infamous. The grisly videos of beheaded journalists, or of prisoners being crucified, pushed off rooftops, or set ablaze in cages; the terrorist rampages in Western capitals and the copycat attacks in nightclubs and beach resorts—all this was still to come. But ISIS had never been coy about its plans and methods. McGurk knew the group's appetite for brutality from its earlier incarnation as al-Qaeda in Iraq, and he had observed the group's remarkable transformation in Syria from up close. More than most observers, he understood the implications of the jihadists' astonishing victory at Mosul—the biggest and most frightening of the cascade of disasters to spring from Syria's civil war.

One summer afternoon, as the ISIS onslaught was still under way, McGurk sat with an administration colleague who, like him, had come up against the terrorist group when it was confined to Iraq and went by a different name. They talked soberly about what the jihadists might do with their newly won territory and about the challenge of trying to dislodge them. Within weeks, McGurk himself would be appointed as the White House's special envoy to an international military alliance that would battle ISIS for the next four years. As the coalition leader, the United States would at last send its warplanes and ground troops to Syria. But they were there to fight a terrorist group, not a dictator.

For six months, McGurk had sounded the alarm about the resurgence of an old terrorist menace that had become newly powerful in the violent, ungoverned enclaves of eastern Syria. Now ISIS was bigger and stronger than even McGurk had imagined was possible. By seizing cities and military bases in Iraq and Syria, Baghdadi's Islamist warriors controlled oil fields, banks, communications networks, and vast quantities of weapons—along with factories and laboratories that could be commandeered to make new ones.

"It's al-Qaeda in Iraq on steroids," McGurk told his friend. "This is going to be really bad."

On July 7, the fourth day of the voyage out of Italy, the *Cape Ray* reached a spot west of the island of Crete that was judged to be far enough from land to begin its mission.

On the bridge, the officer of the watch noted the weather exactly at noon. Only a slight northeasterly breeze tugged at the colors atop the ship's mast. Yet the sea itself was choppy, with moderate swells of up to six feet, a bit rough for the Mediterranean in midsummer. Captain Rick Jordan had already extended the ship's stabilizers to smooth out the ride. Now he slowed the ship to just over six knots, a virtual crawl. This would be the ship's cruising speed until the last barrel of Syrian chemicals was destroyed.

One routine entry on the ship's log for July 7 was never filled in. Under the spaces reserved for noting latitude and longitude, the officer of the watch wrote only the word "CLASSIFIED." For the next forty-five days, the *Cape Ray*'s geographic coordinates would be regarded as an official secret.

Tim Blades's men put on their protective suits and slipped through a plastic airlock to get into position, while others took their seats in the control room and checked their monitors and gauges. Then, at exactly 1:16 p.m., someone flipped a switch and the first of the ship's two Margarita Machines hummed to life. A dusty tank containing 528 gallons of binary sarin precursor was wheeled into place and connected by tubes to the hydrolysis machine. Pumps shot twin streams of poison and water through a maze of pipes, forcing the liquids to mix under pressure. The diluted fluids then spilled into a mixing tank in which caustic soda was added to neutralize the still-lethal hydrofluoric acid—the "bone-seeker." At last the final product, a relatively harmless broth the color of watery blue Kool-Aid, was pumped through hoses into storage tanks arrayed across the ship's decks. It took less than five hours to process the first batch. Then another eight-thousand-pound vat of sarin precursor was wheeled out, and the process was repeated.

Blades hovered over his creation like a nervous parent, watching and offering suggestions. In one hand he clutched a roll of paper strips. These were pH testing papers, of the kind used in school laboratory experiments. The strips are formulated to turn bright red in the presence of a strong acid, or blue when exposed to an alkaline substance such as lye. As he walked, Blades kept his head down, looking intently for the stray droplet or sweaty pipe fitting that might signify that a valve or joint was about to blow, spewing deadly chemicals everywhere. When he saw something suspicious, he dabbed the moist spot with pH paper. He walked and dabbed, walked and dabbed throughout much of the first day.

So far, so good, he thought. *Just seventy-six more containers to go.*

On the bridge, the mission's other leaders were beginning to contemplate a potential crisis of a different order of magnitude. Among the deck officers, there was a growing fear that the ship, under certain circumstances, might be at risk of suddenly rolling on its side, filling up with water, and sinking.

Every modern container ship employs a computer program that charts the weight distribution of cargo, fuel, and ballast to ensure that the vessel remains upright. Normally, the calculations are made at the start of the voyage and then forgotten, because—in almost all cases—cargo doesn't move around. Roll-on/roll-off ships—ro-ros—are notoriously top-heavy, and special care has to be taken to ensure that the vessels remain stable as they burn off fuel, which is stored on a lower deck and helps preserve the ship's stability. Over the years, maritime records have documented the capsizing of several large ro-ros in relatively calm seas, accidents often blamed on the crew's failure to achieve a proper balance on board.

The *Cape Ray* was no ordinary ro-ro. Tanks holding millions of gallons of liquids were dispersed over all five of the ship's decks, and those liquids were constantly moving around. Each day, workers emptied at least two of the eight-thousand-pound vats of liquid poisons into Blades's hydrolysis machines. They also drew thousands of gallons of fresh water from ballast tanks below the ship's hold and pumped prodigious quantities of liquid waste into empty storage bins, many of which were stacked away on the top deck. Meanwhile, the *Cape Ray*'s supply of diesel, also stored belowdecks, diminished a little each day as the ship burned through its fuel supply. Slowly but surely, much of the ballast was shifting from the bottom of the ship to the top.

The daily changes were recorded on a spreadsheet kept by the *Cape Ray*'s second mate, and the new figures were scribbled on a whiteboard outside Jordan's cabin and entered into a computer program that rendered the ship as a two-dimensional animation: a large green boat resting on a flat plane that represented the ocean. In the animation, green meant stability, while a crimson ship was at risk of capsizing. The trend was unmistakable: each day, as the liquid cargo shifted around, the boat was inching closer to the red.

Jordan could feel it happening. As the chemical processing continued, a noticeable change occurred in the *Cape Ray*'s response to ocean swells. Instead of the usual rhythm—roll right, recovery; roll left, recovery—it stayed in the roll much longer, only gradually returning to the upright position.

"The ride actually feels smoother," Jordan said. "But that's when you really start to worry." At some point, he knew, there was a risk that a large swell could push the ship to one side and it might not come back.

And so each morning, the senior officers, including Blades, would meet to discuss the day's progress and chart the latest changes in weight distribution. Refueling to add ballast was not an easy option;

no port would grant entrance to a ship loaded with chemical weapons. From now on, they would be in a race to finish the work before the fuel level dropped below the point where stability was lost.

Blades had mentally calculated how long it would take to destroy the entire load of chemicals from Syria. It would be about thirty-nine days, plus a few additional days for maintenance and repairs, and then more time to get to a port where the ship could unload the waste and refuel.

He let his eyes run along the lines of the graph. This would be close. According to his calculations, by the time everything was finished, the *Cape Ray* would be three days away from turning red.

"Once we reach the point where we've burned that much fuel," he said, "we're screwed."

The deck officers had another problem, much nearer to hand. On the day of the *Cape Ray*'s departure from Italy, news stories about the American ship and its cargo of poisons had ignited a furor in countries up and down the Mediterranean. Anger over the mission intensified with word that the destruction work had officially begun. On both the Greek mainland and on the island of Crete, activists vowed to do more than carry picket signs. Older inhabitants could still recall the wholesale dumping of old chemical munitions into the Mediterranean at the end of World War II, and the possibility of a fresh threat to fishing and tourism touched a nerve. In the Cretan city of Chania, a large band of civic organizations and unions began preparing to mobilize a fleet of vessels to intercept the American ship at sea. The organizers called on "fishermen and anyone else who has a boat" to join in.

"We warned them long before they started," read a statement released by the combined opposition groups in Chania on July 10. "They decided, using concealment and silence by the mass media, to move on; we decided to meet them at sea. We are coming!"

Getting close to the *Cape Ray* would not be easy. The vessel was accompanied by U.S. and European naval frigates whose task was to keep outsiders well away. But no one believed that NATO gunboats would ever open fire on fishing boats filled with unarmed protesters. If some got through, the *Cape Ray* under normal circumstances could simply outrun them. But with the hydrolysis machines running, the boat was cruising at less than a third its normal speed. It was at least plausible that a few of the trawlers and yachts could maneuver themselves into the *Cape Ray*'s path and force it to turn or stop.

In the weeks that followed, and especially as the planned protest date approached, Jordan and Dromerhauser kept a continuous lookout for the flotilla, knowing all the while that there was little they could do if they spotted it.

"Oh well," Jordan said to Blades one day as the two digested the latest news about the protest ships, "you can't please everybody."

By the end of the operation's first week, the work aboard the *Cape Ray* had settled into a predictable, if exhausting, routine. Blades divided the Edgewood contingent into two teams—the day workers and the "night walkers," as the men called themselves—and assigned each to a twelve-hour shift. The crews working inside the hydrolysis tent began emptying vats of sarin precursor at a steady clip, while other workers ran the control room, moved the barrels, or tested the latest batch of wastewater coming from the machine's pipes to ensure that the treatment had reached its minimum standard: a neutralization level of at least 99.9 percent.

During their free hours, the men slept in their trailers, binged on movies, worked out in the small gym, or simply walked the decks to take in fresh air—or not-so-fresh air, on days when pungent odors from the chemical process belowdecks wafted along the ladderways. Alcohol was strictly banned aboard the ship under Navy rules, but the workers could wander into the ship's two galleys at any time to grab sandwiches, cookies, and perhaps a piece of fruit, until the supply of fresh produce ran out two weeks into the voyage. Jordan had brought along his favorite steward, New Orleans chef Louis Johnson, who dished out hot meals that served as either dinner or breakfast, depending on whether the workers were starting their shift or just ending it.

Blades worked both shifts, squeezing in a few hours of sleep in his cabin from about 3 a.m. to 9 a.m. He had just received disturbing news from home as the mission was starting: his seventeen-year-old stepson had been in a farm accident and had broken his backbone in several places. The family was distraught, and Blades offered to his wife, Karen, that he would find a way to come home if she needed him. "I want you to, but I know you can't," she said. Blades stayed on the ship and kept tabs on the youth's slow recovery in daily calls to his house over the ship's WiFi connection. He was tired, but despite the troubles at home, he was growing steadily more optimistic. His machines were working, and the stack of empty tanks that once held ready-to-mix sarin was growing steadily larger. He was beginning to mentally picture the finish line, just over a month away.

Then everything went wrong, all at once.

The first sign of trouble came during one of the night shifts, when a worker noticed a problem with the hydrolysis system. Attached by hoses to the Margarita Machines were huge, six-thousand-gallon tanks made of a corrosion-resistant nickel alloy. These were the tanks that caught the diluted poison and then blended it with caustic soda to neutralize the dangerous acids still in the mix. But something strange was happening inside the tanks. Each day the crews were having to shut off the flow of liquid into the containers because they were already filled up. Either the tanks were somehow shrinking, or there was something inside them that blocked them from taking on a full load of fluids.

Blades's deputy Lloyd Pusey and a few other workers put on their protective gear and began to investigate. After removing the heavy metal lid, they peered inside one of the tanks with a flashlight. The sight that greeted them was surprising and deeply disturbing.

The interior of the tank should have been empty. Instead, Pusey saw a mountain of clay-like sludge, so big it took up half the tank. The mound of goo was white, and it was cut with channels and gorges made by the streams of pressurized liquid coming into the container.

"It looks like the Grand Canyon," Pusey said.

To Blades, it looked like a disaster.

Blades and his chemists had always known that the mixing of alkaline and acid in the tank would create a silt-like by-product, or precipitate, that would eventually settle out and drop to the bottom of the tank, like pulp in a jug of orange juice. In lab tests back in Maryland, the pulpy stuff was swept along with the fluids and was never noticeable until the end stage, when the liquids were already in storage casks ready for disposal. Somehow, things had turned out differently aboard the ship, where the volumes of liquid in play were much larger. The solids were dropping out immediately and forming a dense, sludgy mess inside the mixing tank. The men tried flushing it out and then scooping it out, but nothing worked.

It was a potentially fatal problem for the operation. There was only a limited number of the nickel-alloy tanks aboard the ship, and because they were too big for airlifting by helicopter, the chances of bringing new ones aboard were nil. Eventually the tanks would fill up with sludge. When it happened, the processing of chemicals aboard the *Cape Ray* would grind to a halt.

Blades was floored. He began scrambling for solutions, phoning scientists back at home to ask for advice. It already was clear to him that he would have to change the system he had painstakingly built, perhaps by rerouting the liquids in some way. But that would mean shutting down the hydrolysis machines, and probably a delay of days, or maybe longer. He was already in a race to finish the work before *Cape Ray*'s fuel level dipped below the danger line. A delay of any significance was simply not possible.

As he was working furiously to plug this unexpected hole in his operation, another one suddenly appeared. Blades had just fallen asleep in the early hours of July 19 when one of his crewmen knocked on his cabin door. There had been a serious spill on the main trailer deck. Blades checked his watch. It was just before 5 a.m.

His first glimpse at the problem was through a TV monitor in the control room. From there he could see both hydrolysis machines clearly. To his astonishment, the area all around one of his machines was blanketed in white. It was as though a sudden snow squall had dropped its load on the deck.

"It looks like a blizzard!" one of the control-room operators said.

Blades suited up quickly and ran to the trailer deck. The sight was surreal. The deck was covered with what looked like powdery snow but was actually sodium carbonate, an ash-like substance used to treat acid spills. Men in biohazard gear were spreading the material everywhere while swabbing furiously at a large puddle. Blades watched transfixed as two workers picked up a third man and held him upside down over a plastic barrel liner. The man had become nauseated and was throwing up inside his protective suit.

It took some time to discover that the crisis was not as bad as it first appeared. About twenty gallons of fluid had spilled on the deck, but the liquid was a waste product, not sarin precursor. The fluid was highly acidic, but it was contained within a berm that had been installed around the hydrolysis machines before the *Cape Ray* set sail. The processing of chemicals halted while workers scooped up the vats of now-soggy sodium carbonate covering the floor and repaired the damage. The cleanup was a manageable problem, if unpleasant. No one had been killed or even seriously hurt.

For Blades, however, the repeated setbacks had taken a toll. He was still wrestling with the sludge problem in his tanks, which had cost precious time and forced him to reach deeper into his dwindling supply of chemicals and spare parts. The solution he eventually came up with entailed new risks. It required running hoses filled with poisonous liquids across all five decks of the ship so the crew could mix some of the chemicals manually in smaller containers. Every day, a worker in protective gear would have to climb atop a tank filled with acids heated to near boiling, then reach into the tank with an air hose to make sure the contents were properly blended. The harsh acids were eating through the equipment at a faster rate than Blades anticipated, and the crew had to wait until each valve and pump was on the edge of failure before replacing them. Meanwhile the *Cape Ray* was running out of storage tanks and fuel, both of which factored into the ship's gradual slide toward instability. On top of it all, the crew would soon receive word that the activists' flotilla had departed Crete and was heading in the direction of the American ship.

In his entire career, Blades had never felt so discouraged. There was a real possibility that the entire mission would now fail. If it did, much of the blame would undoubtedly fall on him.

"I pulled a lot of rabbits out of my ass over the years," Blades confided in a phone call to his wife, "but I'm not sure I can do it this time."

By July 25, the day the environmental activists departed the Cretan port of Chania, their planned flotilla was much diminished. Only two boats were deemed sturdy enough for the voyage, and these quickly filled to the maximum with protesters, about twenty-two people in all. They set sail on a balmy Friday and headed west to the spot where they believed the *Cape Ray* might be found.

The boats covered more than one hundred miles that day, and by Saturday morning they were within an easy day's sail of the American ship's location. Then the weather turned. A strong wind began to blow from the northwest, with sustained speeds of nearly twenty knots. Beating into the wind, the small vessels began to encounter even larger swells that sent sea spray splashing over the decks. By early Sunday morning, the activists had had enough. They set buoys adrift bearing protest signs, then turned to head home.

The organizers, while disappointed, believed they delivered a message.

"If you don't fight, you don't achieve anything," said Pavlos Polakis, a *Cape Ray* opponent and mayor of the town of Sfakia.

The flotilla had disappeared as a threat, and soon enough, with Blades's adjustments, the Margarita Machines were functioning at full speed. An average of six tanks of sarin precursor were being emptied each day. On the best days the total rose as high as nine.

Blades was back to his old self. He prowled the decks at all hours with a fistful of pH papers, checking for leaks. Each morning he sat with Jordan and Dromerhauser to look at the computer program to see how much time was left before the fuel level slipped below the danger zone. At the current rate, they could just about make it, the three decided.

Then it was done. On Sunday morning, August 17, one of the hydrolysis teams inserted a tube into the last of the barrels of Syrian chemicals. The pumps did their work, and in a few hours, the leftover wastes poured into a storage tank. It happened to be the last empty container for chemical waste on the entire ship.

There was little fanfare aboard the vessel at the end. After more than forty days and nights of nonstop work, the crew was exhausted. Even the normally outspoken Blades was subdued. For most of the voyage he had maintained an unshakable faith in the competence of his men, and in himself. Yet at the end he had to acknowledge the role of other forces, some of which he had always been powerless to control. He knew that he and the crew had been fortunate.

"It was a perfect storm of luck," he said. "We were lucky with the weather. Lucky with everything. You'd never be able to replicate what we did."

There was an awkward pause as Pentagon officials briefly debated waiting until Monday, a workday, to announce the milestone. But word leaked, and soon Blades and his deputies were receiving congratulatory emails from coworkers and friends. Among the well-wishers was Major General Jay Santee, who had left DTRA for a new assignment but took a moment to try to put the achievement into perspective.

"Five months to create a first-ever field-deployable hydrolysis system; Sixty-six days to outfit the vessel; Forty-two days to destroy 600 metric tons of Syria's most dangerous chemical weapons at sea," Santee wrote. "The number we will never know: the number of men, women and children in Syria who were saved from death by chemical weapons."

Defense secretary Chuck Hagel's message in a phone call to Dromerhauser was short and to the point.

"With the world watching, they performed flawlessly every step of the way," Hagel said.

The world would actually hear little of it. The destruction of the final barrels of binary sarin was noted in a press release, but senior officials at both the White House and the Pentagon decided to keep the pronouncements modest, even low-key. The news out of Syria and Iraq was simply too horrific. In Iraq, U.S. military aircraft had begun bombing ISIS positions in northern Iraq in an attempt to halt an ongoing massacre of ethnic Yazidis who had taken refuge in the Sinjar mountains. ISIS fighters had kidnapped an American journalist named James Foley, and in two days the group would release a graphic video showing the man's beheading in a desert near Raqqa. The Syrian army was continuing its campaign of chlorine attacks on rebel villages, undercutting any possible claims about protecting innocents against chemical weapons.

At the Defense Department, a member of the public affairs staff reached out to Andrew Weber's office for guidance on what, exactly, to say about the day's milestone achievement aboard the *Cape Ray*. How should the Pentagon play up the historic destruction of a vast arsenal of nerve agents over forty-two days at sea?

Weber already had been pulled into a new crisis, the emerging ebola epidemic in West Africa, so his deputy, Christine Parthemore, replied with a quick word of advice.

"Just read your morning's intel brief," she said. This was no time for celebration.

And the mission was not quite complete. The *Cape Ray*'s crews still had to drop off the wastewater tanks at facilities in Germany and Finland, then thoroughly clean the ship and return to Virginia. Meanwhile, they had received a small but immensely important new assignment from the Pentagon.

In the mission's waning hours, it had occurred to the Defense Department's senior staff that it might be useful to preserve a few samples of the Syrian chemicals for future study. These poisons had come directly from Bashar al-Assad's arsenal, and it was important to know exactly what was in them. That way, if an identical type of sarin was used in a future attack anywhere in the world, investigators would immediately know whether it came from Syria.

The request made sense, but fulfilling it would not be easy. The *Cape Ray,* now hauling millions of gallons of chemical waste, could not simply pop into port to drop off a package. There also were strict OPCW rules governing how all chemical weapons must be handled, even in small quantities.

The handoff was finally made on August 26, as the *Cape Ray* was steaming past the southwestern tip of England on its way to Germany. It was just past dawn, and a gale was blowing in the English Channel as two of Blades's men stood by a small pilot door on the ship's starboard side, clutching their bags and a pair of large wooden boxes. Each of the crates contained a three-foot-long cylinder of thick steel, sealed with bolts and gaskets and sturdy enough, it was said, to survive a plane crash. Inside the two cylinders were thirty-two plastic vials filled with liquid poisons drawn straight from the Syrian tanks in which they had been originally stored.

At 8 a.m., after hours of weather delays, the two men began climbing down a rope ladder toward a rubber dinghy waiting in the roiling sea below. One of the men, Wyatt McNutt, a thirty-six-year-old laboratory worker from southeastern Pennsylvania, found himself suddenly dangling from the end of the ladder when the dinghy dropped away at the bottom of a twelve-foot swell. Then the small boat shot back up, and someone in a black survival suit grabbed McNutt's legs. It was his escort, a frogman with the British Royal Navy.

"Enjoy the ride!" the man said. Minutes later, as the dinghy pulled away, the men dropped into a trough so deep that the massive American ship briefly disappeared from sight.

Awesome! McNutt thought.

The adventure was not over. Minutes later, as McNutt was warming up inside a British frigate, he was jarred by the sudden clanging of alarms and rushing of men in protective gear. He had survived the *Cape Ray* voyage, only to find himself off the English coast on a ship with an engine fire. The blaze was contained, but it took nearly eight hours for McNutt and the two cylinders to make it to shore.

The next morning, the *Cape Ray*'s men walked into a laboratory in Holland to officially turn over the samples to the OPCW. The contents of the cylinder would undergo weeks of forensic analyses at laboratories in multiple countries and then be stashed away. No one at the time imagined the day when the samples would become vital evidence in a renewed effort to bring Syria's dictator to justice.

Blades and the rest of the Edgewood team departed the *Cape Ray* after it dropped off its load in Germany, and most boarded commercial planes for the trip back to the United States. In later months there would be ceremonies, awards and medals, but more immediately, many crew members were met with unpleasant news. There had been another shutdown of the federal government, and many Defense Department employees had been forced to take unwanted furloughs. Blades and his men were told to plan on taking some time off, without pay.

Jordan likewise learned that his union had denied his request to return to his normal ship assignment in New Orleans. He was told to go on immediate leave and to forgo pension benefits he believed he had accrued during eleven months at sea.

"We all want to thank you for your service," Jordan said, summarizing the news he received upon his homecoming. "Now get lost."

As a final indignity, the *Cape Ray* itself experienced an engine failure—the first of the entire voyage—during the return crossing of the Atlantic. The big freighter limped along on a single engine until repairs could be made.

During the weeks that followed, a few of the former crew members decided to look again at the weight-distribution problem that had pushed the *Cape Ray* to the brink of instability. Back at Portsmouth, trailers that had been bolted to the top deck to serve as living quarters were reweighed and found to be significantly heavier than the initial estimates. Edgewood's engineers, meanwhile, checked their metering equipment and discovered another flaw: the machines had routinely underestimated the amount of liquid in many of the tanks on the ship's upper decks.

Out of curiosity, one of the *Cape Ray*'s officers entered the correct figures onto a spreadsheet and ran the numbers through the computer program that predicted when the ship would start to become unstable. The results were sobering. According to the revised calculations, the *Cape Ray* had dipped into the red zone in late August, about a week before it finished the mission.

Exactly how close the ship came to flipping over will never be known. But to the crew members who saw the figures, one thing was certain: At the end, the vessel was well outside its safety margin.

"There was more weight in places where it wasn't supposed to be," one officer said. "The question might arise as to why *Cape Ray* did *not* capsize."

The *Cape Ray* had not yet returned to Portsmouth when news broadcasts from Iraq reported a fresh conquest for the Islamic State. Following on its surge across northern Iraq, the black-clad fighters had swept into the ancient Euphrates River city of Hit, seizing control of the town in less than a week. The militants paraded scores of captured policemen and soldiers through the main street and then executed them, dumping their bodies in a mass grave.

Then, looking around the town, the invaders spotted an opportunity. Hit was home to a sizable hospital. The building was damaged, but its clinical laboratories remained intact and functional. In the following weeks, ISIS converted the space into something unique in the group's history: a professional lab for making chemical weapons. A university laboratory in Mosul was soon commandeered for the same purpose, and a few scientists and engineers were put to the task of figuring out what kinds of weapons they could possibly make.

Just upstream from Hit, in the Syrian city of Raqqa, ISIS was putting a different set of technicians to work, devising plans for spectacular terrorist attacks against the group's enemies in the West. One of the planners was a young Danish engineer and bomb maker named Basil Hassan. Before his thirtieth birthday, he would come up with an idea for a terrorist weapon designed to release lethal gases in a confined space, such as a movie theater or an airplane cabin. Hassan had a recipe for poison gas and aspirations for carrying out an attack against the West. All he lacked were foreign accomplices. Soon he would begin looking for them.

ISIS had missed an opportunity in Syria, arriving too late to snatch away the lethal poisons manufactured by the government and stored in bunkers around the country. But soon it would try a different approach. Instead of stealing Assad's weapons, it would steal his idea. Beginning in the fall of 2014, ISIS would find ways to create chemical weapons of its own.

PART III

16

A Day "perfect for a chemical attack"

KESIK KUPRI, IRAQ. JANUARY 23, 2015

The Kurdish fighters dug in along Highway 47 could hear the truck from far off and knew the attack was coming. The defenders crouched behind their vehicles or squatted along a low ridge, rifles trained on the narrow road. From the ridge to the earthen barrier across the highway were perhaps five hundred men, skilled veterans of Iraq's Kurdish Peshmerga brigades as well as teenagers and elderly volunteers from neighboring villages who had come in their civilian coats, sneakers, and checkered scarves to reclaim their homes from the men of ISIS. In two hard days of combat they had seized a strategic crossroads and now effectively controlled the main route between the Iraqi city of Mosul and the Syrian frontier. The Islamists would do whatever they could to take it back.

The afternoon was nearly spent when the suicide vehicle appeared. The Kurds positioned along the ridge could see it clearly: a red farm truck with steel plates welded to the front for ramming and a trailer bed stacked high with metal tanks. The truck picked up speed as it approached the Kurdish line, and from the ridge the defenders unleashed a volley of rifle fire aimed at the passenger cabin. The fusillade kicked up rows of dust spouts in the nearby field, but some bullets found their mark, pinging against the cab and punching holes in some of the metal tanks. From the back of the truck came a ribbon of greenish smoke, like the contrail of a distant jet.

The dirt berm in the middle of the highway forced the driver to slow for a moment, and that was all the defenders needed. Two Kurdish fighters were waiting with a thirty-five-pound antitank rocket, and they fired the projectile directly into the truck's side. The vehicle disintegrated in an instant. When the smoke cleared, the truck's twisted undercarriage lay on the asphalt fifty yards from the impact crater, and metal fragments and bits of the driver's remains were scattered across the nearby fields.

The commanding officer, a Peshmerga colonel named Sabri, cautiously inspected the debris with a few of his aides. The men discovered that the metal tanks in the truck's rear had blown clear of the vehicle when it exploded and landed haphazardly in the dirt. Some of the containers were leaking the same pale-green smoke the men had seen earlier. All around the leaking tanks the soil and grass bore a yellow coating, as though someone had spilled a jar of watery paint. A few men who ventured close to the damaged tanks detected a pungent odor and immediately fell ill.

Sabri could offer his men no protection other than surgical masks, which were useless, so he moved everyone back and radioed for help. Soon afterward, other Kurds arrived carrying respirators and sampling kits, the latter being used to scoop up a few grams of contaminated soil from around the leaking tanks. Weeks passed before the colonel learned precisely what had happened on that late-January afternoon. ISIS had tried to break his line by means of a chemical bomb: a suicide truck loaded with twenty canisters of deadly chlorine gas.

The attack near the crossroads village of Kesik Kupri represented the first known attempt by the newly resurgent ISIS to use a chemical weapon in combat. It was a modest effort, causing no serious casualties and barely drawing notice from outside northern Iraq. But its leaders had signaled their intentions to the Kurds, and to the world.

ISIS was officially in the business of using chemical weapons.

From outside Iraq, it was hard to know what to make of such reports. Was it really possible that the Islamic State was using poison gas on the battlefield? No army had used chemicals against troop formations since the Iran-Iraq War in the 1980s. No militia or terrorist group had done so, ever. Even if the accounts were true, where had the chemicals come from, and how did ISIS manage to get them?

Among the many experts to ponder the questions was Hamish de Bretton-Gordon, the retired British army colonel and WMD expert who had helped train Syria's first responders, including the young physician known as Chemical Hazem. De Bretton-Gordon had been angling to investigate for himself, and during a trip to Iraq, he managed to catch a ride to the front as a guest of a Peshmerga general who had sought him out for advice. The two drove together through desolate towns that weeks earlier had been occupied by ISIS. At last they arrived in Gwer, a village on the southern bank of the Great Zab River, just thirty miles from Mosul, the terrorist group's Iraqi capital. The Islamists' forward position lay less than half a mile away.

The Kurds were winning here, steadily reclaiming territory they had lost months earlier to ISIS. But the campaign was constantly being slowed, the Kurdish officer said, by poison-gas weapons that ISIS was now using with astonishing regularity. Since the first chlorine attack in January, the jihadists had moved into more frightful terrain: blister agents. These consisted of a kind of sulfur mustard that was loaded in large mortar shells and lobbed directly into Kurdish fortifications. Later, ISIS added chemical-laden artillery rockets to the mix so they could fire from longer distances. More than one hundred shells loaded with mustard or chlorine had been hurled at the Kurds in the space of a few months.

The attacks had taken a toll. Fewer than five people—all of them noncombatants—had died, but hundreds had been wounded, including dozens of fighters who suffered searing chemical burns after being splashed with the shells' oily brown contents. Where the liquid touched the victims, their skin erupted in painful blisters, some as big as golf balls.

The psychological injuries were worse. Most of the fighters were old enough to remember the massacres of the 1980s, when Iraqi leader Saddam Hussein used sarin against Kurdish settlements, killing more than three thousand people. Decades later, the very mention of chemical weapons evoked fear and dread among many Iraqi Kurds.

"My lads and lasses don't like chemical weapons," the Kurdish general told de Bretton-Gordon as they walked.

The battlefield visit was still under way when the general learned of a fresh skirmish farther up the line. “There’s an attack going on over there,” he said, pointing. The small entourage climbed into vehicles and rushed toward the action, arriving in time to witness a volley of mortar fire coming from the opposite riverbank. Shells began landing about six hundred yards from where de Bretton-Gordon was standing. But they weren’t exploding, exactly. There was a muffled pop, followed by the emergence of a cloud of greenish smoke that began drifting in the Kurds’ direction.

In all his years of training, the Briton had never witnessed a chemical weapon fired with harmful intent. The sight was mesmerizing.

“The day was perfect for a chemical attack: clear, with a light breeze,” he recalled afterward. “What was fascinating was, you could see the downwind hazard. It was about thirty to forty meters wide and maybe thirty to forty meters long, moving with the wind. I was excited. The Peshmerga thought I was loony.”

The vapor was beginning to disperse as the men watched, so de Bretton-Gordon tried to reassure the Kurds near him.

“We’re all going to die,” one of the fighters said mournfully.

“No,” the British weapons expert replied. “The danger will be gone by the time it gets here.”

“How do you know?”

“When the greenish-yellow stuff disappears, it’s gone,” he said. “It’s not sarin or something that you can’t see.”

With the nearest American outpost miles away, there was no one close by to call in an air strike. So the men just watched quietly as the gas plume thinned and then disappeared altogether. No one had been hurt, but the effect on the Kurdish lines was as profound as though the defenders had suffered a direct hit.

“It’s a horrific thing to see someone die from a chemical weapon,” de Bretton-Gordon said afterward. “The Kurds can tell you about the thousands of people Saddam Hussein killed with chemical weapons in Halabja, and in forty other chemical attacks during the Iran-Iraq War. Everyone in that area knows about chemical warfare. For the Kurds, it’s absolutely in their psyche.”

How did ISIS obtain the weapons? The Kurds could not say. Obtaining chlorine was no problem, as the industrial chemical could be found in Iraqi factories the terrorists now controlled. But what about sulfur mustard? Had the terrorists stumbled upon abandoned munitions from Saddam Hussein's time? Had they managed to steal something from Syria's stockpile of poisons?

Some answers began to emerge in the following months, as delegations from the OPCW arrived in Baghdad to investigate the reported attacks on Kurdish forces at the Iraqi government's request. The investigators swabbed yellow residue from recovered mortar fragments and tested the greasy soil in the spots where the projectiles had landed. They interviewed Kurdish soldiers and examined the ugly scars left behind wherever the foul-smelling liquid had touched human skin. They examined one soldier whose legs were utterly covered with chemical burns, from his waist to the crisp line at mid-calf where his army boots had offered some protection.

The lab tests and interviews yielded a confirmation, and also a surprise. The oily liquid in the mortar shells was sulfur mustard, no doubt, but it differed from the kinds of military-grade blister agents the OPCW's experts were familiar with. Its formula was relatively simple, even crude. It lacked enhancers and stabilizers that military weaponeers typically use, which meant that it tended to break down more quickly when exposed to the environment. It was neither Syrian nor Iraqi, judging from its chemical composition, yet it clearly had been made by someone with access to modern laboratory equipment, a working knowledge of toxic weapons, and a grasp of basic chemistry.

All the signs pointed in the same alarming direction. Somewhere in Iraq or Syria, ISIS was manufacturing its own chemical weapons. The terrorists had not yet mastered all the elements. But they were learning.

De Bretton-Gordon had spent his career thinking about how to protect soldiers and civilians against a chemical or biological attack, and now he struggled to wrap his brain around the concept of a terrorist state with its own dedicated facilities for making poison gas. So what if the weapons weren't yet perfect? Even a chlorine attack on a subway line in London or New York could unleash mayhem.

After returning home, de Bretton-Gordon was commissioned by officials in both of those cities to help lead planning exercises to assess the possible consequences of such an attack on a major transit system. The results were sobering.

"Even if it doesn't kill many people outright, it will terrorize," the retired colonel said of his findings. "In the panic, you've got fifteen hundred people rushing to get out of a tiny area. There could be a hundred deaths from crush injury alone. And then the question becomes, 'How do you decontaminate?'"

Already, more than a year had passed since the *Cape Ray* began its mission to eliminate Syria's nerve agents. Yet as one crisis receded, new ones cropped up like brush fires on a windy plain. Chemical weapons in the hands of terrorists was just one of them. OPCW investigators were beginning to focus on curious gaps in the official records of Syria's chemical weapons production, gaps that raised doubts as to whether Assad had truly given up everything. And at the same time, his army was dropping a chlorine bomb on a Syrian town or village nearly every week, rarely bothering to make an effort to hide it.

Most galling of all, more than a year after the events at Ghouta, Assad had never paid a price for—or even acknowledged—his role in the worst chemical weapons atrocity in a quarter-century.

By 2015, Houssam Alnahhas was ready to give up his perilous existence on the civil war's front lines, though he could never quite free himself from the obsession that earned him the nickname Chemical Hazen. That previous August, a few weeks after his risky evidence-gathering trek across northern Syria, he married Yasmin, the woman he had met in his hospital's pharmacy department, and the two moved into an apartment in Turkey so she could begin university classes. Now twenty-seven, Alnahhas decided that he should obtain a proper medical license, so he taught himself Turkish, researched medical schools, and then crisscrossed the country, driving some two thousand miles to apply in person at twenty-eight different institutions. Two of them sent letters of acceptance.

One day while waiting to begin his studies, a friend passed along an urgent message from one of his former trainees, a radiologist named Mohamed Tennari. The man now ran a field clinic in Sarmin, a small town outside the northern Syrian city of Idlib, where he managed to sustain a practice despite being bombed out of business four times. Just days earlier, on March 16, there had been a deadly chlorine attack on the settlement, with one bomb crashing through a ventilation shaft and killing six people from the same family, including three young children. Alnahhas's student had learned well. While it was too late for some of the injured, Tennari had worked skillfully to save other victims, using techniques he had learned and medicines he stockpiled for the purpose. And as he worked, he documented everything to preserve a record. He collected videos and photographs of the attack site, the victims, and the rescue attempt, as well as blood, clothing, and hair samples from the living and the dead.

As evidence, it was an impressive trove. It also was a rare one. Since Alnahhas's close call, few of Syria's medical workers were willing to put themselves in that kind of danger.

"After our experience in 2014, no one had wanted to do criminal documentation," Alnahhas said. To many of his trainees, collecting evidence no longer seemed important. Why risk one's life over matters that people outside Syria no longer seemed to care about?

But Tennari had taken the risk, and his results might just be powerful enough, Alnahhas thought, to command international attention.

After the message from Tennari, Alnahhas helped organize a relay that couriered proof of the attack to Western embassies in Turkey. The evidence, in sealed vials packed inside an insulated box, was hand-delivered to Alnahhas at his hospital. He tucked the container inside a suitcase and buried it under clothes, then set off for Ankara in an ordinary commuter bus, the bag with its priceless contents resting by his feet. He made it safely to the Turkish capital and, after a few terrifying minutes at a police checkpoint, arrived at the café where the first of his contacts, an American, accepted the parcel with a nod and a quiet "thanks." What happened to the specimens after that, Alnahhas never knew.

Yet the most compelling evidence from Sarmin was not contained in vials of hair and blood samples. Tennari was a passionate and articulate witness to the events in his hometown, and he possessed powerful images of the night's three youngest victims, all siblings under five years of age, lying on a bed in Tennari's clinic, lifeless as dolls. The photos were both awful and unforgettable, a devastating summation of the suffering endured by Sarmin and scores of similar towns over the last year. With help from the Syrian American Medical Society, a flight was arranged, and Tennari and his photos were soon on their way to America.

On April 17, almost exactly a month after the attack on his town, the radiologist stood before a closed session of the UN Security Council in New York to describe the worst night of his professional life. Speaking through an interpreter and using videos as props, he told of hearing helicopters overhead, and of the warning over the loudspeaker at the local mosque that prompted him to leave his house at 11 p.m. to rush to his clinic.

"When I arrived at the hospital, a wave of people had already begun to arrive," said Tennari, narrating the events of the night. "They were all experiencing symptoms of exposure to a choking agent like chlorine gas. . . . Dozens of people had difficulty breathing, with their eyes and throats burning."

The most seriously injured, he recalled, were members of the family who had been trapped in their basement apartment when the chlorine barrel bomb tore through the ventilation shaft and exploded into their kitchen. In a video taken inside Tennari's small clinic, medics are seen working frantically to save the youngest victim, a one-year-old baby, using a squeeze bag to force oxygen into the child's lungs. Nearby lay the baby's two siblings, ages two and three, both on the same bed with their grandmother. There were shouts and cries as physicians also tended to rescue workers who had become sick while pulling the family out of an apartment that had turned into a gas chamber.

For the family whose dwelling suffered a direct hit, the effort ultimately was futile. By the end of the night, all three children lay lifeless next to one another on a shroud, the youngest one's eyes still open. The entire family—mother, father, grandmother, children—were dead. Later, the Syrian government would dismiss reports of a chemical attack on Sarmin as "propaganda" and claim that the six victims had died in a propane gas explosion, though none of the victims in the video showed signs of burns or blast injuries.

"The patients we received in these attacks had symptoms of exposure to choking agents, so they had respiratory symptoms," Tennari said. "They did not have injuries related to bombs and bullets."

By the time the presentation ended, several in the UN audience were visibly weeping. Among them was Samantha Power, the U.S. ambassador to the United Nations. Even before the Ghouta attack in 2013, Power had been among the Obama administration's most vocal advocates for American intervention in Syria. When the presentation ended and she stepped out of the room into the glare of waiting TV cameras, her eyes were red.

"If there was a dry eye in the house, I didn't see it," she said later.

Lingering afterward to answer reporters' questions, Power repeated the usual complaints about Syrian brutality and Russian complicity and promised again that a reckoning was coming.

"Individuals who are responsible for attacks like that will be held accountable," Power said, jabbing a finger for emphasis. "The documentary record is being built. The testimonies are being gathered."

Privately, though, she was longing to try something new. With a small staff that now included Wa'el Alzayat, the Damascus-born diplomat who had served as U.S. liaison to rebel groups, she began to brainstorm about new ways to show the world what Syria was doing and somehow make the accusations stick. The OPCW's Fact-Finding Mission was now regularly turning up intriguing new evidence, but the panel was so hobbled by restrictions that its reports were meaningless, Power's aides thought. Syria not only was able to avoid punishment, but it also was able to continue claiming that it had never used its chemical weapons—not at Ghouta, not in Saraqeb, and certainly not in the village of Sarmin where a family of six had recently died.

"It was the most ridiculous thing ever," Alzayat said. "The reports would say, 'Chemical weapons were used,' but not who used them. Or 'A helicopter dropped something,' but not who flew it. It was a waste of a lot of people's time and money, but that was the position we were in, and that's the way the world is run."

But perhaps not forever. That spring, Power and her team began to map out a possible new strategy for holding Assad accountable for his chemical crimes. The plan would require months of quiet lobbying in Washington, and enough diplomatic savvy to maneuver a way around an obstacle so enormous that it stretched across eleven time zones: Russia.

In fact, Assad's cheating was broader and deeper than anyone knew. It wasn't just the chlorine bombs, though there would be nearly three hundred chlorine attacks in the four years after Syria publicly foreswore the use of chemical weapons. It was also the government's elaborate attempts to conceal what else its military scientists had been up to in thirty years of secret research.

From the beginning, U.S. intelligence officials had known about gaps in the records turned over by Damascus as part of the U.S.-Russia deal in 2013. The Syrians had left out key facilities and experimental programs that the CIA had known about since the 1990s, thanks to the agency's talented spy inside the country's weapons complex. After quiet prodding, the initial reports were amended to include some of the missing details, but a few curious omissions remained. Assad refused, for example, to list the country's main military laboratory—the one known as CERS, where the agency's spy had worked—as a chemical weapons facility. Even as other production centers and testing sites were dismantled and destroyed, CERS remained firmly off-limits.

When the OPCW's inspectors entered Assad's munitions factories and began to ask questions, the depths of Syria's deception became clear. The more information the experts gathered, the more Syria's official account of its weapons research began to unravel.

In some cases, the stories literally did not add up. For example, by Syria's own accounting, the country's factories had produced a massive amount of sulfur mustard—about 385 metric tons—over the years. But official inventories in 2013 listed just twenty metric tons, the same amount that was later surrendered and destroyed aboard the *Cape Ray*. What happened to the rest of it? The Syrians claimed to have destroyed it all in 2012 as the civil war was breaking out, and they led inspectors to incinerators where at least some of the toxic material had been burned. Yet they could produce only vague records in support of the claim, leading the OPCW to question whether all of it had truly been destroyed. More perplexing was the absence of any munitions for using sulfur mustard in battle. If the Syrian military produced nearly four hundred tons of the poison, then surely it also manufactured special bombs and shells to disperse it. Where were they now? The government's official inventory listed only fifteen warheads designated for sulfur mustard, not enough to carry even 2 percent of the total amount Syria admitted making. Unable to come up with a more plausible explanation, the Syrians simply blamed bureaucratic errors and "bad planning," the OPCW said in a confidential report.

The Syrians also offered shifting explanations when confronted with evidence of a secret program to manufacture ricin, an extremely potent toxin derived from castor beans. At first they declined to acknowledge making ricin. Then they admitted to making a little ricin "for medical research purposes," the OPCW report said. Finally, after months of prodding, Assad's men confessed to having launched an ambitious and costly program to develop a ricin bomb, one that could deliver thousands of lethal doses either as a liquid aerosol or a fine powder. Scientists eventually produced nearly two thousand gallons of a liquid ricin solution. Yet they decided to abandon the program and destroy everything—so the government claimed—because they could never find a way to stabilize the concoction so it would remain potent during long periods of storage. The Syrians produced no hard evidence to back the claim that the ricin was destroyed.

But a far more damaging discovery came as inspectors began conducting forensic tests inside Syria's weapons facilities. Beginning in May 2014, and continuing over a series of twenty-seven other visits in the following months, the OPCW's Declaration Assessment Team was allowed to enter some of Syria's most sensitive facilities to ask questions and take samples using kits that collect tiny dust particles on sterile swabs. After gaining permission to inspect the main CERS lab, one of the agency's technicians reached up into a laboratory exhaust hood and scraped off a bit of sooty debris from inside the vent. The swab was placed inside a bag, secured with a tamperproof seal, and dispatched to a laboratory in Europe, along with similar samples collected from a dozen now-empty weapons factories and storage bunkers. The test results, detailed in confidential OPCW reports, confirmed past research on entirely new lines of nerve agents that had never been publicly acknowledged.

The scrapings from the exhaust hood, for example, contained traces of a substance called pinacolyl alcohol. The finding immediately set off alarms, because this rare alcohol is chiefly known as a precursor for soman, a deadly nerve agent. The Syrians had never mentioned soman. How much did they make, and where was it now? Other tests found residues of two types of VX different from the common variety the government acknowledged making. The official record said nothing about experimental forms of VX.

The documents turned over by the Syrians created still more mysteries. Paper records revealed that the country had manufactured more than six hundred metric tons of DF, the ready-to-mix precursor for binary sarin. But only 580 metric tons of DF were brought aboard the *Cape Ray* to be destroyed. Where was the rest?

When confronted, Damascus offered up explanations that evolved as the evidence grew clearer. Asked about the pinacolyl alcohol, Syrian officials at first simply disputed the OPCW's findings. Later they acknowledged making a tiny amount of soman so they could calibrate their chemical-detection equipment. Then they blamed the anomalies on a now-dead scientist who once ran the program—an apparent reference to the CIA's fallen "chemist" spy. Having been executed years earlier, the man was no longer around to answer questions.

To account for the missing twenty tons of DF, the Syrians proffered excuses that were almost laughably far-fetched. A full fifteen tons were said to have been used in tests—a preposterous figure, unless the military had lobbed scores of sarin warheads into the desert. As for the remaining five tons, roughly enough to fill a small swimming pool, the bulk of it had been "lost during transportation, due to traffic accidents," an OPCW report quoted Syrian officials as saying.

The stories were extracted mostly from hapless bureaucrats and scientists who were offered up as expert witnesses when the OPCW's teams traveled to Damascus for their investigations. One official who sat through multiple interviews recalled the pained expressions of the Syrians across the table as they were pressed to reveal details that were not part of the official script.

"We'd have guys put in front of us who clearly had been briefed on 'the story,'" the official said. "You'd get so far and scratch the veneer a little more, and you'd get to the point where the guy couldn't answer the questions. You'd see him look at the others and you know he has gone as far as he's been briefed, and now he's not quite sure what to say."

The investigators followed each new twist in the trail until they inevitably reached a dead end. In some cases, the Syrians could plausibly claim that the paperwork was simply missing; the chemical weapons program had always been secretive and compartmentalized, and since the outbreak of war, records and personnel had been scattered and sometimes lost. But more often, Assad's aides simply refused to budge from explanations that the OPCW inspectors, in their confidential reports, described as "implausible." In the end, even as they ferreted out scores of new details, the inspectors were unable to formally close even one of their investigations into Syria's past weapons research.

Thus, some nine months after the destruction of the last barrels of binary sarin aboard the *Cape Ray,* the existence of a residual cache of sarin, tucked away somewhere in the Syrian countryside, was viewed as plausible, and even likely. Meanwhile, the giant CERS laboratory complex on the hill outside Damascus would continue its secret research, without serious challenge. More chlorine bombs would fall, more Syrians would die, and the OPCW would faithfully document the crimes, without ever identifying a suspect. There was simply no institution with the legal standing to weigh the facts and, when warranted, point a finger of blame.

Until suddenly, almost miraculously, one came to exist.

If Samantha Power had been a more traditional ambassador—or if she had served long enough to become steeped in the culture and traditions of the UN Security Council—the question probably would have never come up. But by the summer of her second year as chief U.S. diplomat to the United Nations, Power had seen enough images of dying children in Syria. It was time to try something different.

If there is no UN body that can hold Syria accountable for its use of chemical weapons, she asked her staff one day, why can't we create one?

The question followed one of the many endless discussions at Power's New York office about Assad's unrelenting campaign of chlorine attacks on besieged Syrian cities. In 2015, the worst year, there were more than one hundred such attacks, part of a ruthless campaign to depopulate residential neighborhoods in opposition-held areas. When criticized about the tactic, Syria would deny using poison gas and insist, absurdly, that the rebels were bombing their own neighborhoods. Then Russian officials would simply parrot the claim while, in their private offices in New York, UN officials shook their heads and lamented their inability to do anything about the attacks.

Power thought the restriction was ridiculous and said so, in meetings with UN counterparts and with White House colleagues. If there's clear evidence of guilt, why not say it publicly?

The UN doesn't have a mandate, Power was repeatedly told.

"Well, that should be a conversation-starter," she replied one day. "What we at the UN do is create mandates."

The problem, of course, was Russia. But here, Power had an unexpected ally. The head of Russia's UN delegation was a veteran diplomat named Vitaly Churkin, the Security Council's longest-serving ambassador and a forceful and frequently caustic defender of the Kremlin's policies in Syria. A former child actor, he had served as a Russian diplomat since the 1970s and possessed a keen understanding of American politics and culture from a long stint in the Soviet Union's embassy in Washington in the 1980s. He had a ruddy complexion, a thinning mane of cottony hair, and a disposition that shifted easily from wryly cheerful to fiercely combative. By the summer of 2015, the sixty-three-year-old Muscovite was also Power's good friend.

When she started the UN job, Power's predecessor, Susan Rice, encouraged her to cultivate a good working relationship with her Russian counterpart. "He will drive you crazy," Rice had said of Churkin, "but you will need each other." Power did so, and the two were soon frequent companions at lunches and cocktail hours and over long, candid conversations in their respective missions in New York. On many a week, as Power would later say, she spent more time with Churkin than with her own family. A camaraderie developed over time, and Power began to perceive Churkin as more than just a skillful diplomat who faithfully advanced his government's policies. In his own way—which usually meant working behind the scenes—Churkin was someone who liked to get things done.

"Vitaly didn't go to work in the morning looking to block things," Power said. "He wasn't a person who liked vetoing resolutions." Despite his country's record of protecting and empowering Assad, Churkin, in private moments, could appear genuinely sympathetic about the suffering of ordinary Syrians, and he was sensitive to the public view of Moscow as an accomplice to genocide. "He didn't want to be the bad guy all the time," she said.

Sensing an opportunity with her new friend, Power began to push the idea of an international panel of experts that would objectively examine the evidence surrounding chemical attacks in Syria and, whenever possible, render a judgment about who was responsible for the crime. If Russia truly believed that Assad was innocent and that all the gas attacks were carried out exclusively by jihadists and other rebels, why not allow the exculpatory evidence to be presented to the whole world?

"What is there to lose?" she asked.

At the White House, Power was advised to save her breath. Even some Obama advisers were not persuaded that chlorine was truly a chemical weapon. "You'll never get the Russians to agree," she was repeatedly told. But in their private conversations, Churkin seemed surprisingly open to the idea, or at least unwilling to rule it out. Power wondered whether the Russians were growing weary of the chlorine attacks, which, after all, sullied the diplomatic victory they had achieved in securing the deal to eliminate Syria's stockpile. Could the mere threat of exposure and public shaming lead the culprits to abandon the tactic?

"If you want to deter, then why don't we do this together?" Power asked Churkin one day. "Why don't we try to create something?"

Churkin paused, considering. The ruddy face brightened.

"Why not?" he said.

Over the following weeks, the two sat together to draw up an outline for the new investigative panel. It would again be jointly run by the United Nations and the OPCW, and it would have a one-year mandate to study evidence collected after previous attacks to see if it was possible at last to identify a guilty party. The results would be presented to the UN Security Council, where Russia could always cast its veto to prevent any real harm from befalling its Syrian ally. But the reports themselves would be public, and everyone would know what the investigators had found.

Power never fully understood why the Russians went along with the plan or knew what kinds of contortions Churkin put himself through to win the Kremlin's approval. The Russian's own aides seemed wary of the proposal, so much so that the two ambassadors sent their deputies out of the room when negotiating the most delicate parts of the agreement.

"The staff is not going to be able to do this," Churkin explained. "It's Samantha and Vitaly."

By early August, they had finished. On August 7, the Security Council unanimously approved the creation of the OPCW-UN Joint Investigative Mechanism, soon known simply as the JIM. In the authorizing resolution, the multinational staff would be charged with identifying "to the greatest extent feasible individuals, entities, groups, or governments who were perpetrators, organizers, sponsors or otherwise involved in the use of chemicals as weapons, including chlorine."

Power was relieved. The JIM could do nothing to stop the fighting in Syria, but at least the perpetrators behind the most grievous offenses finally would be named. After 1,400 people died at Ghouta, the United Nations had been constrained even from saying who was behind the deed, let alone to bring the guilty party to justice. That failure "has allowed conspiracy theories to arise; it has allowed those perpetrators to go free," Power told reporters outside the council chambers after the JIM was voted into existence.

Now, thanks to a rare moment of unity at the United Nations, there would be a "shared international factual basis for eventual prosecution," Power said.

A turning point was indeed at hand. But it was not one that Power and other U.S. officials hoped for. Days after the vote, Russia would radically alter the course of the Syrian conflict. Moscow had decided that henceforth it would back Assad not only with words and diplomacy but also with force.

17

A "catastrophic success"

On the Turkish coast southeast of the city of Adana stood a large villa that functioned for years as a portal into one of the biggest and most secretive CIA operations of recent times. The house was well-appointed, with numerous bedrooms, a swimming pool, and a spacious table near the front entrance where the Americans held meetings with an endless parade of bearded visitors in grubby combat fatigues. The CIA's men would sit around the table to unfurl their maps, discuss tactics, and, when the talking was done, dispense envelopes filled with cash.

The money was mostly salaries for ordinary fighters, ones who gained acceptance into the CIA's program but never saw the villa where their leaders went to receive guidance and draw their unit's share of guns and grenades. These ordinary men crossed the border farther south, near the Turkish town of Reyhanli, and after a quick pat-down and questioning, filed into buses for training camps as far away as Ankara, the capital city some four hundred miles to the north. As many as three hundred Syrians made the trek each week, eventually taking their places in classrooms or at firing ranges where CIA paramilitary trainers demonstrated how to read a topo map, blow a bridge, or use a night-vision scope. By the spring of 2015, thousands of rebels had completed the training and disappeared again across the border, often never to be seen again.

Over time the CIA's Turkish operation acquired a nickname:

MOM, from a Turkish acronym used by the host country's intelligence service. But the official code name was Timber Sycamore. Other than the physical destruction of Syria's chemical stockpile, it was the most significant action taken by the United States in response to Bashar al-Assad's poison-gas attacks. That spring, after months of struggles, it seemed to be working. Aided by a highly secretive American arms program, the rebels suddenly were winning. Syrian soldiers were dying, and government-controlled towns falling, in numbers not seen since the start of the war.

Yet those gains were making some in Washington very nervous. The rebel surge was real enough, but it was not exactly as it seemed.

The reasons for the Americans' anxiety were on display that March when an alliance of rebel militias, some of them with links to MOM, went on the attack against government garrisons around Syria's northern provincial capital of Idlib. The invaders dispatched suicide bombers to destroy checkpoints while hundreds of fighters poured into the city from three directions. When Assad's forces counterattacked with tanks, the militias struck back with a powerful new weapon: TOW antitank missiles designed and built by the United States. In less than a week, Idlib was in rebel hands, becoming the first provincial capital outside ISIS-controlled eastern Syria to fall to the opposition.

Such a resounding defeat for Assad's forces should have been regarded as good news for an American administration that had secretly funneled weapons to Syria's rebels since 2013. Yet among the throngs of victorious gunmen in Idlib, only a few carried the banners of U.S.-backed secular brigades. The overwhelming majority belonged to a coalition of Islamist groups led by al-Nusra Front, the Islamic State offshoot that had allied itself with al-Qaeda. The militants raised black flags over municipal buildings, smashed Assad statues with hammers, and declared Idlib to be under Islamic law. In four days, they had captured the city with the help of arms intended as aid for Syria's moderate rebels. Whether through theft, trickery, or corruption, al-Nusra's fighters had the weapons now.

From the Turkish border to the Damascus suburbs, the story was the same. The rebels possessed real momentum for the first time in two years, thanks in part to weapons purchased by the United States and its allies and administered through the CIA's most ambitious arm-and-equip program since at least the 1980s. Yet the wrong rebels seemed to be benefiting.

U.S. intelligence agencies had monitored the ominous rise of Islamist militias for years, and they had hoped to change the trajectory by supplying better weapons and pay to the Free Syrian Army and other secular rebel groups. But now every assumption about the conflict was being challenged. At first there had been near-universal predictions of a quick collapse of Assad's government. Those gave way to forecasts of stalemate and partition, with Assad left controlling a rump state in the Alawite heartland along the coast. Now analysts worried that Syria could share the same fate as Libya, the North African country that freed itself from dictatorship in 2011, only to see ISIS and other Islamist groups seize control of major cities while the rest of the country fragmented into warring fiefdoms.

In Washington, President Barack Obama was being castigated by pundits on both right and left for failing to do more to help Syria's rebels. In reality, the White House was doing vastly more than anyone knew, and its covert efforts were paying off—just not in the way the administration had hoped. By the spring of 2015, the president's national security team was beginning to contemplate the possibility of a sweeping rebel victory in which Syria's secular dictator would be replaced by Islamists with ties to al-Qaeda. Senior advisers to the president minted a term to describe such an outcome.

They called it "catastrophic success."

In April 2015, Brett McGurk traveled to Jordan to attend an urgent gathering of the leading countries in the international military campaign against the Islamic State. It was one of his first overseas trips since being appointed as a special presidential envoy to the anti-ISIS coalition, and at that moment, the momentum in the fight against militant Islamists seemed to be going in two different directions at once.

In Iraq, U.S.-backed government soldiers and militiamen had nearly completed the liberation of Tikrit, Saddam Hussein's birthplace in Iraq's Sunni heartland, while separately a large fighting force was preparing for an assault on Mosul, the Islamic State's Iraqi capital. Yet in Syria, nearly all the news was bad. In the west, al-Nusra Front was well on its way to capturing Idlib and would soon claim the surrounding countryside, up to the Turkish border. ISIS had taken control of a large Palestinian refugee camp on the outskirts of Damascus, and its fighters would soon overrun the government-held town of Palmyra in the country's center. U.S. intelligence agencies meanwhile had calculated that more than twenty thousand foreign fighters, including thousands of Europeans, had crossed into Syria to join the terrorists.

"This is a problem that is off the charts historically," McGurk told a television interviewer just after his return from Jordan. In Iraq, the eventual defeat of ISIS appeared certain. But Syria was a disaster. Tens of thousands of refugees were fleeing the country each month, while large swaths of northern and eastern Syria were firmly in the hands of Islamist militias with historical ties to al-Qaeda.

How things had gone so badly in Syria was a complicated story, but missteps by Western countries had clearly made matters worse. In the thinking of some of Obama's advisers, including McGurk, any accounting of the West's epic policy collapse in Syria would begin with those few simple words uttered amid a burst of optimism in the uprising's early months: "Assad must go."

President Obama as well as the leaders of Britain, France, Germany, and the European Union had each used those words, with slight variations, in August 2011, five months after the uprising began. They were intended as a statement of support for the democratic aspirations of millions of ordinary Syrians, including the many thousands who had been arrested, beaten, or shot while participating in peaceful protests throughout the country. But McGurk had found the statements deeply worrying. The sentiments were noble, but he knew they were only sentiments, while many who heard them would perceive an implicit promise of help.

As the violence in Syria worsened, McGurk watched with growing concern as different leaders and factions across the Middle East began acting on their own interpretations of "Assad must go." In Syria, millions of street protesters took solace in the belief that the United States and other Western countries ultimately would intervene on their behalf, just as they had done in Libya. From the Turkish capital to the Persian Gulf, governments also perceived a coming intervention and began shaping their own policies accordingly. Some countries—and in some cases, private individuals with pet causes and big bank accounts—were emboldened to throw support to individual militia groups that mirrored their political and religious views. Other officials, particularly Iraqi Shiite leaders whom McGurk knew from his days working the Iraq file, worried that the awful-but-predictable Assad might be replaced with something worse, perhaps a radical Sunni regime openly hostile to them. The Kurds and many Iraqi Sunnis were nervous as well, fearing that Assad's collapse would unleash chaos just as the United States was preparing to withdraw its forces from Iraq. Iraqis from all backgrounds called McGurk asking for reassurance.

"What does it mean, 'Assad must go'?" they demanded. "What's the plan? What comes after?"

In reality, the Obama White House had no appetite for another military entanglement in the Middle East, and the administration offered few ideas beyond the initial call for Assad to step down. Even in 2013, when McGurk was named the State Department's deputy assistant secretary for Iraq and Iran, the prevailing view at Syria policy meetings was that Assad was doomed, locked in a war of attrition that he inevitably would lose. By then, the dictator had lost half his country, along with his cash reserves and best military units, and was forced to depend on Russia and Iran for his survival. Calling for him to go was simply positioning the United States on the right side of history.

"The assumption was that he wouldn't be able to withstand the pressure—the diplomatic isolation, the military pressure, the economic pressure—and eventually he'd have to negotiate himself out of power," McGurk said. "But it was a total misreading. We did not understand the dynamics of Syria, or Assad's readiness to hold on to power at all costs. Short of an invasion, he wasn't going anywhere."

Ultimately Obama had been unable to resist the gravitational pull of Syria's disaster. By now, in 2015, Timber Sycamore had amounted to more than $1 billion worth of weapons and gear for the anti-Assad opposition.

While many of the president's aides were sympathetic to the fighters, many were beginning to see the operation's massive flows of guns and cash as the equivalent of a gasoline tanker spraying its load onto a burning house. Barring direct military intervention by the United

States—a prospect that both the American public and the U.S. president were anxious to avoid—Syria's moderate rebels simply could not defeat a Syrian army that enjoyed unwavering support from Iran and Russia. Dumping more arms into the country, these aides believed, would only prolong the war, deepen Syria's suffering, and strengthen radical elements on both sides.

From its origins to its peak in 2015, as advisers to Obama later described it, Timber Sycamore was like an astronomical black hole whose sheer mass warped time and space around it. Among the president's national security advisers, it was a topic of countless hours of often heated debate, particularly after investigations revealed rampant corruption, incompetence, and theft. Government officials in Turkey and Jordan were caught skimming off the top, stealing small arms and selling them for profit on the black market. Costlier weapons systems, such as the BGM-71 TOW antitank missile launchers, crossed the border into Syria and promptly vanished, with many of them purchased or stolen by Islamists. White House officials were horrified when a rebel unit trained by the Pentagon in a parallel arm-and-equip program run by the military was immediately wiped out by al-Nusra Front, and the survivors kidnapped.

"We created, perhaps inadvertently, the expectation that the United States was coming, particularly as the revolution militarized," McGurk later said. "Then, with so much money, weapons, and tens of thousands of foreign fighters pouring into Syria with little control or accountability, it becomes a total disaster."

Still, there was hope, during the months when the opposition was racking up victories, that Assad might yet be driven from power. As McGurk sat through State Department meetings and secure video conferences, Syria analysts would dutifully parse the latest battlefield gains and note with satisfaction that the "rebels" had won again. There was genuine excitement in Washington when an alliance of opposition fighters captured Raqqa, the first provincial capital to fall entirely under rebel control.

But which rebels? After a few weeks of intermural competition between rival groups, a single victorious faction emerged to pull the entire city into its grasp.

"It was ISIS. ISIS flags, ISIS control," McGurk said. In the northwest, the al-Qaeda-aligned al-Nusra Front and its Islamist allies had become the dominant military force on the rebel side, while in the east it was the terrorist leader Abu Bakr al-Baghdadi and his thuggish lieutenants running entire provinces and seemingly on the march everywhere.

In neighboring countries, from Jordan and Israel to Egypt and Iraq, the nightmare scenario had long been that Syria's cruel and vengeful dictator might "win" by retaining control over Damascus and the coastal cities and perpetuating the civil war indefinitely. Suddenly, in the spring of 2015, that worry was replaced by a new one:

What would happen if Assad lost?

Syria's close-in neighbors were not the only ones alarmed by the change in fortunes in the country's civil war. Iran's Major General Qasem Soleimani also was growing increasingly worried, and he decided in late spring to do something about it.

By 2015, Soleimani had cemented his reputation as the master strategist most responsible for keeping Assad in power. In 2012, when Assad's army began to crack under the strain of the uprising, it was Soleimani who had come to its rescue, directing a patchwork force of Hezbollah fighters, Shiite militias, and Iranian special-forces operators to shore up the defense of government strongholds and gradually help Assad regain lost ground. Soldiers under his direction were later blamed for some of the war's worst atrocities, including the siege of Madaya, a small rebel-controlled town that was sealed off from food and medicine until its ragged inhabitants literally began dropping dead from starvation.

Soleimani, like the rest of Iran's leadership, viewed Syria as a vital ally to be defended at all costs. But to him, there was more at stake than the rule of a strongman whose Alawite religion is actually viewed by pious Iranians as heretical. Soleimani viewed Syria as part of a greater "Shiite Crescent" that enabled Tehran to extend its influence through the Middle East. In furtherance of that goal, he ordered construction in Syria of a new highway that he hoped would become part of a land route for Iranian military supplies and hardware, stretching from Tehran to the Mediterranean coast.

These gains appeared to be suddenly at risk in early 2015 when a better-armed and well-disciplined rebel force began pushing south from the Turkish border toward Damascus and into the staunchly pro-government Alawite provinces on the coast. Soleimani was famously contemptuous of the Syrian military, calling the army "useless" and disparaging its counterproductive use of poison gas, which the Iranians viewed as ineffective militarily and likely to invite Western intervention. But Soleimani had secret weapons of his own.

Convinced that Syria was on the brink of failing, the Iranian general began putting together a new Syrian army, made up of twenty thousand foreign Shiite mercenaries recruited from poor neighborhoods in Afghanistan and Pakistan. These would complement an expanded force of seven thousand Islamic Revolutionary Guard Corps soldiers and Hezbollah fighters that could soon be ready to step into the breach.

Then, while the new divisions were being organized, Soleimani flew to Moscow to personally urge President Vladimir Putin to put his warplanes behind the effort to drive back the rebel advance. The diminutive, snowy-haired Iranian pulled out a map of Syria to highlight the urgency of the rebel threat against Damascus and to show how a coordinated Iranian-Russian counterstrike could break the offensive. It was getting late, but the Russians and Iranians together could still prevail. "We haven't lost all the cards," a Middle Eastern official summarized the Iranian's pitch to Putin.

It worked. Russia began preparations for its first foreign intervention since the Soviet Union's invasion of Afghanistan. And almost no one in Washington saw it coming.

The CIA did detect numerous signs of a Russian military buildup and believed at the time that Moscow was preparing to counter the effects of Timber Sycamore by shipping in more weapons, ammunition, and aircraft. In June, more than three months before the intervention officially started, Russian officials privately secured a treaty with Syria granting Moscow open-ended, rent-free rights to its Khmeimim Air Base, a little-used military installation near the coast just south of Latakia. They then went on a construction spree. Over the summer and early fall, Khmeimim sprouted dozens of new structures, including a new control tower, helicopter pads, a new runway, and housing for 1,500 personnel. Cargo ships and transport planes arrived carrying Russian soldiers and technicians as well as thousands of tons of what Moscow described as "humanitarian aid" for Syrians.

Russian officials meanwhile began an elaborate disinformation campaign to tamp down speculation about a possible military intervention. As late as mid-September, Foreign Ministry spokeswoman Maria Zakharova derided such talk as a "strange hysteria."

"Russian military specialists are in Syria to help them master the weapons being supplied"—and nothing more, she said.

Within the White House, occasional arguments erupted over the meaning of the buildup. U.S. surveillance networks over the summer picked up an additional clue: the Russians were beginning to use a sensitive communications system that normally was reserved for use during military engagements. "They're going into combat in Syria," one official told a meeting of Obama's National Security Council. The finding was debated but ultimately discounted. Yes, Russia appeared to be building a full-fledged military base at Khmeimim, but if Moscow was truly preparing to go on the attack, surely there would be evidence of a more tangible sort: Russian Su-27 fighter planes parked on the runway.

Yet it was happening. Russia perceived its Syrian investments—its Arab ally, its navy base and warm-water port, its surveillance network and listening posts—as being gravely at risk. And it was ready to defend them.

"As we saw the signals, it occurred to me, 'Oh God, they're getting ready to go in,'" said the official who sounded the warning at the White House. "They're not going to let Assad lose."

The U.S. embassy in Baghdad lies on the west bank of the Tigris River inside a compound that is easily the largest, costliest, and most fortified diplomatic mission in the world. Surrounded by high blast walls and patrolled by Iraqi soldiers and U.S. Marines, it is normally off-limits to all except invited visitors and guests. The sentries at the main gate were thus surprised one late September morning when a Russian army officer arrived unannounced by diplomatic car and demanded to be let in. With no calling card other than his dress uniform and a parade's worth of military ribbons and medals, the visitor insisted that he needed to speak with the senior American military officer on post. It is a matter of great urgency, the visitor said.

The request was relayed to the embassy's Office of Security

Cooperation, and then to the man who happened to be the highest-ranking U.S. soldier in all of Iraq at the moment. Lieutenant General Sean MacFarland was the new chief of the multinational coalition battling the Islamic State, and he had just arrived in Iraq a week earlier to begin the mission. A plainspoken New Yorker and former armored-division commander, MacFarland had been a genuine hero of the last Iraq conflict, having led a combat brigade in a grueling, months-long fight to wrest the Iraqi city of Ramadi from the terrorist army that called itself al-Qaeda in Iraq. That same year he helped engineer the "Anbar Awakening" movement, in which western Iraq's Sunni tribal leaders formed alliances with U.S. troops to finally defeat the Islamists. Now, at fifty-six, MacFarland was back to lead another anti-insurgency campaign in Iraq, this time, ironically, against ISIS, a rebranded version of the same terrorist group. It was clear from the outset that his to-do list would also include managing the Russians, who in recent weeks had been moving assets into Syria with the obvious intention of taking on a larger role in the region's wars. The true scope of Russia's ambition was something that MacFarland and other U.S. officials were only beginning to find out.

The Russian visitor was by now waiting in an embassy reception room to deliver his message. He was a three-star general, like MacFarland, but under the Russian system his rank was a full grade lower than that of a U.S. Army lieutenant general. Technically he was an inferior, so MacFarland—who by now had an inkling about the purpose of the visit—decided to play it cool. He dispatched one of the embassy's military attachés, a colonel, to greet the guest from Moscow and try to discern the nature of the "urgent" business that had prompted a Russian officer to show up unannounced like an ordinary Iraqi looking for a travel visa.

"Let me know how it works out," MacFarland said wryly as the colonel left for the meeting.

The Russian general was led to an empty conference room, where he began to explain the two reasons behind his unusual visit. The first reason, he said, was to extend an invitation of sorts. Russia was setting up an intelligence headquarters in Baghdad for the fight against ISIS, parallel to the vastly larger operations center run by the United States along with the dozens of other countries that had signed up to fight the terrorist group. The new Russian entity would include representatives from Iran and Syria. Iraq had signed up as well, he explained, and perhaps the United States would like to join, too, in the interest of coordinating attacks against the Islamists?

It was ludicrous, as the Russians surely knew, to suggest that the United States might consent to joint military operations with leaders from Iran and Syria, two countries Washington regarded as state sponsors of terrorism. The Americans already knew about Russia's newly opened "antiterrorism" command center, located in an office building in central Baghdad, adjacent to the Iraqi Ministry of Defense and about two miles from the U.S. embassy. And they would have nothing to do with it.

The other message was more worthy of an unannounced visit. Moscow had decided to plunge into the four-year-old conflict on the side of Bashar al-Assad, and its warplanes were already in the air, or soon would be, striking "terrorist" strongholds in northern Syria, in an area where military aircraft of the United States and its coalition allies were also active. Any foreign aircraft encountered in Russia's area of operation might be at risk, the general said.

"If you have forces in the area, we request they leave," he told the American.

The Russian had barely departed the compound before news of the warning was swirling through Washington. At the Pentagon, officials vowed publicly that they would ignore the Russians and continue with normal operations against ISIS targets in Syria. In reality, the Obama administration worried about the chances of an accident or misstep that could trigger hostilities with Russia.

Within hours of the Russian general's visit, bombs began to fall.

After that, Russian fighter planes departed daily from the new air base near Latakia to fire missiles at rebel strongholds. Heavy bombers from southern Russia, their fuel tanks replenished after stopovers in northern Iran, crossed into Syria with five-hundred-pound gravity bombs. Russian cruise missiles launched from ships in the Caspian Sea streaked across northern Iraq to targets near Aleppo, one thousand miles away.

Within weeks, the intervention had fundamentally changed the character of Syria's civil war. The great rebel offensive of 2015 sputtered to a halt, and one by one the regime reclaimed many of the towns and villages it had lost, with the exception of Idlib, the rebels' principal stronghold. The CIA-backed covert army continued to train and to receive new weapons, but Damascus never again came under a serious rebel threat.

The reversal spared the Obama administration from having to confront the "catastrophic success" of an al-Nusra army marching into the Syrian capital with black banners and U.S.-supplied antitank weapons. Still, it was a sobering demonstration of the limits of the White House's ability to change the outcome of Syria's civil war, or even to bring about conditions that might force Assad to compromise.

"It turns out that Russia also had a red line, and it was Assad," said a senior White House official who participated in dozens of sensitive discussions about the Syrian war. "They were not going to let Assad fall, and they were willing to bear the cost of intervening to keep him in power.

"In the end," the official said, "they were more committed to keeping him in power than we were committed to making him go."

18

An ISIS "wonder weapon"

MOSUL, IRAQ. FEBRUARY 2016

Suleiman al-Afari woke up on the morning of February 8 with an unusually long to-do list, which put the forty-nine-year-old ISIS weapons-maker in a peevish mood. As a scientist and lifelong bureaucrat, he liked keeping a routine, even in wartime, but on this morning there were errands and obligations that would keep him on the road and out of the office for half the day. His mother was ill, which meant an hour's drive to her village to visit with her, and perhaps to try to negotiate medical care with the jihadists who now ran the local hospital. He also had to drop his wife off at work, pick up cakes, and navigate a gauntlet of checkpoints that clotted the highways all around Mosul, forcing motorists to wait in lines while bearded militiamen peered suspiciously inside their vehicles. As a final chore, he had to stop at an industrial supply warehouse to load up his car with jugs of liquid soap. For the peculiar kind of factory he ran, soap is considered essential safety equipment. His workers made sulfur mustard for the Islamic State's artillery rockets and bombs, and in case of a spill, the lye in the soap could help neutralize the chemical toxins and lessen the number of severe burns and disfiguring scars.

In his former life, Afari never dreamed of having such a job, and he certainly never asked for it. In that fateful summer of 2014 when ISIS took over his city, he had worked as a geologist and midlevel functionary in the Mosul office of Iraq's Ministry of Industry and Minerals.

He was a family man, gregarious and gray-haired, who had spent his entire life in Mosul and had chosen not to flee, as thousands of his neighbors did, when an Islamic State army swept through the city, defeating an Iraqi troop garrison that was at least fifteen times larger.

Thousands of Iraqi troops had been killed that day, many of them shedding their uniforms and trying to escape, only to be rounded up and slaughtered by the assailants. Afari rode out the invasion in his villa, listening to news reports and the sounds of fighting. When it was quiet again, he and other citizens of Iraq's second-largest city ventured outside to find black flags fluttering in the main square and terrorists running the police stations and government ministries.

At first, most Iraqi government employees stayed home, their salaries continuing to show up automatically in their bank accounts. But when the payments stopped, many were left with a choice of either working for the Islamic State's newly proclaimed caliphate, or doing without. For his part, Afari decided to go back to work and claim his desk and job title before someone else took them. He sat in his nearly empty office day after day and waited for ISIS's emissaries to show up.

Mosul's new rulers were inevitably drawn to Afari's Ministry of Industries and Minerals as a gateway to northern Iraq's factories, mines, and oil infrastructure—assets of immense value to an organization that was less interested in governing than in enriching itself and expanding its military capability. Already, some of Afari's colleagues had been put to work restoring production at damaged oil wells in the desert outside town, and some of the department's machine shops had been commandeered as manufacturing hubs for building roadside bombs. Eventually a delegation arrived at Afari's office. The caliphate's representatives told the scientist he could keep his job and salary, if he was willing to accept an important new mission.

Help us make chemical weapons, the men from Islamic State demanded.

Afari knew almost nothing about the subject, but he was reluctant to refuse.

"I was afraid that I would lose my job," Afari said, explaining his decision years afterward. "A government job is hard to get, and it was important to hang on to it."

Thus Afari the geologist became Afari the chemical weaponeer.

High on his list of weekly duties was finding and collecting supplies, which is why he went looking for liquid soap on February 8, 2016.

There was a back road through the desert that bypassed some of Mosul's military checkpoints, and that afternoon Afari opted to take it, hoping to save a little time. He eased his Chevrolet Optra onto the nearly empty expanse of highway and popped a cassette into his tape player to break up the monotony. He was fiddling with the player's controls when, in his rearview mirror, he caught a glimpse of something strange. In the sky behind him were four helicopters, flying very low, just behind his vehicle.

Two of the helicopters moved forward until they were nearly parallel to his car, while the other two hovered overhead. The skids of the nearest one were now almost at eye level, and its big rotors kicked up such clouds of dust that it was difficult to see. Afari was bewildered. ISIS had no helicopters. Were these Iraqi government forces? Why were they flying so close to him?

He was still trying to make sense of it when he felt something hit the car. There was a loud bang, then a series of pops as bullets hit the side panels and hood. A searing pain shot through his left leg, and he felt the car veer sharply as one of its tires blew. Afari pulled off the road and cut the engine, and with uplifted hands he climbed out of the car and into a whirl of sand and rotor wash. A huge dog suddenly appeared from nowhere and seized him by the arm.

"I wasn't afraid that they would kill me," Afari said afterward of the lunging canine and its handler, an American commando in body armor who grabbed his other arm to cuff him as he lay on the ground. "I never saw myself as an important figure. Anyway, at the moment, I was busy with the dog."

Another soldier shoved a picture—an ID photo—in Afari's face and asked in English if he was the man in the photograph.

"That you?"

"Yes," Afari replied.

Then a cloth bag was slipped over his head and the world went dark. He felt himself being dragged onto a helicopter and strapped into a seat. And then with a roar the big machine lifted off the ground, climbing so rapidly it made his stomach churn.

When the blindfold was removed about a half hour later, he was surrounded by U.S. and Kurdish soldiers at an Iraqi detention camp, many miles away. It was day one in Afari's years-long ordeal in prison, and a breakthrough day for the U.S. and Kurdish forces who had just netted one of the most important ISIS weapons-makers ever to be captured alive.

It took only a few hours for Afari to fully grasp his choices, and then the words started to flow. The Iraqis ultimately would seek the death penalty for the ISIS weaponeer, but with a stay of execution as long as he cooperated. So he cooperated.

The picture he painted over the following weeks was of a weapons program that was at once ambitious and amateurish; one that was often mismanaged and disorganized, but malevolent in its intention. The group's propaganda machine had never uttered a word about chemical weapons, but beginning in the fall of 2014, the United States learned, ISIS had been working diligently to make them.

The interrogations took place in Iraq, inside the fortress-like headquarters of the Kurdistan Regional Government's Counterterrorism Department. Afari, sipping tea and wearing prison-issued sweat clothes and sandals, recounted in matter-of-fact detail the terrorist group's attempts to make mustard gas, part of what he described as a broader effort to create novel weapons and delivery systems to defend the caliphate and terrorize its opponents.

On the day that Mosul's conquerors arrived at the Ministry of Industries and Minerals that fall, Afari had been running the acquisitions office in the ministry's metallurgical division, he recalled. The visitors from ISIS who sat with him seemed particularly fascinated to learn details about his job and asked lots of questions. A few weeks later they returned to present him with a new assignment and a list of specialized metal equipment that he was to find and procure. Included on the list were stainless-steel tanks, pipes, valves, and tubes, all with technical specifications that would enable them to withstand corrosive chemicals and high temperatures.

Afari had an inkling of how the materials were to be used. But all doubt was removed when the geologist was partnered with other scientists and experts, including chemists, a biologist, and at least one technician who had worked inside the weapons program of former

Iraqi dictator Saddam Hussein. Together, he said, the team was to design and build a production complex that could make sulfur mustard for the Islamic State. The chemical itself was no mystery to the older men in the group. Iraq manufactured the poison by the ton in the 1980s, with substantial help in the form of equipment and supplies from Western Europe, and with the full knowledge of U.S. governments at the time. During the Iran-Iraq War, Saddam Hussein used mustard gas to drive back "human wave" assaults by Iranian soldiers, killing or wounding them by the tens of thousands in the marshy wastelands near Basra. In 1987, Iraqi jets dropped mustard-gas bombs on civilians in the Iranian border town of Sardasht, killing 113 people and leaving thousands of others with permanent injuries ranging from blindness to severely damaged lungs. Many of the victims were children.

Afari would tell his interrogators that he believed the assignment was nonnegotiable. "You have no choice but to become one of them," he later said. So he went to work organizing a supply chain and equipping a small cluster of labs and workshops that stretched from Mosul University to the suburbs. The job in many ways felt similar to what he had been doing as a manager for the Iraqi government.

Afari's new boss was an Iraqi engineer with an impressive background and big plans. His name was Salih al-Sabawi, but everyone called him by his Arabic *kunya* name, Abu Malik—literally "father of the king." It was easy to see why he had been picked for the job. He was an ISIS insider, having joined the terrorist group in 2005 when Zarqawi was still the leader. Before that, back in the 1990s, he had worked inside Saddam Hussein's chemical weapons complex. In Abu Malik, ISIS had found a leader with solid terrorist credentials and rare, hands-on experience manufacturing poison gas on an industrial scale. The Iraqi was given an office and a lab on the grounds of Mosul University, and he began making a list of critical supplies and equipment that would enable him to replicate his former weapons factory somewhere in the Islamic State's eastern capital. Abu Malik also would need deputies, including seasoned technocrats who understood metallurgy and supply chains. And so ISIS identified experienced managers such as Afari and brought them aboard, willingly or not.

Within weeks, Afari began to feel at ease with his new life. According to his own account, he liked the work, and he gradually came to admire his ISIS overseers. A religiously observant Sunni Muslim, he was grateful to see ISIS chase away the Shiite soldiers and corrupt police officers who ran checkpoints to shake down motorists for small bribes. He was exultant one day to see an ISIS crew hauling away a large rubbish pile that had partially blocked his street for years. Crime was down, and despite chronic scarcities of many consumer goods, workers were regularly getting their paychecks and basic services, from electricity and water to trash collection and medical care. Like everyone else, Afari heard stories about ISIS carrying out public beheadings and other acts of cruelty, but he never personally saw them, and he didn't much care.

"To be honest, it was the best year of my life—the best," he said afterward. "We felt free. Since the U.S. occupation things had never been as calm as this. ISIS showed us something we had never seen."

As for the business of making chemical weapons, Afari managed to make peace with that as well. The mustard gas he was helping create was not an instrument of genocide, he reasoned, but rather a psychological weapon that usually kills only a fraction of the people exposed to it. ISIS was surrounded by larger, more powerful enemies, so it needed to project itself as fearsome. Chemical weapons, he said, were "about creating horror"—about making rivals too frightened to fight.

The reality was even more terrifying. By early 2015, ISIS was exploring a variety of uses for its newly acquired poisons and even trying them out on Iraqi prisoners to assess the poisons' potential as terrorist weapons. In conversations secretly monitored by spy agencies, Abu Malik enthused about unleashing lethal gases on the cities of Europe, and perhaps the United States. The same idea occurred to others, including Basil Hassan, the young engineer from Denmark whose potential as a bomb maker had quickly drawn the attention of ISIS commanders in Iraq and Syria. Hassan's vague idea for a poison-gas device had not yet taken shape, but the youth had been assigned to a foreign-operations unit and put to work researching ways to attach explosives to drone aircraft. Ambitious and cold-blooded, Hassan eventually earned a nickname from the Western intelligence agencies who tracked his online communications but did not yet know his real identity. They called him "The Controller."

The plans were ambitious, but they were slow to bear fruit. The truth was, the mustard gas Afari and his friends were making was not all that good—at least not yet. It was difficult to find high-quality equipment and supplies in the caliphate, and many of Mosul's experienced chemists and lab workers had fled the city. On the week he was captured, Afari had visited one of the main production sites in Mosul and was struck by how inadequate it seemed. *Very primitive and simple,* he thought to himself. He wondered how long it would take to transform the place into a truly professional operation.

Still, it had been a promising start. Despite the program's rawness, Afari was not displeased with what he had helped accomplish.

"Do I regret it?" he mused afterward in his Kurdish prison. "I don't know if I'd use that word."

Over several weeks the interrogation of Afari yielded a trove of precious details, including specific locations of chemical facilities and the names of the scientists and functionaries who ran them. Each day's summaries were transmitted to analysts at the CIA and Pentagon, and then back across the Atlantic to the Baghdad operations room from which Lieutenant General Sean MacFarland, leader of military forces in the anti-ISIS coalition, managed the war.

MacFarland read the reports carefully. The CIA and Defense Department were now working to disrupt the Islamic State's weapons program, and they already had achieved a crucial success: the killing of Abu Malik. Alarmed by the engineer's talk about gassing Western cities, the Pentagon quietly dispatched special-forces teams into Iraq to find him, and then ordered an air strike that obliterated his Mosul office. Abu Malik was dead, but as Afari's confessions revealed, ISIS had not given up. Newcomers, including foreign scientists, had been tapped to fulfill Abu Malik's terrible vision. MacFarland parsed the latest intelligence in daily conference calls with other Pentagon officials who separately arrived at the same grim conclusion: Given enough time, the ISIS weaponeers would eventually succeed.

"We began to recognize that ISIS was pulling in not just fighters but people with unique skills: technical skills, scientific skills, financial skills," said General Joseph Votel, the Pentagon's special-operations chief at the time and a regular participant in the discussions. "That gave us pause. We all witnessed the horrific things they were doing. You had to make the presumption that if they got their hands on a chemical weapon, they would use it."

By early 2016, under pressure from the U.S.-led military campaign, the caliphate's soldiers were retreating everywhere, but the chemical threat appeared ever more significant. The worry among both American and Iraqi commanders was that a collapsing ISIS would try to avenge its losses by unleashing its chemical weapons, either on the battlefield or in terrorist attacks in Western cities, delivered perhaps by one of the scores of small drones the militants had gone to great effort to acquire. "They were hoping for some kind of a wonder weapon," MacFarland said later, "one that might save the caliphate."

MacFarland faced enormous pressure to act. In Washington, the president's national security advisers now were well aware of how a poison-gas weapon could transform the terror campaign that ISIS had already unleashed in European cities. Even a relatively minor attack in New York or Los Angeles would generate such an outcry that the White House would be compelled to expand the war and send another generation of U.S. ground forces into battle in Iraq and perhaps Syria. In Baghdad, Prime Minister Haider al-Abadi's government was equally anxious. Iraq's frontline troops already were jittery about the possibility of chemical attacks, so much so that senior commanders worried about the effect on morale. In MacFarland's visits with Iraqi counterparts, the subject almost always came up. The older officers had seen the effects of sarin and mustard gas during the Iran-Iraq War, and the memory was seared into their brains.

"They would talk about it, and the Iraqi press would make a big deal about it," MacFarland said. "They all knew how terrible it can be."

Taking out the group's capability would not be easy. The weapons facilities described by Afari were not hidden away on military bases or in underground bunkers, as they had been in Syria. The most important ones were in cities, inside lightly protected civilian facilities in the middle of residential neighborhoods. The Islamists had hidden a sizable production center inside a wing of a civilian hospital in Hit, a city of sixty thousand people. Another was on the grounds of Mosul University, in the heart of Iraq's second most populous city. Any air strike against sites such as these carried a risk of releasing clouds of dangerous chemicals that could drift through homes, schools, and playgrounds. If civilians were killed, the U.S. military and its partners would be blamed.

But MacFarland was out of time. Waiting for Iraqi troops to recapture the sites would mean a delay of many weeks, perhaps months. ISIS would surely use the time to build more weapons, or better ones. Or it might simply move its factories somewhere else.

A strike package was carefully assembled, with special kinds of bombs selected for the unusual mission. Beginning in March, just over a month after Afari's arrest, MacFarland's team was ready to act.

The spring's rolling air strikes began without fanfare and gained little notice in U.S. newspapers. The first target was the Iraqi city of Hit, where hundreds of government troops and tribal militiamen already were waiting on the outskirts to liberate the town from its ISIS occupiers. U.S. warplanes swooped in on March 25, 2015, to attack strategic targets around the city ahead of the ground assault, and over the following five days the Americans struck seventeen sites, one of which was blandly listed by the Pentagon as an "improvised weapons facility." On April 12, Iraqi forces fought their way into central Hit, capturing the hospital and its now-ruined chemical lab.

Next on the list was Mosul. The Islamic State's Iraqi capital was, even in wartime, a densely populated city of more than a million people, and the terrorists had positioned their most important laboratories at Mosul University, on the east bank of the Tigris River and smack in the middle of town. Mindful of the high risk of civilian casualties, the mission's planners selected special incendiary bombs designed to generate a small blast radius but intense heat, to vaporize weapons, supplies, and any residual gases that might otherwise escape. Then they waited for conditions to be just right. The time of day, the wind's speed and direction, the humidity level—any one of these could be the margin between a clean strike and a calamity for an innocent Iraqi family.

The strikes occurred sporadically as conditions allowed and new targets emerged, beginning in late spring and continuing through fall. The biggest strike, on September 13, involved a dozen U.S. aircraft and more than fifty bombs and missiles that tore apart a large manufacturing complex for pharmaceuticals on Mosul's outskirts.

Then it was over. By late 2016, U.S. military commanders were confidently asserting that the Islamic State's industrial capacity for making chemical weapons had been eliminated. On January 14, 2017, six weeks before the end of the Obama presidency, Iraqi troops captured Mosul University, the heart of eastern Mosul and the epicenter of the Islamic State's chemical weapons program.

The impact of the Pentagon's bombing campaign was direct and measurable. Researchers ultimately would attribute more than seventy poison-gas attacks to ISIS forces in Iraq and Syria. After the liberation of eastern Mosul, the number of incidents dropped to zero.

Yet in the assessment of MacFarland and the other generals behind the bombing campaign, there was little doubt about the threat that remained. Several key ISIS figures were known to have escaped to Syria, including a French national named Joe Asperman, one of the Europeans recruited by ISIS for his scientific expertise. The caliphate's leaders were so protective of Asperman and his projects that they issued a statement falsely claiming that the Frenchman had been "martyred." Now dispersed across the Middle East and perhaps beyond, Asperman and other operatives would simply be harder to find.

"They had all this capability and technical knowledge. Where did it go?" asked Votel, the former special-operations commander who would soon become the CENTCOM chief. "We know that some of their people were killed and others went home. But some may still be out there."

Iraqi troops were clearing the last ISIS renegades from eastern Mosul when a new commander in chief stood on the Capitol's West Front terrace to take the presidential oath. Donald J. Trump, now the forty-fifth U.S. president, had run a nontraditional campaign and promised a radically different approach to governing. As a candidate, Trump styled himself a rhetorical flamethrower who torched political opponents, U.S. allies, and international institutions with equal abandon. Still, many in Washington believed that Trump, who lacked any military or foreign-policy experience, would shed his reality-TV persona after taking office and follow the path of other conservative U.S. presidents, adhering to the traditions and decorum of the office and the rules of Washington statecraft. But Trump had his own ideas, and he would not be so easily constrained.

In a few areas, Trump turned out to be surprisingly conformist. Candidate Trump had regularly savaged the Obama administration over its counter-ISIS strategy, at one point claiming, preposterously, that Obama had been the "founder of ISIS" and his Democratic rival Hillary Clinton was the group's "most valuable player." (He later qualified that he was being sarcastic.) He told a cheering crowd in 2015, "I know more about ISIS than the generals do, believe me," and he later said he had a secret plan for defeating the terrorists quickly. But once in office, the new president followed the same strategy, with minor tweaks, that had been adopted by his predecessor two years earlier: using a combination of local ground forces and allied air power to slowly liberate ISIS-held cities in Iraq and Syria. His hand-picked secretary of defense, retired Marine Corps general James "Mad Dog" Mattis, turned out to be a thoughtful and cautious commander who—despite his colorful nickname—worked closely with allies and pushed back against Trump's more aggressive ideas.

Trump showed little interest in the Syrian conflict. Before announcing his candidacy, he publicly opposed bombing Syria over its chemical weapons attack at Ghouta, and he said it would be "stupid" to get involved in the country's civil war. During his presidential campaign he argued the Russia and the Arab League were better equipped to handle the Syria crisis, while the United States should "stay the hell out." If the Kremlin wanted to trouble itself with sorting out Syria's problems, they could have the place. "Let them get rid of ISIS. What the hell do we care?" he said in an interview. Taking to Twitter, his preferred means of communication, Trump expressed distrust of Syria's opposition and antipathy toward its refugees, while showing no interest in ongoing negotiations seeking a peaceful resolution to the war.

The Obama administration had been a big proponent of diplomacy, though it had little to show for more than five years of effort. Secretary of State John F. Kerry continued his nearly quixotic quest for a negotiated settlement until literally the last day of the administration. Samantha Power, the U.S. ambassador to the United Nations, cashed in the last of her chits with her Russian counterpart, Vitaly

Churkin, to secure a one-year extension for the Joint Investigative Mechanism, the UN-OPCW team that was now making steady progress in identifying the culprits behind Syria's chemical attacks. Power could not, however, resist scolding her friend over Russia's unrelenting support for Syria's murderous regime. "Is there literally nothing that can shame you?" Power asked, turning to Churkin in her final public remarks in the Security Council chamber. "Is there no act of barbarism against civilians, no execution of a child that gets under your skin, that creeps you out a little bit? Is there nothing you will not lie about or justify?"

Kerry and Power stepped down officially at noon on January 20, the day and hour of Trump's swearing-in. But the fate of other key officials and experts on Syria policy was not immediately clear. Thomas Countryman, the State Department's top WMD official and a key player in the U.S.-Russia deal to remove Syria's chemical stockpile, submitted an official letter of resignation, as is customary for assistant secretaries at the change of an administration. But Countryman had been a career civil servant under Republican and Democratic administrations, and he hoped to stay on. He wrote briefing papers for Trump's transition team, outlining the key arms-control issues currently in play, and found there was no one to give the papers to. Weeks passed without a word from anyone from the transition team. No one turned up at all until just a week before the inauguration.

Lacking instructions to the contrary, Countryman proceeded with his normal duties. A week into the new administration, he boarded a plane for a long-planned trip to Jordan and Italy for a pair of international meetings on WMD proliferation. He had just arrived in Amman, the Jordanian capital, when he received an email from a State Department colleague asking him to call the office at once.

"Tom, sorry to do this, but we've been notified by the White House that they've accepted your resignation," the colleague said.

Countryman was surprised. He was scheduled to represent the State Department at meetings that evening, then fly to Rome.

"Should I go to the meeting or just come home?" he said.

"Just come home," came the reply.

Countryman did come home. Two days after his return he cleared out his office, turned in his badge, and left the State Department. A year passed before the Trump administration named a new assistant secretary to take his place.

One of the rare political appointees who did keep his job was the chief civilian official in charge of the counter-ISIS campaign. Brett McGurk spent the transition managing a fragile, seventy-nation coalition through the battle to retake eastern Mosul. One day, as Obama was preparing to depart, the president summoned McGurk to the White House to say that he had encouraged Trump to keep him on the job, if McGurk was interested.

Of course, McGurk said. If asked, he would stay.

Weeks passed, and finally, six days before the inauguration, Trump's incoming national security adviser, Michael Flynn, invited McGurk to his office for an interview that turned into a three-hour discussion of ISIS and the Middle East. On inauguration eve, just hours before his government appointment was set to expire, White House spokesman Sean Spicer formally announced that McGurk would stay on as Trump's choice for special envoy to the counter-ISIS campaign.

Not long after that, McGurk was back in Baghdad with orders to carry out two extraordinarily difficult assignments: overseeing the final phases of the war against the Islamic State, and helping create a postwar regional framework that would preserve peace and prevent the terrorist group from threatening the security of the Middle East and the world beyond.

Of the two assignments, one would prove to be infinitely more challenging than the other.

19

"Like Judgment Day"

KHAN SHEIKHOUN, SYRIA. APRIL 4, 2017

Physician Mamoun Morad was driving to work just after sunrise when the warning came over his radio scanner. The sixty-five-year-old liked to listen to the chatter among the rescue workers and volunteer civil patrols to get an early sense of what his day would be like. This bright, chilly April morning already was shaping up to be a memorable one.

There was a volunteer spotter who lived near Syria's al-Shayrat air base and kept an eye out for outgoing military sorties. Around 6:30 a.m., the lookout reported seeing a lone, Russian-made Su-22 fighter-bomber taxiing on the runway. "There's an airplane from Shayrat about to take off," the spotter was saying. "To the people in north Hama, be careful. To the south Idlib people, be careful."

Morad, bald and ruddy-faced with soft brown eyes that were often obscured behind thick reading glasses, ran two hospitals, including one in Khan Sheikhoun, a town of sixty thousand about twenty miles from Hama. The town was near the front line, nominally controlled by Islamist rebels but frequently targeted by government warplanes and helicopters. The spotter's alert meant there could be fresh casualties that morning, perhaps even for him and his overstretched medical staff.

Morad was still driving minutes later when he heard the plane. Craning for a look, he could see the bomber as it flew in a tight circle directly over Khan Sheikhoun. Then it flew away again. Ten minutes later, the doctor's scanner erupted with desperate cries for help.

Civil defense patrols on the north side of town heard the whistling of the bomb and felt the impact. It was a big bomb, and it landed in a street near a bakery shop, gouging a hole in the pavement and sending up a plume of dust and smoke. Yet, curiously, it did not explode. The smoke drifted south on the morning breeze toward a residential street of modest two-story villas and apartments. Suddenly a small boy was seen tearing out of one of the buildings, racing as though escaping a fire. The child ran about thirty feet, then stumbled and fell. He recovered himself, took a faltering step and fell again, and did not get up. Minutes later, scores of people were staggering out of their houses, some gasping and wheezing and others collapsing onto the pavement in agony.

By the time Morad arrived, there were perhaps four hundred people in the street, including rescue workers and volunteers who rushed out of their houses to help. The doctor organized a triage while medics turned spray hoses on victims to remove as much of the poison as possible from their hair and skin.

"This is for sure chemicals," Morad told his team.

But it was not the kind of chemical attack that medical workers in northern Syria were accustomed to seeing. Morad moved from patient to patient and saw an identical set of symptoms: extreme respiratory distress. Involuntary twitching and convulsions. Foaming around the mouth and nose. Pupils narrowed to pinpoints. Morad knew what chlorine exposure did to the human body. This was far worse.

Unmistakably, the victims had been stricken by a nerve agent.

Most distressing were the children. There were dozens of them, many of them toddlers still in their pajamas. Morad watched as rescue workers squeezed ten tiny forms, all of them drenched and as limp as dolls, into the back of a truck that was being used as a makeshift ambulance. The physician administered an atropine shot to a young boy of about six, a handsome child with light brown curls. His breaths came in painful, heaving gasps, but his frightened eyes appeared not to see the medical workers tending to him. The boy died on his way to the hospital.

Ninety-one others would die that day, many of them in Morad's clinic or in makeshift triage centers set up on the street. Among the hundreds who were sickened but survived were rescue personnel, nurses, orderlies, and Morad himself, who had rushed to help without taking time to find gloves or a mask. As he labored, he felt his throat tighten, as tiny traces of poison from victims' clothes and skin found their way into his own nervous system. Soon he could no longer speak at all, and his hands became so painfully cramped that he had to give himself cortisone shots in order to continue working.

Days would pass before Morad could speak again. By then, images and video recorded on cell phones had spread virally, and the world—prime ministers, UN officials, diplomats, and even a newly installed U.S. president in Washington, D.C.—had witnessed the horrific scenes for which Morad had neither the voice nor the words.

"Can you imagine what the end of the world will be like?" said Morad, smoking a cigarette as he sat weeks later with a camera crew in Turkey to talk about the ordeal. "Do you think anyone can guess what it will look like?"

Later with his family, on rare occasions when he could be induced to speak about the events, he said only this:

"It was like Judgment Day."

Since the sarin attack on Ghouta in August 2013, there had been no verified claims of the use of nerve agents anywhere in Syria. Any sarin that remained in the country after June 2014—and any precursor ingredients that weren't destroyed on the *Cape Ray* that summer—remained locked away and out of sight for nearly three years.

But then something changed. A few days before Trump's inauguration, human-rights groups reported a possible sarin attack on a pair of villages in ISIS-controlled territory near the city of Palmyra. No inspector dared enter the area to investigate, so the accounts were never confirmed. Similarly, a week before lethal gas was released at Khan Sheikhoun, a bomb filled with a suspected nerve agent landed in a farmer's field about fifteen miles south of the town. Dozens of fighters nearby were treated for possible exposure to sarin, but no deaths were reported and no formal inquest was made. Then came the dramatic, and clearly calculated, attack on Khan Sheikhoun. The Russian-made Su-22 that flew over the town on April 4 dropped a single chemical bomb—later determined by independent experts to be a specialized

Syrian munition known as the M4000, designed for dispersing sarin. It carried a relatively small amount of poison, roughly enough to fill a standard household water heater. But that was sufficient in theory to deliver thousands of lethal doses. Dictator Bashar al-Assad surely knew that images of the victims would reach the West, touching off waves of outrage. And yet he felt comfortable in taking the risk.

Was Assad emboldened by the new U.S. president's apparent disinterest in his country's civil war? During a televised debate with Democratic rival Hillary Clinton, then-candidate Trump appeared to signal a willingness to tolerate Assad's brutal tactics. While he disliked the dictator, "Assad is killing ISIS," Trump said, in a remark that echoed the dictator's own defense of his brutal war against any and all "terrorists" who would seek to overthrow him. Days after taking office, Trump made clear his views toward Syria's suffering multitudes when he announced plans to close U.S. borders to all Syrian refugees seeking to escape their country's civil war, including those who had been vetted and approved for entry into the United States. Then, just days before the Khan Sheikhoun attack, two prominent White House officials publicly distanced themselves from the "Assad must go" stance that had long been a pillar of the Obama administration's Syria policy.

"The longer-term status of President Assad will be decided by the Syrian people," Secretary of State Rex Tillerson said during a visit to Turkey in March 2017.

"Do we think he's a hindrance? Yes," Nikki Haley, Trump's newly appointed UN ambassador, said of Assad that same day. "Are we going to sit there and focus on getting him out? No."

Yet when the images of Khan Sheikhoun's victims appeared on digital screens on April 4, Trump's response seemed hardly that of a man determined to stay out of Syria's affairs. His immediate reaction, according to multiple accounts, was personal and visceral. Trump's daughter, Ivanka, had seen the videos of dying children, and she was so horrified she walked into her father's office with her cell phone to show him. By the time the new president spoke with his national security advisers that morning, he was raging. Phoning his defense secretary, retired Marine Corps general James Mattis, he demanded an all-out military assault on Syria and its president.

"Let's go in!" he told Mattis. "Let's kill the f—king lot of them."

Mattis believed that Obama had erred by failing to order a military strike after his chemical weapons "red line" was crossed in 2013, and the general assured Trump that he would look at options. But Mattis had no intention of unleashing U.S. military firepower on the scale that Trump was envisioning, aides later said. Such a strike would risk further destabilizing Syria and—given the presence of dozens of Russian planes and thousands of Russian personnel—potentially trigger a military clash with Moscow, or perhaps with Iran.

"We're not going to do any of that," Mattis told an aide. "We're going to be much more measured."

Over the next two days, Trump's advisers argued furiously over the appropriate response. Some pressed for a crushing blow that not only would punish Assad but also potentially shift the war's momentum in favor of the rebels. At the other extreme, chief White House strategist Steve Bannon cautioned Trump against taking any action that might draw the United States into another Middle Eastern war. By the end of the second day, the debate was reduced to haggling over the number of cruise missiles to launch, with various aides advocating figures ranging from zero to two hundred.

The final plan called for sixty missiles, all of them aimed at a single air base: al-Shayrat, the Syrian installation from which the chemical attack was launched. The target list, an updated version of the one prepared for Obama four years earlier, included aircraft bunkers, surface-to-air missile batteries, and fuel depots. The strike's planners cautioned against bombing a suspected chemical weapons storage site on the base, fearing—just as their predecessors had in 2013—that an accidental sarin release might kill innocents in nearby villages.

A pair of Navy warships moved into position, and beginning at 4:40 a.m. Damascus time, fifty-nine cruise missiles—one of the original sixty malfunctioned and crashed into the Mediterranean—began streaking across the darkened Syrian coastline. When it was over, satellite images confirmed successful hits on a dozen aircraft hangars and about twenty of Syria's warplanes, as well as missile batteries and fuel tanks. Western news reports put the number of dead Syrians at fewer than ten.

Trump and his aides immediately sought to reap a political advantage from the air strike, contrasting the Republican president's decisive response to a chemical weapons attack to Obama's. Tillerson quickly clarified that the administration's position on Syria had not changed, and that there were no plans for a broader use of military force against Assad. Still, the news of the first international military response to Assad's brutality drew widespread support, including, quietly, from weary UN officials and aid workers who had witnessed the regime's brutality up close. Syrian opposition groups were ecstatic, and some expressed hope that Trump's first taste of military action would whet his appetite for more.

Among those applauding the loudest was Kassem Eid, the young Syrian activist who had been caught up in the 2013 sarin attack at Ghouta. Eid had stood before the UN Security Council in 2014 to bear witness to the horrors of chemical weapons as a guest of Ambassador Samantha Power. But after two years of pleading with U.S. officials for more military aid for Syria's rebels, he had become so disillusioned that he left the United States to apply for refugee status in Germany. When asked by a journalist to describe his feelings about Trump's decision to strike, his impromptu response went instantly viral. "I'll name my son Donald," he said.

"I cried out of joy. I thanked God. I don't know—I was overwhelmed," Eid told CNN. "We've been asking for protection. We've been asking for consequences for more than six years and today for the first time it happened. For the very first time we see Assad held accountable, just for once."

Eid urged Trump to keep going. Destroy all Assad's warplanes, he pleaded. Create a no-fly zone where refugees could be kept safe. "Please don't stop," he said.

But there would be no further U.S. military strikes that year. Indeed, within hours of the April 7 missile barrage, it was clear that the attack on al-Shayrat was less than it initially seemed. Assad lost a few aircraft, but the base's runways escaped major damage. By the next morning, Syrian warplanes were again taking off from al-Shayrat for their daily bombing runs. Pentagon officials acknowledged that they had warned the Kremlin in advance about the impending attack, allowing Russian personnel, and perhaps Syrians, to slip away from the base before the missiles struck.

For the anti-Assad opposition, nothing had changed—or so it seemed at first. The war ground on without a pause. Even the chlorine attacks resumed after a break of a few weeks. But in reality, the spring of 2017 was the moment when Washington began to divest itself of any significant role in determining Syria's future, other than concluding the war against ISIS.

In May, less than a month after the air strike and four months into the Trump administration, a new phase of peace talks for Syria began in the Kazakh capital of Astana, with the United States notably absent. For nearly six years, Washington had led international peace efforts through multiple rounds of negotiations in Geneva or Vienna. From now on the center of the action would be Central Asia, with Russia, Iran, and Turkey serving as the main guarantors and referees. With the Americans having sidelined themselves, the three powers agreed on a "de-escalation" strategy that involved carving Syria into zones. Within each zone, regional opposition groups could sue for peace with the Assad government in exchange for a promise of protection. In practice, the Astana agreement became an exercise in divide-and-conquer: one by one, rebel factions were persuaded to accept terms that ostensibly included guarantees of protection for towns and cities that had known only war for six long years. Russian soldiers moved in to supervise the disarming of local militias and allow safe passage for remaining fighters to Idlib, the last remaining rebel stronghold near the border with Turkey. Then, with the combatants gone, Syrian forces moved in, often with an entourage of Iranians, Lebanese, and other foreigners looking to settle in deserted neighborhoods where Sunni Arab families once lived.

A more profound policy shift occurred in June. After a meeting with his then CIA director, Mike Pompeo, Trump decided abruptly to pull the plug on Timber Sycamore. The reasons for abandoning the covert arms program for Syria's rebels were never explicitly stated, though Trump, in a move that astonished his intelligence advisers, confirmed the existence of the top-secret program in a Twitter posting, and then disparaged it as "massive, dangerous and wasteful." The decision to cancel Timber Sycamore came just days before Trump was due to meet Russian leader Vladimir Putin in Germany to discuss, among other topics, Syria. Putin, of course, strongly opposed the covert operation to bolster anti-Assad militants.

By any objective measure, the CIA's $1 billion arm-and-equip program was already in serious trouble. Plagued by scandal and riddled with corruption and waste, it supported secular rebels who were no longer capable of mounting a credible bid for power in Syria. Obama had remained skeptical of the program to the end, and some senior advisers to the Democratic president said Obama probably would have halted it himself in time.

Yet even Trump administration officials were surprised by the abruptness with which the decision was made. The Russians knew all about Timber Sycamore and brought it up frequently in private discussions with American counterparts. Why not at least use the program as leverage in negotiations? And what about the thousands of rebels who no longer would receive salaries? Surely some would take up arms with the jihadists—which, in fact, many eventually did.

"It was like a guillotine," said one former Trump official who said he supported the goal of eliminating the program, but not the means. "We should at least have gotten a soft landing, or a cease-fire with the Russians to buy time. We might have thought a little about the people who worked with us and made sure they were safe and were able to get out of there."

Another Trump official, blindsided and exasperated, described the outcome of the decision more bluntly.

"Putin won," the official said.

The other potential beneficiary was Iran. Even more than Moscow, Tehran was deeply committed to ensuring Assad's survival. By Western calculations, the CIA-trained force had killed as many as one hundred thousand Syrian troops and pro-Iranian militiamen over its four-year history. Now those fighters were effectively gone.

Ironically, ending the program dashed hopes for achieving the one policy goal that mattered most to Trump: curbing Iranian influence in Syria. After Trump took office, the White House repeatedly demanded the removal of all Iranian troops and military advisers from the country. Instead, Iran now found itself in a far stronger position in Syria than it had been at the start of the war. Iranian troops and Iranian-trained Shiite militias were now entrenched throughout the country, and Assad, a weakened leader utterly dependent on Tehran for aid, lacked the leverage to ask them to leave.

Iran's long dream of a "land bridge" across the Levant, allowing unrestricted movement through northern Iraq and Syria and a direct physical link to its Hezbollah allies in southern Lebanon, was coming closer to reality. Only a few hundred U.S. forces stood in the way: the Pentagon kept a small force of commandos and trainers in Syria to assist the Kurds in ongoing efforts to destroy the Islamic State's remaining strongholds. Those Americans were clustered in forward-operating bases in northern Syria, near the Turkish border, and in the south near the Jordanian frontier at al-Tanf. Straddling the two main thoroughfares leading from Iraq to the Lebanese coast, the U.S. troops were among the few remaining physical impediments to the Levantine bridge that Tehran longed to build.

If Trump could be persuaded to withdraw U.S. forces from Syria, as the president had frequently promised to do, even this last obstacle would finally be gone.

The men with the black flags were not so easy to defeat. By the spring of 2017, fighters aligned with al-Nusra Front, the al-Qaeda offshoot, dominated the entire northwestern city of Idlib along with the surrounding countryside up to the Turkish border. Now rebranded as Hayat Tahrir al-Sham, or the Organization for the Liberation of the Levant, the Islamists commanded a battle-hardened army of thirty-one thousand linked by a network of trenches and tunnels dug beneath the city's ruins. Awash in weapons and cash, they ran their territory as an Islamist fiefdom and all but dared the Syrians to try to dislodge them.

On the opposite side of the country, fanatical elements of the Islamic State waged a fierce, street-by-street defense of Raqqa, the caliphate's Syrian capital, while stubbornly clinging to a shrinking corner of Mosul's historic west bank. Like Japanese defenders in the Pacific Island battles of World War II, the militants nearly always fought to the death, forcing Kurdish and Iraqi troops to halt their advance to clear a building of a single ISIS sniper. Relentlessly brutal to the end, they used civilians as human shields and exacted a gruesome toll on their opponents with elaborate booby traps, suicide bombers, and small, remote-controlled drones that dropped grenades on troop transports.

The mustard gas that ISIS had worked so hard to create was only rarely used, as the group's weapons factories and stockpiles had been almost entirely destroyed. But the men who created the poisons had not given up. In the spring of 2017, they began to look outside the region for a new project, one that required no factory or infrastructure that America's bombers could discover and destroy. It was a change in strategy that U.S. security officials had anticipated, and greatly feared.

The militants had managed to keep many details of their chemical program hidden, including where and how they obtained the ingredients for mustard gas. From now on, disrupting the group's plans would be even harder. "They had made and used mustard as a battlefield weapon, but without a lot of effect," said Laura Holgate, the point person on WMD terrorism at the Obama White House. "We knew there was a point where they could flip and use it for terrorism."

All that was needed were trusted and capable collaborators overseas. And by April of that year, ISIS had found them. In a working-class suburb of Lakemba, just outside Sydney, Australia, there lived a Lebanese immigrant with a close family connection to the Islamic State. Khaled Khayat was a forty-nine-year-old handyman and football enthusiast who lived a quiet life with an extended family that included two younger brothers who had immigrated with him to Australia, hoping to start a new life on the far side of the world. The Khayat men had another brother, Tarek, who had stayed behind in Lebanon. In 2014, after getting into some legal trouble, Tarek had moved to Syria with his three sons to join ISIS. Within a few months he had risen within the terrorist group to become a midlevel commander and sheikh. Using an encrypted texting platform called WhatsApp, Tarek kept in touch with his brother Khaled, and the two discussed ISIS and its ambition to become a modern incarnation of the ancient caliphates of Islam's past. Khayat listened and was sympathetic but showed no interest in joining the group.

Then, in March, Tarek's son Mohamed, just seventeen, was killed while fighting for ISIS in Syria—the second of Tarek's sons to die that way in a span of less than six months. As the Khayats grieved, Tarek sent video messages to his Australian kin hailing the boy's death as an act of martyrdom. He began prodding his brothers on their familial obligation to honor his sons' sacrifices. To Tarek, that meant taking up the boys' cause and striking a blow on behalf of the Islamic State.

Khaled Khayat finally agreed. Over the following days, he waited as Tarek turned to another ISIS official with experience in such matters to plan an operation. And that's how the operative known as the Controller came to have a willing accomplice and a clean canvas on which to draw up and execute the most ambitious chemical terror plot ever attempted by the Islamic State.

20

A Smoking Gun

NEW YORK, NEW YORK. APRIL 2017

In the spring of 2017, the world's best hope for holding Bashar al-Assad legally accountable for gassing Syrian civilians resided in a sixty-six-year-old Guatemalan diplomat who knew next to nothing about chemical weapons. A onetime newspaper columnist, Edmond Mulet had limited experience in the Middle East, but he had served as a legislator, an ambassador, a UN mission chief in Haiti, and the head of UN peacekeeping operations around the world. Now he was being tapped to lead the hunt for elusive evidence that might prove, once and for all, who was behind one of the most horrific crimes of the twenty-first century.

Mulet, earnest and dapper with a meticulously groomed silver mustache, had retired from UN work and was back in his native Guatemala when the new UN secretary-general António Guterres telephoned him with the job pitch. It would be a brief assignment, perhaps as short as six months, but it would be important and high-profile, if perhaps unpleasant at times.

Was Mulet interested?

He was, and weeks later Mulet flew to New York to begin his appointment as head of the Joint Investigative Mechanism, the UN-OPCW panel tasked with assessing blame for Syria's chemical attacks. The JIM was the now–fully realized product of UN ambassador Samantha Power's brainstorming sessions with her Russian counterpart, Vitaly Churkin, in 2015. In its first eighteen months, the panel had produced a series of reports that, for the first time, directly linked the Assad government to three chlorine attacks. The reports stirred controversy, as Russia and Syria immediately assailed the findings, but now the investigators were on a roll. And in April, the panel would take on new energy in the form of a dogged new director and a formidable new challenge: investigating the nerve-agent attack that had just occurred in the Syrian town of Khan Sheikhoun.

To Mulet, the task didn't at first seem that hard. As he read up on the JIM's short history, he could see how the process was supposed to work. Another branch of the OPCW—its "Fact-Finding Mission"—would collect testimony, blood samples, and other data to verify whether a chemical weapon had been used. The JIM would then sort through the same evidence and conduct additional scientific analysis to try to determine who was behind the attack. Obtaining evidence in an active war zone was never easy, but from a casual reading of Western news accounts, the facts seemed clear enough: a Syrian warplane had dropped a bomb, and immediately afterward, hundreds of people developed symptoms of exposure to a nerve agent. More than one hundred ultimately had died.

The problem was that Syria and its allies perceived a reality completely at odds with those accounts in Western newspapers and TV newscasts. Syria insisted, repeatedly, that it had no sarin, having destroyed its stockpile under international supervision in 2014. Yes, a Syrian warplane had dropped bombs on rebel positions in Khan Sheikhoun. But if anyone died of exposure to a nerve agent, it was not Damascus's doing. Syrian officials offered multiple alternative theories to explain the images of dead children in the town's streets. In one version, a Syrian bomb had struck a warehouse and released sarin gas that the rebels had collected and stored. Another, touted by Assad himself, held that the attacks had been staged, and the "dead" children were actors. The stories seemed far-fetched, but they were repeated and validated by a member of the UN Security Council: Russia. The Kremlin sought to block or discredit official investigations of Syria's chemical weapons use, and it built a powerful propaganda machine—a social-media network of troll farms and Internet "bots"—to flood Facebook and Twitter with postings and fake news articles promoting Syria's version of the truth.

Despite the background noise, Mulet was convinced he could build an unassailable case with hard facts and a rigorous scientific process. But on one of his first days on the job, he came to discover just how difficult that would be.

Mulet was still getting settled into his new office when he received a visit from a senior member of Russia's UN mission. The official from Moscow ostensibly was calling to congratulate Mulet on the job.

"We supported you," the official said.

But then he delivered a message of astonishing frankness.

"Don't take this personally," the diplomat said, "but we're going to destroy you."

After the initial visit, Russian officials made a point of regularly calling on Mulet, as though to remind him of their close scrutiny of his work. Mulet was quizzed about the progress of his investigation, cautioned against drawing unhelpful conclusions, and, at times, given not-so-subtle hints about the reach of Moscow's intelligence services into all matters pertaining to Syria. Once, after Mulet dispatched a confidential letter to Syria's foreign minister discussing a possible visit to Damascus, he received an immediate reply—from the Russians. The missive went out on a Monday afternoon, and at 10 a.m. the following morning, a diplomat from the Russian UN mission was standing at his door.

"The letter you sent yesterday is unacceptable," the official said.

Mulet had experienced official intimidation in previous jobs, and he was determined not to let it affect him. He drew up plans for investigating the Khan Sheikhoun attack and, with his team, began methodically laying out the evidence and resources that would serve as the starting point. Mulet soon discovered that he had an extraordinary asset in the person of one of the JIM's senior deputies. Scientist Stefan Mogl was the head of the chemistry division at Switzerland's Spiez Laboratory, one of the world's premier institutions in the study of chemical, biological, and radiological threats, located in an Alpine village on the shores of Lake Thun. The Swiss government had offered Mogl's services to the United Nations as a technical adviser to the JIM, meaning that Mulet's investigation would be aided by an experienced and highly regarded expert on the forensic chemistry of military nerve agents.

Mulet and Mogl agreed on an approach that could settle the

question of the sarin's origins. The JIM team had access to environmental samples of the nerve agent used at Khan Sheikhoun. Some of them had been provided to the OPCW by doctors and rescue workers in the town, and others were supplied by the Syrian government itself, which said it would cooperate with international investigators in order to prove its innocence. If the JIM's experts could obtain samples from Syria's original stock—material that indisputably had come from Syria's production line—they could run tests to see if the Khan Sheikhoun samples were chemically related. But where could the JIM's scientists go to obtain a few grams of vintage binary sarin from Syria's original production line?

Fortunately, Stefan Mogl knew exactly where to find it.

The sealed tubes that two of Tim Blades's crew members had carried with them in the storm-tossed English Channel had been delivered to The Hague and locked away in the OPCW's laboratory. It was now part of the organization's reference collection, available to investigators in the event that Syrian-made nerve agent would turn up in a terrorist attack somewhere in the world. The preserving of the samples was done without fanfare, and few people knew about it.

But Stefan Mogl knew. Earlier in his career, the Swiss chemist had run the OPCW's lab in The Hague. He knew where the samples were and, more than anyone, understood their value and what they could potentially achieve.

Mogl needed help, and he called on the OPCW's lab chief to ask for advice. The two of them decided to work together to see what clues could be found in the samples taken from the *Cape Ray.* With a small team of investigators, they would begin the search for impurities and any other distinctive features that could be matched against the sarin used at Khan Sheikhoun. Then, as a final experiment, lab workers in protective gear would pour some of the *Cape Ray* liquid into a beaker and add a few drops of isopropyl alcohol. Using the same formula the CIA's "chemist" spy had developed decades earlier, they would create a tiny amount of actual Syria-style sarin.

At nearly the same moment, on the opposite side of the world, one of the most ambitious terrorist plots ever attempted by the Islamic State was just getting underway. At just past 9 a.m. on April 21, Khaled

Khayat picked up his mobile phone to transmit a quick text to his younger brother, Mahmoud, then at home in a different Sydney suburb a few miles away.

"Come over so we can open it," he wrote.

Mahmoud understood and was soon on his way. "It" referred to the mysterious package that had just been delivered to the older brother's house a few days before. The heavy box bore stamps and labels showing that it had originated at a post office in Turkey and traveled halfway around the world. The address had been slightly botched, which prompted hours of panicked searching after a deliveryman tried to drop off the parcel at the wrong house. But at last Khaled had it, and with his brother next to him, it was time to carefully remove the wrappings and examine the long-awaited contents.

Mahmoud was the only brother whom Khaled could trust to help with such an assignment. The third of the Lebanese brothers in Australia, named Amer, was the black sheep of the family, a man who liked nightclubs and drinking and who had, after a divorce, come out as gay. Amer would be told nothing about the package, or his brothers' contact with the man known as the Controller.

The mastermind had mentioned two mighty blows the brothers could help ISIS inflict, and the package he sent them contained a starter kit for the first one. The Khayats opened the box to find what appeared to be a portable welding machine, the kind that can be purchased at a hardware store for a few hundred dollars. But after removing the metal sides they found, concealed behind copper coils, the small cylindrical device they had been expecting. This was the bomb. Or it would be, once the Lebanese men carried out the intricate instructions on how to assemble it.

That same day, Tarek, the brother who joined ISIS, sent a coded message from Syria on what their next task would be.

It was a photograph of a timer.

The brothers spent the next two weeks finding parts and slowly assembling the bomb in Khaled's garage. They were still at work on May 6 when a ping on Khaled's phone alerted them to new instructions. The Controller had sent a video with details about the second phase of the plot. It was a chemical bomb.

It was impractical to send sulfur mustard or any other manufactured poison through the mail from Turkey, but there were certain deadly gases that the Khayats could easily make at home, as the Controller explained. One such was called hydrogen sulfide. It is relatively easy to make and required no special laboratories or production centers, yet in a confined space, such as a train car or airplane cabin, it could be exceedingly deadly. Historically, its lethal qualities had attracted the attention of British army scientists, who had used it at least twice in gas attacks against the Germans in western France during World War I.

Suddenly, Khaled began to lose his nerve. The idea of mixing toxic chemicals struck the Lebanese immigrant as difficult, even dangerous. Without telling the Controller, he set aside the poison plot and decided to finish the conventional bomb first.

By early July, the brothers were ready for the plot's first phase. The bomb, now with a timing device and batteries attached, was hidden inside a meat-grinding machine Khaled had obtained. The plan was to smuggle the device into the cabin of a commercial airliner and set it to detonate twenty minutes into the flight. But there was yet one more obstacle to overcome: to get the bomb inside the plane, they needed to secure the unwitting assistance of a passenger, someone to carry the device aboard the plane for them.

They found a perfect candidate: their own brother, Amer.

The party-loving younger Khayat was planning a trip to Lebanon, and he had bought a ticket for an Etihad Airways flight from Sydney to Beirut, connecting through Abu Dhabi. As he was preparing to leave, Khaled asked a favor: Would Amer mind delivering the meat grinder as a gift for a Lebanese friend?

On July 15, Khaled helped Amer pack the grinder inside his carry-on luggage and quietly, when no one was looking, connected the bomb's battery and switched on the timer. The three brothers drove to the airport together. Mahmoud stayed with the car while Khaled walked with Amer to the Etihad check-in desk and prepared to say good-bye.

It was all going perfectly, right up to their arrival at the baggage counter. A harried young woman in an Etihad uniform studied Amer's hand luggage, checked the scale, and then cast a skeptical eye on the two brothers.

It's too heavy for the passenger cabin, the agent announced. Amer's two bags would have to be either lightened and repacked, or one of them would have to go into the airplane's cargo hold. Khaled stared at the woman as she made a note flagging Amer's carry-on bags for rechecking at the departure gate. The handbags would be reweighed, screened, and possibly searched. What if the bomb was discovered?

Khaled racked his brain while the two walked back toward Mahmoud and the waiting car. There was no choice. Inside the vehicle, Khaled removed the meat grinder, placed it in the backseat, and repacked Amer's bag without the bomb. The two men embraced, and Amer walked into the terminal alone, not knowing how close he had just come to death at the hands of his own brothers.

Back at his house minutes later, Khaled took apart the meat grinder and carefully disconnected the bomb's battery pack, using tape to secure the wires so they did not accidentally reconnect. His plan had failed, by the narrowest of margins. Had it not been for the baggage agent, Amer Khayat and four hundred other Etihad passengers would already be entombed in their plane at the bottom of the Indian Ocean.

Phase One of the ISIS plot had been thwarted. But the Khayats and their Syrian "Controller" were not defeated yet.

Khaled Khayat tried to be cautious in communicating with his ISIS handler overseas, but occasionally he forgot himself. Once, pleased with the way his meat-grinder bomb turned out, he took photos of the device, proudly texted them to the Controller—and promptly received a scolding in return.

"You should not have sent me a picture of the item, brother," the operative replied.

But the transmission of the bomb's image could not be undone. Thousands of miles away, at a military listening post in northern Israel, someone was scanning the encrypted channels used by ISIS and saw a lengthy series of exchanges between Sydney and a mobile phone associated with a suspected terrorist operative. The man whom investigators would call the Controller was known to the Israelis and the Americans. Basil Hassan, the young engineer from Denmark who had been chosen by ISIS to plan terrorist attacks overseas, was now one of the group's top specialists in aviation plots. On his own, he had acquired expertise in drone aircraft, poison gases, and the construction of miniaturized bombs that could be hidden inside ordinary objects as small as a soda can. A few months earlier, in November 2016, the U.S. State Department had formally listed Hassan as a "Specially Designated Global Terrorist," elevating him to the top of the country's most-wanted list. A senior official said of him: "Hassan is one of the most dangerous people we've ever designated at the Department of State."

Only thirty at the time of his contact with the Khayat brothers, Hassan seemed to possess almost limitless potential as a killer. Born into a middle-class family with Lebanese Palestinian roots, he grew up in a Copenhagen suburb where he drew attention from an early age for his intellectual abilities and extremist views. In 2011, the first year of the Syrian uprising, he was a newly minted engineer and a pilot trainee who hacked computers as a hobby. He was also, as police later confirmed, a member of a small cell of Danish Islamists with ties to radical groups abroad. In 2013 Hassan acquired a gun and a postman's uniform and tried to shoot Lars Hedegaard, a Danish historian and author known for his outspoken criticism of the Muslim religion. The assassination attempt failed, and Hassan fled to Turkey and then to Syria, where he eventually joined ISIS. Settling in Raqqa, the caliphate's Syrian capital, he went to work assembling a fleet of small drone aircraft that could be used for surveillance or for carrying out terrorist attacks. Danish court documents suggested that he also helped plan the bombing of Russia's Metrojet Flight 9268, which exploded over the Sinai Peninsula in October 2015, killing 224 passengers and crew members. The attack on the Etihad jet in Australia would have cemented his reputation as one of the Islamic State's most feared killers.

At the moment, though, Hassan was preoccupied with his amateur accomplices and their sluggishness at carrying out Phase Two of the terrorist plot. He pressed his Australian partners to get on with the task of assembling the materials.

"We should be a bit fast," he told Khaled in a text message.

Compared to putting a bomb on a plane, the blueprint for building a chemical weapon was simple, if risky. It involved a kind of poison gas that is easy to make, using ingredients available in many grocery stores. Hydrogen sulfide gas is common in nature, and in low concentrations it has few deleterious effects beyond its off-putting rotten-egg smell. People exposed to higher doses often describe a vaguely sweet odor—if they live to tell about the experience. Unconsciousness and death come quickly, sometimes after only a couple of breaths. So potent is the gas that, for a time in the early 2000s, it became a faddish way to commit suicide for hundreds of Japanese youths. Parents and rescue workers who tried to save the victims often were stricken as well.

On July 24, just nine days after the failed bombing attempt, Khaled jotted down Hassan's instructions for making the gas and calculated the amount of supplies he would need to guarantee a lethal dose. Five days later, with the necessary materials in hand, he was ready to test his formula by preparing a small batch in a barbecue pit in his backyard.

"Rejoice, brother," he wrote in a text to the Controller that morning, July 29. "God willing, I will let you know the results."

Recounting the events of the day afterward in statements to investigators, Khaled's neighbors would describe a sweet smell and what appeared to be white barbecue smoke wafting over the handyman's fence. From a nearby balcony, another observer, an undercover police officer, recorded the moment on video. Alerted by the Israeli government, Australian authorities were now monitoring Khaled's every movement. They watched him as he worked and trailed him as he left the house and climbed into his car, carrying something with him in a plastic bag.

Two hours later, police swarmed Khaled's car as he sat parked in a neighborhood not far from his apartment. He gave up without a struggle, as did his brother Mahmoud, picked up separately a few miles away. Next to Khaled on the front seat, police said, were the materials from the afternoon's poison-gas experiment, a partially successful trial intended to help the Khayats calibrate their device to achieve the deadliest possible results.

Twice in two weeks, Australians had avoided a catastrophic act of terrorism, by the slimmest of margins: this time thanks to a chance interception of a text message by eavesdroppers working in a country nearly nine thousand miles away. Forensics experts later testified that the Khayats' weapon, when fully ready, would almost certainly have done the gruesome work for which it was designed. Very possibly, the results would have ranked among the deadliest chemical attacks by a terrorist group of all time.

"Had the gas been produced in accordance with the instructions," the Australian prosecutor's office concluded in an official summary of the case, "it would have been lethal."

But the plot's real mastermind was in Syria, well beyond the reach of Western law-enforcement agencies. Just days earlier, the last sector of ISIS-held western Mosul had fallen to the Iraqi army, all its black-clad defenders having been captured or killed. That same week, Kurdish fighters began battling their way into central Raqqa, the Syrian provincial capital that served as the caliphate's administrative headquarters. Yet the group was not vanquished. Nearly all its senior leaders and many of its fighters had already moved on, some hiding out in scattered Euphrates River towns near the Iraqi border, and others in the countryside in northwestern Syria, where crossing into Turkey and farther into Europe could still be as simple as hailing a taxi.

Did the Controller follow them? Police records revealed that Basil Hassan continued to send text messages to Khaled Khayat right up to the hour of his arrest, when he vanished from view. There were vague reports suggesting that he had died, but no proof.

What is certain is that Hassan's idea for unleashing a killer cloud on one of the world's great cities did not end with the arrests of two brothers in a working-class Australian suburb. Months later, after Kurdish fighters overran the caliphate's last enclaves in Syria, ISIS issued an official pronouncement declaring a "new stage" in the group's terror campaign against its enemies, especially Israelis. The message promised new tactics and weapons, and included, for the first time, an explicit call for the use of poison gas.

"O soldiers of the caliphate everywhere," it said, "below you are the settlements and markets of the Jews. So make them a testing ground for your weapons: your chemical-bearing rockets."

Police in Australia were just beginning their forensic work when Edmond Mulet's investigators discovered the clue they had been looking for.

The experiments conducted over the summer at Stefan Mogl's

direction had borne fruit. In the tests of environmental samples taken after the Khan Sheikhoun attack, the investigators consistently found traces of a now-familiar ingredient: the chemical additive hexamine. It was, as Swedish scientist Åke Sellström had discovered in his Ghouta investigation in 2013, a unique signature of Syria's manufacturing process, dating back to the 1980s when Ayman, the CIA's Syrian "chemist" mole, ran the program and developed his novel method for making sarin. But Mogl was not yet satisfied. The problem was that Syria's use of hexamine in its nerve agents was now publicly known. Anyone looking carefully could find it mentioned in UN reports available on the Internet. If someone were to try to frame Syria for a sarin attack, they might be clever enough to sprinkle some hexamine into their product to make it look convincing. In Mogl's mind, the presence of hexamine was interesting, but it did not cinch the case.

Then the investigators spotted something else. Present in samples from Khan Sheikhoun was a chemical called hexafluorophosphate, or PF6. It was a curious finding, and not easily explained. The PF6 was clearly an accidental by-product of some kind, a residue from the reaction of two chemicals during some phase of the manufacturing process. But how was it formed, and where else did it exist? The scientists searched through the summer, and eventually found the same impurity in a most interesting place: in the vial of sarin the researchers had made using liquid precursors taken from the *Cape Ray.*

It took weeks of additional experiments to piece together the full story, but the PF6 revealed something important. The sarin used at Khan Sheikhoun was, without doubt, a binary sarin. It had been made from precursors that had been manufactured at an industrial scale. And its chemical makeup included impurities and trace elements that were identical to those found in the liquids that had been taken aboard the *Cape Ray* for destruction at sea. The sarin used in the 2017 attack was not the fruit of some mad scientist's basement experiment, nor was it something cooked up in a garage by would-be terrorists. It was a military-grade nerve agent that was created in bulk by someone who planned to keep it in a storage bunker for years, or even decades.

As an impurity, the PF6 was harmless. As a means of identifying a made-in-Syria nerve agent—one that could have originated only in one of the country's now-destroyed weapons factories—it was the chemical equivalent of a fingerprint.

Unless a thief had stolen something from Syria's original stockpile—something that officials in Damascus repeatedly swore had never happened—then there was only one plausible conclusion:

Syria, despite its assurances, had failed to give up all its nerve agents. And nearly four years after the murder of fourteen hundred innocents at Ghouta, it had used its chemicals to kill again.

Mulet had his smoking gun, but he remained anxious. The discovery of the impurity was kept secret for weeks as the JIM's investigators completed their case. As they worked, Mulet and Mogl worried that word would somehow leak out, giving the Syrians and Russians time to concoct a plausible-sounding explanation that might cause some on the Security Council to doubt.

"It was a very small group that knew about it," Mogl said. "We kept it very, very tight."

Not everyone in Mulet's team was delighted by the way the investigation had turned out. The JIM was about to publicly accuse Syria of multiple lies and deceptions, and, far more consequentially, of committing a war crime. Some aides, fearing Russia's response, urged Mulet to consider taking a softer approach, to buy the investigators more time to do their work. We could just say that findings aren't yet conclusive, one staff member suggested.

Mulet refused to wait. The victims of the attacks deserved the truth, he said.

"I have a mandate," he said. "This is our job. This is what we have to do."

As he held his regular meetings with Russian diplomats in the early fall, he began to suspect that the Kremlin knew that his investigators had found something important. In one meeting, Mulet was told that a negative report would result in his blacklisting at the United Nations, and his staff could well suffer the same fate. His report would be vetoed—rendered meaningless, essentially. And the JIM itself would be put out of business.

"It would be a shame for your career, and for your staff," Mulet was told. "The people working for you? They will be left without a job. That would be a pity."

Mulet shrugged off the warning and offered advice of his own.

"This is going to be a stain on you forever," Mulet said to the Russian. "And if you don't stop the Syrians, someday you'll have chemical weapons in your backyard, maybe in Chechnya. Stop it now, or eventually you will be the victims."

Mulet and his team spent weeks turning their findings into the dry prose of a UN report. On November 7, flanked by his top deputies Mogl and Malaysian diplomat Judy Cheng-Hopkins, the Guatemalan walked into the Security Council chambers in a navy suit to present his findings. The meeting would rank among the most difficult of his career.

Mulet happened to be seated at the same table as the man who would be his harshest critic during the afternoon's proceedings. Syria's ambassador to the United Nations, Bashar Jaafari, scowled at his copy of the report as Mulet began to describe the main points, reading with a slow, deliberate cadence. The JIM, he said, had been able to assess blame for two incidents involving chemical weapons: a mustard-gas attack by the Islamic State in 2016 and the use of sarin in Khan Sheikhoun in April. The clear culprit in the latter event, he said, was Syria.

Mulet proceeded to lay out the key evidentiary pieces, from the flight log of the Russian-made Su-22 bomber, to the blood samples taken from victims, to the dimensions of the bomb crater. Turning to Mogl's forensic work, he described in simple terms the "in-depth laboratory study" revealing that "the sarin used in Khan Sheikhoun was very likely to have been made from the same precursor" that came from Syria's pre-2014 stockpile. The discovery of the PF6 was described in detail in the body of the JIM's thirty-three-page report.

"Taken together, all these elements constitute clear evidence that the Syrian Arab Republic is responsible for the use of sarin at Khan Sheikhoun," Mulet said. Then, setting aside the report, he tried a different tack. The choice before the Security Council was a moral one, transcending the usual UN politics, he said.

"Consider the victims of those insidious acts," Mulet said. "Attaining a world without chemical weapons is an imperative requiring concrete and unified action. The Security Council has a unique responsibility in that regard, including to deter all those who continue to believe that there is something to be gained from their use.

"This is not a political issue, but an issue about the lives of innocent civilians," Mulet said. "Impunity must not prevail."

After he finished, representatives of more than a dozen countries, including the United States, Britain, and France, spoke out in support of Mulet and his findings. Then it was Russia's turn, and it was clear that not everyone had been moved by the Guatemalan's eloquence. Deputy Russian ambassador Vladimir Safronkov called the JIM's report "deeply disappointing" and riddled with "circumstantial evidence" and "gross errors."

"Its conclusions cannot stand up to any serious criticism," Safronkov said in Russian, wrapping up a lengthy tirade. Mulet's panel should have focused on the real perpetrators of chemical atrocities—the "terrorists"—rather than seeking to please those who "continue to try to find these imaginary chemical weapons in Damascus," he said.

The last word belonged to Syria's perpetually dour ambassador. Jaafari, a slim, balding man with a gray goatee and mustache, had a habit of glaring at council members over the tops of his glasses while lashing out about the latest indignity his government was being forced to endure. It was quickly clear that the target of Jaafari's insults on this day was the man sitting next to him. Mulet had been scribbling in the margins of his notes, as he often did, and Jaafari seized the opportunity to belittle the Guatemalan, implying that the JIM leader wasn't paying attention to the debate over his own report. He addressed his desk mate as "Mr. Mulet, who is seated right next to me, doodling!"

"I can almost see Machiavelli here today, standing and observing the behavior of some United Nations committees that are supposed to be neutral, professional, and credible, while their work and reports prove that they are biased, politicized, and immoral," he said. "They excel in using false witnesses, sources they call 'open,' and fabricated evidence."

The personal attacks on Mulet continued. Why hadn't the JIM leader bothered to visit Khan Sheikhoun to see the evidence firsthand? The suggestion was that Mulet had been lazy or cowardly, though, as

Jaafari well knew, the town was held at the time by al-Nusra Front, the al-Qaeda-linked terrorist group that opposed the panel's work in Syria.

"Can a crime be investigated remotely, like a PlayStation game, without visiting the scene of the crime?" Jaafari continued.

The insults were over, but the most painful blows were still to come. Russia, keeping its promise to Mulet, cast its veto blocking the UN Security Council from temporarily extending the JIM's mandate. Then, on November 17, the week after Mulet presented his findings, it cast a second veto that effectively terminated the panel altogether. Bolivia joined Russia in blocking the extension, and China and Egypt abstained. As of midnight, Mulet and the other panel members were unemployed.

Mulet returned to his native Guatemala to dive into local politics, eventually running for president on an anticorruption platform. The effort failed, but throughout it—and, indeed, for years after he left New York—he regularly found hate messages in his Twitter account, as well as occasional trolling campaigns—perhaps by computer "bots," though it was hard to tell for sure—attacking the "fake" JIM report and accusing him of being a mindless puppet of the Americans.

Even for Mulet, a man who in his UN peacekeeping days had often seen humanity at its worst, the cynicism and dysfunction he had witnessed at the United Nations was deeply unsettling. In 2013, the world's leaders had come together in a rare moment of unity to eliminate a deadly arsenal that had snuffed out hundreds of lives in Ghouta and held the potential for killing many thousands more. But four years later, the last vestiges of post–Cold War optimism had evaporated, with Russia and its allies occupying one side of the new divide and Western countries on the opposite side, while nonaligned countries made calculated decisions based on their own self-interests. The disarming of Syria, imperfect as it was, had been one of the young century's great triumphs of multilateralism. And it was quite possibly the last of them.

Mulet, frustrated, sat at his computer to sum up his feelings in an op-ed essay that became his farewell to an institution he had served for twelve years. The headline aptly captured the tone of the piece: "How the Security Council Failed the Syria Chemical Weapons Investigators and Victims." The events of 2013 had proven that countries can still act decisively in a moment of crisis, he wrote. But in addressing the difficult, everyday challenges of upholding civilized norms, protecting innocents, or seeking accountability for war crimes, the world body had shown itself to be incapable. Indeed, it had lost ground.

Mulet occasionally returned to New York afterward to visit family, and sometimes he would ride past the United Nations headquarters, the thirty-nine-story tower overlooking the East River in Manhattan. Whenever he saw it, he would take some comfort in knowing that the evidence collected by the JIM was still there, in a vault or database somewhere in the building. It would remain there as a witness to the crimes that he and the other panel members had documented.

"All of it was kept: all the facts and findings, the photographs, the videos, the lab tests—it's all there," Mulet said. "That is one small achievement of the JIM, to have compiled all the evidence, and to make accountability possible.

"One day," he said, "it will all be out in the open."

21

The Unraveling

DAMASCUS, SYRIA. APRIL 14, 2018

Just after four o'clock on a moonless Saturday morning, Damascus was jarred awake by a terrific explosion in the hills just north of Syria's capital. It was an ominous sound, even for a city accustomed to war, and thousands took to their windows and balconies to see what had happened. The sight they witnessed was an unforgettable one: just beyond the familiar hulk of the city's Mount Qasioun, an entire ridgeline appeared to be on fire.

More blasts shook the city as missiles—dazzling streaks of white against the dark skyline—found their target. When the sky brightened with the approach of dawn, a huge pall of black smoke could be seen rising from the hilltop. For years, the ridge was home to a modern laboratory complex, one noted for its commanding views of Damascus and extreme secrecy. Workers there knew it by its acronym in French: CERS. The research center in the Barzeh suburb was the newest branch of the weapons complex once led by the CIA's "chemist" spy. Now it was gone, erased entirely by more than seventy missiles launched by U.S., British, and French warships off the coast.

President Donald Trump's second missile strike against Syria in just over a year was again prompted by a chemical attack. A week earlier, on April 7, Syrian helicopters had dropped barrel bombs on the Damascus suburb of Douma as the army attempted to drive Islamist rebels from one of the last pockets of resistance near the capital. About seventy people died, at least some of them from exposure to what initial reports described as a mixture of chlorine and sarin. Trump's previous use of airpower had garnered widespread praise, and the U.S. president appeared intent on hitting Syria again. But this time, White House officials faced tougher choices on nearly every front, and it was far from clear what, if anything, a strike would accomplish.

The murkiness began with the nature of the attack itself. With street battles raging around Douma, it was impossible in the initial hours for independent fact-finders to examine bodies or gain access to the apartment building where many of the victims lived. The OPCW's experts—chased off by gunfire during their first attempt to visit the site—ultimately confirmed the use of chlorine, but they found no trace of sarin or its residues. No one would ever know how many of the seventy dead actually succumbed to poison gas and how many died from blast injuries or shrapnel.

Trump and his aides would not wait for answers. Instead, the White House began preparing for a strike, only to become embroiled in bitter arguments over the proper scale of the response. This time, there was a new national security adviser at the White House who had big ideas, and the president's ear. John Bolton, a sixty-nine-year-old ex-diplomat, was an unrepentant backer of the 2003 Iraq invasion and a man known in Washington for his consistently hawkish views. Just two weeks into his new job, he seized on the opportunity to push for a series of devastating strikes targeting not just Syrian air bases but the command-and-control facilities and military operations centers from which Assad and his generals ran the war.

"What he really wanted was to topple the regime," acknowledged a Trump adviser who attended meetings at which targets were discussed. Bolton would later clarify that he had no interest in getting involved in Syria's war, which he called a "strategic sideshow." But he acknowledged that he had advocated dropping bombs not just on runways and aircraft hangars but also on targets that "threatened the regime itself, such as by attacking Assad's palaces." And it should be a "sustained—not just a one-shot—effort," he later wrote. Trump initially agreed, according to Bolton, and urged his security adviser to make the rounds on news shows to win public backing for an aggressive air campaign. "Do as much TV as you want," Trump said. "Go after Obama as much as you want."

Others in Trump's cabinet, worried about blundering into a war with Russia or Iran, quietly scuttled the idea of attacking Syria's civilian leadership. Defense secretary James Mattis ultimately recommended just three targets, all of them at least symbolically linked to Syria's chemical weapons past: the CERS research center in the Damascus hills, and two obscure bunkers where intelligence analysts suspected some of Assad's missing chemicals might have been hidden. Yet, as the hour for launching the strike drew closer, Trump appeared to waver, fretting aloud about "chemical plumes" and suggesting to aides that he should perhaps just warn Assad instead.

"I nearly imploded," Bolton recalled afterward. It was too late to back out, he told Trump.

Still, Mattis promised the president a big strike, and he delivered. More than one hundred missiles—overkill, by any measure—fell on the three targets, obliterating them. But not a single Syrian was killed, and none of the buildings where Assad and his generals lived and worked were touched.

Trump, however, seemed satisfied with the outcome. At news conferences, senior aides again commended the president for using bombs and missiles to enforce the chemical weapons "red line," in contrast with Barack Obama's more nuanced response. Trump took to Twitter to congratulate himself, using a phrase that, perhaps unwittingly, echoed the words his Republican predecessor, George W. Bush, had used to prematurely declare victory in Iraq in 2003.

"Mission accomplished!" Trump tweeted.

But what mission, exactly, had Trump accomplished?

Trump's air strikes in 2017 and 2018 cheered Assad's foes in Syria and demonstrated resolve in enforcing international norms. But there was no proof that either strike resulted in the destruction of nerve agents, and the missiles' deterrent effect on the country's dictator proved to be only temporary. Indeed, as Bolton would later acknowledge, Syria resumed using chlorine the following spring, so the two air strikes at best bought a respite of a few months. "Did we succeed in deterring Assad?" Bolton asked. "Ultimately, we did not."

Obama destroyed vastly more chemical weapons through diplomacy than Trump did with missiles. But ultimately neither president succeeded in changing Assad's behavior, or shortening Syria's war. The United States and its allies proved unable or unwilling to halt the use of barrel bombs or starvation sieges. They were powerless to stem refugee flows or prevent extremists from exploiting the crisis to win converts and pursue violent agendas, from terrorism to attacks on immigrants.

Neither administration could prevent Russia and Iran from capitalizing on Syria's war to expand their influence in the region at the West's expense. After Washington removed itself from negotiations on Syria's future in 2017, Russia stepped fully into the role of the region's power broker, dictating terms to the warring factions and forging cooperative partnerships with America's chief allies in the region, including Jordan and Israel. Reaching deeply into its Soviet-era playbook, it deployed its own chemical weapons in a botched assassination attempt on British soil in early 2018: Russia's military intelligence service dispatched a pair of operatives to southern England to poison turncoat Russian spy Sergei Skripal with a Cold War nerve agent called novichok. Skripal and his adult daughter were sickened but survived. However, a British woman who was accidentally exposed to the substance later died.

The other indisputable winner in Syria was Iran. The cagey Quds Force commander Qasem Soleimani gambled on Assad in 2012, then doubled down three years later when the Syrian regime appeared to be at risk. His returns included a vastly expanded network of pro-Iranian militias, including thousands of young Shiites from Iraq, Lebanon, and South Asia who were now radicalized and battle-hardened. By late 2018 Soleimani's dream of an Iranian land bridge had been all but realized. Only those one thousand American troops, based in eastern Syria in a handful of strategically placed outposts near the Iraq border, still stood in the way.

Then President Trump astonished his security advisers by announcing that those, too, were soon departing.

Just before the Christmas holidays in 2018, Brett McGurk flew to Ottawa for a gathering of military and diplomatic leaders of the international coalition against ISIS. The group's once-vast caliphate now consisted of a few villages on the Euphrates River in eastern Syria, and those would fall to Kurdish ground troops within weeks. McGurk's task at the meeting was not to cheerlead, though, but to reassure. Trump had startled the coalition over the previous months with off-hand comments suggesting that he was considering withdrawing all forces from Syria. McGurk, along with defense secretary James Mattis, was in Ottawa to tell U.S. allies that it wasn't true. The White House had just organized a policy review on Syria, led by Bolton, and the official message to allies was that U.S. forces would remain until ISIS was entirely defeated and all Iranian-backed fighters had left the country.

"We're staying for the foreseeable future, and we need your continued support," said McGurk later, summarizing the message he delivered to the gathering. "On that, everybody was unanimous. This wasn't over."

At that moment, a Kurdish-led army was preparing for what would become a grinding, weeks-long assault to liberate Baghouz, the last Syrian town fully under ISIS control. Once that was accomplished, months, perhaps years, of hard work remained: finding the terrorist group's surviving leaders as well as up to thirty thousand fighters who had scattered across Iraq and Syria as the caliphate collapsed. Syria's stateless Kurds could not accomplish the task without American help, and if they failed, both ISIS and Iran would be free to do whatever they wanted in southeastern Syria. There was no choice: the United States had to stay engaged.

After the Ottawa meeting, McGurk flew to the Middle East to repeat the same essential message. He was at a conference in Qatar when another diplomat mentioned something that startled him: Turkey was telling its allies that Trump was about to announce an immediate withdrawal of all U.S. forces from Syria. McGurk, the top U.S. civilian official overseeing the anti-ISIS campaign, heard nothing about it until the following day when Secretary of State Mike Pompeo phoned him personally to break the news. Trump had made a snap decision after a conversation with Turkey's president, Recep Tayyip Erdogan. The Turkish leader had convinced Trump he could now handle the ISIS problem on his own.

McGurk made arrangements to fly back to Washington at once. He barely made it home when Trump announced the new policy using his favorite communications platform, Twitter.

"We have defeated ISIS in Syria, my only reason for being there during the Trump Presidency," he wrote. In a second posting Trump added, "Our boys, our young women, our men—they're coming back, and they're coming back now."

McGurk was astonished. He was also angry. How could he tell the Syrian Kurds that their fates had been abruptly consigned to Erdogan, who regarded their militia army as a terrorist group?

"My counterparts in coalition capitals were bewildered," McGurk wrote soon after the policy change was announced. "Our fighting partners in the [Kurdish-led] SDF, whom I had visited regularly on the ground in Syria, expressed shock and then denial, hoping Trump would change his mind."

"Trump tweeted, 'We have defeated ISIS in Syria,' " McGurk continued, "but that is not true."

McGurk pondered how he could support a policy change that required abandoning a critical U.S. ally in the still-active fight against the terrorist group. At last he arrived at an answer: he couldn't. It would have to fall to someone else.

"I ultimately concluded that I could not carry out these new instructions and maintain my integrity," he wrote in an email to friends.

On December 20, a day after the announced troop withdrawal, Secretary of Defense Mattis tendered his resignation in a letter to Trump. The following day, McGurk did the same. Trump would later change his mind and order only a partial withdrawal. He would repeat the pattern months later with still another withdrawal order, followed by another partial reversal. But as far as McGurk was concerned, the damage was done.

The diplomat formally left government service on New Year's Eve, departing as one of the last senior U.S. officials to witness the Syrian conflict in its entirety, from the earliest pro-democracy uprisings through the rise of the Islamic State; from the regime's first experimental use of sarin to the dramatic, if incomplete, mission to destroy Syria's chemical stockpile; from the hopeful declaration that "Assad must go" to the despairing reality of an entrenched Syrian dictatorship propped up by Russian and Iranian protectors intent on reshaping the region in their own image.

Trump accepted the resignation but could not pass up a chance to publicly insult the man he had named as special envoy.

"Brett McGurk, who I do not know, was appointed by President Obama in 2015," he wrote in a Twitter posting. "Was supposed to leave in February but he just resigned prior to leaving. Grandstander? The Fake News is making such a big deal about this nothing event!"

—

The war in Syria was effectively over. The entire country was in ruins, with a scale of devastation rivaling that of Germany and Japan after World War II. By 2020, the dead would number at least half a million. Another seven million were permanent refugees, many of them shunned by their adopted countries and facing uncertain futures. An entire generation of children was growing up with little or no formal schooling, leaving them vulnerable to poverty, radicalization, and violence.

The people and places victimized by chemical weapons would remain forever scarred. Saraqeb, the northern city that witnessed a strange canister of poison gas falling from the sky in April 2013, was bombed and shelled so many times that the entire town was deserted, with only rubble covering the spot where Maryam al-Khatib had tended her grapevines.

Mazen al-Hamada, the engineer-turned-prisoner who endured hellish days inside an aircraft hangar as the Syrian government awaited a possible U.S. military strike, sought refuge in Holland after winning his release. But later he suffered a breakdown that doctors attributed to post-traumatic stress. After a long hospital stint, he tried to restart his life, but then was lured back to Syria by diplomats who gave him a passport and promised him a role in negotiating a future amnesty for the country's political prisoners. He flew to Damascus and was immediately arrested and returned to prison.

Kassem Eid, the young man stricken by sarin at Ghouta, applied for permanent asylum in Germany. Increasingly embittered by the West's failure to intervene in Syria, he announced to his Twitter followers that he was finished as an activist.

"I have decided to stop," he wrote in a Twitter posting. "I will no longer do interviews or write. I am almost consumed."

Houssam Alnahhas's escape plan was to get as far away from Syria, physically and emotionally, as he possibly could. His parents and siblings followed him to Turkey to try to start new lives, and soon after they were devastated to learn that the family home in the Damascus suburbs had been destroyed, with even the wires and fixtures torn from the walls by looters. Alnahhas, after finally earning his medical degree, left with Yasmin and their baby girl for the United States, where he continued his studies at Harvard University and Johns Hopkins University's School of Public Health.

Once, while in Boston, he happened to catch a lecture by Robert Ford, the by-then-retired U.S. ambassador who had advocated unsuccessfully for U.S. intervention in Syria. When it was time for questions, the young physician could not restrain himself. But you *did* intervene, he corrected. You gave the people false hope.

Yet he would not allow himself to dwell on Syria and the awful events he witnessed there. "It's easy to blame everyone," he said.

There were reasons to keep going and to focus on possibilities that still lay ahead. He had a new daughter and a career that was devoted to saving lives. In The Hague, the OPCW had created yet another investigative team, this time with an explicit mandate to review past chemical weapons attacks in Syria with the goal of assessing guilt, as the JIM had attempted to do years before. Near the top of the new panel's list was the April 2014 attack in Kafr Zita, for which the OPCW's evidentiary files included recordings and documents collected by a young Syrian medical intern who had risked his life to obtain them. "All the things we did—it's now part of history," Alnahhas said.

The young doctor had meanwhile kept his own personal archive, mementos and artifacts from the time when he was known as Chemical Hazem. It includes a time line of the events in Syria, many of which he witnessed himself, and dozens of videos. In one of them, a young man in a physician's coat can be seen climbing onto a makeshift riser before a crowd of demonstrators to pay tribute to three murdered friends whose burned bodies had been discovered the day before. "If they died for you, then it is our honor to die for you as well," he tells the crowd in Arabic.

When his daughter is old enough, he will show the videos to her, Alnahhas said. He will tell her about the tragic country where her parents had lived, suffered, and grieved, a country to which the couple still hoped to return.

"I will tell her why it was that we just couldn't give up," he said. "I'll tell her how, when the crisis happened, we tried to help, wherever we were, in any way we could. Because we were thinking then about a future that we know some day will come."

ACKNOWLEDGMENTS

When writing about a historical event as complex as the one that unfolds in *Red Line,* one of the hardest challenges is deciding which parts to leave out. The story at the book's core—the investigation of the Syrian chemical attacks and the removal and destruction of the country's declared stockpile—is a tale with many thousands of characters, including government officials, diplomats, scientists, technicians, politicians, soldiers, spies, activists, medical workers, and countless ordinary citizens. Only a fraction of these appear in the pages of this book. Among the excluded are a large number of extraordinary individuals who played vital roles, some of whom generously shared their memories and insights with me. I owe a debt of gratitude to each of them and regret that their contributions could not be fully acknowledged in this limited and somewhat narrow account.

The story contained in these pages was constructed from material gathered over more than two years of reporting, including more than 250 interviews, thousands of documents, and tens of gigabytes of digital files, photos, and videos. Very early in this process, several key participants emerged as guides and interpreters to the events, providing important context as well as introductions, suggestions, and resources. Some of them cannot be identified here because of sensitivities related to their jobs. While I am unable to thank them publicly, each of them knows how grateful I am. Among the many who helpfully provided early insights and assistance regarding the disarmament mission were Laura Holgate, Andrew Weber, Thomas Countryman, Jay Santee, John Gower, Rebecca Hersman, Jeffrey Feltman, Susana Malcorra, Angela Kane, and Toby Harward. A special thanks is owed to Tony Banbury, Jannell MacAulay, Karen Cullison, Simon and Julia Limage, and Chelsea Goldstein for their exceptional generosity in this regard. I am also especially indebted to the following: the management and staff of the U.S. Army Combat Capabilities Development Command Chemical Biological Center at Edgewood, Maryland, especially Richard Arndt; Tim Blades and his entire team at the Chemical Biological Application and Risk Reduction unit; the U.S. Department of Transportation's Marine Administration and Keystone Shipping Co., operators of the MV *Cape Ray;* Master Mariner Rick Jordan and the former officers and crew of the *Cape Ray;* the current and former leadership of the Organization for the Prohibition of Chemical Weapons, most especially Ahmet Üzümcü, Robert Fairweather, and Deepti Choubey, as well as numerous former OPCW officials; and the current and former senior management at the Defense Threat Reduction Agency. I also was greatly helped at the start of my journey by a number of published and unpublished reports and studies, most especially Albert Mauroni's "Eliminating Syria's Chemical Weapons," by the U.S. Air Force's Center for Unconventional Weapons Studies (2017); the monograph by Karim Makdisi and Coralie Pison Hindawi titled "Creative Diplomacy Amidst a Brutal Conflict: Analyzing the OPCW-Joint Mission for the Elimination of the Syrian Chemical Weapons Program" (Issam Fares Institute for Public Policy and International Affairs, 2016); and the extraordinary investigative work and insightful analysis by Eliot Higgins and his fellow researchers at Bellingcat. A great many sources—Middle Eastern, European, and American—were helpful with insights and context on the Syrian conflict and on White House, UN, and OPCW decision-making and the larger geopolitical context. I am indebted to numerous current and former officials and experts whose writings, memoirs, and insights were particularly helpful, including Gregory Koblentz, Ben Rhodes, Samantha Power, Derek Chollet, Wa'el Alzayat, Brett McGurk, Jake Sullivan, David Petraeus, John Kerry, Susan Rice, William Burns, Hamish de Bretton-Gordon, Nikolaos van Dam, Christopher Phillips, Mallory Stewart, Tony Blinken, Jon Finer, and numerous other Obama and Trump administration officials who cannot be credited publicly. I am also unable to publicly thank several individuals from the classified world, in the United States and abroad, who offered invaluable assistance, including one in particular who was unfailingly generous in providing context, ideas, reassurance, and occasional inspiration. Finally, I was helped immensely by numerous individuals who provided an all-important Syrian perspective, most especially Kassem Eid, Houssam Alnahhas, the Syrian American Medical Society (SAMS), and Mouaz Moustafa and the entire staff of the Syrian Emergency Task Force.

This book would not have been possible without the support of two great Washington, D.C., institutions. I am enormously grateful to my employer, *The Washington Post,* for granting me a leave of absence to work on this project, and also for the privilege of working with so many U.S. and Middle East–based journalists whose work was a daily source of ideas and inspiration. I am especially indebted to Marty Baron, Cameron Barr, Tracy Grant, and Steve Ginsberg, and to friends and colleagues who offered invaluable advice and feedback, especially Peter Finn, David Hoffman, Souad Mekhennet, Steven Luxenberg, Larry Roberts, Paul Scicchitano, and Anders Gyllenhaal. I also was extraordinarily fortunate to have the support of the Woodrow Wilson International Center for Scholars, which generously offered me a scholarship, an office, and a wealth of research resources, all of which were indispensable to the completion of the book. I am most thankful to director Jane Harman and senior vice president Robert Litwak, and also to the Wilson Center's researchers, Janet Spikes and Michelle Kamalich, and many talented and generous colleagues, especially Meg King, Kim Connor, Michael Morrow, Alexander Bick, David and Marina Ottaway, and Haleh Esfandiari. A special tip of the hat goes to my amazingly gifted and resourceful intern, Sean Morrow, who worked tirelessly with me on this project for more than six months.

I am fortunate to be associated with one of the industry's best literary agents, Gail Ross, who was crucial in helping me refine and structure my initial idea for a book about Syria's chemical weapons, and who, together with the staff of the Ross Yoon Agency, offered support and encouragement throughout this journey. I am also indebted to the management and staff of Doubleday and the rest of the Penguin Random House team, including editor in chief Bill Thomas, Michael Goldsmith, Lauren Weber, Nora Reichard, Amelia Zalcman, Daniel

Meyer, and, most especially, my remarkable editor, Kris Puopolo, whose perception, skill, and seemingly endless patience were the special sauce that helped bring this project's diffuse elements together. For this book, as with my two previous ones, she has been a true partner, collaborator, and friend.

My work on this book required extensive travel and many long days of absence—physically, and more often mentally—from family. I am forever grateful to my children, Victoria and Andrew, and to my wife, Maryanne, for their love, patience, encouragement, and counsel. I am blessed beyond words.

It would be impossible to work on a project such as this one without being profoundly touched by the suffering and hardship endured by the people of Syria during a vicious war that, as I write these words, is now entering its tenth year. I have been inspired and moved every day by their stories, and by the bravery of the incredible men and women who have devoted themselves to alleviating suffering and seeking to bring this terrible conflict to an end.

NOTES

Prologue: The Chemist

1 He was known to the CIA's: Details of the Syrian spy's life and relations with his handler were provided to the author in confidential interviews with three former intelligence officials with detailed, contemporaneous knowledge of the spy's recruitment and case file. The author also extensively interviewed a former Syrian colleague who worked with the spy and was familiar with his personal story and scientific accomplishments.

2 Call me Ayman: The chemist's surname was withheld upon request because of concerns about reprisals against surviving family members.

3 hinted about a new "deterrent": Dany Shoham, "Guile, Gas and Germs: Syria's Ultimate Weapons," *Middle East Quarterly* (Summer 2002).

4 as the Nazis learned: See Jonathan Tucker, *War of Nerves: Chemical Warfare from World War I to Al-Qaeda* (New York: Pantheon, 2006).

4 twenty-six times deadlier than cyanide: "Public Information: Biological & Chemical Threats," World Health Organization, 2003, https://www.who.int/csr/delibepidemics/biochem_threats.pdf?ua=1.

6 The interrogation began: Details of the chemist's interrogation, confession, and execution were described in interviews with the former Syrian colleague, a CERS scientist present at the time of the events.

Chapter 1: "Like watching a freight train coming"

11 where inmates were locked away: "Torture Archipelago, Arbitrary Arrests, Torture, and Enforced Disappearances in Syria's Underground Prisons since March 2011," Human Rights Watch, 2012, https://www.hrw.org/report

/2012/07/03/torture-archipelago/arbitrary-arrests-torture-and-enforced-disappearances-syrias.

11 it was dubbed the "Sheraton": Neil MacFarquhar and Hwaida Saad, "2 Car Bombs Open Deadly New Front in Syria Conflict," *International Herald Tribune,* May 11, 2012.

11 The blast was so powerful: "Syria: 56 Dead in Suicide Bomb Attacks," Associated Press, May 11, 2012.

12 "We kept our promise:" Ben Hubbard, "Militant Video Claims Deadly Syria Bombings," *The Independent,* May 12, 2012.

12 "An al-Qaeda presence in Syria": Panetta's public comments as reported in Bassem Mroue, "Twin Car Bombs Kill 55 in Damascus," Associated Press, May 11, 2012.

14 *There are multiple potential disasters:* Author interview with Andrew C. Weber.

14 "It was like watching a freight train": Author interview with former U.S. intelligence official who participated in the briefings.

14 "a well-organized al-Qaeda affiliate": Author interview with Weber.

15 "a religious duty," he said: "Osama bin Laden Interview (1998)," www.abcnews.go.com, accessed August 26, 2019, https://abcnews.go.com/2020/video/osama-bin-laden-interview-1998-13506629.

15 "They are within our reach": Aimen Dean, Paul Cruickshank, and Tim Lister, *Nine Lives: My Time as MI6's Top Spy Inside al-Qaeda* (New York: One World, 2018).

15 "The question that lurked": Dean, *Nine Lives.*

16 "The prototype confirmed their worst fears": Ron Suskind, *The One Percent Doctrine: Deep Inside America's Pursuit of Its Enemies Since 9/11* (New York: Simon & Schuster, 2006).

17 a plan to release a cloud of poison gas: For an account of the chemical plot, see Joby Warrick, *Black Flags: The Rise of ISIS* (New York: Doubleday, 2015).

Chapter 2: "Something fell from the sky"

18 faint whir of a lone helicopter: The attack, including the dropping of the device and the reaction of onlookers and the subsequent treatment of victims, was recorded multiple times on cell-phone video, several of which were reposted by Brown Moses Blog at http://brown-moses.blogspot.com/2013/04/links-between-alleged-chemical-attacks.html.

19 The mistress of the house: A narrative of the April 29, 2013, events at Maryam al-Khatib's house was reconstructed from extensive videotaped interviews with family members and neighbors, conducted by Syrian

citizen-journalists and volunteers, and provided to the OPCW. Copies of the videos were obtained by the author.

21 "Hold his legs!": Conversations and treatment procedures as recorded on amateur cell-phone video and reposted by Brown Moses Blog.

23 doctor noted Maryam's death at 10:45 p.m.: United Nations Security Council, *United Nations Mission to Investigate Allegations of the Use of Chemical Weapons in the Syrian Arab Republic,* Final Report A/68/663, S/2013/735, December 13, 2013.

23 His first patient: Author interview with Houssam Alnahhas.

24 "What do you think is happening": Alnahhas, author interview.

25 "Made in China" imprinted on the metal lid: As seen in video of unexploded munition, obtained by the author.

25 "What is the world waiting for?": Family interview, obtained by the author.

26 Seven men in green scrubs and surgical masks: Details of the autopsy obtained from OPCW video footage of the procedure, seen by the author.

28 "a slip on a banana peel": Author interview with Åke Sellström.

30 "Throw us out and we'll have another war": Sellström, author interview.

31 "What have you said yes to now?": Åke Sellström in TedX Umea talk, YouTube.Com, May 20, 2015, https://www.youtube.com/watch?v=zq9kOFWp2T0.

31 "That's when we realized": Sellström, author interview.

32 denoted on the lab sheets simply as "GB": UN Security Council report, December 13, 2013.

34 "For one hundred years": Author interview with Andrew C. Weber.

34 known to history as Project Sapphire: For a detailed account of the Project Sapphire operation, see David E. Hoffman, *The Dead Hand* (New York: Doubleday, 2009).

35 all of them enriched to "weapons grade": Hoffman, *The Dead Hand.*

36 "The guy was brilliant": Weber, author interview.

36 "Hey, where's Lugar?": As recounted by Weber.

37 Moscow ended its participation: David M. Herszenhorn, "Russia Won't Renew Pact on Weapons with U.S.," *New York Times,* October 10, 2012.

37 "time has come for President Assad to step aside": Barack Obama spoken remarks, August 18, 2011, archived at https://obamawhitehouse.archives.gov/blog/2011/08/18/president-obama-future-syria-must-be-determined-its-people-president-bashar-al-assad.

37 "No shooting": Verbal instructions to rebels recounted in author interview with former State Department official who attended meetings with rebel leaders in 2011.

39 "Assad, or we burn the country": See Sam Dagher, *Assad or We Burn the*

Country: How One Family's Lust for Power Destroyed Syria (New York: Little, Brown and Co., 2019).

40 Israeli officials rushed thousands of gas masks: Adiv Sterman, "Syria fears send gas mask demand north," *Times of Israel,* January 30, 2013.

40 "Think outside the box!" Derek Chollet, *The Long Game: How Obama Defied Washington and Redefined America's Role in the World* (New York: PublicAffairs, 2016).

40 spokesman warned that Damascus possessed special weapons: "Syria Says Chemical or Biological Weapons Could Be Used If There Is 'External Aggression,'" CBSnews.com, July 23, 2012, https://www.cbsnews.com/news/syria-says-chemical-or-biological-weapons-could-be-used-if-there-is-external-aggression/.

41 Syria would be "held accountable": Obama remarks as recorded in "Remarks by the President to the 113th National Convention of the Veterans of Foreign Wars," July 23, 2012, https://obamawhitehouse.archives.gov/the-press-office/2012/07/23/remarks-president-113th-national-convention-veterans-foreign-wars.

41 "We have been very clear to the Assad regime": Obama remarks as recorded in "Remarks by the President to the White House Press Corps," August 20, 2012, https://obamawhitehouse.archives.gov/the-press-office/2012/08/20/remarks-president-white-house-press-corps.

41 "a U.S. president says millions of words": Ben Rhodes, *The World as It Is: A Memoir of the Obama White House* (New York: Random House, 2018).

42 "You will be held accountable": Obama remarks at the National Defense University, as recorded in "President Obama Pushes for Nonproliferation," December 4, 2012, https://obamawhitehouse.archives.gov/blog/2012/12/04/president-obama-pushes-nonproliferation.

42 "How many trucks?": Author interview with Andrew C. Weber.

Chapter 3: The Machine

43 "I never heard of the place": Author interview with Jay Santee.

44 he perceived a serious gap: Author interview with Richard Falkenrath.

45 "The answers were lousy:" Falkenrath, author interview.

45 made their way to a large conference room: Events and conversations at the December 28, 2012, Edgewood meeting were described in author interviews with six participants.

47 *These are highly operational, no-nonsense guys:* Falkenrath, author interview.

48 "These guys think they can deploy a mobile system": As recounted by Weber in author interview.

48 The first crude design was scrawled: Author interview with Tim Blades.

49 "What do you need to go forward with this?": Details of the exchange described in author interviews with three participants in the meeting.

50 Alnahhas arranged for the fake chemical attack: Aleppo drill described in author interview with Houssam Alnahhas.

51 "This is a new start for us": Alnahhas, author interview.

52 "probably suffering from internal bleeding": Alnahhas, author interview.

52 "Kill me before you go": Alnahhas's mother's words as recounted by himself in "Stoop Storytelling Series: In Search of Safety," Johns Hopkins Center for Humanitarian Health, March 9, 2020, https://www.youtube.com/watch?v=jic9Z-cWTxY.

53 "on a small scale against the opposition": White House findings as summarized in "Statement by Deputy National Security Advisor for Strategic Communications Ben Rhodes on Syrian Chemical Weapons Use," June 13, 2013, https://obamawhitehouse.archives.gov/the-press-office/2013/06/13/statement-deputy-national-security-advisor-strategic-communications-ben-.

53 "Legally, we couldn't say what the support was": Rhodes, *The World as It Is.*

54 He signed a secret document: Obama's actions increasing covert training and aid under Timber Sycamore were described in author interviews with four senior Obama administration officials with direct knowledge of the program.

54 "What if, all of a sudden": Author interview with senior administration official involved in brainstorming sessions at the White House.

54 "How does it end?" Obama would repeatedly ask: The president's views about various kinetic options were described in author interviews with four senior administration officials who participated in the discussions.

55 "did not want direct U.S. military intervention": Author interview with Wa'el Alzayat.

57 *Beautiful,* Santee thought: Author interview with Jay Santee.

58 "We paid a lot of money": Author interview with Tim Blades.

Chapter 4: "Help, please—they're dying!"

59 mission was finally on: An account of the Sellström team's journey to Damascus was described in author interviews with four members of the delegation.

60 "Don't get lost in your thoughts": Author interview with Diarmuid O'Donovan.

62 "We were invited here": Author interview with Åke Sellström.

64 "We don't have those kinds of problems": As recounted by Sellström; author interview.

66 "They kept explaining very basic concepts": Author interview with Sellström team member present in the meeting.

66 "Is it possible that 'terrorists' ": Author interview with Sellström team member present in the meeting.

66 "We are going nowhere": Author interview with Åke Sellström.

66 could not sleep: Cairns's account of the night as described by a former member of the Sellström team.

68 Sellström rolled out of bed early: Åke Sellström in TedX Umea talk, YouTube .Com, May 20, 2015, https://www.youtube.com/watch?v=zq9kOFWp2T0.

69 Eid heard the incoming rockets as well: Kassem Eid's experience of the chemical attack at Ghouta were described in an author interview and also in Kassem Eid, *My Country: A Syrian Memoir* (London: Bloomsbury Publishing, 2018).

70 "Wake up!" he screamed: Eid, *My Country.*

71 "I held him:" Eid, *My Country.*

Chapter 5: "No one is coming out alive"

72 "We've got a real issue here": Author interview with Tony Blinken.

73 Everyone at the meeting: Accounts of White House discussions of the Ghouta attack were provided in author interviews with three officials present.

73 "about to go over another Middle East waterfall": Author interview with senior Obama administration official present.

74 *This is so horrible:* Author interview with Åke Sellström.

74 "You have to let us in": As recounted by Sellström; author interview.

75 "Wake up!" his boss said: Author interview with Houssam Alnahhas.

76 "get those UN inspectors out of Syria": Exchange with Obama recounted in Samantha Power, *The Education of an Idealist: A Memoir* (New York: HarperCollins, 2019).

76 "This is a moot mission": Author interview with Samantha Power.

77 "You need to pack it up": Obama's words as recalled in author interview with senior aide to Ban Ki-moon.

77 "We cannot *not* proceed": Power, *The Education of an Idealist.*

77 "But for the ongoing presence of the inspectors": Power, author interview.

78 No one doubts that poison gas was used: Vladimir V. Putin, "A Plea for Caution from Russia," *New York Times,* September 11, 2013, https://www.nytimes.com/2013/09/12/opinion/putin-plea-for-caution-from-russia-on-syria.html.

79 "this thing is going to start up": Author interview with Tim Blades.

80 "What are you doing": Blades, author interview.

82 he was forced onto a bus: The prisoners' ordeal in the aircraft hangar was described in an author interview with Mazen al-Hamada.
83 "What's going on?" he asked: Hamada, author interview.

Chapter 6: "We go in again"

85 "Once we step into those cars": Author interview with Åke Sellström.
86 "officially consider your team persona non grata": Revolution Leadership Council in Damascus, open letter addressed to "Mr. Sellström," August 21, 2013.
87 Two men riding in the lead vehicle: A detailed description of the Sellström team's August 26, 2013, journey to the Ghouta attack site was described in author interviews with four team members.
91 "It was like the Beatles had come": Author interview with Åke Sellström.
92 "He was holding this bundle of sticks": The incident was described in author interviews with two Sellström team members present.
94 Eid awakened: Eid's encounter with the Sellström team was described in an author interview and also in Kassem Eid, *My Country: A Syrian Memoir* (London: Bloomsbury Publishing, 2018).
94 "I couldn't tell if I was proud or sad": Eid, *My Country.*
95 "What are you seeing right now?": Author interview with Wa'el Alzayat.
95 "We're sorry we can't bring you food": Eid, author interview.
96 "They were professionals": Eid, author interview.
96 The target this time: Details of the Sellström team's August 28, 2013, journey to east Ghouta were described in author interviews with four team members.
99 traces of an unusual additive: hexamine: United Nations Security Council, *United Nations Mission to Investigate Allegations of the Use of Chemical Weapons in the Syrian Arab Republic,* Final Report A/68/663, S/2013/735, December 13, 2013.

Chapter 7: "The eye of a hurricane"

102 "It was like we were all in the eye": Confidential author interview with Sellström team member.
103 "Engaging our military in Syria": Matt Fuller, "116 House Members Sign Syria Letter to Obama," RollCall.Com, August 28, 2013, https://www.rollcall.com/news/policy/87-house-members-sign-syria-letter-to-obama.
103 "left on a limb": Ben Rhodes, *The World as It Is: A Memoir of the Obama White House* (New York: Random House, 2018).
104 "It spooked everyone": Author interview with former White House official present during the discussions.

105 "We've had enough of presidents": Transcript of Obama's October 12, 2007, speech, retrieved from https://www.cnn.com/2007/POLITICS/12/21/obama.trans.iraq/.

105 "Congress," Rice told the president: Ben Rhodes, "Inside the White House During the Red Line Crisis," *Atlantic,* June 3, 2018.

105 "It would give President Obama": Samantha Power, *The Education of an Idealist.*

106 "Mr. Secretary-General": Author interview with UN official present during the meeting.

106 "He felt the pressure": Author interview with senior UN official.

107 McConnell would praise Obama's: Robert Farley, "McConnell Revises History on Syria," FactCheck.Org, April 7, 2017, https://www.factcheck.org/2017/04/mcconnell-revises-history-syria/.

107 "I can't find anyone": Samantha Power, *The Education of an Idealist.*

108 25 percent of Americans favored bombing: Lesley Wroughton, "As Syria War Escalates, Americans Cool to U.S. Intervention," Reuters, August 24, 2013, https://www.reuters.com/article/us-syria-crisis-usa-poll/as-syria-war-escalates-americans-cool-to-u-s-intervention-reuters-ipsos-poll-idUSBRE97O00E20130825.

108 over 51 percent: Gallup survey as reported by Gallup.com; see Andrew Dugan, "U.S. Support for Action in Syria Is Low vs. Past Conflicts," Gallup.com, September 6, 2013, https://news.gallup.com/poll/164282/support-syria-action-lower-past-conflicts.aspx.

109 "this menace must be confronted": *Washington Post* staff, "Transcript: President Obama's Aug. 31 Statement on Syria," *Washington Post,* August 31, 2013, https://www.washingtonpost.com/politics/transcript-president-obamas-aug-31-statement-on-syria/2013/08/31/3019213c-125d-11e3-b4cb-fd7ce041d814_story.html?utm_term=.5a6787f52fc2.

109 "Why not try to secure the dismantlement": Author interview with Samantha Power.

110 the inspectors quietly loaded their gear: Events of the Sellström team's departure from Damascus were described in interviews with three participants.

111 *We managed it:* Author interview with Åke Sellström.

111 "There is a threat against you": Sellström, author interview.

113 "After careful deliberation": *Washington Post* staff, "Transcript: President Obama's Aug. 31 Statement on Syria," *Washington Post,* August 31, 2013.

114 "I began to doubt": Kassem Eid, *My Country: A Syrian Memoir* (London: Bloomsbury Publishing, 2018).

114 languishing with hundreds of other prisoners: Author interview with Mazen al-Hamada.

114 "There was one man": Hamada, author interview.

Chapter 8: The Deal

116 "Sergey, you have to do this": Atmosphere at poolside talks related during author interviews with two former U.S. officials present in Geneva at the time.

118 Steinitz summoned Russia's ambassador: Account of the meeting provided in author interview with former senior Israeli official.

118 brief exchange between Putin and Obama: Obama's account of the meeting was described in author interview with senior aide to the president.

119 "He could turn over every single bit": Transcript of John F. Kerry's London news conference with Foreign Secretary William Hague, on September 9, 2013, https://2009-2017.state.gov/secretary/remarks/2013/09/213956.htm.

119 "This is not a change in policy": Author interview with former State Department official familiar with the events.

119 "I saw your comments": Account of phone conversation provided in author interview with former Kerry aide.

120 the talks began in earnest: Detailed account of the meetings in Geneva was provided in author interviews with six U.S. officials present or briefed on the events.

121 "on the border between feasible and insane": Author interview with Thomas Countryman.

123 "Move over": Author interview with Colonel John Cinnamon.

123 "The parties agree": UN Security Council, "Framework for Elimination of Syrian Chemical Weapons," A/68/398 S/2013/565; September 19, 2013, https://www.securitycouncilreport.org/atf/cf/%7B65BFCF9B-6D27-4E9C-8CD3-CF6E4FF96FF9%7D/s_2013_565.pdf.

124 "We were all for doing it fast": Author interview with Rebecca Hersman.

124 "the Russians really believed we couldn't do it": Hersman, author interview.

125 "We're now committed": Cinnamon, author interview.

125 "It just sounds impossible": Hersman, author interview.

126 "six hours of just 'no, no, no, no' ": Hersman, author interview.

126 "you know how to make the Syrian government behave": Conversation described in author interview with former senior State Department official.

Chapter 9: "No one is coming to help you"

127 "The findings are beyond doubt": Video press statement by UN secretary-general Ban Ki-moon, September 16, 2013. Reposted by *The Guardian*, https://www.theguardian.com/world/2013/sep/16/syrian-chemical-attack-sarin-says-un.

128 "We need not jump to any conclusions": Rick Gladstone and C. J. Chivers, "Forensic Details in UN Report Point to Assad's Use of Gas," *New York Times,* September 16, 2013, https://www.nytimes.com/2013/09/17/world/europe/syria-united-nations.html.

128 the scientist took his audience of reporters on a virtual tour: Details of closed UN briefing described in author interviews with two UN officials present.

128 traces of the additive called hexamine: As described in the "Report on the Alleged Use of Chemical Weapons in the Ghouta Area of Damascus" by the United Nations Mission to Investigate Allegations of the Use of Chemical Weapons, September 2013. https://www.un.org/zh/focus/northafrica/cwinvestigation.pdf.

129 "In his mind": Author interview with former UN official.

130 "extensive efforts to eliminate chemical weapons": Press release, The Nobel Peace Prize for 2013, NobelPrize.org, October 11, 2013, https://www.nobelprize.org/prizes/peace/2013/press-release/.

130 "No, I didn't get it": Author interview with Åke Sellström.

131 "We cannot resolve someone else's civil war": *Washington Post* staff, "Full Transcript: President Obama's Sept. 10 Speech on Syria," *Washington Post,* September 10, 2013, https://www.washingtonpost.com/politics/running-transcript-president-obamas-sept-10-speech-on-syria/2013/09/10/a8826aa6-1a2e-11e3-8685-5021e0c41964_story.html.

131 "I didn't have the heart": Kassem Eid, *My Country: A Syrian Memoir* (London: Bloomsbury Publishing, 2018).

132 "For these groups": Author interview with Kassem Eid.

132 "You relied on the West": Author interview with Houssam Alnahhas.

Chapter 10: "An elephant with a tick on its back"

137 towering superstructure and a mast: "Welcome Aboard the CAPE RAY (T-AKR 9679)," Maritime Administration data sheet, U.S. Department of Transportation, https://www.army.mil/e2/c/downloads/326584.pdf.

138 "It was not 'Plan A'": Author interview with former Pentagon official actively involved in the *Cape Ray* project.

138 "He was typical Tim": Author interview with civilian employee who worked closely with Blades in 2013.

138 "Don't worry about it": Author interview with participant in the exchange.

139 scouring the globe for countries: The multicountry mission to find a place to park Blades's machines was described by six Defense Department and State Department officials who participated in the search.

141 "It's perfect": Author interview with Andrew C. Weber.
142 "Build a plan and show me": Author interview with Jay Santee.
143 "Sir, it looks like this could work": Author interview with Tina Schoenberger.
143 "an equally low likelihood of accidents": Defense Threat Reduction Agency, "Field Deployable Hydrolysis System (FDHS) Ship-Board Option," final version, October 28, 2013.
144 "We are not a bin for chemical weapons": Staff article and photo, "US Offers to Destroy Syria's Most Lethal Weapons Offshore," Associated Press, November 20, 2013.
144 "I really wanted to do this": Rama's words to Kerry as recalled by a senior Kerry aide who listened to the conversation.
144 "We're going with the ship!": Author interview with Julia Brown.
145 "Enjoy your Thanksgiving": Author interview with Tim Blades.
147 *These are my kind of people:* Author interview with Rick Jordan.
147 "It was like a huge science experiment": Author interview with Chris Myers.
148 "You can't just go around cutting holes in ships!": Jordan, author interview.
149 "I'll come up with something": Blades, author interview.
149 "high potential" for an accident: Key conclusions of the Navy report were described in author interview with two Defense Department officials who read it.
150 "A ship is like an elephant": Jordan, author interview.
151 "It's just FUD": Santee, author interview.
152 "Most of us wished for death": Author interview with Edgewood crew member.

Chapter 11: "A technical delay"

154 "A technical delay": United Nations on YouTube.com, "Progress Continues Despite Likely Technical Delays (OPCW-UN Special Coordinator Sigrid Kaag)," December 29, 2013, https://www.youtube.com/watch?v=pNuQSa_m4T4.
155 "The tragedy continues unabated": Sigrid Kaag speech, "Eliminating Syria's Chemical Weapons," Georgetown University, September 30, 2013, https://www.c-span.org/video/?321781-1/discussion-eliminating-syrias-chemical-weapons.
156 "almost no one connected to this mission": Author interview with Sigrid Kaag.
158 "The fact that she's a woman": Author interview with Susana Malcorra.
159 *"Okay, I can do this":* Kaag, author interview.
160 "like bringing a patient to a nonexistent hospital": Kaag, author interview.

160 "I don't need these kinds of weapons": Karim Makdisi and Coralie Pison Hindawi, "Creative Diplomacy amidst a Brutal Conflict: Analyzing the OPCW-UN Joint Mission for the Elimination of the Syrian Chemical Weapons Program," Issam Fares Institute for Public Policy and International Affairs, American University of Beirut, 2016.

161 "This is a bit like a date": Author interview with Joint Mission team member present at the meeting.

161 "If they're planning to whack us": Author interview with a participant in the October 6 inspection.

163 a claim sourced to an Iraqi informant: See Bob Drogin, *Curveball: Spies, Lies, and the Con Man Who Caused a War* (New York: Random House, 2007).

163 "all this beautiful, gleaming equipment": Author interview with a participant in the October 6 inspection.

164 Team leader Jerry Smith was considering: Smith's effort to destroy the munitions was described by two officials present and a former UN official with access to field reports on the October 6 site visit.

165 "They just launched a barrage": Author interview with Joint Mission team member who witnessed the exchange.

167 "This is not a place": Exchange as recalled by former Joint Mission team member present.

168 "the Joint Mission is now satisfied": OPCW news release, "Syria Completes Destruction Activities to Render Inoperable Chemical Weapons Production Facilities," OPCW.org, October 31, 2013, https://www.opcw.org/media-centre/news/2013/10/syria-completes-destruction-activities-render-inoperable-chemical-weapons.

Chapter 12: Ghost Armies

171 *The Iraq-Syria border is being erased:* Summary of diplomatic cable described by former U.S. official with access to sensitive State Department reports.

171 "We face a real problem": Brett McGurk testimony, official transcript of the House Committee on Foreign Affairs, subcommittee on the Middle East and North Africa, November 13, 2013.

172 "Part of solving the security situation": Anne Gearan, "During Maliki Trip, Balancing Act for U.S.," *Washington Post,* October 31, 2013.

172 "Why do we care anymore": Representative Dana Rohrabacher comments, official transcript of the House Committee on Foreign Affairs, subcommittee on the Middle East and North Africa, November 13, 2013.

172 "You have a youthful population": McGurk, House testimony, November 13, 2013.

173 "Extremists linked to al-Qaeda": OPCW-UN Joint Mission in Syria, "Security Risk Assessment," January 2013.

173 "talking about acquiring" nerve agents: Author interview with a Western security official who read the report at the time.

175 "I'll see what I can do": Discussion with Russian ambassador described in author interview with Joint Mission team member present.

176 "Inside those containers": Author interview with Torben Mikkelsen. See also Mikkelsen's Danish memoir, *Tohundrede Dage,* August 2020.

179 "The boats may have been loaded": Author interview with Per Rostad.

180 "Welcome to Syria": Arrival of the *Ark Futura* and exchange with Danish officers described in author interview with Joint Mission official present at the time.

182 "Conditions this morning are TERRIBLE": emailed status "Update" to *Cape Ray* team, January 22, 2014.

182 "We briefed POTUS on this tonight": Confidential email to *Cape Ray* team, January 22, 2014.

182 "Which is faster—snails": Confidential email to *Cape Ray* team, January 13, 2014.

183 "Don't spill a drop": Author interview with Richard Dromerhauser.

184 "Holding folks this long": Author interview with Rick Jordan.

184 "I plan to become a bullfighter": Confidential email to *Cape Ray* team, January 29, 2014.

184 "Take care of yourselves": Confidential email to Rick Jordan, January 27, 2014.

Chapter 13: "A perfect loophole"

185 "This is for us": Author interview with Houssam Alnahhas.

186 "There *is* no more sarin": Alnahhas, author interview.

188 "It's brilliant": Author interview with Hamish de Bretton-Gordon.

189 "It was far away from us": Alnahhas, author interview.

190 "This is one of the best things": Alnahhas, author interview.

191 "We have found evidence of chlorine": De Bretton-Gordon, quoted in Ruth Sherlock, "Syria Chemical Weapons: How the Telegraph Found Evidence of Chlorine and Ammonia Gas Bombs," *Telegraph,* April 29, 2014, https://www.telegraph.co.uk/news/worldnews/middleeast/syria/10796150/Syria-chemical-weapons-how-the-Telegraph-found-evidence-of-chlorine-and-ammonia-gas-bombs.html.

192 "This is a chance": Author interview with Samantha Power.

193 "Qusai's account": Samantha Power's statement as recorded in UN Security Council, 7180th Meeting transcript, May 22, 2014.

194 "I really wanted to scream": Kassem Eid, *My Country: A Syrian Memoir* (London: Bloomsbury Publishing, 2018).

194 "The debates can seem clinical": Power, author interview.

Chapter 14: Race to the Coast

195 *Groundhog Day:* Author interview with Tim Blades.

195 "It's a slam dunk": Author interview with Rick Jordan.

196 "The next time you see Maryland": Jordan email to Tim Blades, June 4, 2014.

197 "Destroyed 1,279 gallons": Confidential email to *Cape Ray* team, June 18, 2014.

198 "Many of the original ship's crew": Confidential email, June 18, 2014.

198 "If we don't sail soon": Blades, author interview.

200 "That's bull!": Tim Blades, 2015 interview, courtesy of Chelsea Goldstein.

200 "Umm. No": Blades, author interview.

201 "I can't keep them here": Blades, author interview.

203 The rebel force pushed on: Assessment of security situation in June 2014 described in author interviews with two Joint Mission team members.

203 "move it out or sell it": Author interview with State Department official with insight into Syrian security situation.

204 "NOT a particularly safe": Discussion of options for dealing with Site Two chemicals as laid out in confidential OPCW email obtained by the author.

204 "will not consider airlifting": Confidential OPCW email.

205 "The deadline will not be met": UN news release, "As Syria Deadline Nears, OPCW-UN Mission Focuses on Swift Removal of Remaining Chemicals," News.UN.org, June 4, 2014, https://news.un.org/en/story/2014/06/469952-syria-deadline-nears-opcw-un-mission-focuses-swift-removal-remaining-chemicals.

205 "We know our obligations": Syrian government position as relayed in author interview with Joint Mission official.

205 "We will work within the parameters": Kaag, author interview.

206 "It is no longer sufficient": Kaag, author interview.

206 "The removal of the chemicals": Confidential email to *Cape Ray* crew, June 20, 2014.

207 "Never before:" Ahmet Üzümcü statement, OPCW.org, June 23, 2014, https://www.opcw.org/media-centre/news/2014/06/announcement-media-last-consignment-chemicals-leaving-syria.

208 "I hope the people of Syria can forgive us": Kaag, author interview.

210 "So it begins": Blades, author interview.

Chapter 15: "The number we will never know . . ."

212 "You will conquer Rome": Damien McElroy, "Rome Will Be Conquered Next, Says Leader of 'Islamic State,'" *Telegraph,* July 1, 2014.
212 "You have to let the Peshmerga": Author interview with Brett McGurk.
215 "It's al-Qaeda in Iraq on steroids": McGurk, author interview.
216 Margarita Machines hummed to life: The start-up of the machine and subsequent destruction of the chemicals were described in author interviews with six crew members aboard the ship.
217 "the ride actually feels smoother": Author interview with Rick Jordan.
218 "Once we reach the point": Jordan, author interview.
218 "We warned them": Petition as quoted in Apostolis Fotiadis, "Pollution: Syria's Chemicals Haunt the Mediterranean," Inter Press Service, July 11, 2014.
219 "you can't please everybody": Jordan, author interview.
220 "It looks like the Grand Canyon": Author interview with Lloyd Pusey.
222 "I pulled a lot of rabbits": Blades, author interview.
223 "If you don't fight": Pavlos Polakis quoted in Nathalie Savaricas, "Bad Weather Stymies Activists' Attempt to Stop Syrian Chemical Weapons Ship," *Independent,* July 27, 2014.
223 "It was a perfect storm of luck": Blades, author interview.
224 "Five months to create": Santee message as provided to author by a participant in the *Cape Ray* mission.
224 "With the world watching:" Author interview with Richard Dromerhauser.
225 "Just read your morning's intel brief": Author interview with Christine Parthemore.
226 "Enjoy the ride": Author interview with Wyatt McNutt.
226 "We all want to thank you": Jordan, author interview.
227 "There was more weight": Author interview with a participant in the *Cape Ray* mission.

Chapter 16: A Day "perfect for a chemical attack"

231 The defenders crouched: Account of the ISIS chlorine attack was provided by two Kurdish regional government officials and gleaned from video footage.
233 "My lads and lasses don't like chemical weapons": Author interview with Hamish de Bretton-Gordon.
234 "The day was perfect for a chemical attack": de Bretton-Gordon, author interview.

234 "It's a horrific thing": de Bretton-Gordon, author interview.

235 "Even if it doesn't kill many": de Bretton-Gordon, author interview.

237 "After our experience": Author interview with Houssam Alnahhas.

238 "When I arrived": Mohammed Tennari, quoted in Somini Sengupta, "U.N. Security Council Sees Video Evidence of a Chemical Attack in Syria," *New York Times,* April 17, 2015.

239 "If there was a dry eye in the house:" Power, quoted in "Syria War: 'Chlorine' Attack Video Moves UN to Tears," BBC News, April 17, 2015, https://www.bbc.com/news/world-middle-east-32346790.

239 "Individuals who are responsible for attacks like that": From Power's videotaped remarks at April 17, 2015, UNSC news conference, https://www.bbc.com/news/world-middle-east-32346790.

239 "It was the most ridiculous thing": Author interview with Wa'el Alzayat.

240 "bad planning": "Report on the Work of the Declaration Assessment Team," OPCW, July 4, 2016.

242 "We'd have guys put in front of us:" Author interview with former Declarations Assessment Team official.

242 described as "implausible": "Report on the Work of the Declaration Assessment Team," OPCW, July 4, 2016.

244 "Well, that should be a conversation-starter": Author interview with Samantha Power.

244 "He will drive you crazy": Rice as quoted in Samantha Power, *The Education of an Idealist: A Memoir* (New York, HarperCollins, 2019).

244 "Vitaly didn't go to work": Author interview.

245 "The staff is not going to be": Author interview.

246 identifying "to the greatest extent feasible": Press release, "Security Council Unanimously Adopts Resolution 2235 (2015)," United Nations, August 7, 2015, https://www.un.org/press/en/2015/sc12001.doc.htm.

Chapter 17: "A catastrophic success"

247 stood a large villa: A description of the facility and broader program was provided in author interviews with three current and former U.S. officials.

249 "catastrophic success": Author interview with former Obama administration official involved in dozens of Syria meetings.

250 "off the charts historically": McGurk quoted in Jim Sciutto, "U.S. Official Calls ISIS a Problem 'Off the Charts Historically,'" CNN Wire, April 13, 2015.

251 "What does it mean": Author interview with Brett McGurk.

252 "We created, perhaps inadvertently": McGurk, author interview.

254 expanded force of seven thousand: Sam Dagher and Asa Fitch, "Iran Expands Role in Syria in Conjunction with Russia's Airstrikes," *Wall Street Journal,* October 2, 2015, https://web.archive.org/web/20171130060756/https://www.wsj.com/articles/iran-expands-role-in-syria-in-conjunction-with-russias-airstrikes-1443811030.

255 "strange hysteria": Zakharova quoted in Shaun Walker and Ian Black, "Russia Complains of 'Strange Hysteria' over Its Presence in Syria," *Guardian,* September 9, 2015, https://www.theguardian.com/world/2015/sep/09/russia-complains-of-strange-hysteria-over-its-presence-in-syria.

255 "They're going into combat": Author interview with senior Obama official present in the meeting.

256 "Let me know how it works out": Author interview with official present.

257 "If you have forces in the area": Jennifer Griffin and Lucas Tomlinson, "Russia Launches Airstrikes in Northern Syria, Senior Military Officer Says," FoxNews.com, Sept. 30, 2015, https://www.foxnews.com/world/russia-launches-airstrikes-in-northern-syria-senior-military-official-says.

258 "It turns out that Russia also": Author interview with senior Obama administration official.

Chapter 18: An ISIS "wonder weapon"

260 "I was afraid": All quotes from author interview with Suleiman al-Afari, in Iraqi Kurdish custody on December 12, 2018. The interview was conducted at the counterterrorism division headquarters of Iraq's Kurdish Regional Government, with Kurdish officials present.

262 So he cooperated: Details of Afari's interrogation were described by two Kurdish Regional Government officials directly familiar with the events.

263 Saddam Hussein used mustard gas: Borzou Daragahi, "1987 Chemical Strike Still Haunts Iran," *Los Angeles Times,* March 19, 2007, https://www.latimes.com/archives/la-xpm-2007-mar-19-fg-sardasht19-story.html.

265 "Do I regret it": Afari, author interview.

265 MacFarland read the reports: MacFarland's interactions with the Iraqis described in author interview with former Defense Department official.

265 "We began to recognize": Author interview with General Joseph Votel.

266 "hoping for some kind of a wonder weapon": Author interview with General Sean MacFarland.

267 The biggest strike: Barbara Starr and Nicole Gaouette, "U.S. Bombs ISIS Chemical Weapons Plant," CNN.com, September 13, 2016, https://www.cnn.com/2016/09/13/politics/isis-chemical-weapons-plant/index.html.

268 "They had all this capability": Votel, author interview.

269 "founder of ISIS": Lori Robertson and Eugene Kiely, "Trump's False Obama-ISIS Link," Factcheck.org, August 11, 2016, https://www.factcheck.org/2016/08/trumps-false-obama-isis-link/.

269 "I know more about ISIS": Donald Trump at Fort Dodge, Iowa, political rally, as carried by CNN on November 13, 2015, https://grabien.com/file.php?id=64904.

269 "stupid" to get involved: Nicholas Fandos, "Trump's View of Syria: How It Evolved, in 19 Tweets," *New York Times,* April 7, 2017, https://www.nytimes.com/2017/04/07/us/politics/donald-trump-syria-twitter.html.

269 "Let them get rid of ISIS": Donald Trump interview with *Sixty Minutes,* CBSNews.com, September 27, 2015, https://www.cbsnews.com/news/donald-trump-60-minutes-scott-pelley/.

270 "Is there literally nothing": Samantha Power, *Education of an Idealist: A Memoir* (New York, HarperCollins, 2019).

270 "Tom, sorry to do this": Author interview with Thomas Countryman.

Chapter 19: "Like Judgment Day"

272 Morad was driving to work: Mamoun Morad's depiction of the day's events was obtained from the physician's children and a recorded interview with Australian Broadcasting Corp. See Sophie McNeill and Brigid Andersen, "Khan Sheikhoun Chemical Attack: Doctor Tells of 'Day from Hell,'" ABC.net.au, May 2, 2017, https://www.abc.net.au/news/2017-05-02/day-from-hell-khan-sheikhoun-chemical-attack/8489214.

272 a lone, Russian-made Su-22 fighter-bomber: Details of the attack described in "Seventh Report of the OPCW-UN Joint Investigative Mechanism," UN Security Council, October 26, 2017, https://www.securitycouncilreport.org/atf/cf/%7B65BFCF9B-6D27-4E9C-8CD3-CF6E4FF96FF9%7D/s_2017_904.pdf.

273 a small boy was seen tearing out: Witness accounts as described in "Death by Chemicals: The Syrian Government's Widespread and Systematic Use of Chemical Weapons," Human Rights Watch, May 2017, https://www.hrw.org/report/2017/05/01/death-chemicals/syrian-governments-widespread-and-systematic-use-chemical-weapons.

274 "Can you imagine": Sophie McNeill and Brigid Andersen, "Khan Sheikhoun Chemical Attack: Doctor Tells of 'Day from Hell,'" ABC.net.au, May 2, 2017, https://www.abc.net.au/news/2017-05-02/day-from-hell-khan-sheikhoun-chemical-attack/8489214.

274 "It was like Judgment Day": author interview with Morad's son-in-law, Dr. Amjad Rass.

275 Syrian munition known as the M4000: Eliot Higgins, "The Open Source Hunt for Syria's Favourite Sarin Bomb," www.bellingcat.com, April 21, 2020.

275 "Assad Is killing ISIS": Michael Crowley, "Trump's Praise of Russia, Iran and Assad Regime Riles GOP Experts," Politico.com, October 10, 2016, https://www.politico.com/story/2016/10/trump-praise-russia-iran-assad-criticism-229546.

275 "The longer-term status of President Assad": Michael R. Gordon, "White House Accepts 'Political Reality' of Assad's Grip on Power in Syria," *New York Times,* March 31, 2017, https://www.nytimes.com/2017/03/31/us/politics/trump-bashar-assad-syria.html.

275 "Do we think he's a hindrance? Yes": Michelle Nichols, "US Priority on Syria No Longer Focused on 'Getting Assad Out': Haley," Reuters, March 30, 2017, https://de.reuters.com/article/us-mideast-crisis-syria-usa-haley/u-s-priority-on-syria-no-longer-focused-on-getting-assad-out-haley-idUSKBN1712QL.

275 "Let's go in": Donald Trump as quoted in Bob Woodward, *Fear: Trump in the White House* (New York: Simon & Schuster, 2018).

277 "I'll name my son Donald": Eid comment to journalist Ruth Sherlock as related on Sherlock's Twitter account @Rsherlock, April 6, 2017.

277 "I cried out of joy": Eid's live interview on April 7, 2017, with CNN anchor Brooke Baldwin, as posted on RealClearPolitics.com on April 11, 2017, https://www.realclearpolitics.com/video/2017/04/11/syrian_refugee_to_cnn_anchor_thank_you_trump_establish_safe_zones_to_help_syrians_stay_in_their_country.html.

278 "massive, dangerous and wasteful": Donald J. Trump Twitter posting, June 24, 2017.

279 "It was like a guillotine": Author interview with Trump administration National Security Council official.

279 "Putin won": Greg Jaffe and Adam Entous, "Trump Ends Covert CIA Program to Arm Anti-Assad Rebels in Syria, a Move Sought by Moscow," *Washington Post,* July 19, 2017, https://www.washingtonpost.com/world/national-security/trump-ends-covert-cia-program-to-arm-anti-assad-rebels-in-syria-a-move-sought-by-moscow/2017/07/19/b6821a62-6beb-11e7-96ab-5f38140b38cc_story.html.

279 killed as many as one hundred thousand: David Ignatius, "What the Demise of the CIA's Anti-Assad Program Means," *Washington Post,* July 20, 2017, https://www.washingtonpost.com/opinions/what-the-demise-of-the-cias-anti-assad-program-means/2017/07/20/f6467240-6d87-11e7-b9e2-2056e768a7e5_story.html.

281 "They had made and used mustard": Author interview with Laura Holgate, director for WMD terrorism, White House National Security Council.

281 Khaled Khayat was a forty-nine-year-old handyman: An extensive narrative of the Khayat case was obtained from Australian court records, chiefly sentencing documents for the case *R v Khaled Khayat; R v Mahmoud Khayat,* New South Wales Supreme Court docket 1817, December 17, 2019.

Chapter 20: A Smoking Gun

282 António Guterres, telephoned: The interaction was described in an author interview with an official knowledgeable about the conversation.

284 "We supported you": Author interview with Edmond Mulet.

286 "Come over so we can open it": Khaled Khayat's text as recorded in sentencing documents for the case *R v Khaled Khayat; R v Mahmoud Khayat,* New South Wales Supreme Court docket 1817, December 17, 2019.

287 could be exceedingly deadly: Sentencing documents for the case *R v Khaled Khayat; R v Mahmoud Khayat,* New South Wales Supreme Court docket 1817, December 17, 2019.

288 "You should not have sent me a picture": The Controller's text as recorded in sentencing documents, Dec. 17, 2019.

288 The man whom investigators would call the Controller: For a detailed account of Hassan's role in the plot, see Andrew Zammit, "'Operation Silves': Inside the Islamic State Sydney Plane Plot," *CTC Sentinel,* April 2020; and Mette Mayli Albaek et al., "The Controller: How Basil Hassan Launched Islamic State Terror into the Skies," *CTC Sentinel,* May 2020.

289 "one of the most dangerous people": State Department Counterterrorism Finance and Designations director, as interviewed in "Dronekrigeren: Danmarks farligeste terrorist," Part 1, Danish broadcaster DR, April 7, 2019.

290 faddish way to commit suicide: Stavroula Papadodima et. al., "'Detergent Suicide' by Adolescent as Instructed by Internet: a Case Report," *Forensic Science and Criminology* 2, No. 10 (March 2017), https://www.oatext.com/Detergent-suicide-by-adolescent-as-instructed-by-internet-A-case-report.php#Article_Info.

291 "it would have been lethal": Prosecutor's conclusion as summarized in sentencing documents, December 17, 2019.

291 "O soldiers of the caliphate": ISIS communiqué as reported in "IS Spokesman Boasts of Group's Longevity," SITE Intelligence Group, January 28, 2020.

291 The experiments conducted over the summer: Accounts of the JIM's forensic investigation were based on author interviews with Stefan Mogl and a second JIM official who participated in the probe.

293 "It was a very small group": Mogl, author interview.

293 "I have a mandate": Mulet, author interview.

294 "It would be a shame for your career": Author interview with former UN official present at the meeting.

294 "Consider the victims of these insidious acts": Testimony of Mulet and other speakers as recorded in UN Security Council official meeting transcript for November 7, 2017.

296 "How the Security Council Failed": Edmond Mulet, "How the Security Council Failed the Syria Chemical Weapons Investigators and Victims," *New York Times,* December 29, 2017.

297 "All of it was kept": Mulet, author interview.

Chapter 21: The Unraveling

299 "What he really wanted": Author interview with Trump administration National Security Council official.

299 "strategic sideshow": John Bolton, *The Room Where It Happened: A White House Memoir* (New York: Simon & Schuster, 2020).

300 "Mission accomplished": Donald J. Trump Twitter posting, April 14, 2018.

302 "We're staying": Author interview with Brett McGurk.

302 "We have defeated ISIS in Syria": Donald J. Trump Twitter posting, December 19, 2018, TheHill.com, https://thehill.com/policy/defense/435402-16-times-trump-declared-or-predicted-the-demise-of-isis.

303 "My counterparts in coalition capitals": Brett McGurk, "Trump Said He Beat ISIS. Instead, He's Giving It New Life," *Washington Post,* January 18, 2018, https://www.washingtonpost.com/outlook/trump-said-hed-stay-in-syria-to-beat-isis-instead-hes-giving-it-new-life/2019/01/17/a25a00cc-19cd-11e9-8813-cb9dec761e73_story.html.

303 "McGurk, who I do not know": Donald J. Trump Twitter posting, December 28, 2018.

304 "I have decided to stop": Kassem Eid Twitter posting, January 11, 2020.

305 "It's easy to blame": Author interview with Houssam Alnahhas.

305 "I will tell her why": Alnahhas, author interview.

INDEX

al-Abadi, Haider, 266
Abdullah II, King, 40, 139–40
Adra, 162
Adra Prison, 8, 82–83, 114–15, 162
al-Afari, Suleiman, 259–61
Afghanistan, 108, 131, 254
Alawites, 249, 253–54
Albania, 140–41, 143–44
Aleppo, 6, 23–24, 26, 29, 33, 49–53, 55, 59, 74–75, 132, 257
Alnahhas, Houssam ("Chemical Hazem"), 23–26, 49–53, 74–75, 132–33, 185–91, 236–37, 303–4
  arrest of, 51–52
  chemical weapons drill set up by, 49–51
  chlorine attacks and, 186–91
  de Bretton-Gordon and, 187, 188, 190–91, 233
  health-care worker training organized by, 49–51, 132
  helicopter and, 185, 190
al-Nusra Front, 11–14, 131–32, 248, 250, 252–53, 258, 280, 295
al-Qaeda, 14–17, 33, 172, 173, 248–50, 252
  chemical weapons and, 15–17, 33–34
  September 11 attacks by, 7, 14–16
al-Qaeda in Iraq, 12, 17, 170–71, 214–15, 256
al-Qusayr, 55
al-Safira, 33–34
Alzayat, Wa'el, 55–56, 95, 239
Amman, 17
Anbar Awakening, 171, 256
Ankara, 247
anthrax, 36
Arab Spring, 37–39, 108, 166
Ark Futura, 176, 177, 179–82, 198, 199, 201–2, 207–10
Asperman, Joe, 268
al-Assad, Asma, 158
al-Assad, Bashar, 7, 37–39, 44, 55, 61, 62, 158, 174, 175, 251
  "Assad must go" policies, 37, 250–51, 275, 302
  jihadists and, 38
  Obama and, 37

Russia's support of, 239, 246, 251, 252, 254–58
Soleimani and, 55, 253
U.S. air strikes and, 299
U.S. proposals targeting, 54
al-Assad, Bashar, chemical weapons of, 13–15, 25, 31, 33–34, 37–42, 50, 53, 56, 76–78, 83, 109, 130–31, 208, 303
agreement to surrender arsenal, 117–20, 126, 131, 139, 160
and delay of destruction of chemicals until entire arsenal is removed, 198–99
Ghouta attacks and, 99–100, 108, 127
ISIS and, 228
Joint Investigative Mechanism and, 243–46, 270, 282–85
Khan Sheikhoun attack and, 275, 283
lack of acknowledgment and justice for use of, 236, 239
preservation of samples of, 225–26, 285, 291–92, 294
Sellström and, 73–74, 76
UN inspections and, 73–74, 84, 86, 102
U.S. air strike proposals and, 104–8, 113, 131
see also Syrian chemical weapons
al-Assad, Hafez, 7, 38, 158
Astana, 278
atropine, 21, 53
Aziz, Tariq, 30

Baghdad, 255–56
al-Baghdadi, Abu Bakr, 12–14, 171, 211–12, 215, 253
Baghouz, 301
Bahrain, 16
Baiji, 169
Ban Ki-moon, 74, 76–77, 105–6, 127, 158, 159
Bannon, Steve, 276
Beirut, 59–61
Belgium, 140
Benghazi, 108
bin Laden, Osama, 15, 17
Black Sea, 121–22
Blades, Karen, 58, 219–20, 222
Blades, Timothy, 44–49, 56–58, 79–81, 122, 125, 226, 285
on *Cape Ray*, 137–39, 141–43, 145–46, 148–51, 182–84, 195–202, 210, 215–26
disillusionment with government, 199–200
Jordan and, 146
near-fatal sarin encounters of, 79–81
Blinken, Tony, 72
Bolton, John, 298–300
bombs, bombings, 264
barrel, 24, 186, 297, 299
of Branch 235 in Damascus, 11–14
IEDs, 60
Khayat brothers and Etihad Airways plot, 286–89
roadside, 97, 108
of Russian Metrojet, 264, 288–89
Brahimi, Lakhdar, 208
Britain, 29, 250
in air strikes on Iraq, 30
and air strikes proposed against Syria, 78, 103–4, 113
Iraq War and, 104
MI6 in, 15, 16
VX precursor and, 149
Brown, Julia, 141, 145
Burns, William J., 41

Bush, George W., 16, 30, 163, 170, 200, 299

Cairns, Scott, 62, 66–69, 91–92, 129, 167
Cameron, David, 103–4, 113
Cape Ray, 137–39, 142–53, 175, 177, 179–84, 195–202, 208–10, 211, 215–27, 236, 240, 242, 243, 274, 291
- description of, 142–43
- engine failure of, 226–27
- environmental activists and, 197, 218–19, 222–23
- fuel supply of, 217, 223
- hydrolysis machines on, 142–43, 148–50, 197, 216–24
- inspection by naval experts, 149–50
- sludge problem on, 220–22
- spill on deck of, 221–22
- weight distribution and capsize risk of, 217–18, 227

Carter, Ashton, 34, 48, 118
CBARR (Chemical Biological Application and Risk Reduction), 45–49, 57
CERS (Scientific Studies and Research Center), 2–7, 205, 240, 241, 243, 297–99
chemical obscurants, 43
chemical weapons
- al-Qaeda and, 15–17, 33–34
- Chemical Weapons Convention, 38, 120, 204
- chlorine, *see* chlorine
- Cooperative Threat Reduction program and, 35–36
- Edgewood Chemical Biological Center, 43–49, 56–58, 79–81, 122, 138, 139, 146–52, 201, 219, 226, 227
- environmental protests and, 197, 218–19, 222–23
- "fixers" and, 44
- hydrogen cyanide gas, 15–16
- in Iraq, 17, 28, 30, 45, 47, 233–35, 263
- of ISIS, 227, 228, 232–36, 259–68, 280, 281, 286–87, 289–91, 294
- Khayat brothers and, 286–87, 289–90
- mustard gas, 3, 6, 47, 117, 125, 140, 148, 187, 233, 235, 240, 259, 263, 265, 266, 280, 286, 294
- nerve agents, *see* nerve agents
- OPCW and, *see* Organization for the Prohibition of Chemical Weapons
- ricin, 240–41
- in Russia, 35–36, 67, 118, 122
- Saddam's use of, 233–35, 263
- Sardasht attack, 263
- sarin, *see* sarin
- soman, 241
- in Soviet Union, 3, 4, 118, 122
- training drill for dealing with, in Aleppo, 49–51
- U.S. development of, 3, 4
- U.S. dumping of, 199
- VX, *see* VX
- in World War I, 3, 15, 140, 187, 286
- in World War II, 218
- *see also* Syrian chemical weapons

"chemist, the" (CIA spy), 1–8, 14, 121, 240, 242, 292, 297
Cheng-Hopkins, Judy, 293
China, 193, 295
chlorine, 235, 236
- ISIS's use of, 17, 232, 233
- Syria's use of, 186–92, 224, 236–39, 243, 277, 298, 299

Churkin, Vitaly, 128, 244–45, 270, 282–83
CIA (Central Intelligence Agency), 12, 16, 257–58, 265
 "the chemist" spy and, 1–2, 4–7, 14, 121, 240, 242, 292, 297
 Syria's chemical weapons and, 1–2, 4–7, 13, 39–40, 53, 72, 121, 240
 Timber Sycamore operation of, 54, 247–48, 251, 252, 254, 278–79
Cinnamon, John, 123–25, 141, 146
Clinton, Bill, 35, 199
Clinton, Hillary Rodham, 41, 53–54, 269, 275
Cold War, 4, 35–36, 47
Colvin, Marie, 166
Congress, U.S., 104–7, 109, 113–14
Constitution, U.S., 103
Controller, the (Basil Hassan), 228, 264, 268, 281, 286–91
Cooperative Threat Reduction program, 35–36
Countryman, Thomas, 121–24, 141, 270–71
Curveball, 163
cyanide, 4
 hydrogen cyanide gas, 15–16
Czechoslovakia, 36

Damascus, 2, 3, 24, 29, 39, 59, 63–64, 67–68, 173, 204, 206, 248, 250, 253–54, 258, 297
 Adra Prison at, 8, 82–83, 114–15
 Branch 235 bombing in, 11–14
 CERS (Scientific Studies and Research Center) in, 2–7, 205, 240, 241, 243, 297–99
 Douma chemical attack, 297–98
 Four Seasons Hotel in, 63, 66, 84–86, 101–3, 110, 159, 173
 Russian embassy in, 174–75
 security zone in, 63, 174–75
 Sheraton Hotel in, 63, 65, 160
 U.S. air strike feared in, 101–2, 112
 see also Ghouta
Damascus Spring, 7
Dean, Aimen, 15–16
de Bretton-Gordon, Hamish, 187, 188, 190–91, 233–36
Defense Department, U.S., 44, 49, 124, 138, 144, 145, 200, 209, 224–26
Democrats, 105–7
DF (methylphosphonyl difluoride), 4, 148, 163–64, 197, 201, 203, 242, 292
Diyala Province, 17
Douma, 297–98
Dromerhauser, Richard, 183–84, 210, 219, 223, 224
DTRA (Defense Threat Reduction Agency), 44–45, 56, 123, 125, 139, 141, 143, 144, 224
Ad-Dumayr, 203
Durrës, 141

Ebola, 224–25
Edgewood, Md., 199
Edgewood Chemical Biological Center, 43–49, 56–58, 79–81, 122, 138, 139, 146–52, 201, 219, 226, 227
Egypt, 37, 39, 253, 295
 Muslim Brotherhood in, 108
Eid, Kassem, 69–71, 94–96, 112–14, 130–32, 192–94, 277, 303
 Alzayat and, 95
Erbil, 212
Erdogan, Recep Tayyip, 301
Esbern Snare, 175, 179, 181

Etihad Airways, 287–89
European Union, 250

Fadil, Abdullah, 160, 207
Falkenrath, Richard, 44–45, 47, 48
Fallujah, 211
Feltman, Jeffrey, 106
Field Deployable Hydrolysis System (FDHS; "Margarita Machine"), 46–49, 56–58, 79, 122–25, 139, 141–43, 146–50, 197, 216–24
Fitzgerald, USS, 183
Flynn, Michael, 271
Foley, James, 224
Ford, Robert, 55–56
France, 29, 250
  acceptance of Syrian chemical weapons refused by, 140
  and proposed air strike against Syria, 78, 103

G20 summit, 118
Gaddafi, Muammar, 156
Geneva agreement between U.S. and Russia, 116–26, 127, 130, 131, 137, 139, 156, 240, 270
Germany, 225, 226, 250
Germany, Nazi, 4
Ghouta, 63, 69, 98
  artillery barrage on, 81–82
  chemical warfare attacks in, 67–71, 72–79, 81–83, 94–100, 101–4, 106–8, 110–13, 117, 118, 127–33, 192–94, 236, 238, 239, 246, 269, 274, 277, 292, 296, 303
  response to U.S.-Russia agreement in, 130
  see also Moadamiyeh
Gioia Tauro, 208–9
Golan Heights, 3
Goldstein, Chelsea, 141, 144–45
Great Britain, *see* Britain
Gulf War, 28, 45, 142, 164, 199
Guterres, António, 282
Gwer, 233

Hagel, Chuck, 125, 184, 224
Hague, The, 67, 125–26, 174, 182
  OPCW in, *see* Organization for the Prohibition of Chemical Weapons
  resolution to prosecute Syria at, 192–94
Halabja, 234
Haley, Nikki, 275
Hama, 186, 190, 272
al-Hamada, Mazen, 82–83, 86, 114–15, 303
Harris, Jeff, 122–23
Hassan, Basil ("the Controller"), 228, 264, 268, 281, 286–91
Hayat Tahrir al-Sham, 280
Hedegaard, Lars, 288
Helge Ingstad, 176, 178
Hersman, Rebecca, 120, 124–26
hexafluorophosphate (PF6), 291–92, 294
hexamine, 33, 99, 128, 291
Hezbollah, 24, 39, 40, 55, 111, 156, 166, 173, 253, 254, 279
Hit, 227, 266, 267
Holgate, Laura, 34, 281
Homs, 166–67
hydrofluoric acid (HF), 79–80, 151
hydrogen cyanide gas, 15–16
hydrogen sulfide, 286, 289–90
hydrolysis (Field Deployable Hydrolysis System; "Margarita Machine"), 46–49, 56–58, 79, 122–25, 139, 141–43, 146–50, 197, 216–24

Idlib, 236, 248, 250, 257, 272, 278
IEDs, 60
Iran, 14, 24, 34, 37, 39–41, 109, 111, 156, 166, 172, 174, 251, 276
  Iran-Iraq War, 232, 234, 263, 266
  land bridge goal in, 279–80, 300
  in peace talks for Syria, 278
  Quds Force in, 24, 300
  Russian collaboration with, 254
  Syria supported by, 39, 251–54, 279, 298, 299, 300, 302
  Timber Sycamore and, 279
Iraq, 139, 169–73, 253, 256, 266
  air strikes on, 30
  al-Qaeda in Iraq, 12, 17, 170–71, 214–15, 256
  Assad and, 251
  chemical weapons in, 17, 28, 30, 45, 47, 233–35, 263
  Coalition Provisional Authority in, 170
  Gulf War, 28, 45, 142, 164, 199
  Hit, 227, 266, 267
  Iran-Iraq War, 232, 234, 263, 266
  Kurdistan region of, *see* Kurdistan, Kurds
  Mosul, 211–14, 227, 231, 233, 249, 259–68, 271, 280, 290
  Operation Desert Fox in, 199–200
  Sunnis in, 171, 214, 249, 251, 256, 264, 278
  Syria's border with, 171
  U.S. invasion and war in, 7, 16, 30, 73, 104, 105, 108, 131, 163, 170, 200, 299
  U.S. withdrawal from, 171
  WMD in, 28, 30, 35, 45, 47, 163, 164, 199, 263
  WMD in, as reason for U.S. war against, 200
ISIS (Islamic State), 7, 17, 33, 55, 108, 131–32, 169–73, 179, 211–15, 224, 227–28, 231, 248–50, 252, 256, 257, 259–71, 274, 278, 280–81, 301, 302
  Afari and, 259–67
  al-Nusra Front and, 12
  chemical weapons of, 17, 227, 228, 232–36, 259–68, 280, 281, 286–87, 289–91, 294
  Foley kidnapped by, 224
  Hassan ("the Controller") in, 228, 264, 268, 281, 286–91
  in Hit, 227, 266, 267
  international coalition against, 300–302
  Khayat brothers and, 285–90
  Kurds and, 231–35
  official pronouncement by, 290–91
  Trump and, 269, 275, 301–2
  U.S. air strikes against, 267–68
Islamic Front, 203
Islamist extremists and jihadists, 38, 39, 60, 78, 96–98, 105, 108, 131–32, 179, 196, 203, 205, 248–50, 252–53, 256–57, 279
  al-Nusra Front, 11–14, 131–32, 248, 250, 252–53, 258, 280, 295
  al-Qaeda, *see* al-Qaeda
  al-Qaeda in Iraq, 12, 17, 170–71, 214–15, 256
  Hayat Tahrir al-Sham, 280
  Hezbollah, 24, 39, 40, 55, 111, 156, 166, 173, 253, 254, 279
  ISIS, *see* ISIS
  TOW missile launchers and, 252
Israel, 33, 39–41, 78, 139, 253, 300
  nuclear weapons of, 3, 117–18
  Syria and, 3–4, 117, 118
Italy, 198, 208–10, 218

Jaafari, Bashar, 193, 294, 295
jihadists, *see* Islamist extremists and jihadists
Johnson, Louis, 219
Joint Investigative Mechanism (JIM), 243–46, 270, 282–85, 292–96, 304
Joint Mission, 156–68, 173–84, 203, 204, 207, 208
Jordan, 17, 33, 40, 51, 54, 139–40, 252, 253, 280, 300
  Syrian refugees in, 140
Jordan, Rick, 146–52, 182–84, 195, 196, 210, 215, 217, 219, 223, 226

Kaag, Sigrid, 154–60, 167, 173–75, 196, 204–8
Kafr Zita, 185–91, 304
Kane, Angela, 30, 64
Kazakhstan, 34–35
Kennedy, Christopher J., 166
Kerry, John F., 116–17, 119, 120, 123–26, 144, 160, 269–70
Kesik Kupri, 232
al-Khafagi, Mohammed, 87–90, 92–93
Khan al-Assal, 29, 64
Khan Sheikhoun, 272–75, 283–85, 291–95
al-Khatib, Ahlah, 19–22
al-Khatib, Ibrahim, 19–22, 25–26
al-Khatib, Maryam, 19–23, 99, 303
  death and autopsy in Turkey, 22–23, 25–27, 31–33, 59, 64
al-Khatib, Mohammad, 21
Khayat, Amer, 286–88
Khayat, Khaled, 281, 285–90
Khayat, Mahmoud, 285–87
Khayat, Mohamed, 281
Khayat, Tarek, 281, 286
Khmeimim Air Base, 254–55
Kulmuhametov, Azamat, 175
Kurdistan, Kurds, 212–14, 231–35, 251, 262, 280, 290, 301–2
  ISIS and, 231–35
  Peshmerga brigades, 212–13, 213–34
  Saddam's chemical attacks against, 233, 234
Kyiv, 36

Latakia, 254, 257
  chemical weapons removal at, 154–55, 173–81, 195, 199, 201–4, 206, 207
Lavrov, Sergey, 116–17, 119, 120, 121, 123–26, 160
Lebanon, 24, 39, 110–11, 196, 279, 300
  Beirut, 59–61
Libya, 39, 108, 156, 249, 250
  Benghazi, 108
Lugar, Richard, 35, 36, 118

MacAulay, Jannell, 141
MacDill Air Force Base, 265
MacFarland, Sean, 256, 265–68
Madaya, 253
Malcorra, Susana, 106, 158–59
Malik, Abu (Salih al-Sabawi), 263, 264–65
al-Maliki, Nouri, 171–73, 212–14
"Margarita Machine" (Field Deployable Hydrolysis System), 46–49, 56–58, 79, 122–25, 139, 141–43, 146–50, 197, 216–24
Maritime Administration, 142
al-Masri, Abu Khabab, 15, 16
Mattis, James "Mad Dog," 269, 275–76, 298–300, 302

al-Mazzeh aircraft hangar, 82–83, 86, 114–15, 303
McConnell, Mitch, 107, 108
McDonough, Denis, 104, 105
McGurk, Brett, 170–73, 212–15, 249–52, 271, 300–302
McNutt, Wyatt, 225–26
Mekdad, Faisal, 65, 160
al-Menagh, 33
Merkel, Angela, 103
MI6, 15, 16
Middle East, 7, 14, 54, 73, 107, 251, 253
  Arab Spring in, 37–39, 108, 166
Mikkelsen, Torben, 175–79, 199
Mikulak, Robert, 120
Moldova, 34
Moadamiyeh, 82, 85–87, 91–93, 98
  chemical warfare attack in, 69–70, 82, 94–99, 112, 113, 128, 193
  famine and desperation in, 91–92, 102
  rebel council in, 95
Mogl, Stefan, 284–85, 291–94
Morad, Mamoun, 272–74
Mosul, 211–14, 227, 231, 233, 249, 259–68, 271, 280, 290
Mosul University, 266–68
Muallem, Walid, 41, 159
mubtakkar al-farid, 16
Mulet, Edmond, 282–85, 291–96
mustard gas, 3, 6, 47, 117, 125, 140, 148, 187, 233, 235, 240, 259, 263, 265, 266, 280, 286, 294
Myers, Chris, 147–48

National Defense University, 41–42
National Security Council, 34, 144, 182, 255
NATO, 40, 78, 140, 141, 187, 218
Nazi Germany, 4
nerve agents, 3, 17, 28, 45–46, 50, 117, 163, 187, 203, 241, 274
  novichok, 300
  soman, 241
  see also chemical weapons; sarin; VX
Netanyahu, Benjamin, 40
New York City, 16, 235, 266
New York Times, 78
9/11 attacks, 7, 14–16
Nobel Prize, 129–30, 157
North Korea, 37, 109
novichok, 300
nuclear weapons, 13
  Cooperative Threat Reduction program and, 35–36
  of Israel, 3, 117–18
  of Russia, 36–37, 118
  of Soviet Union, 34–35, 118

Obama, Barack, and administration, 12, 35, 53, 104–5, 141, 144, 182, 250, 255, 257, 258, 268, 269, 271, 299
  air strikes against Syria considered by, 76–79, 83, 101–9, 112–13, 117–19, 131, 194
  "Assad must go" stance of, 37, 275
  chlorine attack and, 192
  covert action against Syria authorized by, 54
  Ghouta attack and, 72–73, 76–78
  ISIS and, 213, 214
  Maliki and, 172–73
  McDonough's South Lawn walk with, 104, 105
  McGurk and, 170, 213, 302
  and possibility of Syrian chemical warfare attack, 39–40
  Power and, 76
  and proposals targeting Assad, 54

Obama, Barack, and administration *(continued)*
  Putin's meeting with, 118–19
  "red line" warning to Syria, 25, 33, 40–42, 43, 50, 53, 56, 76, 105, 107, 131, 132, 276, 299
  and Sellström's evacuation from Syria, 76, 77
  speeches on Syria, 37, 41–42, 43, 108–9, 112–14, 130–31
  Syrian rebels and, 249
  Timber Sycamore and, 279
  and U.S.-Russia agreement to eliminate Syria's weapons, 118, 125
  Weber and, 35–36
  WMD as priority for, 35–37
O'Donovan, Diarmuid, 60–61, 65, 67, 87–92, 97–98, 110, 161–62, 165, 167
One Percent Doctrine, The (Suskind), 16
Organization for the Prohibition of Chemical Weapons (OPCW), 38, 67, 85, 120, 123, 124, 129–30, 157, 204–8, 235, 236, 239–43, 298, 304
  chlorine and, 191
  Fact-Finding Mission of, 239, 283
  forensic tests of Syrian weapons facilities by, 241
  Joint Investigative Mechanism (JIM) with UN, 243–46, 270, 282–85, 292–96, 304
  Joint Mission with UN, 156–68, 173–84, 203, 204, 207, 208
  sarin samples preserved at, 225–26, 285, 291–92, 294

Palmyra, 250, 274
Panetta, Leon, 12–13
Parthemore, Christine, 225
Peshmerga, 212–13, 231–34
Petraeus, David, 54
pinacolyl alcohol, 241, 242
plague, 36
Polakis, Pavlos, 223
Pompeo, Mike, 278, 301
Powell, Colin, 200
Power, Samantha, 76–78, 105–7, 109, 192–94, 238–39, 243–46, 270, 282
  Churkin and, 244, 270, 282–83
  Eid and, 192–94, 277
  and OPCW-UN Joint Investigative Mechanism, 243–46, 270
  "A Problem from Hell", 76
Project Sapphire, 34–35
Pusey, Lloyd, 220
Putin, Vladimir, 7, 37, 78–79, 118, 127, 160
  Obama and, 118–19
  Soleimani and, 254
  Trump and, 278, 279

Qalamoun, 196
Qatar, 29

Rama, Edi, 141, 143–44
Ramadan, 198, 205, 207
Ramadi, 256
Raqqa, 55, 132, 173, 211, 228, 252, 280, 290
Republicans, 105, 107
Reyhanli, 22, 26, 32, 247
Rhodes, Ben, 41, 53, 103, 104
Rice, Susan, 72, 105, 244
ricin, 240–41
Rohrabacher, Dana, 172
Rostad, Per, 178–79
Rota, 183, 195–202

Russia, 41, 156, 206, 276, 296
acceptance of Syrian chemical weapons refused by, 121–22, 125, 139
Cooperative Threat Reduction program and, 35–36
Damascus embassy of, 174–75
Ghouta attack and, 76, 78
Iranian collaboration with, 254
Joint Investigative Mechanism and, 243–46, 270, 283, 284, 292–94
Khan Sheikhoun attack and, 283
in peace talks for Syria, 278
and resolution to prosecute Syria at The Hague, 192–94
Skripal poisoning and, 300
Syria supported by, 39, 128, 239, 246, 251, 252, 254–58, 269, 299–300, 302
Timber Sycamore and, 279
U.S. agreement with (Geneva agreement) to eliminate Syria's weapons, 116–26, 127, 130, 131, 137, 139, 156, 240, 270
weapons in, 35–37, 67, 118, 122
Russian Metrojet bombing, 264, 288–89

al-Sabawi, Salih ("Abu Malik"), 263, 264
Saddam Hussein, 30, 163, 169, 212, 249, 263
chemical weapons used by, 233–35, 263
Safronkov, Vladimir, 294–95
Santee, Jay, 43–48, 56–57, 123, 125, 139, 141–43, 146, 149–51, 197, 224
Saraqeb chemical warfare attack, 18–23, 25–27, 31–33, 53, 99, 129, 239, 303
Sardasht chemical warfare attack, 263
sarin, 3–6, 8, 13, 14, 17, 34, 37, 40, 50, 55, 117, 125, 173, 186, 187, 196, 203, 204, 234, 274, 298
binary, development of, 4
Blades' near-fatal encounters with, 79–81
DF precursor of, 4, 148, 163–64, 197, 201, 203, 242, 292
Ghouta attacks, 67–71, 72–79, 81–83, 94–100, 101–4, 106–8, 110–13, 117, 118, 127–33, 192–94, 236, 238, 239, 246, 269, 274, 277, 292, 296, 303
hexamine added to, 33, 99, 128, 291
hydrofluoric acid precursor of, 79–80, 151
hydrolysis system to destroy, 46–49, 56–58, 122–25, 139, 141–43, 146–50, 197, 216–24
Khan Sheikhoun attack, 272–75, 283–85, 291–95
lack of hospital resources to deal with, 50, 75
possibility of residual cache of, 243, 292
preservation of samples of, 225–26, 285, 291–92, 294
Saddam's use of, 233
Saraqeb attack, 18–23, 25–27, 31–33, 53, 99, 129, 239, 303
see also Syrian chemical weapons
Sarmin, 236–39
Sayqal (Site Two), 196, 202–7
Schoenberger, Tina, 141–43
Scientific Studies and Research Center (CERS), 2–7, 205, 240, 241, 243, 297–99
Sellström, Åke, 28
campaign to pressure Assad to allow UN investigations, 73–74

Sellström, Åke *(continued)*
  departure from Syria, 73, 76–77, 105, 110–12, 130
  investigation of Syria's chemical weapons, 28–33, 53, 59–66, 68–69, 73–74, 77, 82, 84–87, 89–93, 96–97, 99, 100, 101–3, 106, 110–12, 157, 160, 191, 192, 291
  report of, 127–30
September 11 attacks, 7, 14–16
al-Sharif, Hassan, 65, 74, 110, 165, 174, 179–81, 204–7
Shawkat, Assef, 6–7
al-Shayrat air base, 276–78
Shiites, 111, 170, 172, 251, 253, 254, 264, 279, 300
Skripal, Sergei, 300
Smith, Jerry, 161, 164–65, 180
smugglers, 179
Soleimani, Qasem, 24, 55, 253–54, 300
soman, 241
Soviet republics, former, 13, 34
  Cooperative Threat Reduction program and, 35–36
Soviet Union, 244, 300
  Afghanistan invasion of, 254
  collapse of, 34–35
  weapons in, 3, 4, 34–35, 67, 118, 122
Spain, 200
Spicer, Sean, 271
Spiez Laboratory, 284, 291
State Department, U.S., 95, 121, 141, 144, 170–72, 193, 251, 252, 270–71, 299
Steinitz, Yuval, 118
subway systems, 16, 235
sulfur mustard, 3, 6, 47, 117, 125, 140, 148, 187, 233, 235, 240, 259, 263, 265, 266, 280, 286, 294
Sunnis, 171, 214, 249, 251, 256, 264, 278
Suskind, Ron, 16
Syria
  Aleppo, 6, 23–24, 26, 29, 33, 49–53, 55, 59, 74–75, 132, 257
  Americans' opposition to involvement in, 108, 251–52
  analyses of U.S. decision-making on, 107
  CIA's Timber Sycamore operation and, 54, 247–48, 251, 252, 254, 278–79
  civil war in, 11, 13, 17, 18–19, 23–24, 37–39, 53–57, 59, 74, 78, 87, 94, 108, 130–31, 171, 186, 203, 240, 248–58, 269, 275–77, 299, 302, 303
  Damascus, *see* Damascus
  Ghouta, *see* Ghouta
  Iran as ally of, 39, 251–54, 279, 298, 299, 300, 302
  Iraq's border with, 171
  Israel and, 3–4, 117, 118
  military airports in, 82–83
  Military Intelligence Directorate in, 11
  Mukhabarat intelligence service in, 6–7
  peace talks for, 278, 299–300
  refugees from, 108, 140, 250, 269, 275
  Russia as ally of, 39, 128, 239, 246, 251, 252, 254–58, 269, 299–300, 302
  shabiha militiamen in, 26
  Trump and, 107, 269, 275–78, 280, 297–302

UN relief convoys and aid workers in, 59
U.S. air strikes against, 276–78, 297–99
U.S. intervention requested by rebel leaders in, 55–56
West's policy collapse in, 250
Syrian chemical weapons, 3, 15, 24–25, 37–42, 117, 254, 299, 303, 304
air strikes considered as response to, 76–79, 83, 101–9, 112–14, 117–19, 131, 194
al-Qaeda and, 15, 33–34
Assad and, *see* al-Assad, Bashar, chemical weapons of
"the chemist" spy and, 1–8, 14, 121, 240, 242, 292, 297
chlorine, 186–92, 224, 236–39, 243, 277
CERS and, 2–7, 205, 240, 241, 243, 297–99
CIA and, 1–2, 4–7, 13, 39–40, 53, 72, 121, 240
delivery systems for, 42, 128, 129, 240
Douma attack, 297–98
Foreign Ministry statement on, 40–41
gaps and discrepancies in official records on, 236, 239–43
Ghouta attacks, 67–71, 72–79, 81–83, 94–100, 101–4, 106–8, 110–13, 117, 118, 127–33, 192–94, 236, 238, 239, 246, 269, 274, 277, 292, 296, 303
ISIS and, 235
Joint Investigative Mechanism and, 243–46, 270, 282–85, 292–96, 304
Kafr Zita attack, 185–91, 304
Khan al-Assal attack, 29
Khan Sheikhoun attack, 272–75, 283–85, 291–95
lack of acknowledgment and justice for use of, 236, 239
lack of hospital resources to deal with, 50, 75, 132, 133
and Maryam al-Khatib's death and autopsy, 22–23, 25–27, 31–33, 59, 64, 99
Moadamiyeh attack, 69–70, 82, 94–99, 112, 113, 128, 193
mobilization of mixing trucks for, 40, 42
Obama's "red line" warning on, 25, 33, 40–42, 43, 50, 53, 56, 76, 105, 107, 131, 132, 275–76, 299
Obama's speeches on, 41–42, 43, 108–9, 112–14, 130–31
OPCW's forensic tests of facilities for, 241
quantity of, 121, 125
ricin, 240–41
Saraqeb attack, 18–23, 25–27, 31–33, 53, 99, 129, 239, 303
sarin, 3–6, 8, 13, 14, 17, 34, 37, 40, 50, 55, 117, 125, 173, 186, 187, 196, 203; *see also* sarin
Sellström's investigation of, 28–33, 53, 59–66, 68–69, 73–74, 77, 82, 84–87, 89–93, 96–97, 99, 100, 101–3, 106, 110–12, 157, 160, 191, 192, 291
UN investigation of, 27–33, 53, 59–69, 64–65, 73–74, 76–78, 82, 84–100, 101–3, 105, 106, 110–13, 127–30
UN resolution calling for war-crimes prosecution at The Hague for, 192–94

Syrian chemical weapons *(continued)*
U.S. intelligence community's assessment of, 78, 104, 108, 239–40
Western fears about use against Syrian population, 39
Syrian chemical weapons, removal and destruction of, 154–68, 173–84, 283, 296, 302
Albania proposed as site for, 140–41, 143–44
Ark Futura in, 176, 177, 179–82, 198, 199, 201–2, 207–10
Assad's cooperation with, 117–20, 126, 131, 139, 160
bulldozer photo op in, 164–65
Cape Ray in, *see Cape Ray*
completion of destruction of chemicals, 223–24
completion of removal operations, 207–8
destruction of chemicals delayed until removal of entire arsenal is completed, 198–99
destruction of production, mixing, and filling equipment, 163–68
discussion on possible methods of, 42, 44–46
discussion on securing authorization for, 109
environmental activists and, 197, 218–19, 222–23
fighting near operations of, 165–67, 177–78, 196
first day of, 161–62
hydrolysis in, 46–49, 56–58, 122–25, 139, 141–43, 146–50, 197, 216–24
Latakia harbor operations, 154–55, 173–81, 195, 199, 201–4, 206, 207
leaking containers and, 201–2
logistical challenges in, 120–22, 125, 139, 173–74
military crisis and, 196, 202–5
OPCW-UN Joint Mission in, 156–68, 173–84, 203, 204, 207, 208
and possibility of residual cache of sarin, 243, 292
preservation of samples for study, 225–26, 285, 291–92, 294
problems and delays in, 182, 183, 196–98, 205, 207, 220–22
Ramadan and, 198, 205, 207
Russia's refusal to accept weapons in, 121–22, 125, 139
shipping container size and, 197
at Site Two (Sayqal), 196, 202–7
at Site 7 ("Dr. Evil's Lair"), 162–65, 180
sludge problem and, 220–22
timeline for, 117, 121, 123–25, 148, 174, 182, 197–98, 204, 206, 207
transfer of cargo between ships, 177, 179–81, 195, 198, 208–10
U.S.-Russia agreement (Geneva agreement) on, 116–26, 127, 130, 131, 137, 139, 156, 240, 270

Taiko, 176–79, 198–99
Talmenes, 187
Tangaere, Julian, 159–61, 165, 166, 207
Tartus, 121, 205
Telegraph, 191
Tennari, Mohamed, 236–38
Tikrit, 169, 249
Tillerson, Rex, 275–77
Timber Sycamore, 54, 247–48, 251, 252, 254, 278–79
Tirana, 144

TOW antitank missiles, 248, 252
Trump, Donald, and administration, 268–71, 274
  Countryman and, 270–71
  ISIS and, 269, 275, 301–2
  Khan Sheikhoun attack and, 275
  McGurk and, 271
  Putin and, 278, 279
  Syria and, 107, 269, 275–78, 280, 297–302
  Timber Sycamore program ended by, 278–79
Trump, Ivanka, 275
Tunisia, 37
Turkey, 14, 33, 51, 54, 55, 78, 190, 252, 275, 280, 301
  Maryam al-Khatib's death and autopsy in, 22–23, 25–27, 31–33, 59, 64
  in peace talks for Syria, 278

Ukraine, 35–36
United Nations (UN), 30, 109, 117, 154–57, 204, 206, 208, 209, 238, 243–44, 277, 296
  and Geneva agreement on removing Syria's chemical weapon arsenal, 123–24
  Iraqi weapons and, 28, 30, 200
  OPCW Joint Investigative Mechanism (JIM) with, 243–46, 270, 282–85, 292–96, 304
  OPCW Joint Mission with, 156–68, 173–84, 203, 204, 207, 208
  relief convoys and aid workers in Syria, 59
  resolution to prosecute Syria at The Hague, 192–94
  Syrian chemical weapon investigations of, 27–33, 53, 59–69, 64–65, 73–74, 76–78, 82, 84–100, 101–3, 105, 106, 110–13, 127–30
United States
  air strikes considered as response to Syrian attacks, 76–79, 83, 101–9, 112–14, 117–19, 131, 194
  air strikes on Iraq, 30
  air strikes on Syria, 276–78, 297–99
  chemical weapon development in, 3, 4
  chemical weapon dumping in, 199
  Russian agreement with (Geneva agreement) to eliminate Syrian weapons, 116–26, 127, 130, 131, 137, 139, 156, 240, 270
  September 11 attacks on, 7, 14–16
  Soviet nuclear agreement with, 36–37
  Syrian rebels' request for intervention from, 55–56
  see also Obama, Barack, and administration; Trump, Donald, and administration
uranium, 34–35
Üzümcü, Ahmet, 157, 206, 207

Venezuela, 109
Veterans of Foreign Wars, 41
Votel, Joseph, 265–66, 268
VX, 3, 6, 13, 17, 30, 34, 47, 117, 203, 241
  precursors for, 148–49, 176

Washington Post, 172
weapons of mass destruction (WMD), 34, 44, 120, 187, 270
  Cooperative Threat Reduction program and, 35–36
  Defense Threat Reduction Agency and, *see* DTRA

weapons of mass destruction (WMD) *(continued)*
in Iraq, 28, 30, 35, 45, 47, 163, 164, 199, 263
in Iraq, as reason for U.S. invasion, 200
in Russia, 36–37, 67
in Soviet Union, 3, 4, 34–35, 67
see also chemical weapons; nuclear weapons
Weber, Andrew C., 13–14, 33–36, 42, 118, 139, 141, 143, 144, 201, 224–25
hydrolysis system and, 48, 49
Obama and, 35–36
in Project Sapphire, 34–35
World Health Organization, 85
World War I, 3, 15, 140, 187, 286
World War II, 218, 303

Yazidis, 224
Yom Kippur War, 3
Ypres, 140

Zakharova, Maria, 255
al-Zarqawi, Abu Musab, 7, 16–17, 170–73, 264
al-Zawahiri, Ayman, 16, 173

ALSO BY

JOBY WARRICK

BLACK FLAGS

The Rise of ISIS

In a thrilling dramatic narrative, the award-winning reporter traces how the strain of militant Islam behind ISIS first arose in a remote Jordanian prison and spread with the unwitting aid of two American presidents. Drawing on unique high-level access to CIA and Jordanian sources, Warrick weaves gripping, moment-by-moment operational details with the perspectives of diplomats and spies, generals and heads of state, many of whom foresaw a menace worse than al-Qaeda and tried desperately to stop it. *Black Flags* is a brilliant and definitive history that reveals the long arc of today's most dangerous extremist threat.

Political Science

THE TRIPLE AGENT

The al-Qaeda Mole Who Infiltrated the CIA

In December 2009, a group of the CIA's top terrorist hunters gathered at a secret base in Afghanistan to greet a rising superspy: Humam Khalil al-Balawi, a Jordanian who had infiltrated the upper ranks of al-Qaeda. For months, he had sent shocking revelations from inside the terrorist network and now promised to help the CIA assassinate Osama bin Laden's top deputy. Instead, as he stepped from his car, al-Balawi detonated a thirty-pound bomb, instantly killing seven CIA operatives and giving the agency its worst loss of life in decades.

Current Affairs

ANCHOR BOOKS
Available wherever books are sold.
anchorbooks.com